# TERRIAN JOURNALS'
# NEWS TO ME

(missing facts, stories, questions, and details)

by DONALD MURRAY ANDERSON

Terrian Journals'
News To Me

A Mythbreaker Book

First Edition

© Copyright 2024 by Donald Murray Anderson

ISBN 978-1-989593-40-0

All rights reserved. Without limiting rights under copyright reserved above, no part of this book may be reproduced, stored in or introduced into a retrieval system, or transmitted in any form or by any means (electronic, mechanical, photo-copying, recording, or other-wise) without prior written permission of the copyright owner.

For information address:
mythbreaker@mail.com

**"At last the story can be told." But who will read it? Who will believe it? And who will learn from it?**

...

**"Better to write for yourself and have no public than to write for the public and have no self."**

- Cyril Connolly <u>The New Statesman</u>. February 25, 1933

"The news" offers "the audience" information providing "them" with a vague awareness of the outside world from the perspective of complete strangers vaguely aware of "them".

Occasionally, "the news" also offers "a feature" or "special report" glimpse, "a snapshot" of reality.

# Before Endless News

There's a time, a very long time, in fact most of human history, when not almost anyone, almost anywhere could make, report, invent, or fabricate news by simply pointing a portable telephone camera lens and microphone at anyone and anything, or submit news with a hunt-and-peck keyboard like an experimental test animal seeking food.

Of course the quality of journalism is no more perfect now than then.

At times, "yellow" journalism goes rampant like a virus and gullible, uninformed, and ignorant audiences react with strong emotional outbursts, plaguing others with injustice and other suffering.

In great contrast, reporting and journalism are at their best when led by fastidious, nit-picking, dedicated editors who are fluent in good grammar and spelling; who only agree to publish verified and substantiated stories with credible sources; and who are working with reporters devoted to the basic principle of news – getting it right, i.e. accurate and unbiased copy.

In that spirit, the present volume isn't a review, a retelling, or a rewrite of "first" world mass media's "big stories" of my time.

This book tries to be a first telling of stories ignored, downplayed, missed, buried, or untold by the "first" world mass media, and a presentation of story questions, angles, and perspectives not asked, not seen, and not revealed by the "first" world mass media.

## Community Journalism Dedication

For the community correspondents, amateur scribes who love to tell us all the details of what's happening to whom in the smallest villages and towns which are barely dots on the most local of maps.

For the journalists with various degrees, or none at all, who seek out and respond to every local person and every event visible and to those local news tips that arrive by phone, by mail, and by someone walking into the office to tell a tale.

For the owner-editors, who invest themselves and their incomes in keeping the independent weeklies alive; protect their staff reporters; and encourage the spread of accurate news and constructive criticism in the community.

For all the readers and subscribers who support their only source of authentic, local community news.

For the only form of journalism that is truly close up and personal, enabling writers and readers to interact face-to-face on a daily basis, in the streets and at home, and to learn the inside story of what writers and readers are doing, communicating to each other, and contributing to enriching both the writing and reading experiences, while spreading the news with the most meaning to local everyday reality.

Community journalism is the alternative to anonymous mass media news in which writers and readers are largely complete strangers who know almost nothing about each other and yet who try to convey and understand news that seems so far away and remote from daily lives here and now, even if the stories are related to those very lives.

A global climate crisis is felt in every locality, not just somewhere else. Only community journalism can provide the missing link between here and there.

Communities in the "mass" share much in common. It's so common that it can go unrecognized and thus unreported in mass media.

Consequently, it becomes news that's not received or taken to heart because it seems to have no relationship to local life.

In mass media, reporters and news organizations are as overly isolated as any other bureaucracy, rendering news writers apart, where they work so hard that they can lose themselves and become no more than distant observers of other people's lives.

I'm never interested in writing for mass media and daily news publishers because that type of reporting is trapped in the artificial world of a daily grind deadline.

Every day, a writer must jump from topic to topic, story to story, unlikely to ever return to "old new" that "we've already done".

Editorial, op-ed, and column writing are obliging news writers to produce daily opinions-on-demand just to fill the regular, fixed spaces requiring routine filling in the daily and periodical news media.

If s/he writes a column, s/he must either actually have an opinion or express an opinion on anything that comes up every day, a perspective of everything.

It's column deadline time. I must have an instant opinion.

Would you want to have a conversation with someone who offers an opinion on everything you say? Who would?

Deadline approaches to writing never appeal to me. That's why I choose not to try to work for daily news organizations.

Deadline writing can be no more than just that, writing dead lines.

Lines become dead if writers and editors don't carefully reflect upon themselves and carefully scrutinize what they're doing at all times.

But deadline writing makes that very difficult.

By its very nature, deadline writing tends to inhibit or block that care altogether. So deadline writing easily slips into errors and inaccuracies.

I marvel at the work of professional editors who make sure that billions of words in millions of newspapers and magazines are almost flawless every time.

Deadline writing also slips into depending on "news makers" to make news deliveries.

Deadline news can also slip into making up news.

Both the mass media news reporters and the mass media news audience share in the deadline dictated news behaviour.

For news readers, listeners, and viewers, paying some attention to the daily mass media news becomes only a routine, habitual behaviour.

They rush to buy the latest daily newspaper edition because they always do that.

Their urge to tune in or turn on the mass media news reports is not a yearning for news and information.

If it were, the mass media audience would be highly informed and aware activists motivated and moved to action every day by the news that they consume.

Unfortunately, people are not consuming mass media news because they want to pay attention to it; to learn something they don't know; to change their point of view or opinion; and to take decisive, positive action to influence the world.

If they did, the world would be in a constant state of deliberate change and thoughtful improvement.

The easily distracted and inattentive mass media con-sumer has selective reading and listening skills, at best waiting only for one particular item to grab the eyes and ears among the ads and commercial messages.

News is reduced to its four primary points: north, east, west, and south, in almost exactly that order.

In "first" world locations, the more accurate word for news is nwes, since "the north" and "the west" are emphasized most often. They are the centre of the world.

Mass media gives far less serious attention to the south and east, unless they are perceived as weirdly entertaining, threatening, or tragic.

## First News Assignment

My personal involvement in community journalism starts at a young age. I'm about 13.

It's my first paid job and my last until I graduate from senior secondary school.

Barely into my teen years, I begin delivering a weekly newspaper in a larger Canadian city.

At the time, I live in a commercial-residential area about two blocks from the weekly's office.

My delivery route is mostly to small shops along the same street and a few nearby apartment buildings.

It's easy work, requires little time, and has some perks. The weekly gives me free movie passes for a theatre in the area.

I still have one of the passes. I wonder if it's still valid or if the theatre still exists.

Why do I get involved in community journalism so early in life? I have no idea. Maybe I know at the time, but I don't now.

I didn't need the money and I had homework to do. Since I don't recall any particularly rainy weather, perhaps I only make deliveries in the summer months of the cloudy city.

But delivering the weekly is only once a week, on Thursday, and the small business people are friendly and always seem happy to see me.

They advertise in the weekly too. So their subscriptions are included in the advertising rate they pay?

The only grumpy subscriber I encounter is an older woman in an apartment building.

She claims that she doesn't receive the paper I deliver every week to her door.

One month she disappears without notifying the newspaper. So I can't collect her monthly subscription fee. But the weekly's office worker isn't upset and doesn't charge me.

Another time, someone in the street asks me if he can buy a paper from me. That's the first and only time I hear that request.

I sell it, but when I take his money to the newspaper office, the clerk says the paper doesn't have a permit for street sales. So she splits the 10¢ with me. It's fair and square.

I leave my weekly paper route job when my parents move us more than ten blocks from the newspaper office. It's no longer convenient for me.

Yet this isn't long before I start taking much longer walks, working up to the 80 km walk that a former U.S. P.T. boat commander recommends for everyone. He's JFK.

I get closer to completing the walk over the years that follow, but I'm still working on it.

As for my involvement in community journalism, it takes more than ten years before I start working as a reporter for a small town weekly paper in Ontario, as described in detail in <u>Terrian Journals Origins</u> (volume two).

**Discomfort zone**

Mass media news reporters face imminent, life-threatening dangers during some assignments. Others are surprised by unexpected and unanticipated hazards in much safer zones.

**Harmer Ridge**: I don't speed, but I drive too fast for the comfort of a visiting television newscaster from Lethbridge (Alberta).

We're in a Suburban van, going along a coal mine haul road built for 100 tonne Terex trucks.

I ask the news reader if he's nervous. He replies, "No, I twitch like this all the time."

## Front page cover story

### Why's news wise

**Cartagena:** I walk out of the beach strip into the edge of the old-looking walled town.

Although I'm largely illiterate in Spanish, I buy a local newspaper to carry, to give any malicious types the impression that I know the language well.

I watch how locals pay, and note the price, then indicate with a simple gesture that I am buying one too.

The paper has a story about the current Argentina vs. U.K. war. I understand the pictures.

There's also news about the "presidente norte-americano". Canada, U.S.A., Mexico, etc. elect a president during my flight here?

No matter where you are and how little you know of the language(s) there, always buy and carry a local newspaper and try to look as if you understand what's going on around you.

This way you can help both yourself and maybe local journalism, if there is freedom of the press locally.

### Who's and whose news

Wherever I am, I try to get my news from more than one source.

Different news publishers and broadcasters cover different angles and provide different details of ostensibly exactly the same stories.

**Berlin (East):** Someone I meet from what is then called "East Germany" tells me that my approach to news has special merit for her.

Without an objective or impartial source of news in her home city, she can only listen to the U.S.-slanted and C.C.C.P.-slanted news. She listens to both, not believing either side.

When the two news sources agree on a story, she concludes that it's probably true.

**Rio de Janeiro, Rio de Janeiro:** During one of the first elections in Brasil after nearly 20 years of military dictatorship, getting news from more than one source on election night is essential.

Polls open at 7 a.m. and close at 5 p.m., but no results coverage are broadcast yet. It's 10:30 p.m.

Television news and specials provide an excellent description of the number of positions being filled and the mood of the day. But there is no poll by poll results reporting.

Regular programmes are aired. The latest newscast is giving exit-from-polls numbers now, not actual counts.

Radio Jornal do Brasil and Globo TV news have significantly contradictory results for tonight's election.

On Jornal do Brasil, I hear that the PDT's Lionel Brizola is winning the governorship in Rio de Janeiro State.

My Carioca friend Zita comes home with Globo-watchers reports of a PDS, Moreira Franco win.

I'm watching Globo too. Every time they cut from national results to the Rio governor's race, the announcing becomes rather vague.

Globo says that it's either a PDS win or too early and/or too close to call.

Radio Jornal do Brasil presses ahead with current results and a growing lead for nearly Governor-elect Brizola.

There's too much difference in reporting to be believable.

Globo news already has a reputation for being in favour of the status quo, whatever it is.

In this case the PDS is the preferred political party of the withdrawing military dictatorship.

Suspicions are raised.

Then the big story breaks.

<u>Jornal do Brasil</u> newspaper publishes a front page article stating that the government electoral office has been trying to persuade <u>Jornal do Brasil</u> to hold back election results.

The clear implication of the Jornal do Brasil article is that Globo is bowing to the military dictatorships' request, but Jornal do Brasil is not.

Globo TV watchers still watch. I don't know why.

After the Jornal do Brasil article appears, Globo still holds back, but almost imperceptibly recognizes that Brizola has won, referring to him as "governor-elect" at one point.

Globo has no credibility for me now. I deliberately do not watch their newscast anymore.

Globo put itself in a position where the military dictatorship could have rigged election results and nobody would have known about it.

Jornal do Brasil made election rigging less likely.

Despite my boycott of Globo "news", I do see the Globo anchor who hosts the election night coverage again, quite by accident.

While visiting a friend who leaves on the television during my visit, I notice that the former anchor is now hosting a different sort of broadcast.

Will he spend the rest of his life as the host of that quiz show, repeatedly saying, "resposta certa" to contestants, as if they were the news attachés of the military dictatorship?

**Montevideo**: Local newspapers report that visiting Rio PDT Governor Brizola is concerned that the generals in Brasília are forming a parallel government in response to the recent elections.

**São Paulo**: There are reports of looting and rioting just outside the governor's palace. Evidently a demonstration against unemployment gets out of hand.

There is some press speculation about outside agitators, i.e. PDS supporters inciting the riot to embarrass three renowned opposition parties' governors who are meeting in the São Paulo palace.

One news photo shows a looter wearing a PDS T-shirt. (That's not conclusive evidence, since the poorer people accept free, albeit advertising clothes, from any politician.)

The logic behind this speculation is that some generals are not pro-elections.

But even Globo TV, the PDS-ally news service, has headlines about right-wing agitators in São Paulo.

**Update**: The incidents in São Paulo were evidently not looting in the sense of U.S. cities, but destruction of food in a supermarket.

Do hungry, unemployed people destroy food?

Stores close early in Rio tonight for fear of similar events. We have first-hand reports of vandalism and extra military police in our central city.

But I see no problems while in downtown Rio myself today. Yet I do pass a couple of store display windows, and minutes later find them in fragments, being cleaned away. Coincidence?

...We were had. Nothing seems to happen except early closings and the arrival of shock police.

We walk through the Rio centre and find all peaceful, no signs of damage, and business as usual.

...Tonight the president/general makes a five minute TV speech against violence and for democracy. Governor Brizola congratulates Cariocas, residents of Rio, for not being violent.

...Both the military dictators and the Soviet Empire lose if the liberal governors succeed in Brasil.

Gallop opinion polls say that the public wants direct presidential elections, not the indirect ones that the generals plan for three years hence; and, if the newly-elected opposition politicians can be made to look as if they are under siege, and incompetent at maintaining the peace, the military could say the clock is turning back 19 years and it's time for another coup d'état.

**Córdoba**: Our hosts Eduardo and Eli have a multi-band radio, which he often leaves in the kitchen so that we can listen to short-wave radio.

This includes the Radio Canada International broad-casts in Portuguese and Spanish. It's my first time listening to R.C.I.

Tonight they say that people arriving in Canada from other countries will soon have to fill out a form.

The U.S. will reciprocate, so every time you go across the U.S. border for a drive you would have to spend hours in line-ups.

How stupid. This law is to appease ignorant people who claim that world unemployment is a distinctly Canadian problem, caused by "foreigners" entering Canada illegally.

In other nation-states the same claim is made. If true, it means that all the nation-states have unemployment due to "foreigners" entering illegally.

How can that be true? Logically it would mean that if all nation-states had no "foreigners" entering illegally there would be no unemployment anywhere, including the "foreigners" homelands.

Trying to eliminate illegal entry is going to mean more costly bureaucracy for taxpayers.

This is a good reason to write to the government minister responsible and other members of parliament to disagree with this scheme of increased government spending.

The politicians are hearing too many ignorant voices in Canada.

Bureaucrats tremble. The human beings are at the gate.

...

At mid-morning we receive short-wave news from France, as well as Radio Beijing and Moscow in French.

There is also German. So we hear many official-style newscasts on the same items.

...

News of Canada doesn't appear most days and ignorance of it is unimportant in the outside world. I only find out about three or four Canadian news stories in two years abroad.

Conclusion: Apart from Pierre Trudeau's retirement, knowing what's happening in Canada is of no importance outside of Canada. There are no repercussions.

**Fukuoka**: Here, as in Córdoba, we listen to the short-wave broadcasts on a borrowed radio.

We hear some NHK International news broadcasts in Portuguese and Spanish, destined for a southern Americas audience.

It doesn't strike me as such an interesting novelty anymore. It's a static interrupting human communication.

The short-wave band is full of nationalism.

On occasion there are interesting items, e.g. The Great Wall of China is more than 6,000 kilometres long. It could thus be stretched across Canada.

The United Nations and the Organization of American States broadcast short-wave radio news in Spanish here too, from their headquarters in the U.S.

But so much of SW is uninteresting or official news only.

Listening to Radio Canada International, Radio Japan, Beijing, Kiev, or The Voice of America is all the same.

The radio band could be better used in other, non-national ways instead of drumming up prejudices.

Short wave ought to be taken out of the nation-states' hands. Their broadcast licenses should be cancelled and handed over to denationalizing interests.

**Córdoba**: Partisan jingles are becoming apparent on the local radio stations. They are all paid, not all "free time" like Brasil.

The little TV we do see also has only paid political ads.

I see a portion of the TV news of one network on Eli and Eduardo's television.

Two newscasters stand telling each other the news as if the audience were a standing, listening third person.
Radio Nacional has a CBC Radio sound, with some very similar sounding broadcasts.

...

Teachers are demonstrating for more pay in Buenos Aires today. Córdoba municipal police are in their fifth day on strike.

These are stories that we see reported during the first full-hour of television news broadcasting that we watch in Argentina.

The international news stories on TV are simply photos pulled out of a U.P.I. news service transmitter machine and then placed in front of a camera as the announcers speak.

Brasil news telecasting is far more global and detailed.

...

Letters from Rio de Janeiro and stories in Buenos Aires newspapers tells us what's happening in Brasil.

The Cruzeiro may drop three zeros, like the peso does here.

There's now such a growing street market business in Rio, encouraged by Governor Brizola, that there's even a sidewalk dentist.

**Mendosa:** The military dictators in Buenos Aires, who ruin the economy and try to divert attention from their imminent demise, (just like Thatcher in the U.K.), by promoting the War of Las Malvinas, are finally disappearing tonight.

Unfortunately, the war prolongs Thatcher's incumbency beyond the one term that U.K. opinion polls are predicting before the war.

Every street in Mendosa is a parade ground tonight.

Election results are broadcast and posted in the streets by local newspapers, to cheering crowds.

At the same time, honking cars start parading back and forth, filled with waving partisans and brandishing national flags and banners. Then the pedestrians take over.

Police in groups of six or seven help the cars leave. Shredded paper is thrown from the crowds or building windows.

People sing, shout, dance, and jump like pogo sticks.

Drums are brought and beat hard, until they have holes in them.

It's the first time in my life that I see a truly spontaneous demonstration of people's feelings.

This isn't one of those institutionalized, staged demonstrations which provide to-ken participation; ease other-wise suppressed consciousness; and temporarily activate people who are usually far away from direct knowledge and experience of what they are demonstrating about.

Such demonstrations are commonplace in the comfortable, isolated north-lands.

We pass Radicalista party headquarters and see the newly-elected governor and mayor speak.

Around the corner at Peronista headquarters, half a dozen police and dogs block access to the defeated party's street.

Radio has no national or international news all day, just turnout figures, and then results after 6 p.m.

Radicalistas take an early lead of 53% to 39%, depending on the region, and never trail.

The big Peronista rallies are only wakes for Juan and Eva Peron. A ghost cannot really be elected, even on this Hallowe'en eve election night.

Voting is compulsory here, as in Brasil. But voters here have an enthusiasm that makes even Trudeaumania pale in comparison. It's votemania in the south.

**San Rafael**: We have our first good radio reception since Mendoza, on Zita's tiny transistor radio, and find out that the previously daily Las Malvinas propaganda jingle has gone off the air with the election commercials.

The programme director of Radio Nacional is apparently not a general.

There will be no more of the constant reminders of war. Las Malvinas are to be peacefully negotiated, newly-elected President Alfonsin says.

Some local people say the war is to hide the generals' incompetence, and explain the enormous national debt.

A "patriotic" fund, to pay for both, apparently gets pocketed by the military dictators.

The Argentinian Jewish community is said to have unwittingly contributed 50 tons of gold.

Months earlier, during the war, I'm in Buenos Aires walking past a live broadcast of a fundraising event.

Much news comes from our casual conversations with various local individuals in various places.

I don't reveal their full names in letters that become <u>Terrian Journals</u> because it is legal for the dictators to open mail, and I don't want my writing to lead them to more victims.

I mail letters critical of one military dictatorship in a neighbouring nation-state with a different military dictatorship that doesn't like its neighbouring one.

**Valparaíso**: I read about the war-made-majority U.K. Prime Minister Thatcher's visit to Canada in one of the newspapers here.

If the prime minister actually says, as quoted in Chile and Argentina, that Las Malvinas are rarely not U.K. colonies with only U.K. residents, then why would the U.K. government bother negotiating with Argentina or any other country?

...

The national map of Chile indicates Chilean possesses a large chunk of Antarctica which is the same land claimed on Argentina's national maps.

Brasil runs a television ad about the Antártica Brasileira.

The ice market is up? Let the snowball fights begin!

...

News says Santiago's power is cut off by sabotage bombings of transmission lines.

We don't know if it's the military dictatorship trying to make the opposition look bad, or the opposition trying to alienate the public so that they'll support the military dictatorship.

Which seems more plausible?

Some credit the military dictatorship for improving literacy and introducing a school lunch programme.

Tomorrow's soldiers must be strong and capable of reading orders.

**Coihaique**: Moments after arriving in Coihaique, a radio journalist comes over to the bench where we're sitting in the plaza.

He points a microphone at us and asks us about our adventure.
Excerpts of our taped interview are to be aired in two days.

It's surprising that we're chosen for an interview, considering the number of backpackers we see here eroding natural contact and creating tourism.

**Puerto Aisen**: Today the radio features news of us. We're famous!

We just hear our entire, unedited interview broadcast on the region-wide Radio Patagonia. It's about 12 minutes long.

We recount highlights of all our adventure to date, and I speak of our objective to reach Tierra del Fuego, "porque esta alla", because it's there, I say, mixing Portuguese mais with Spanish mas.

I also say that for a Canadian, from the most northern landmass in the Americas, it's important to reach the southernmost lands of the continent. We speak only Spanish for the entire interview, with my Portuguese words keep intruding.
The people here at the residencial enjoyed listening to us. Whoopee!

When the reporter singles us out, in a plaza full of backpackers I'm puzzled.

But the other people in the plaza all come on the 17 hour boat. They're not en route for 153 days, like us.

And, after hearing us tell our story, even I'm impressed.

**Concepción del Uruguay**: A horseback parade of couples in costumes greets us when we arrive in this town. It's the local carnival and bronco-busting festival.

This, I think, is the evening's highlight. But, as I began writing about it, a radio reporter is already tapping on our hotel room door.

We walk out front for a live-from-the-streets-of-Concepcion del Uruguay radio night show interview. The tourist office must have tipped off the radio station.

We talk to the reporter and the in-studio announcer for about 10 minutes. Since it's a live broadcast, we won't be able to listen to it later.

Our adventure is news! The reporter calls us "hermanos en el ejército de la paz." It's such a great compliment.

The reporter wants us to talk to us on the radio again in the morning, live from the gaucho festival at the town's five kilometre river beach,.

Unfortunately, we carry on north the next morning, missing the next radio interview and leaving our fame behind.

...

I'm so impressed by our radio experience that I send a couple of post cards and some words on the crossing of the 45th parallel south to the Herald-Gazette newspaper, in Bracebridge (Ontario).

When I live in Bracebridge, the people there prided themselves on living at 45 degrees north, "half way between the equator and the north pole".

I wonder if the newspaper will print my short item about the Carretera Austral.
Years later I'm delighted to find out that they do print an abbreviated version, with only a few typos, such as missing

the "5" in 45 degrees and the final "e" in Chile. I correct the errors:

I enclose my report from halfway between the Equator and the South Pole. If you have space for the words and picture please include my best wishes for all who treated me so well when I wrote for *The Herald-Gazette.*
Don Anderson
Coihaique, Chile.

Cross 45°S Latitude
January 4, 1984
Muskoka's southern hemisphere counterpart in southern Chile is also a land of rivers, lakes, and forests. But here the resources have yet to be exploited. Here perhaps is what the Muskoka hills were like before the mills, the railway, or the ships. But, unlike 45°N latitude, the 45th parallel south crosses few areas of land, only in Chile, Argentina, and New Zealand. It's precious territory.

Halfway between the Equator and the South Pole is the raw frontier land of southern Chile. Great tracts of uninhabited land predominate. The scenery varies from wild seashore to snowy mountains, with a seemily endless number of waterfalls. The Austral Highway at 45°S latitude was only cut into the mountains two years ago and still remains a narrow, rocky trail. Construction crews work in the heavy summer rains of January, staying one to three months.

**Caleta Olivia**: The news we see along the way reports President Alfonsin's news conference about human rights, and the trials of the generals.

It's like Greece after the military regime falls, in recent years.

The military get "due process" of law, unlike the civilians who they murder during coups and subsequent dictatorships.

The last elected president of Chile gets no "due process", just bullets.

**Puerto Madryn**: ...Bodies from the military regime times are turning up in unmarked graves in Córdoba, and sunken in oil drums in Ushuaia.

...

News reports that the U.S. presidents of about 30 years earlier fear that Peron would unite the southern Americas. This unity would not be in the U.S. interest, the U.S. is said to have said at that time.

**Uruguaiana to Porto Alegre**: In the bus we can barely hear a radio newscast beginning a report about the earth/moon gravitational system. We theorize that the earth is closer to the sun because even Zita is sweating heavily.

Or, have we chosen the ideal moment to leave artifact for reality, to see earth while it's still here?

It's time to buy a newspaper.

**Caxias do Sul**: According to the Buenos Aires newspapers that we read before coming here, the Brasilia military cabinet which still controls Brasil's decision-making is afraid of direct presidential elections, such as those held in Argentina.

They must think that another Alfonsin and trials of generals like those in Athens and Buenos Aires would follow.

But, a campaign for direct elections continues in Caxias do Sul. Petitions and t-shirts circulate from open air booths in this city.

...

The <u>Folha de São Paulo</u> newspaper reports the long-expected retirement of Canada's Prime Minister Pierre E. Trudeau.

The paper's New York correspondent writes that Pierre is a grand leader "in face of the mediocrity of the contemporary U.S. president, U.K. prime minister, French president, West German chancellor, and the rest who today orient our world".

How true.

The big difference is that Pierre is not a posturer or a phony.

He openly reveals his personality and natural reactions, instead of just hiding behind a title and filling a role.

Pierre holds office for about 16 years, and no Canadian dies abroad due to any of his government's international policy decisions. He keeps Canada out of the empires' wars.

No one of Pierre's humanity or intelligence has ever held a prime minister's title in Canada during my adult lifetime.

Perhaps some day Canadians will appreciate Pierre as the founder of a Canada liberated from domination by a minority of greedy, ethnocentric, unilingual anglophones, and by other anachronisms of the U.K.'s long-defunct empire; and, as the founder of a Canada which is, instead, united realistically as a multicultural, i.e. fully planetary land, where francophones and other non-U.K. people have the equal opportunity they deserve with the perhaps 40% of people of U.K. origin in Canada.

Perhaps Pierre will be recalled as the prime minister who recognizes Canada as the Brasil of the north, a land where all humans can be at home.

For this work alone, even without his recent peace tour of the nations, Pierre Trudeau should receive the nomination for an Albert Einstein Peace Prize.

**Rio de Janeiro**: Jornal do Brasil runs a long column article and photo of Pierre Trudeau.

It describes Pierre as someone who fascinates Canadians, "a serious student of law and politics, intellectually brilliant, and many times surprising..."

What a hard act to follow, for any future Canadian prime minister.

...

The U.K is finally given its monarch a job? News reports say that she and her husband are in Jordan, selling U.K. arms. Isn't she radiant? Isn't she lovely?

...

Some of Brasil's indigenous people are on the war path, no joking.

In Matto Grosso, a TV news team and their aircraft crew are met by warriors, armed with lances and knives. The crews look frightened in front of the TV news cameras.

(We pass through Matto Grosso when we start out from São Paulo, heading for Bolivia, many months ago.)

The warriors paint the crew's faces with war paint, telling them that they'll cut off the Brasilia government representative's ear if he comes to visit.

The Brazilian colonial-national-based regime is constantly reducing the territory open to aboriginal civilizations.

In a huge place like Brasil, with so many empty hectares, how is this possible?

…Mario Juruna is an aboriginal person originally from Matto Grosso, and a federal deputy elected to represent Rio state in the elections of 17 months ago.

He never sees a person from outside his indigenous community until he's six or seven years old.

Before then, he says, he doesn't realize there are other people or places in the world. He's about 40 years old now.

What did any of us know at five or six years old?

How many "first" worlders now carry on their daily habits as if the "outside world" did not exist?

Fascinating.

My Carioca friend Zita corrects my understanding of Juruna's age when he first sees an outsider. He's then 16 or 17 years old, not 6 or 7 years old.

His story is thus so much more remarkable.

Juruna should be able to help resolve the dispute in his home state.

Apparently, there are about two million aboriginal people living in Brasil 500 years ago.

…Aboriginal cultures still exist in Brasil. Matto Grosso's indigenous people have, in some cases, distorted lips similar to those of the black Africans of some African civilizations.

Brasil's Amerinds still paint their bodies, sing, and dance for themselves, not for show, not for tourists, and not for multicultural festivals.

The only things commercialized are their store-bought shorts.

They are survivors of humanity, in an age of artifact. Would they survive the northerners' radiation diseases?

It's intriguing to see the very articulate aboriginals dressed in superficially "primitive" ways.

…The aboriginal affairs departments of governments in the Americas should be headed by people elected by the aboriginals.

Their civilizations have nothing to do with the European forms of government in places like Brasil and Canada.

...

My Carioca friend Zita says that she does not recall ever seeing so much news in the past about indigenous people on TV news.

She's 32 and only spent a couple of years abroad, studying for her doctorate at La Sorbonne in Paris.

Although technically a member of the formally-educated elite in Brasil, she's working as a secretary now.

Her parents are landless peasants.

He father has a sítio, a very small plot of land like many given to landless locals by the government. Her mother now works in a sewing sweat shop.

...

The current problem in Matto Grosso seems to be resolved.

The head of the aboriginal affairs department has resigned. The minister of the interior has made a land deal with the indigenous people. He's a presidential candidate.

...

...According to Canadian government information, the Canuck north has Inuit and other First Nations who are still living traditional lifestyles.

I would like to learn from them.

...

...Tonight the Carnaval desfile has a delay.

A report says the military police "accidentally throw tear gas" at the samba school now entering the reviewing area, to sing a song which calls the military cabinet "os tripalões", (Brasil's equivalent of "the three stooges").

A nervous-looking Governor Brizola, standing beside a uniformed police supervisor, says the police are telling him they have no tear gas, (not now? they used it all?), and are looking for suspects.

...

Television news cameras are focusing on Candelária.

Political desfiles are due today, before the national diréitas já demonstrations. The favela groups who dance in the carnaval will come out in full fantasias again.

They are dancing in favour of having the direct presidential elections that the outgoing military dictators don't want.

Brizola constructs a very colourful speech platform,, and closes half the downtown streets.

Another political party, PT, pays Cr. 9 million to give free bus and ferry service to all people who are going to Candelária during the demonstration hours.

This party is also attributed with pushing for a general strike soon.

But all of the opposition party people who are interviewed in the news say that the strike is a bad idea, and not necessary. (It could just encourage brute force reactions.)

We see the last, great, orderly demonstration in the Candelária of 20 years ago, in the film "Jango", short for João Goulart. Jango was Brasil's last elected president.

He announces a social reform programme that day in Candelária. The generals don't like it.

The U.S. Empire, official U.S. documents indicate, send in navy ships on a stand-by basis. The coup d'état happens a few weeks later.

People in Copacabana celebrate the "revolution", as the military like to call their illegal seizure of power from the elected government.

While Copacabana residents are jubilant in their streets, police attack and are attacked by people in the streets downtown.

A retired general, interviewed in the documentary film, says the military was pre-empting a political party coup, a "communist" take-over.

Jango is called pro-"communist" by the Copacabana and

military crowd, because, as J.K.'s vice-president, he makes an official visit to China.

He makes a speech there saying that China, Brasil, and other countries have poverty problems in common, despite ideological differences.

He also visits Moscow as president of Brasil. So far, Jango's "pro-communist" activities look the same as maybe 99 per cent of the world's nation-states leaders.

Jango also lets Argentina's and Cuba's Ché come for a visit, and treats him like the representative of a foreign government. So?

Ché was a representative of the unelected government of Cuba, and someone who might have helped overthrow Jango, not support him.

Locals say the Copacabana crowd fear "communism" 20 years ago because "communism" represents the U.S.S.R. Empire, loss of liberty, elimination of free speech, and prohibition of demonstrations.

Today the Copacabana crowd fears "communism" because it means the return of liberty, free speech, and demonstrations, versus the Copacabana supported military dictatorship which prohibits liberty, free speech, and demonstrations for 20 years, after the coup.

So "communism" has nothing to do with Marx. It's just a code name for anything you don't like, or find threatening.

When the military dictators roll in, Jango and J.K. are exiled. J.K is later allowed back in. He's killed in a car accident.

Jango dies of a heart attack, 12 years after the coup d'état. His body is returned to Brasil. No one will ever know what Jango might have done for Brasil.

It's astonishing to me that a government be elected, then ignored and replaced by a military dictatorship for 20 years, solely on the basis of bogeyman fears.

...

Somewhere in the masses showing on the live TV news coverage, my Carioca friend Zita and I are two in a million, in Candelária.

En route to tonight's demonstration downtown, I see more smiling bus passengers than ever, entering by the front door instead of the usual back turnstile, all for the joy of a free ride.

The demonstration is festive, but too congested. There are some people in costumes, performing street theatre.

A Chinese-style, nine-person dragon circles around. A huge, goofy effigy of the military's finance minister, from carnaval, is making another appearance here.

Showers of telex and shreded paper streamers fill the air between the tops of high office towers. It's a peaceful protest.

...At one point, some bank employees, who are looking out their view windows above us, start pointing at someone in the crowd, and making urgent gestures, mouthing the word "ladrão"(thief).

I look around for an armed robber, but see none. Other people grab someone, rip his shirt, and bring him before the window.

The bank people cheer, indicating - "That's him". The "thief" is terrified, saying "Not me".

Three young men pursue him in flight, capture him 10 metres from us, and give him some heavy punches.

I tell Zita that I think robbers should thus be made too frightened to rob. Robbers, not potential victims, should live in fear.

She says she agrees, so long as the vigilantes catch the real robber. A few weeks earlier a mob catches and beats up the wrong person.

More recently, a German couple goes to hospital because they try to resist giving away $50 to Flamengo area robbers.

In response to crime, one must evaluate the dangers in response.

...

One diréitas já T-shirt features the pictures of an evolving human, as shown in natural history museums, under the caption "diréitas já".

We're joining the a million people between Candelária and Central do Brasil train station, a distance of two and a half kilometres, sitting across seven lanes of road, standing over 16 meters of sidewalk, to support diréitas já.

It's the biggest demonstration since Jango's final meeting. We're here for three and a half of the six and a half hours of speeches and song.

We leave early to get uncrowded transportation back to Iacir's place, and because we have enough of the crowd and poor sound where we sit near the speech platform.

The problem in the sidewalk crowds is congestion. Some people are bored, drunk, partying, foolish, mindless, or just disrupters pushing too much.

They almost make dominos out of Zita, me, and a few hundred others who are half a road away from the speakers' stand, on a street corner.

When the problem recurs, an organizer on the stand interrupts a speaker.

He points at the problem area and tells the pushers to come to the front of the platform to pass through the crowd.

In the heat and annoyance of the crowd, the people who nearly fall shout "Calma!" at those pushing and pushed. People police themselves.

We find out there are scuffles earlier in the day, but only when we see them on the TV news.

A million people crowded together is a test of everybody's patience.

Rio Branco and Av. do Brasil are lined with loud speaker systems.

Off these streets, in the quieter areas, people are just sitting quietly on curbs, some with dress shirts and briefcases, listening to the 50 speakers.

We hear the final speakers, Brizola and Neves, in the comfort of Iacir's living room, with the good sound and view of live, multi-channel TV coverage.

Even Rede Globo, the military's friend is there, claiming to be giving an "exclusive" broadcast.

Brizola is a ghost of democratic form past, the governor of Rio Grande do Sul State before the military coup d'état of about 20 years ago.

Brizola now returns to haunt the military by making a moving speech.

He says that public pressure is now evident. The military dictatorship's 20 years are over. It's time to restore the legitimate government.

As the event ends with an emotional singing of Brasil's national anthem, it begins to rain.

I'm moved by the spirit and finale of the throngs who want nothing more than to vote for a president, directly.

Elected politicians are in denial.

Meanwhile, in Brasilia, the military's allies in the PDS governing party are saying they will not even vote on renewal of the direct elections.

Fearing passage of a diréitas já bill, they plan to stay away from congress to prevent a quorum and thus prevent a vote.

The bill, due to be voted on in a few days, is introduced by opposition party representatives and has support from both opposition and many PDS reps.

The military cabinet and president plan to declare their own law, versus direct elections now.

If demonstrations planned for other cities are like the one in Rio, the public cannot be expected to accept a non-vote.

Tensions could rise. Another coup, or a real revolution, or both could follow.

It might even get a column centimetre in the northern newspapers.

This is the first day of President-General Figuereido's emergency measures days in Brasilia and in access towns nearby.

There are to be 59 more emergency measures days to come.

A meeting is planned for this Easter Sunday to decide how to apply the censorship of all news from and to Brasilia.

The emergency measures law isn't even submitted to the congress elected 17 months ago.

The military dictators thus shows the falseness of its promise to restore responsible government to Brasil.

The president-general says he wants to prevent "unfair" pressure on congress from the diréitas já demonstrations.

Vice-President Chaves says the emergency measures are also unfair pressure. He's brave.

Chaves also says he will only be a presidential candidate if there are diréitas já.

General Figuereido says, during his previous TV speech, that diréitas já could be held four years from now. Later he warns that there could be emergency measures.

So we have emergency measures now, instead of diréitas já.

The London Times newspaper reports that the military dictators fear that diréitas já could produce a Brazilian Alfonsin, i.e. prison for the criminals who overthrow the elected government 20 years earlier.

The vote on diréitas já in congress will have censored news coverage. No one will ever know if the vote is rigged. It's closed to public view.

So the military have declared a state of siege in their last hold-out, Brasilia.

How ironic it is that J.K.'s capital of the future should be the last stand site for a discredited, outmoded, anachronistic concept such as military dictatorship.

Brasileiros/as are powerless? In at least one way, yes.

Electric power fails in four states for one or two hours during the night. São Paulo and Rio are hit. I'm just leaving the metro at Cinelândia when it happens.

I come home a while later on the bus through downtown Rio without traffic lights. What difference? Radio is running ads against reckless driving.

The "blecaute" remains unexplained.

Quarantine is the new word for censorship and gagging news reporters.

Apparently censorship begins right away on TV news reaching Brasilia.

Jornal Manchette loses a segment of interviews, seen here in Rio, critiquing the emergency measures. This is democracy?

If Ottawa declared an emergency every time that a big demonstration was planned to influence members of parliament, Ottawa would be in a permanent state of emergency measures.

Military dictators don't understand the meaning of the word democracy. They are not qualified to establish or oversee the return of responsible government.

Brasilia is now encircled by a police quarantine.

All cars, buses, etc. entering the city are searched. Passengers are all checked for documents.

Reporters are filming and interviewing the police in action. The police seem very polite, cooperative, and responsive.

...Demonstrators carrying signs reading "Jesus por diréitas", in front of the Brasilia cathedral, are arrested. They're later released.

...Television news people say their technology doesn't lend itself to external censorship.

Also, censorship regulations seem to be out of date. They don't cover everything currently used in TV technology.

So it might be technically possible to legally communicate news which is meant to be censored. If everyone in Brasilia had a satellite receiver and transmitter...

...Some municipal leaders are at the J.K. monument, saying that they are military reservists who think diréitas já is simply good for Brasil, not an anti-military idea.

Even a general who was a state governor now says he wants diréitas já. So the military is not unanimous in its fear of responsible government now.

...

The news reports that some northern hemisphere journalists are now out on strike.

Journalists here would like the luxury of having such easy access to information that they could go on strike with a clear conscience.

Some local people tell me there may be no further news from Brasilia soon. The censors are sharpening their pencils, in waiting.

Two days from now we'll know, and places outside Brasil might, or might not.
We do get news reports about what I call the coup math.

In Brasilia early this morning, after 16 to 17 hours of debate, the congress votes 298 for diréitas já, 65 against.

So those against win by 22 votes. Only in a military run government could this occur.

A half hour before the vote, military police surround the congress building, to show their support for democratic processes?

The diréitas já vote loses because there's no quorum. About 113 PDS members don't show up. Incredible.

If MPs didn't show up in Ottawa, they would be pressured to resign and/or be thrown out by voters if they ever ran for office again.

...So, generals, what's the difference between the day in Brasilia and the day in Moscow (C.C.C.P.)?

During the day, about 8,000 people gather in and around the building in a silent demonstration.

Some students form the words diréitas já with their bodies on the lawn. Passing cars and buses honk enthusiastically.

The general in charge of emergency measures says it would cost them dearly. About 100 cars and seven buses are seized. The tires are shot on one car.

...Broadcasters who put on news without going through censors are temporarily taken off the air.

Radio Jornal do Brasil runs a disclaimer before every newscast, announcing that the censors have forbidden them from broadcasting any political items.

Censorship is to be lifted Monday, but no news censored up to that time can be broadcast then either.

...Rede Manchette TV news gets an official warning from the military bosses for its use of uncensored political items from Brasilia.

...Squares in most cities are full of people, some watching news, listening to radios, carrying banners, or listening to speeches. I see one square in passing.

Apparently, they stay in the squares until early in the morning, when vote results are announced.

...Some demonstrations continue today, all peaceful. Some thugs in São Paulo break store windows.

Police are moving into the centre this evening. Police interviewed say they can clearly distinguish between the thugs and the non-violent demonstrators.

Protests in one-party regimes aren't always so challenging.

Protests and demonstrations are essential wherever and so long as there is "representative" government, instead of direct democracy.

...When there is only one party which has sufficient public confidence to form a government, and other parties fail to provide effective opposition, the need for protest is increased.

At one point in history, Columbia (Br.) has one-party rule for the better part of 30. The leadership is almost a family dynasty, and one leader is there for 20 years.

Ontario is another example of one-party government for a very long time.

Alberta switches from one long

term one-party rule to another.

In Canada, the same party stays in power in Ottawa for all but four and a half years out of 50. During that era, the leadership is also of long duration, except in one case.

While one party alone seems to be the ticket to being elected, the opposition attracts mediocre candidates, and is chronically ill-prepared to govern.

Demonstrations become the alternative.

...

...A Zurich paper is very critical of the military's mishandling of the diréitas já vote, according to the now resuscitated Radio Jornal do Brasil.

In times of very serious economic troubles, the paper says, the military pressures the elected congress to avoid voting on a democratic process for seeking possible solutions.

The paper suggests that, deprived of rational forms of action, the public could seek more extreme solutions. (...such as another coup?)

...

There are measures of security in the news from elsewhere.

On Rede Manchette TV news, scenes of police violence against residents of Poland and Chile are shown side by side with no commentary on labour day.

Brute force is brute force, "liberty" or "communism".

The empires' obsession with their own security puts human life's security in jeopardy. No one would vote to be oppressed or in favour of a nuclear war.

...

A recent poll gives Vice-President Chaves the most public support as a candidate for the presidency. Brizola, who has suggested Chaves as a transitional president, comes second.

There are a lot of negotiations in progress with the military. There are 250 amendments being proposed to change the current president's proposal on elections.

The next vote on diréitas já will be with a quorum.

Rumour says that the generals will not accept passage of any amendments. The military can't reasonably expect to win a free vote.

Meanwhile, President-General Figuereido is going to visit China. He thus follows in the footsteps of Brasil's last elected president, Jango.

As I mention earlier, one of the excuses that the generals give for their coup d'état, 20 years earlier, is Jango's visit to "communist" China. Is there a little contradiction here?

...

A prominent Brazilian politician tells the real news reporters that Figuereido says he believes opposition governor Tancredo Neves will win the presidency through the indirect elections process.

Figuereido's office says that the politician speaking to reporters will no longer be granted private appointments with the president.

Meanwhile, the presidential elections process becomes more confused each day.

The PDS party leader resigns and moves out of his office after receiving a letter from the president-general.

The resigning leader is also severely criticized for organizing a PDS national convention to hold a primary election within the party to choose a single candidate for an indirect election.

So he should not do what the republicans and democrats do in the U.S. every four years?

An indirect election means that only those PDS members who are in the national congress can vote for Brasil's next president.

Most of these members are the people who blocked the first diréitas já vote by not being present, i.e. preventing a quorum.

So the people who clearly would have lost their fight against direct elections in the vote, had a quorum existed, are now the people in Brasil who can elect the president.

This is not partial democracy. It's farcical democracy!

Under this system, the two candidates vying for last place in the public opinion polls are the front runners to become president.

The resigned PDS chief says that even he would rather vote for an opposition candidate.

...When least popular, but most likely to win presidential candidate Paul Maluf recites the names of Brasil's political parties, PDT, PTB, PDS, PT, PMDB, his physical resemblance to the stuttering U.S. cartoon character Porky Pig is accentuated.

...Now the PDS deputy chief, João Sarney is also resigning after a dispute with Maluf's organizers.

...The military are inventing an indirect form of dictatorship until, maybe, four years from now.

They are tiring the public and risking handing the people over to non-military preachers of violence.

Of course the role of these preachers can be to justify a military comeback, to "restore order".

How can a representative government ever hope to be born in Brasil?

If Brasil were not a nation in a nation-state system; If there were direct, global democracy; the human beings crossing the lands of Brasil would not suffer these political insults to us all.

But the present situation is not completely hopeless. A long-discussed new political party is still in the works.

Brizola can still be interviewed in front of President João Goulart School, calling for diréitas já. Goulart's daughter can still appear on TV in political commercials.

..Maluf, the anti-quorum politicians, and their uniformed chiefs are getting very isolated.

The chiefs are losing their ability to conceal their manipulations of the farcical democracy.

They may soon have to choose between retirement under another Greek or Alfonsin-type government, i.e. end up in court for the coup d'état of 20 years ago; or fake a crisis to justify another coup.

**Anchorage**: We have access to a television and watch a major U.S. network news telecast. There is no word about whether the vote in Brasília takes place or not.

It's difficult to believe the U.S. news people don't know what's going on, especially after all the drama of emergency measures, non-quorum voting, and the withdrawn amendment of General-President Figuereido.

The struggle to renew an elected form of government in indirect/direct elections democracy doesn't even merit a ten-second air space in the U.S. news.

So people in the northern Americas can live on in blissful ignorance and fear, while the generals of the south make their plans, unobstructed by daily scrutiny, to "save" the ig-norant of the northern Ameri-cas from the "spectre of com-munism".

They can save us with the concrete reality of dictatorship and repression, save us with the techniques that a previous generation died to fight, in the 1930s/1940s war.

**Fukuoka**: "Diréitas já" don't materialize this year in Brasília.

But the split and eventual breakup of the military-favoured PDS does keep Maluf, the least popular presidential candidates, from winning the indirect elections vote.

The new president is Tancredo Neves, who is governor of Minas Gerais and prime minister of Brasil before the coup d'état.

President-elect Neves is in the news every day in Nippon. It's not because of his victory. Neves never takes office.

On the eve of his planned inauguration, Neves is rushed to hospital for emergency surgery. For more than a week he undergoes operation after operation.

He's not a young person. There seems to be no clear word on the cause of his initial surgery.

One time we hear that it's an emergency appendix operation. There are other stories.

We wonder who the doctors are and if their loyalty rests with the elected or military patients.
The number of operations seems so great and the information so unclear, at least from these thousands of kilometres away, in Fukuoka.

But when the news of Neves' death reaches us, it's as if we're in Glória again watching Rede Manchette news. It's a very sad day.

José Sarney, the vice-president-elect, will be president.

He's the former PDS vice-president who resigns in disgust for the PDS presidential candidates. So, indirectly, the PDS does win the presidency.

We hope it's truly the better elements of the former PDS who now control Brasília, not the military-puppet wing.

I look at the foreign language newspaper the next day and feel no cheerier.

...

Gareth, a mind-troubling negative person from Wales, uses an item in The Guardian newspaper to support his vehement attacks on Nippon.

His caustic gross generalizations always turn out to be as false and misleading as everything I hear about the southern Americas, from every source, before I go there to learn for myself.

Gareth discounts my real-life positive experiences here as if they were outlandish fiction.

Gareth's isolation from Nippon and local people, despite his marriage to a local person, is surely why he's able to maintain and reinforce his negativity.

Not sharing fluency in the same language saves his marriage and those of other malcontent non-locals?

Gareth waves The Guardian at me as if it were a religionist sacred text that I must believe and blindly accept or suffer eternal damnation.

Within the pages of this otherwise prestigious and

widely-respected newspaper is an item authored by a foreign correspondent who is spouting the same negative gross generalizations as Gareth.

Gareth declares that the article is evidence and undeniable proof that all of his Nippon-bashing is the truth.

The Guardian has a reporter unwilling and unable to apply critical journalistic judgement to complaints with no basis in fact?

The complainers themselves are exempt from the critical eye of investigative reporting?

Complainers' racism and hatred are never exposed by the foreign correspondent from the complainers' part of the world?

Gareth says the reporter writing the negative story is leaving Nippon. So it's a parting shot?!

I write a critique of the article to The Guardian, explaining my positive experiences and challenging the paper to cover the whole story instead of only negative prejudices.

The Guardian never replies to me and to my knowledge doesn't retract or improve the "story".

...I can understand the hostility coming from jealous psychological nationalism that I see displayed by non-locals from the U.S. and other former imperial centres.

It's a legacy of racism pretending that "white" people are superior by nature to everyone else. Nippon proves this is a foolish lie and illusion.

At time of writing, Nippon has the world's number two economy and is poised to replace the U.S. in the top spot; Nippon's auto makers are supplanting the former "big three" U.S. makers; and Nippon's corporations are blowing up a "bubble economy" that is years from bursting.

Even the U.S. Universal Studios and Columbia Pictures are owned by Japanese companies at the time.

...Two years later, while helping a UBC psychology student with an experiment, I mention the apparent psychological problems of non-locals in Nippon.

She smiles and says she can imagine. I'm not the first to notice the problem.

Nipponphobia seems to be a type of phobia experienced by some non-locals around the world, starting with the European era invaders of more than 500 years ago.

I meet the phobic in many different parts of the world.

...

The last two nights, television news specials feature global political, economic, physical, and other issues.

Some are produced by NHK, Nippon's equivalent of Canada's CBC-SRC. Other programmes are imported and translated.

Television news picks up items from BBC, ABC and France's TV. All of these are broadcast in the original languages, with subtitles or voice over.

Very early in the morning there's a "feed" from a U.S. cable TV news network.

During these first months in Nippon, I get up at 6 a.m. and watch the news before going out for the day.

I also read an English translation of Marco Polo's logs.

...

Some of the last news stories attracting my attention while I prepare to leave for Canada are about oil tankers being sunk in Arabian waters.

My Carioca friend Zita notes on several occasions that tanker crews aren't treated as people in the news. They're reported as no more than numbers, total injured and dead.

News concentrates on oil supplies, insurance, and arms.

Commercial sailors, like the ones we meet at Valparaíso's Seamen's' Institute are invisible, forgotten, insignificant lives, on top of being routinely exploited in the ports.

**Rio de Janeiro**: ...A famous Canadian book by a well-known Canadian journalist, but a book not well-written enough for me to read beyond the first pages, calls Canada "unknown".

That seems to be true here in Rio.

Canada is apparently not newsworthy outside of Canada.

I make one of my rare visits to the Canadian consulate today, just to look at the Canuck newspapers.

So I know that Columbia (Br.) currently has unemployment as large as some "third world" countries. It's 20%.

...Of course unemployment is an anachronistic concept.

Employment is merely neo-slavery in a fancy wrapper, an elaborate way to give away a lifetime, which rightfully belongs to the one living it.

...

Letters I receive from Canada and news reports we see in the southern Americas make us wonder if this is the time to visit Canada, to quote back at people saying the same thing about my adventures here in the south.

In Canada: Body guards are protecting the Columbia (Br.) premier; a mad soldier shoots up the Québec legislature; There's hockey violence too.

The northern road that we plan to take to Inuvik in future is "primitive".

In comparison with this news from Canada, Bolivia sounds idyllic.

...

Daily life experiences of the northern hemisphere might seem like dreams to many people in the south. Yet the TV networks here use Star Trek-like special effects.

Rede Manchette introduces its Jornal newscast with a screen full of stars, drifting through space. Then a globe appears, and grows into the spinning earth.

But talk to people in the streets of Rio and you'll find many who have never heard of what's happening in the "outside" world.

When I say I'm from "the north", apparently some Cariocas conclude that I'm from Bahia or somewhere near there.

For these people, and many in the northern hemisphere too, the past, present, and future beyond their daily lives do not exist. All of human history is lost for them.

Their lives are: commuting, employment, eating, sleeping, and maybe watching, or the extremely minimal communication talking which takes place in front of the dulling light of the television screen.
It talks endlessly, says nothing in particular for long periods of time, and makes itself at home. A TV is like the new drinking buddy of the "blue collar" set. TV fits in just fine.

Long after I write those words about TV, PADD, the personal advertising delivery devices such as "smart phones" augment the TV effect by burying minds in an endless foray of images, sounds, and words bombarding the people holding and fixated on PADD everywhere they go.

The role of such people, millions of them, is to serve companies and governments as PADD carriers.

...

The star of the film "Pixote" is in the local news.

"Pixote" is a fictional story based on the actual experience of children who are turned into criminals by unscrupulous adults in Brasil.

The adults use the kids to commit crimes because children can't be tried in adult criminal court. The story occurs in Brasil.

In real life, the young actor playing Pixote lives in a favela. I see him on television in Rio. He's in a commercial helping to raise money for UNICEF. He also has a small acting part in another movie.

But his life as an actor doesn't move fast enough for him.

When Zita and I return from Patagonia, the young actor steals a television set, perhaps just to draw attention to his plight.

A local politician responds by offering to provide both a home for the Pixote actor's family and some acting lessons for him.

The final news of the young actor who plays Pixote is that the police shoot him dead.

**Inuvik:** There's a federal election in Canada this particular year too. I'm in Edmonton when one of the party leaders speaks at a local shopping centre.

I also see some of the election debating and news coverage in this small northern town. The television I have access too is usually tuned to Olympic games coverage.

The excerpts of the election debates between party leaders, that I see in the news here give me a funny impression.

One of the party leaders looks like Steve Martin, the surreal, white-haired U.S. comedian.

The other party leader has a chin like Dudley Dooright, the cartoon version of a Mountie.

**Fukuoka:** My Carioca friend Zita often says that we can learn a lot about a society from its soap operas.

Although she doesn't watch soap operas in Rio, with the exception of the political satyr Bem Amado, she encourages me to do so.

But I spend too much time watching the news in Rio.

The implications of a connection between a society and its soap operas seems ominous to me, in the U.S. context. Many U.S. soap operas are available in Canada too.

These afternoon plays have long depicted superficial, cardboard characters incapable of coping with their lives or with unfamiliar situations.

Problems drag out forever, or until the unlikely event that, some day, a "soap" is cancelled or voluntarily ceases to exist.

Does this mean that people in the U.S. should be considered lacking in depth; incapable of showing their true feelings; having no understanding of the world beyond their routine boundaries; and incompetent as problem-solvers?
Well…

...

Nippon's television news covers the day's/week's

flower-in-bloom as a major story.

It's refreshing to see a real story instead of one cultivated by news and public relations "judgement".

When my partner Mariko sees such "headline news" she often remarks, "What a peaceful country!"

But the advertising sometimes lacks any judgement.

Nicotine and alcohol ads abound, featuring U.S. movie stars who know their message is destructive to health and illegal in their homeland.

One alcohol ad shows a local woman arguing with a man and then going for a drink called, "my friend", which makes her happy.

The implication is that she should take alcohol instead of solving her real problems.

...

The editor of a local newspaper phones me at my workplace one day to ask me how it feels to be the first "U.S. citizen to refuse to be fingerprinted".

Here, finally, is a rumour that I don't start about myself.

I brush aside the insult that I have the right to vote and influence policy decisions in the U.S.

Talk about not getting basic facts correctly- and this is an "editor".

I tell the "editor" I'm just a Canadian, not a representative of the good or bad deeds of the U.S.

Then I ask him to tell me the source of the story that I'm refusing to do something.

He says that some church person hears the story from "my wife".

I ask the "editor" what language the churchist and my "wife" are using to communicate.

I add that the woman in question, who he calls my "wife" is a lusophone who doesn't dominate either English or Japanese.

Therefore, if the churchist doesn't speak Portuguese, I wouldn't put much confidence in any account of what the person he calls my "wife", presumably my Carioca friend Zita "says" about me.

The editor apologizes and hangs up.

All the while I remain unmarried, as does Zita.

When I tell Zita this story she says she does meet a churchist during her Korean visa trip.

Zita also says that she sympathizes with the lack of rights for locals of Korean origin but never says anything about me being from the U.S. or refusing finger-printing.

In Zita's case it's rather a non-issue.

Brazilian locals are obliged to have, and carry at all times, an identification card bearing their photo and fingerprint.

Since the photo is taken when a person is 18 years old, that part is not very effective identification. Only the fingerprint remains the same.

While I think this is all being settled, I'm particularly surprised to find a "reporter" waiting for me in the lobby of my workplace a few weeks later.

She asks me if I'm the "U.S. citizen" who's refusing to be fingerprinted.

I very politely tell her to tell her "editor" that there's been a mistake.

Thus my opportunity to be famous and to gain U.S. citizenship without going through the U.S. immigration department passes. The mass media forget me.

...

Perhaps the Japanese alien registration system is inherited from the U.S. military occupation of Nippon before my birth.

Whatever the origins, it now extends to locals of Korean origin who are not of Japanese parentage.

They have to report for fingerprinting and provide a photo for the little identification card they must carry at all times, by law.

Zita and I comply with the same law, but only because we are non-locals.

I don't consider the fingerprinting and photo alone to be the issue. Fingerprinting is meaningless to me. Who cares if everyone knows what my fingers look like?

What I do take exception to is that the fingerprinting creates yet another nation-state function, another reinforcement of the nation-state illusion of nationality.

And it's basically a waste of everyone's time and resources, as well as tax revenue.

...

News stories about "Koreans" refusing to be fingerprinted continue.

The Hangoo government in Seoul advises Japanese born people of Korean origin to comply with all Japanese government laws.

Perhaps if this group of effectively Japanese locals concentrated on opposing other discrimination issues, their cause would have more chances of attracting more attention and wider support beyond Nippon.

At time of writing, Hangoo's military dictatorship certainly has little to gain by attracting international attention to civil liberties issues involving any Koreans, ethnic or otherwise.

And the issue of nationality-in-question is a threat to the entire nation-state system.

The idea that nationality can become a very abstract and fluid notion becomes a threat to all those having vested interests in the absolute power of the nation-state over a strictly defined group of people.

The "Korean" issue in Nippon could be one of the beachheads for denationalizing relations among human beings.

Ultimately, the locals of Korean origin win their case in the Japanese courts, which rule that the fingerprinting of these local born people is illegal.

True non-locals like me benefit too. We only have to sign our alien registration cards instead of being fingerprinted.

Unfortunately, when the extreme, hysterical, excessive, and paranoid U.S. obsession with "terrorism" and "security" obliges Nippon's government to adopt U.S. immigration rules, years later, fingerprinting and mug shots of almost every non-local arriving in Nippon begins.

Only the "Korean" residents are spared. They are unmolested in this sense, at Nippon's entry points.

Canada becomes one of the most offensive and worst followers of the U.S. lead by fingerprinting and taking mug shots of everyone landing in a Canadian airport.

This includes locals returning from annual vacations abroad.

Thus Canada abandons its former basic justice principle that everyone is presumed innocent until found guilty beyond reasonable doubt in a court of law.

Argentina's now long democratically-elected government also follows the U.S. suit, as reciprocity for the treatment of its citizens visiting that country.

I even see a baby printed and mug shot at one Argentina airport immigration booth.

The airport is using U.S. computers and software. So, the U.S. obsession with "security" is simply a new Yankee Trader sales scheme to sell lower quality U.S. products abroad?

Whatever the case, dictators around the world are licking their lips, ordering equipment on line, and rejoicing at the increased power and longer reign that they can gain thanks to U.S. "security" technology.

Bigger and worse genocide, holocausts, and other crimes against humanity are already in the making due to the "miracle" of technology.

...

Television news has powerful images of politicians and their staff posing for photos in fine suits, watching guns fire, toasting each other, and sitting in luxurious meeting rooms.

All this is to tell us that the nation-state and its inherent problems are more important than humanity and Earth.

No one whose prime concern is humanity would worry about nation-states or their balances-of-power or weapons of mass destruction.

Weapons protect only elite structures, while destroying buildings, history, and the natural environment, and killing people.

Dictators kill dissenters while indirect democracies merely ignore them and absorb them into the nation-state.

In both cases, the ideas are kept from harming the elite struc-tures.

The political TV stars posing in front of cameras should not ask what they can do for the nation-state, but what they can do for the human world. So should all of us.

...Considering the state of the finances of the nation-states, I wonder what results would come of a study of the cost-effectiveness of the nation-state.

How would a cost-benefit analysis go?

These are more unasked questions for the sacred nation-state.

**Taipei:** During the era of my first visit, entry information to visitors says it's illegal to bring in foreign newspapers, which might mention the existence of The People's Republic of China and its government.

It's also illegal to import anything made in eastern Europe or "communist" countries.

They won't be confiscated. You just have to declare them and leave them with customs at the airport, then pick them up on departure.

Is Polish underwear being smuggled in, under cover?

I recall a U.B.C. prof returning from a trip to Taiwan and showing us foreign books that he purchased there. Whenever a book mentioned the PRC it was blank due to Taiwan censors.

This is a strong, free, democratic outpost? It's a greenhouse. All will perish if the door is left open.

Taiwan is not without its contradictions as a closed island. When I show customs that I am carrying foreign newspapers, from Nippon, they just smile and wave me through.

But I am still left wondering about the basis for the continued existence of Taiwan as "The Republic of China", a country which, in real terms, ceases to exist before my birth.

We know what Taiwan is officially against, but what is Taiwan for?

[2024: I'm aware that Chiang Kai Shek and his son rule this island for many years. Only now do I learn that I arrive there during the final year of a very long period of Marshall Law. Shek and the Kuomintang crush a pro-democracy movement and imprison opposition politicians. So, to partially answer my question: Taiwan doesn't stand for democracy. Despite Cold War propaganda to the contrary, Taiwan isn't any more than another military dictatorship promoting itself as "anti-communist" and "pro-western". With allies like these, how can we ever honestly claim to be against totalitarianism?]

**Seoul**: Some very serious and detailed plans for reuniting northern and southern Korea are on page one of the Seoul newspapers when I arrive.

I take a train to Buson, across a wide area of Hangoo for the first time. I'm thinking about the war here, 30 years before my arrival in this land.

How long did it take to rehabilitate the lush, green farmland which now dominates the scenery?

What did the U.S. and U.S.S.R. empires really want in this ancient land of friendly folks?

Why did those empires despoil this land and people for silly ideologies and a few more kilometres of imperial influence?

**Fukuoka**: Death in OBON is the top story in the news.

OBON is the annual festival for the dead, a kind of prolonged and more elaborate form of a west Eurasian "Hallowe'en/All Saints Day".

A fatal "jumbo" jet plane crash during OBON is a macabre moment.

At first no one knows the extent of the human loss. News reports simply state the names and ages of people on the passenger list.

Maps show the location and terrain of the area where the plane loses radio contact with air traffic control.

No one knows who's dead, or how many this night. And no one tries to find out. Rescuers don't attempt to reach the crash site until the following morning.

Anyone who might be alive tonight might not survive until morning, if they require a great deal of medical treatment.

Later, reports indicate that some of the airline passengers may have died overnight at the crash site.

If concealing emotions ever is universal and a constant factor in Nippon, the arrival of television in these green mountain islands may be a cause of its demise.

Smiles, tears, and cheers are close-up on TV here.

The air crash manifests the open expression of emotions in Nippon on a large scale, as special news reports continue.

Sometimes announcers sit in front of a photo of a jumbo jet (Boeing model 737), trying to point out the fault in the plane which seems to be responsible for the disaster.

Sometimes the photo turns into a wall of black and white photos of the 500 victims.

Some telecasts seem to give a body-by-body report as rescuers, faces covered with white towels, hoist bodes, one at a time, into helicopter slings for loading.

A stop-action camera focuses on each body sac and shows a photo of the victim in life who is wrapped inside.

The name, age, and a few words about the victim are shown on screen under each wrapped body sac.

Or, shots of the wreckage freeze and a picture of each

victim is shown, always with name and age.

The scene changes to an airport where a person with a white box in his arms is met by wailing relatives of the dead. It's a box of ashes?

Now there's a large hall scene, full of those white boxes.

Adults and children lift a flap on top of each box – again and again – then go into fits of tears in each other's arms. Some brace themselves in hysteria.

More lucid family members talk before TV cameras.

A photo of a survivor, a flight attendant, is shown as a tape of her voice, from a hospital bed, is played.

I've never before seen such a deep presentation of the emotions of tragedy. It's a moving spectacle which makes the others seem like mere lottery results.

Here every victim is presented as a real, lost life, a person who lived, not just a statistic.

It's more than a body count. It's not just a news item for a few minutes before commercials.

What deep sensibility this culture holds! What humanity! What emotion manifest!

...

OBON is also the anniversary of two days when the U.S. became the first and, to date, last nation-state to commit horrific mass murder by dropping atomic bombs on Hiroshima and Nagasaki.

The only fortunate aspect of the OBON bombings is that they didn't become the first volleys in a U.S. offensive more ambitious than the Japanese military dictatorship was undertaking up until then.

News reports now say the U.S. did have a larger plan. The post-war plan is to use atomic bombs to attack and occupy U.S.S.R. cities between 1945 and 1950.

How little the planners of such atrocious behaviour must have been moved by the human suffering of Hiroshima and Nagasaki.

Likewise the Soviet war planners, who may have had a similar, equally incomprehensible plan on the very heels of the first bombings.

But the U.S.S.R. had no atomic bomb at the time of Hiroshima and Nagasaki.

Recent news that both U.S. and U.S.S.R. empires were apparently eager and willing to offer nuclear weapons to belligerents in the heat of the last Yisra'el-Egypt war shows the great difference between national and human values.

Nation-states and empires are entities in themselves, separated from the facts and sentiments of human life.

Nation-states and empires have no human characteristics or qualities.

Nation-states and their empires are our Frankenstein-type monster. We need to dismantle them, while we are still alive.

OBON is an appropriate time to consider not only previous death, but avoidable future death as well. OBON also makes me think of Brasil's macumba fires and candles.

...

...The news is reporting that food sterilized by radiation might be shipped from the U.S. to here, so that there won't be any spoilage en route.

What about vitamin loss or long-term radiation effects, if any?

The news also shows dehydrated vegetables compressed to pocket size.

I can see the value in pre-space station agriculture, but in the long run would it only further jeopardize our survival as a lifeform by removing us even farther from the ability to harvest our food directly?

We would be one more step removed from the realities of nourishing ourselves.

We would be better off if we followed the example of plants.

This would mean that we could take our sustenance directly from sunlight, rather than via intermediaries such as eating other life-forms.

It seems like a logical step and far superior to the food industry concept now in vogue in the caretaker society.

...

Several days after November 11, the day commemorating the armistice ending the 1914-1918 war, I realize I'm unaware that this day passes unnoticed.

Perhaps I miss the news that day?

In Rio it's only a military ceremony. I see no poppies made by war veterans in Rio.

Maybe I don't notice the eleventh because the wars of the past and present aren't a part of my daily consciousness or my life's experience.

The current wars are just a few seconds of news, often unwatched by residents of the caretaker society who find news "so depressing".

Better not to know? We await Robespierre to bring us the news? Children, the naïve of the world (?), know war today in many places.

The grenade throwers in the recent Egyptian airline tragedy seem like mere crazies, with no possible justification, no ideology for what they learn since childhood.

Near another pole of humanity, the U.S. and U.S.S.R. leaders may now be coming up with a way to divide up their world pie.

Maybe it'll be a trade, Afghanistan for Central America.

The leaders of both world-ruling empires are such charming fellows.

**Macau**: As soon as I cross the border into the People's Republic of China for the first time, I'm immediately disillusioned.

I see flies.

Back at university in Canada, I read a newspaper saying that the late Chairman Mao tells everyone to kill flies. They haven't finished yet!?

Finding a fly in Chuang Hwa is an experience of the same magnitude as, say, finding a rat in Alberta. That too is supposed to be highly unlikely verging on impossible.

**Fukuoka**: The ballot counting for Nippon's Diet election is one ballot at a time, like in Canada, according to the television news images.

The election returns come in slowly. There's no TV coverage of results until the 11 p.m. news. But even then no results are given.

It's more suspenseful than waiting from the results to appear in Rio.

But everyone we talk to during the campaign would be surprised if the incumbent prime minister's party doesn't win the election. They expect his victory.

He dissolves both houses of the diet, which is apparently unusual. The elections are usually separate, locals tell us.

Apparently the prime minister wants to capitalize on his current personal popularity and win a majority for his party in both houses.

Real coverage of actual election results doesn't begin until the day after voting. It's reported in detail, riding by riding, like in Canada.

It's a long time before we know that the party in power has actually won its expected majority of seats in both houses of the diet.

In a quiet country like this one, the electoral process seems like a definite side event.

Maybe in prosperous times the only issue that counts is prosperity.

Election issues seem to be military and education spending, according to one language student I know, who works as a probation officer in family court.

The winning party claims that it's necessary to spend more than the current ceiling on military spending. It's a limit of 1% of the total budget.

The prime minister says raising the limit is only required to cover routine pay increases for self-defence force personnel.

News of two weeks ago reports that Nippon already has the second-highest government spending tally in modern Japanese history.

So 1% of that is already a great deal of money.

The question remains however – At what point will military spending be held now? Will it be 2%, or more?

The U.S. imposed constitution of 40 years earlier obliges Nippon to spend no more than 1% on the military, but now the U.S. wants Nippon to join the space wars scheme, which is very expensive.

That spending is far more than 1%.

Is Nippon to "regulate its trade surplus" in the same manner as military dictatorships in the southern Americas?

Soon after the election, the education minister becomes involved in yet another controversy related to some poorly chosen words about Japan's participation in east Eurasian history during the past 100 years.

Some omissions in text books, the parts describing past Tokyo governments' crimes, are already causing much criticism from Beijing.

Now that the prime minister's popularity has helped his party get re-elected, he's being forced out of office.

His political heirs and rivals seem to be giving him one year's notice of his retirement from politics. This is the final election for Prime Minister Nakasone.

...

The big news is beyond my understanding because I don't have enough vocabulary in Japanese and I don't have a non-Japanese sound track television set.

Visually, I gather that the headline items include an all-night meeting of the Diet. Television news shows politicians asleep, trying to wake up with pep drinks, etc.

Is it the new sales tax debate? Just before leaving office Nakasone wants to put a 5% sales tax on all merchandise, including food. Up to now, there's no sales tax.

Diet members heckle, march to the podium, and slam the name plates on their desks inside the chamber while others chant outside, disrupting others trying to speak.

...Something is happening in Bolivia too, but I don't know what.

...In Argentina, President Alfonsin and former Peronista presidential candidate Luder are standing in front of a mass rally while los militares roll tanks around Bariloche.

The newsreader says, "coup d'état".

Some street interviewers in Buenos Aires, ones I can hear in Castellano, over the Japanese voice-over, are talking about "stopping them", them being the military.

Would the U.S. and U.K. repeat their Granada performance to "protect democracy" in Argentina? Don't bet on it. They just play U.S.-U.S.S.R. games.

The rest of us are only pawns.

The U.S.-U.S.S.R. has no morality. They just guard the nation-state itself. They fear more Vietnam and Afghanistan wars.

They fear uniting the brother generals they put in power in Poland and Chile, the new "Axis Powers".

...Now I know what's happening in Nippon and Argentina.

Here it's a filibuster on the budget, including the sales tax bill.

In Argentina it's an officers' rebellion, like in the Philippines? I'm sure my Carioca friend Zita isn't surprised that the military in Barcelona tries to pull a coup.

She and I have a run-in with a young military guy there during her annual vacation in Argentina and Chile. Fortunately, we're also victorious in that encounter.

After trying to take on Zita, I would have thought they'd

have learned their lesson. Apparently not.

...

...The U.S. agriculture minister is touring supermarkets in Nippon, maybe only in Tokyo's most expensive shops.

He's in the television news showing pictures which ostensibly demonstrate how cheap U.S. farm products could make shopping in Nippon.

After buying Nippon-grown food in Fukuoka for some time, in the Nishijin and Tojin-machi markets, I know that prices are much cheaper here than the ones the U.S. minister is showing.

Who is he trying to kid?

...Have the U.S.-Canada trade talks collapsed yet? When?

...In a way, the U.S. consumer preference for Japanese products reminds me of the former(?) desire of Canadian consumers to buy U.S. products.

**Sapporo**: Ainu daily prayers are religion as journalism. The gods' only source of news about human world events comes from prayers.

So wording and associated rituals were carefully chosen according to strict rules. Holy style guide!

Yet the Ainu gods are in everything, even inanimate objects such as kitchen utensils. There's an Ainu story about a well-cleaned pot rewarding its owners.

Life after death is thought to be the same as life. So things needed in life-before-death are buried with bodies. How Egyptian!

**Paris**: In the place in front of the Ministry of Justice and a tiny branch of the Bank of Montréal, I see the machine-gun-toting police so reminiscent of Santiago under the much-loathed Pinochet military dictatorship.

Yet this is typical of what I'm seeing around Parisien government buildings at time of writing.

Later, near Place d'Iéna, there's a real tour de force around the Conseil économique et social.

I'm coming around the corner to write these words just in case the street full of black-clad swat team police troops get trigger happy when they see me pulling out a pen.

...After taking a close look at a map of Paris and watching the television news reports... I discover that Place d'Iena is just around the corner from the Iranian Embassy.

It's currently under siege by the French police because they believe there's a suspected terrorist hiding out there.

This is how and why I accidentally stumble upon the main attraction in Paris at time of writing.

...

Between a museum and Le Louvre I walk past a million people lining the Champs Elysées, from the larger Arc de Triomphe of l'Étoile to Le Louvre.

They're just standing and waiting before an unusually empty boulevard. I try to look around and over the heads in front of me, but all I can see is empty pavement.

I find this extraordinary. I ask someone what's going on. He uses some words which I know but which have no significance for me as a unit.

Then I see some souvenirs on sale and realize that I am familiar with this event and see recordings of it in a television newscast.

It's a bicycle race called "Tour de France".

**Toronto**: In large type, front page stories, Southam Newspapers and others are reporting research saying that about 24% of Canadians are functionally illiterate.

It's a percentage based on testing, not formal education attained.

About 8% of Canadian university graduates are functionally illiterate, the research says. With my spelling and grammatical errors, am I among them?

Of course one question judges how well people understand The Canadian "Charter of Rights and Freedoms". It's also a test of official languages, not first language literacy.

So a person literate in Portuguese or Chinese could be listed as functionally illiterate in English or French. I qualify for that category in Japanese.

I hope the literacy groups working abroad are using local languages, not European imperial languages.

Otherwise the literacy work is no better than a linguistic equivalent of colonialism and accuturation.

...

It's now three years since Pierre Trudeau takes a walk in the snow and decides to retire. When we arrive in Toronto he seems to be making a comeback.

I hope to watch Pierre when he testifies before the parliamentary committee on what is called the Meech Lake Accord.

Unfortunately, I don't get to see Pierre speak because the current prime minister prevents the parliamentary television channel from broadcasting the event when it happens.

Instead of Pierre talking about the Meech Lake Accord, the parliamentary channel shows only a member of the party in power reading an entire newspaper article.

I only see excerpts from Pierre's views, broadcast on the late night newscasts.

Only one reporter on one of the four TV station newscasts I watch, mentions how the party in power stops the live broadcast of Pierre while he's speaking.

The parliamentary channel does play a recording of Pierre's views the next morning, after most people go to work for the day. I don't know if it's the complete or edited version.

...

The separatist trade continues in Canada.

I see one news report which says younger reporters are "dazzled by the economic wizardry" of a former Péquist (separatist) finance minister who is praising the idea of a free trade deal with the U.S.

People, especially reporters, should be suspicious of the old Péquists who are coming back from the political dead to promote this deal.

It's part of sneaky, soft-sell separatism. The deal can bolster the old separatist slogan, "sovereignty-association".

The current witless prime minister is portraying the deal in classic separatist language. Is this another side-effect of having his friend, a separatist, as his key advisor?

The current prime minister says Canada's well-being depends on signing a trade agreement with the U.S. which both recognizes our <u>sovereignty</u> and provides us with unhampered access to U.S. markets through continued close <u>association</u> with the U.S.

...

I learn something from the unreported news that is persuading me that Canadian politicians and news people are sloppy and lack knowledge of basic facts.

During the final week of the federal election campaign the current prime minister pooh-poohs worries about how a free trade deal with the U.S. could affect Canada's social programmes.

People are worried due to Canada's relatively small population.

The prime minister says, "If Sweden, with its small population, were worried about its many social programmes it would not be-long to the EEC." (European Economic Community)

After the election, I look at a list of EEC member states. Sweden is not a member.

Sweden does not join the EEC's successor, the European Union. until about eight years after Canada's free trade election!

Yet no one challenges the statement about Sweden, made by the prime minister of the time just before the Canadian election. Nobody knows which nation-states belong to the EEC then?

...

Unelected traditions seem to be popular in Ottawa during the "free trade" debate. The main government spokesperson seen in the news is an appointed negotiator.

During news interviews he presents himself as someone who is only capable of out-talking people, instead of out-reasoning them.

This specious approach is the exact opposite of the Trudeau age of reasoning.

...

One of the final opinion polls in the news before election day shows the official opposition ahead of the party in power. The Canadian dollar exchange rate decreases.

News reports connect the poll and the rate.

Then the dollar goes up again, but the news says nothing. Then a poll shows the party in power leading again.

The dollar goes up, but this time the news links the poll and the rate again.

What about the intervening days' rate increase, before the latest poll?

...

Partisan politics and business are getting mixed up in this campaign, but in backwards order, as shown in the private advertising which supports the policy of the party in power.

Democratic institutions should call the shots in business, not vice versa. Otherwise business has the power to interfere with democracy.

Business bureaucracy, like government bureaucracy can become a parallel government.

If democracy is not to interfere with business as conservatives say, then business is not to interfere with democracy.

This means no lobbying, no political issue propaganda, and no revolving doors between cabinet offices and corporate executive suites.

A person can be in business or politics, not in both at the same time.

All this should be the law, but government would call all the shots, as it does now, on labour law, environmental health, product safety, etc.

In all these areas, human rights must always take precedence over business rights.

In fact business is a privilege, not a right. European monarchs give the Hudson Bay Company and others licenses.

Democracy should have a like absolute right over business. Business exploits the creative and then claims glory for "promoting" creativity.

As soon as business feels itself being challenged by democracy it starts shouting "socialist" and "communist".

Now the business clique shouts "anti-free-traders are stupid, disaster-makers".

But democracy, by its very nature, isn't supposed to be minority rule by the business elite.

The real spectre hanging over business is democracy. True democracy defines the role of business, not vice-versa.

That's how CBC, public health insurance, minimum wage, etc. come to be.

They're democracy ruling over business. Free individual enterprise is democratic. I live free individual enterprise.

The conservative business license, in the sense of chaos, is anti-democratic.

Business is not a voter. Business is a parasite living off the lives of its employed and the incomes of everyone.

Business is strictly busy-ness with no productivity in terms of human improvement beyond a hollow existence with material possessions.

The business plan is to pre-vent thinking and probable resulting revolt.

...

News reports show that foreign intervention in Canada's free trade election is unblushing and shameless.

It's amazing to see the conservative parties' desperation to keep their Canadian cohort in office.

The U.K. prime minister and the U.S. president both arrive on cue to tell Canadians to vote for the party in power.

Then the official U.S. business clique newspaper, <u>Wall Street Journal</u> accuses the leader of Canada's official opposition of being the "Juan Peron of Canada" because he opposes the sacred trade deal.

Arch conservatives in the U.S. once call Pierre Trudeau "the Castro of the north".

When I think about the Peron comparison it reminds me that the U.S. is apparently concerned when Peron is in power, that he will unite all the southern Americas.

That would make a formidable competitor in the "U.S.A.'s" world. Competition is all right so long as the "third" world is not competitive?

...

The annual "surprise" arrival of winter is reported in Toronto's dailies again.

...This weekend it's suddenly colder. Weather forecasters call it "unusually cold", and compare temperatures with "the north".

I'm thinking of Inuvik, but in Toronto "the north" is Barrie.

I don't know or notice this comparison, which shows that I'm not very conscious of weather or climate during my first years in Toronto.

I recall only several consecutive years of what the daily newspapers call "surprise" snow storms north of Barrie.

These surprises were always during the same month, which makes me wonder why they are always called "surprise".

...

The media of communication, in today's human and stock market illusions, are helping to bring about the decline of two empires at a rate faster than ever before in history.

Past empires of the U.S.-U.S.S.R. size could last much longer then, when news of imperial decay and fall travelled much slower.

The U.S.S.R.'s experimental system, invented by someone from Deutschland while living in London, is undergoing a desperate overhaul after only 60 years.

The U.S.S.R.'s present empire, beyond its national borders, is only 40 years old.

The U.S.A. Empire's current power is also about 40 years old, and in bad shape economically. Even Canada's resources might not save it.

The U.S. has no history of wise resource use since the arrival and start of the occupation by Eurasian settlers, 400-500 years ago.

Canada's resources will look so inexhaustible that the U.S. will see no reason to start imposing self-discipline now.

The U.S. will despoil Canada as quickly as it did the land now called southern California. The U.S. will be like the military dictatorship of wartime Nippon in Manchuria, in terms of harvesting the maximum for the imperial homeland.

...

Getting too close to the U.S. shouldn't be popular with anyone in Canada, particularly after the U.K. has a strange way of showing motherly love toward Canada during war.

"The Journal", a CBC TV News programme, has some interesting statistics to add to the revelations of the CBC dramatic series "Chasing Rainbows" about that war.

The drama shows the experiences of returning veterans of the 1914-18 European war.

Canada's second European "mother country", the U.K., our then "greatest friend and largest trading partner" automatically put us into that big European war of the monarchies.

More than 300 Canadians suffering from battle stress, trauma, and shock are executed by the U.K. military. That's the

U.K.'s final solution cure for PTSD.

The U.K. war criminal, Haig, orders people from Canada slaughtered. He's promoted for that.

Then he slaughters more Canadians for no reason at Passchendaele.

In the context of the Russian troop revolts and desertions leading to the Russian Revolution, that war can be seen as a monarchy and nation-state war against humanity.

If Canada now gets too close to the U.S., as with the U.K. in the past, will Canada be able to say, "No." to the U.S. the next time that it gets tangled up in war somewhere?

The present Canadian prime minister is no Pearson or Trudeau.

After the election, at least the present prime minister does say, "No." to setting up manufacturing facilities in Canada for the U.S. "missile defence" project.

And the following prime minister refuses to join the U.S. invasion of Iraq.

...

The Toronto Star newspaper publishes a letter to the editor that I write about free trade, Meech Lake, and immigration.

I send another letter to The Japan Times newspaper, suggesting that Canada and Nippon are getting the same threats from U.S. trade negoti-ators.

My words are published in Toronto and Tokyo.

**Québec City**: Living in my building, seeing posters in shops, and watching local television news keeps me aware of my surroundings.

From these sources I have a good idea of the major issues preoccupying people in the city and province.

Most are not that unusual and are common to many cities in the "first" world.

My observations indicate that the prime issues in Québec are:

an aging population; low rents and high vacancy rates in rental housing; minor theft among rental housing neighbours; drug abuse; spouse beating; shoplifting and TV surveillance cameras in small shops; arson; unemployment; demon-strations against sex peep shows (giving a sex industry merchant free publicity); debate over a $12,000 per year tax status for women working at home; and, the start of a discussion about opening shops on Sundays*.

(*When tourists are here, most shops are open on Sunday.)

I know a surprising amount about my surroundings for an ostensibly reclusive writer.

...

In one way, I can relate to one of the main characters in the actual-events-based "Cry Freedom" movie. He's Donald Woods the newspaper editor.

His relationship with the majority of people in his homeland reminds me of my relationship to my fellow humans outside the "first" world.

We of the "first" world rule over a kind of global apartheid.

We keep out the majority of humanity, especially the discouraged refugees and immigrants, via trade policies, through bureaucracy and by police/border guard/military force.

News reports that Canada's military submarines are currently not looking for armed and dangerous adversary naval vessels.

Instead, our submarine fleet is hunting for civilian, refugee ships.

Our allies in this war against the majority are the military regimes kept in power by our ignorance, aid, or disinterested indifference.

They help us to keep the "inferior" majority away from "our", not "their" shores.

Thus we can maintain the economic, topographic, political, and social segregation of the "third" from the "first" world.

The only exceptions are the dreamy, made-by-tourist industry annual vacations and the selective contacts made in moneyed, expatriate and elite ghettos abroad.

When we walk in our lovely parks, eat well, and enjoy first class medical care, it's difficult to consider our "order", systems, way of life, and governments to be anything but good-for-all.

We don't see what our nicotine companies, our other companies, and our governments do elsewhere in order to maintain our special status quo, our distinct society.

If we don't unravel this mess soon, our victims will become our masters instead of our co-human partners. Our equal partnership is the only thing we have to offer them.

We must abandon our greed, careers, nine-to-five-ism, real estate, possessiveness, consumerism, etc. while we can still make our own decisions and set examples and behave positively toward our co-humans.

Let's be remembered for more than a few crumbling buildings and old pots.

...

News reports about the current starvation in Ethiopia make me think that two shipment problems need solving.

Of course make the food shipments move, but to do that work, we have to stop the arms shipments which feed the war, which threatens to cut off the food shipments.

**Postville**: This is the only town in a long way. It's a remote fragile point coming from the southern urban artifact and insular living.

All around is sheer other-creature land.

CBC Radio and TV are the main links between here and an alien, unknown, artificial living zone south of here.

That zone is an enclave which is protected from the awesome reality of the northland.

Parabolic discs can bring in images of places and experiences that are as far removed from the north's remote villages as Star Trek is from a pioneer village museum.

Postville isn't the "conveniences", it's the reality experience. Here, places like Toronto, Vancouver, etc. are as fictional as any other "TV show".

"The news" may be an abstraction.

These are all things which local people can't relate to in their ordinary daily routine experiences or surroundings.

Their society/ies is/are distinct, i.e. separate from what the visual media shows them is Canada and "the world".

Yet the people here live in housing whose shells are identical to the world of television.

How is this superficial alikeness, but profound difference, handled in their minds?

**Sheffreville**: I'm sitting on a new sofa at the train crew house, watching Radio Canada from Montréal.

There's also TV from St. John's.

So far nothing extraordinary. But this non-cable, rabbit ear TV set also picks up Detroit, Michigan (U.S.A.) as if it were a local station.

Earlier in the day, while I'm just flipping channels casually I see a "noon hour" newscast.

The time zones are so confusing lately that I don't notice anything unusual about the name.

Knowing the time during the long days of summer sunlight has become irrelevant to my daily life, more so than usual for an adventurer.

During the moments of "noon news" I see a familiar broadcast symbol, one resembling BCTV in Vancouver. This evening I find out it is in fact that symbol.

So I watch the Pacific Time Zone evening "Newshour". It's a local station in terms of reception. Amazing.

More surprising yet is that the hand-size radio I'm carrying is receiving CFMI-FM, also from Vancouver.

The train crew says this is all done without wires and without a household parabolic antenna. How?

This town of empty streets is a long way toward becoming a 100% ghost town, with so many houses and apartments boarded up.

The exceptional television and radio reception makes the scene even more eerie.

It's living off the news of places which are still alive, like a vampire sucking blood from the living.

Is that Rod Serling out there, alone in the sunny street?

Have my adventures finally lead me to – The Twilight Zone?

A rich, dark blue sky fades to black. Phantom houses vanish. Distant street lamps are fewer and seem farther away than the sky of stars beyond.

This is a distant, deserted station at the edge of the galaxy.

...

Mikhail Gorbachev is the most popular leader in the world today. He's also the lead story and front page news.

People here are calling him by the affectionate name Gorby. He's real star material.

During his current visit to New York crowds are mobbing him when he makes a surprise stop while he's driving through town and jumps out of his limousine to shake hands with everyone nearby.

There's no comparable or so popular leader on U.S. territory since John Kennedy.

Among all the well-known nation-state leaders, Gorby is the only one who comes across as someone who is intelligent and makes the most of his intelligence.

Even through the monotonous translator's voice the global concepts of the speech Gorby makes at the United Nations today has quite an impact.

Fortunately, I'm able to see most of the speech while it's happening, through TVA Nouvelles.

It uses the United Nations translation sound and the visual broadcast from the U.S. cable news station.

I'm impressed by the fact that public broadcaster CBC-Radio Canada doesn't bother to provide such live coverage even though a private, "capitalist" TV network does so.

The private network has such a powerful news department that it can reschedule commercial shows for an hour of public service.

Why can't our publicly-financed television networks do the same?

The news coverage on the national networks is so insignificant on their regular news shows. They miss so much.

Gorby talks about the importance of Nippon and Brasil in solving the global economic crisis. I hear no other world leaders making speeches about these two essential players.

Gorby also talks about the universality and non-national character of environmental threats to human survival on earth.

It impresses me that it only takes the Soviet Union 68 years to produce a world-calibre leader like Gorby, coming from a one-party, multi-faction system that replaces monarchical dictatorship.

Consider that it takes Canada 100 years to produce a world-calibre leader like Pierre Trudeau, coming from Canada's inherited, partial-democracy system designed by barons and monarchy in western Asia's Eur.

Of course it takes the U.S. more than 135 years to produce their first world-calibre although flawed leader, Woodrow Wilson.

I wouldn't be so nationalistic as to attribute Wilson's qualities to the fact that his parents live in Canada for a while.

One might well wonder which governmental organization system is more likely to attract talent to key posts soonest.

The fact that someone of Gorby's world vision can make

it through big government, in a world of mediocre parochialists and ne'er-do-wells like the current U.K. and U.S. heads, makes Gorby a very significant leader for future historians.

**Barcelona**: A few days earlier, we happen upon a coat of arms which looks familiar and find ourselves in front of a building housing the Canadian consulate.

It's next door to the U.S. Institute.

Since we're here, I go into the Canadian consulate to ask to see a Canadian newspaper.

The person who comes to the little office door says, in English, that subscribing to a Canadian newspaper is not in the budget and hasn't been for two years.

"Two years." I reply. "You haven't seen a Canadian newspaper."

How can anyone represent Canada who is out of touch with the daily news there for two years, I'm wondering.

To further distort their impressions, all they have is a U.S. anglophone summary newspaper in the Canadian consulate office.

Reading that one they'd never know that Canada exists.

I add, "Well, there was an election last year..." She says, "Oh yes. We know about that."

Perhaps I'll donate some money to the poor conservative government in Ottawa so they can buy a Saturday only subscription to Le Devoir and The Globe & Mail.

Or the consular office could stop reading the U.S. newspaper and use the savings to buy some Canadian ones.

Is that too novel an idea? The consulate is supposed to be her representing Canada, isn't it?

There's another fundraising technique which the employees of the Canadian government could use. It seems to work here.

People open church doors and hold out their hands. Others

try the baby-on-the-lap technique.

The most dramatic begging I see in this city is a fairly young, reasonably-dressed man who kneels on one or both knees, head down, arm outstretched, with a written sign before him.

The sign indicates that he has two children to feed.

Embarrassed, expensively-dressed people seem to give to all these people. So the Canuck consulate bureaucrats could be put to work, say from 2 p.m. to 5 p.m.

The Canadian consulate is open more hours than that now, from 9 a.m. to 1 p.m.

I would contribute a handwritten sign: "Canadian consulate can't afford Canadian newspapers; Hors d'oeuvres and cocktail budget needs feeding."

How can anyone "represent" Canada abroad without any information about daily events in Canada? What is the mandate of External Affairs?

What are the job descriptions? What is the department's budget? How much money is allocated per item? How many Canadians know the answers to these question?

It seems to be a government department requiring far more public scrutiny, media surveillance.

Multinational companies do not need consulates. So why do nation-states?

The real work is done by political appointees on "shuttle diplomacy" and by other special negotiators, according to the attention they get in news reports.

Embassies are just overnight accommodation for them. Meanwhile, companies make trade work. Governments are like figurehead governor-generals.

They just sign agreements which are already arranged by corporations.

Are the nation-state "representatives" and the national government any more than emperors-without-clothes in the intercorporate, international systems?

...

Since the government-union situation is calming down, the Radio Nacional d'España news seems to be getting shorter.

International news seems to be always so brief, almost as brief as national news. It's like the three-minute hourly CBC Radio news.

But at least R.N.E. regularly mentions news of places formerly occupied by España in the southern Americas.

There are short items about Ecuador and Venezuela now. The rare news I hear about Ecuador in the past comes from an Ecuadorian friend living in Fukuoka, Miriam.

Another story is coming out of Buenos Aires. This time it's about a group of fifty "extreme left" people trying to throw out the elected government of President Alfonsin.

It's only a month since the extreme military tries the same. But the news doesn't call them "extreme".

The news would be better saying that "another one of the elite groups" is trying to destabilize the elected government.

One group of destabilizers is the same as the next.

They're all afraid that elected government can carry on for six more years.

The more that people get used to having elections to change the people in power, the less likely they are to lie down and surrender to potential dictators of any superficial hue.

...

There's no need to listen to the news to notice evidence of an interest in Argentina here.

One major traffic artery near our apartment in Putxet is named for a president of Argentina, albeit a military one, General Mitre.

Despite his title he was an elected president. In fact, he helps overthrow a dictator who has no street named after him in Barcelona.

Mitre is also a convert from Buenos Aires provincial separatism to a supporter of the confederation of Argentina. Catalan separatists may want the street name changed?

Mitre is also an author and founder of the newspaper La Nacion.

...

I'll have to find a more locally-oriented radio station or newspaper to find out what's happening in Barcelona.

There's always a newspaper on the table in the front lobby of our apartment building when I leave in the morning. I'm looking at it and understanding what I read.

After a while I realize it's a Catalan newspaper, not one in Español. How do I understand it? Maybe Portuguese and French help me?

...

This morning, our 24th in Barcelona, we awaken to the news that Asunción is in chaos.

What an unimaginable idea in that sleepy little capital of Paraguay that my Carioca friend Zita and I visit for a few days, four and a half years ago.

What seems more probable is the news that General Stroessner is finally out, although I have the impression he won't fall until a calcium deficiency breaks his hip.

A pattern seems to be continuing in Paraguay. The military is overthrowing its own leader then claiming to be the saviour and restorer of democracy.

They're promising a "Catholic and democratic government" to replace Stroessner. Isn't that a contradiction in terms?

Perhaps the old dictator, like the recently deceased emperor of Nippon, is actually a dead duck for some time. But Paraguay is such a tranquil place that no one notices.

The general is thought to be sitting or sleeping at his desk as usual. Now he'll go into exile in Brasil until someone discovers his death actually occurs quite a while ago.

Should we call this the first act of power of the new U.S.

president, a former CIA director? Is the Chilian dictator's long wooden nose about to crumble into sawdust next?

Does the new U.S. president send his vice to El Salvador because that fellow misses out on Viet Nam because he's too busy with tennis matches at "the club" during those years?

Will Paraguay's former military dictator be able to vote for his successors from his home in exile?

He has quite a time planning his travel itinerary.

Radio Nacional d'España reports that Stroessner is heading for his home in Brasil, in Florianopolis or somewhere in Parana State, until he finds another country.

I doubt that the current president of Hangoo will dare to invite Stroessner to live there just because he let Hangoosaram settle in Asunción.

But Taiwan might welcome the old soldier. Stroessner could fit into the immigration category of "illegal, but legal".

I wonder if the 1972 election signs are still up saying "'Vote for Stroessner", as they are when Zita and I visit Paraguay ten years later.

Maybe Guarani will be used more widely in Paraguay now, like Catalan in España. That will be real freedom of expression.

...

In the news, nationalists versus others in Deutschland seem to be debating the right to vote. Some say that citizenship is the criteria to use in deciding who can and can't vote.

At time of writing, in Canada this isn't the case. Residency takes priority, even though citizenship and age determine eligibility to vote.

A person must reside in a Canadian federal electoral district a minimum number of days before enumeration in order to be able to get on the list of federal electors.

People who leave one address without already having a new address are legally disenfranchised.

The only exception is if the elector is enumerated in a riding and then returns to that riding on election day, or an advance poll station, to vote.

But in a country the size of Canada, if a person moves from one province to another it would most likely be very inconvenient and expensive to return to the province where s/he is enumerated in order to have the right to vote.

That's the loophole in the law according to an electoral official I talk to in Vancouver just before the federal election last year.

A person contributing to Canadian unity by moving among provinces is liable to find him/herself disenfranchised.

Provincial and municipal elections also have residency demands in the provinces I know.

In municipal jurisdictions I can understand why a certain length of residency could make a person more familiar with the place and its realities.

In a big city, residency/ eligibility to vote could just mean having lived in a similarly big city for those who aren't longer term residents of the specific city.

Voting decisions are often made only during election periods, not well in advance. Many candidates are unknown until campaigning begins.

I recognize that eligibility and capability are distinct regardless of duration of residency.

In a provincial election, residency can be argued to be an essential qualification.

Newfoundland, Alberta, Québec, and Columbia (Br.) do have different kinds of issues, unless the political parties are simply dealing in hackneyed, stereotypical generalities such as employment, social welfare, inflation, and development.

If those are the main issues, anyone can vote anywhere.

Those issues aren't location specific in the parts of Canada with permanent settlement.

Indirect, i.e. elected government tends to be limited to generalities such as those just listed, instead of problem-solving.

Thus residency is never really a factor except in large versus small municipality elections. Nor does citizenship particularly matter.

Tourists from other jurisdictions might just as well vote as residents.

Elected governments of all jurisdictions talk about generalities, even though they portray them as exclusive to their particular jurisdiction.

That's why they blame people from other jurisdictions for the local manifestations of generalities common to all.

It's just like politicians and extreme viewpoints that blame "foreigners" for the local branch of the world-wide unemployed.

The companion issue of citizenship versus residency in voting is also a question.

A non-resident citizen of Canada might reasonably lose her/his vote but should therefore also be exempt from taxation.

"No taxation without representation" as the U.S. revolutionaries put it, but a non-citizen resident of a nation who pays taxes, as I do in Nippon, should be able to vote for those who decide taxes and issues effecting residents.

Citizenship and residency should not be a game where nation-states make all the voting rules.

Can Europeans living in nation-states where they don't have citizenship have the right to vote for the European parliament candidates where they reside or only where they have citizenship?

If they have no address of their own in their land of birth where can they vote?

The unifying and enriching contacts of mobile lifestyles should not be penalized by disenfranchising mobile people.

U.S. citizens residing abroad can vote in U.S. elections. But, at time of writing, only

Canadian military and External Affairs ministry elite can vote in Canadian elections while living abroad.

That's autocracy.

This situation is a serious betrayal of the one person – one vote principal of Canada's elected government system.

The current voting rights system gives the privileged and military special status in the electoral system, as if Canada were under military dictatorships.

What member(s) of parliament represents non-residents who are disenfranchised?

Fortunately, this flaw in the electoral system is eventually eliminated. (But it remains in the tax system.)

...

Today's newspapers show a Spanish government minister and the current U.K. prime minister after a meeting about Gibraltar.

Gibraltar is the only leftover European era occupied territory on the European peninsula.

The minister of España seems to have two black eyes in the newspaper photo.

...

No matter where I live in the northern hemisphere, the news is always presented as if I were in the centre of the world, where key decisions are being made which have much wider consequences.

I find out how insignificant Canadian news is for my life when I live in Rio de Janeiro and Fukuoka.

The only thing of importance that happens during all the time that I'm in both of these cities and exploring beyond them is that Pierre Trudeau retires.

The blunders of the U.S.-Canada trade deal and the meek constitutional amendments seem to be unknown stories for news gatherers out-side of Canada.

...

...The publisher of an English-language guidebook, one for companies in España, is pushing the book by saying that España "is expected to be the fastest growing country in Europe in the coming years…"

…España' President Gonzalez seems to be the centre of all the biggest world news events, i.e. the union of '92 in Europe; "P.L.O." terrorists of southwest Asia; the IMF debt; Central Americas.

Gonzalez seems to be busier than the U.S. president. I wonder if there is much news about España's president in Canada. He seems quite young, maybe in his 40s.

…

…Union-government talks about the economy break down, for the moment, despite attempts to overcome the disaccord which leads to the general strike before our arrival.

If I clearly understand Radio Nacional d'España, the meeting between the president and unions is bugged and then broadcast today.

The president seems to feel that the general strike is like an attempted coup against the "socialist" government.

Gonzalez says he wants to keep the boom going in España and doesn't want to compro-mise that plan be agreeing to what the unions want.

He accuses them of breaking the social peace by going on a general strike.

When union leaders say they might withdraw their traditional support for the Socialist Party, the president replies that the government is elected by the most votes of the electorate, not the unions.

Gonzalez later appeals to the members of unions to think in terms of the country as a whole, not union leaders' positions at the bargaining table. Is an election due?

…

…Also in España, questions are being raised about how the European Community accord, to take full effect in about four years, will be a challenge to the U.S. and Nippon.

Our brief forays across the European peninsula make me

wonder who its tailor is and if the new clothes will be ready for the parade four years from now.

But I'm just starting to discover the European Community in Colon's tradition. My arrival here is the second "greatest event since creation"?

...

Canada now does get mentioned in local newscasts as often as once a week here. Recent stories include a refugee from Mexican "death squadrons".

This story catches me un-aware that the ostensibly democratically-elected government of Mexico has death squads.

These squads apparently operate for seven years, ending about ten years ago. Is that when the big IMF debt builds up?

If so, maybe the squads create the same fear of political participation as military dictatorships elsewhere.

Severe scrutiny of government budgets may be discouraged in Mexico to a degree approaching military dictatorship.

Other news items about Canada that are considered newsworthy here include hormone-filled beef.

The E.C. says that kind of beef from Canada and the U.S. is not up to standard for E.C. consumers.

Another story out of Canada is that scientists find a hole in the north pole ozone layer like the one over Antarctica.

...

In Venezuela today the war against the IMF seems to be starting. The violence in the streets is a direct result of the nation-state government complying with IMF demands.

I wonder how that news is read at IMF headquarters.

...

A local newspaper's front page reports that the union of '92, the E.U., isn't really an agreement among 12 nation-states. It's among 15 world-wide corporations.

Thus the status quo of the moment is actually tripolar. There are "capitalists", "communists", and reality. But in reality there are no poles, just two partners, Earth and life.

"Capitalism" and "communism are merely short-lived relics of the European colonial-national era.

...

There's a story in the news about some brave young men who are standing up to the military's compulsory service. They are civilians, armed only with their consciences.

They don't want to be transformed into paid killers and anti-human robots, like Oswiecim guards or the bombers of Hiroshima and Nagasaki.

Once trained, civilians are expected to commit any crime against humanity in order to serve and to "do their duty" to the nation-state.

Compulsory military service or any other form of conscription at any time is anti-human.

It means training people to respond to the order "kill" with only questions such as "Who?" and "How many?"

Military training is the prerequisite and first step on the path to being a guard "just following orders" at a concentration camp.

Training people not to think but to automatically obey is the extreme opposite of education.

It's the same as killing an author because a gangster boss orders the kill.

It's the same as producing internal combustion engines while the environment declines.

Trials of the military criminals in Germany and Argentina stop because everyone who's ever trained to be a soldier would have to be put on trial.

The whole concept of military and nationalism would be on trial. These trials can be held now or by future historians on paper.

...

The anglophone elite gets most of its information about the world through a series of translations and interpretations.

By the time news of the world is turned into English it's far more remote than second-hand or hearsay.

The information is a rather precarious basis upon which to perceive, evaluate, and make decisions that have great consequences for the non-anglophone majority of the human population.

Most U.S. presidents are unilingual anglophones. Little wonder that they make so many gross blunders in world affairs.

The same can be said for most U.S.S.R. leaders?

Neither empire realizes that it could prolong its existence by encouraging language learning and making language skills a prerequisite to leadership.

Now that both empires are in decline, even language learning cannot save them.

...

Nippon is giving one of its famous, generous presents to the U.S.

According to the front page of this morning's newspaper, Nippon is helping to solve both the U.S. IMF and the U.S. financial balance problems.

The solution involves the united efforts of both the economically very strong and very weak, i.e. Nippon plus Brasil and other IMF "debtors".

The solution comes in a single stroke.

The idea is that Nippon will finance the morally-bankrupt IMF with Nippon's hard-earned trade surplus.

This takes the U.S. off the books, eliminates pressure on the U.S. and "third" world "debts", and probably means fewer U.S. salespeople banging on Nippon's doors to coerce Nippon into squandering its fortunes on U.S. arms purchases.

What a deal! Bankers rejoice.

...A general strike is being held in Brasil to protest IMF-imposed policies.

Meanwhile, in Venezuela it's reported that half of the Venezuela money from the IMF is ending up in private bank account in Switzerland and the U.S.

That means Venezuelans are paying back money that never makes it to their national treasury or the IMF. That's a good reason for massive protests in Venezuela and beyond.

The Venezuelan scandal clearly shows how greedy and incompetent the foreign banks really are in their IMF loaning policies.

Obviously they are not monitoring the path of the money they're lending.

In many cases, the IMF also fails to consider the kind of government that they're dealing with when they make decisions to lend out huge amounts of money.

Dictatorships are the banks' preferred clients, good risks, and prime rate customers with great credit ratings?

Why else would the most indebted nation-states be the ones which have military dictatorships during the time that loans are taken out?

Contrast this with personal loan policies.

If I claim to have the right to control all my family's savings, without ever asking my family's permission, would a bank then lend me money for one purpose, and then sit idly by watching me do something entirely different with the bank loan, such as buying a yacht, hiring a crew, and sailing off toward a distant horizon?

Would the bank loan department come to the dock smiling and waving because it's dreaming about all the interest it's going to collect on the loan after I leave?

After I sail beyond the horizon, never to return, would the bank go to the family I'm claiming to represent and tell them to pay back the bank loan I'm using for my endless yacht trip?

Would the family have to pay because I, not they, used all the money I borrowed from the bank to sail away?

Would the family have to pay even if I took along all the family's money in the yacht?

If the bank went after the family, and not me, it would be treating the family exactly like the people ruled by the military dictators who took out loans and left office with no intention of being responsible for paying back the bank.

The banks are not going after the former military dictators. The banks are not freezing or seizing the loan money and assets the dictators stole.

The banks are only interested in forcing the military dictator's victims to pay off the bank loans with interest.

When military dictators ask for loans, the IMF and banks treat the dictators as if they were exactly the same as democratically-elected governments.

Thus the IMF and banks knowingly finance military dictatorships.

Somehow the IMF and banks don't consider dictators to be bad risks.

Somehow the IMF and banks don't consider it bad to cripple elected governments by insisting they pay off the former dictators' loans.

To paraphrase what an Argentinian says here in Barcelona a short time ago, when talking about human rights:

Why is the "third" world paying the moneyed world for the moneyed "first" world's IMF and bank loan policy mistakes?

The moneyed "first" world considers itself such a superior place that it won't admit and pay for its own mistakes?

It's as if the "first" world believes it is providing charity and welfare, for a price.

The moneyed "first" world IMF and banks now claim they are "giving responsibility" to the unmoneyed "third" world for debt management.

It sounds as if the IMF and banks are now claiming that loaning money to criminal gangs called military dictatorships and demanding payment from democratically-elected governments adds up to giving the "third" world a helping hand.

Burdening elected governments and punishing the victims of dictatorship with unpayable debt and interest repayment helps no one, particularly not supporters of democracy and freedom.

...

Among the rare bits of news about Canada that do manage to get reported outside Canada, there's a story about a new supermarket roof that collapses in the Vancouver area.

Fortunately, there are no fatalities. I'm sure the supermarket passes all the building codes.

While the roof is falling in on that structure the favelados of Rio de Janeiro still have solid rooves over them which would pass no codes.

...

According to España's "first" world version of the news, people in Uruguay are voting to decide how to deal with military dictatorship criminals, i.e. war criminals.

The fight for elected government is thus ingeniously democratic.

The vote is compulsory. Exiles returning from neighbouring countries are on the voters' list.

The vote can overturn a law in Uruguay, similar to one passed by Brasil's former, long-term military dictatorship.

There, the former dictators and their fellow thugs in uniform declare themselves immune from prosecution for all crimes before surrendering to elected government.

The crimes are murder, kidnapping, assault with a deadly weapon causing bodily harm, threats of assault, physical intimidation, harassment, false arrest and detention without charge or due process, cruel and unusual punishment, psychological cruelty, etc.

Journalists and well-intentioned activist groups are calling these criminal acts by the polite, innocuous, and nebulous term "human rights violations".

The Uruguay vote is thus merely to call for the implementation of what we casually accept as just routine law enforcement and an effective, functioning court system of justice.

It's an astonishing fact that military dictatorship is so bad that its victim populations have to vote to ensure "norms" of justice and to restore normal law and order by having a referendum.

Worse yet, the victim populations are worrying about whether the military will consider the vote a "radical provocation" that demands a military intervention in electoral processes, the removal of newly-elected government, and the elimination of the justice system.

The Uruguay referendum results are about 57% in favour of forgiving the military and about 40% against. Is it "forget the immediate past"?

Would a referendum on convicted prison inmates who commit violent crimes turn out the same?

Is the vote also motivated by a fear of reprisals after some future military coup?

I wonder what the Uruguay political campaign looks like from inside Uruguay? What are people saying in their parlours and at their tables?

The "first" world will never know?

That kind of information seems to be rarely collected or reported because foreign correspondents without local language skills seem to be people who are parachuted into completely unknown territory.

So instead of landing on their feet running, they have to, or choose to spend their hours with the elite who speak their first language and local journalists in bars, instead of "embedding" in the daily life of most locals.

It's not being objective.

It's being uninformed and relying on second-hand stories; perspectives of the privileged local minority; and hearsay.

This information vaccuum in news reporting is filtered through and filled by all of the preconceived notions carried in the foreign correspondents' heads from abroad.

Journalists abroad are thus always and forever temporary

residents and foreign employees, like so many other corporate/government bureaucrats going to unfamiliar places.

The result is a kind of poorly-informed, deadline and employer money "objectivity" that is essentially ignorance.

I know so little that I can have no biases. I'm a parrot, a recorded message of all around me that I know little or nothing about.

A reporter sent overseas is so busy trying to report, and trying to figure out how to report the unfamiliar, that s/he has little time to adapt to the unfamiliar, enter the heart of a situation, live with it, and understand it profoundly before reporting.

It takes a lot of time to truly sit in parlours and at tables with the non-elite and impartial locals. A "media identification" card is useless for getting this type of intimate encounter.

A reporter would have to behave as if s/he were not a journalist to get close enough to an environment to be able to report a story arising in or from the environs.

A one or two year "foreign correspondent" posting or even a local correspondent stint can't do the job. A reporter has to live the locale before s/he can be an accurate reporter there.

Perhaps living-as-a-newcomer in one's locale of origin is prerequisite to living-as-a-journalist.

**Boston**: When we get to town, one of the first news items catching my eye is about Argentina. President Alfonsin retires after six years of fighting off coups. I hardly blame him.

His would-be Radicalista successor is defeated in elections by the Judicialista candidate Carlos Menem.

Maybe he'll make people forget about "Peron lives" slogans through the success or failure of the new Judicialista government.

The party is on the spot. It has to reprove itself or govern by séance, asking Juan and Evita to say what they want Menem to do.

At least that way they could blame the Perons for their policy mistakes.

**Peace River to Enterprise bus**: A passenger from Wayburn, Saskatchewan says that I look familiar to her. Another asks me to tell him if I'm famous because he never meets anyone famous.

I say, "Okay, I'll tell you. I'm Knolton Nash." (laughter) Nashi is a famous journalist at CBC TV News at this moment.

He begins reporting when I'm still a child. (or before)

**Jakarta**: The local English language daily newspaper today reports that residents of some area of the city are complaining about toxic acid water. Another news story is about an area that has no water supply for months.

My residence and the "school" have drinking water in new looking plastic tanks like the classic office water coolers of the past. There are hot and cold taps.

So a good water supply is easily available to people with money.

The Indonesian government (Suharto) prefers to spend money on concrete and air pollution instead of a good water supply for all?

The official daily also says that the government wants more trees in Jakarta to clean the air. The wider streets in my neighbourhood have many trees breathing the smog now.

It's like treating symptoms instead of curing the pollution at its source.

The people who live here before the Dutch occupation and "developed" era clearly know that activities producing dirty water, smoggy air, and noisy surroundings do not improve human life in these isles.

Bright new buildings bordered with wide streets full of brown fume spewing machines replace both the villages and the knowledge which are here before the "first" world influence takes hold.

The impact of the "first" world on Jakarta is the only thing that's clearly visible in this urbanizing setting.

Formerly healthy villagers become choking, waterless pedestrians in a fabricated environment which produces only negative results.

We end up with holes in the ozone layer protecting earth lifeforms from solar radiation and a "greenhouse" effect destabilizing the delicate balance of climates and temperatures which support life as we know it on earth.

The only consolation for the near-equatorial "third" world, and for myself at the moment, is that the equatorial regions of earth have the thickest atmosphere.

So, I reason, they'll be the last to feel the full effects of environmental collapse.

Perhaps after seeing the "first" world eliminated by environmental disaster, the "third" world can stop the folly of imitating or following the foolish lead of the "first".

Perhaps the "third" world can stop "development" quickly enough to maintain the "third" world as the last preserve for life on earth.

On top of everything else, walking around Jakarta thus gives me some hopeful thoughts that human life can survive the "developed" "first" world era by outliving it in the "third" world.

Unfortunately, Jakarta may be more typical of the last "first" world invented city on earth. I contrast it with Rio de Janeiro.

Rio is so comparatively beautiful, clean, and well-kept, having more than the presence of humans manifesting human-directed rather than "first" world empire directed human life.

My learning in the "third" world is always significant, even from the first day that I set foot anywhere in it. The "third" world is so inspiring, so unlike the "first".

...

Later on the big news story is about poison cookies which are made because there's a mix up between sacs of flour and sacs of sodium nitrate.

The wrong sacs are shipped to the cookie factory. Fortunately, I never eat such foreign-type food. I hope the locals will also avoid this "developed" diet.

It can be fatal to more than the local culture.

A more serious problem threatens local fruit and vegetable markets which supply the truly local diet.

Some people are apparently spraying poison on foodstuffs sold in such places. I meet a local who actually witnesses a spraying.

At the same time, street vendors are coming under attack as a cause of garbage in the streets and poisonous goods.

I never have any problems with vendors' food.

In response, government officials now say all the stories of poison are no more than rumours.

A headline in the government-controlled local press says that "former communists" are behind the poison rumours.

Is that the Perestroika and Gladnost chocolate chip or wafer type?

...

There are a number of radios stations but all carry the same newscast at 10 p.m., like "Hora da Brasilia" – the official news under the military dictatorship.

The local, nation-state government of Indonesia is a residue of some previous U.S.-S.U. rivalry.

Non-locals tell me that journalists from abroad who make critical comments about the Indonesian government are still ending up expelled and having their publications banned here. I don't know if this is true.

Wherever I go, non-locals tend to be usually unreliable sources. A consensus grows around a rumour.

...

Local news stories getting the biggest play now involve fights among senior secondary school students and overexposed photos.

The photographers' subjects, not the films, are apparently too exposed for locals.

I can vouch for the stories. Students from rival schools do seem to be having what the news calls "brawls".

One day while I'm riding on a well-travelled bus route, I'm joined by some students carrying short lengths of wood, holding them like clubs.

These students are fleeing another group which pursues them onto the bus.

Another day, in a different bus ride along the same route, students begin jumping in the windows and climbing to the upper deck of the double-deck bus.

They seem to be joking but the sitting, adult passengers seem genuinely peeved and alarmed, closing windows to keep out the intruders.

The bus employeed who takes passenger fares keeps away from the invaders. They only go about one kilometre and seem friendly.

I also see the overexposed photos on magazine covers and calendars. These show pictures of women exposing some of their skin.

But the skin exposed is so minimal that it would probably attract little notice in the "first" world and elsewhere.

The national government says there's a "danger of sexual excitement". Low threshold or repressed population?

If the photos are banned, will they become an expensive underground commodity or will the birth rate drop because few people in this nation-state can become sexually excited without visual aids?

It would seem better to eliminate the unnatural denial of human sexuality and the consequent enriching of the sex industry in a milieu of sexism.

The only public manifestation of sexuality which seems to be considered ordinary in Jakarta is that exhibited by young local men who hang around a certain department store trying to seduce each other.

One tries to seduce a non-local I meet here, but he replies that he prefers females. Prefers? Tease?

The government's social message is clear. It wants people to be married or gay, but in no other way sexually excited.

...

**Singapura**: The first news hitting me in Singapura is political. Almost all of the places that I live in during the past seven years seem to be having weird experiences.

The new president of Argentina, Menem is contemplating release of the convicted criminals who are part of the former military dictatorship.

It seems a bit premature to put those gangsters and terrorists back on the streets.

It might give heart to a certain U.S. mass murderer who is put away some years ago after killing a movie star in her home.

Are the Greek generals who did the coup d'état some years ago still in prison?

I'm glad to see that after six years of elected government in Buenos Aires, the U.K. is finally restoring diplomatic and air links with Argentina. It's about time.

The war between the U.K. and the former military dictatorship ends several years earlier.

In Brasil, Silvio Santos, the king of mediocre television, a pioneer in introducing U.S. like junk TV into Brasil's otherwise rich culture, could become a presidential candidate.

This would be a tragic end for the direítas já movement during my time in Rio.

Millions of demonstrators gather during that very popular

movement, demanding full restauration of Brasil's democratic system of a popularly-elected president.

Finally, about five years after the movement begins, those elections are to be held for the first time.

Santos is currently the first choice of people polled by a U.S. public opinion survey group. Fortunately, Santos is not declaring himself a candidate.

It would be like a "B" movie star becoming U.S. president. But such an actor is U.S. president for eight years. It's his best role but not a great performance.

Santos intelligently announces that he's not suited for office and not running.

Meanwhile, in my other homeland, Nippon, the power behind the party-in-power in Tokyo isn't personalities but the country's second most popular game, pachinko.

The most popular game is English.

Apparently Nippon's LDP government is financing itself through loans from pachinko parlours.

Some of these parlours are alleged to have yakuza connections. (gangsters) So I finally know what the letters LDP stand for: Loans Derived from Pachinko.

...

The daily English language television news broadcast has a BBC sound. But there are items from U.S. television news too.

One U.S. item tonight is about people in East Germany lining up for goods during shopping trips to West Germany.

Thanks to Gorby, people in East Germany can now get permission to leave there to shop in West Germany.

The U.S. reporter covering this story comments that lining up is already a familiar experience for people living in East Germany.

Only the goods available and the store owners are different.

So lineups are the meeting ground of the U.S. and U.S.S.R. empires' models of caretaker society?

Is Gorby trying to let his subjects learn that prices are higher in the U.S. imperial turf and line-ups can be long there too?

Supermarkets in Canada too have long lineups when my parents go shopping Thursday nights, the only evening shopping day when I'm a child.

Before I leave Toronto for Rio, the banks have such long lineups that they install cattle guards to make customers go around in circle. Airports adopt this system later.

During Gorby's era, East Germans going home from shopping trips in West Germany might conclude that their nation-state's unpleasant status quo has line-ups which at least could lead to products they can afford to buy.

Generally, the current opening of the Soviet associate states in the eastern part of the European peninsula could make the western part seem less mysterious, exotic, attractive, and/or enticing for easterners.

The western part of the European peninsula could be perceived as an interesting place to visit, a good place to shop, but an expensive place to live. "Freedom" means the right to line up and spend more money?

The eastern part of the European peninsula might avoid the sleazy capitalism that I see on an earlier visit to Chuang Hwa by introducing consumer laws to protect eastern Europeans from both bad corporate citizens and an overly-autonomous bureaucracy.

...

Finally the military dictatorship is ending in Chile. The first elections in 16 years are being held.

But the radio news of BBC World Service gives little mention to the event during 10 minute newscasts.

At the same time, the demise of dictators in Eastern Europe is receiving a great deal of attention in the newscasts.

As a U.S. affiliate state, perhaps the U.K. doesn't want its news service to give listeners the impression that it's not just the U.S.S.R. Empire which is falling.

And the Malvinas-saved U.K. prime minister, Thatcher, loves to invite Chile's dictator to tea, calling the bloodthirsty general the U.K.'s "great friend".

News stories about the fall of the U.S.S.R. Empire avoid mentioning that the U.S. Empire begins falling in the southern Americas about six to eight years before the U.S.S.R. Empire falls in eastern Europe.

I see the U.S. Empire falling close up while I'm living in the southern Americas for the first time.

Elected governments are re-emerging then, replacing the U.S. Empire's "friends and allies", i.e. murderous military dictatorships.

The era of both the U.S. and U.S.S.R. empires is ending but all the emphasis in the "free world" news media is on the U.S.S.R. Empire alone.

This helps to ensure that people living in the southern Americas and the eastern part of Europe don't get together and compare notes of their experiences under two empires?

...

News media should go to the arms factories every time there's a story involving death by arms. Arms destroy more lives than drugs.

During the 50 years preceding the moment of the present writing, tens of millions of human lives are destroyed by the manufacturers and traffickers of arms.

Before I leave Rio, a major newspaper tallies up the deaths caused by war since the end of the 1930s/40s war.

This is very rare reporting and provides a shocking picture of war deaths during "world peace".

It adds up Algeria, Korea, Malaysia, Viet Nam, Afghanistan, etc.

...

The local daily newspaper runs an article which defies and belittles progress made against sexist behaviour in recent years.

No wonder so many local women seem to act as if they feel obliged to present themselves as male dependent.

The newspaper article gives a positive account of how a young male improves his job prospects by claiming to be engaged to be married.

His prospective employers apparently feel free to ask the applicant's marital status. This question is illegal in societies which are trying to promote sexual equality.

Both the newspaper and employer would be paying fines elsewhere, for promoting sexual inequality.

Marital status has no direct relationship with a person's ability to work or produce.

Marital status has no place in the rational processes of matching persons with work skill requirements. Marital status is not a measure of merit.

Employers have no place I the employeed's homeplace.

In the past, companies used people's marital status to force compliance with company demands and to trap the employeed in debt, dependency, and security fear behaviours. This is obedience training.

At the time of this writing from Singapura, even governments with human rights codes have taxation and social services which discriminate on the basis of marital status.

Our lawyer friend Jan of Malmø (Sverige) advises clients not to marry because of the government income tax advantages of a couple living together remaining single.

But when the Sverige government reverses the marital status tax rules, Jan reverses his advice.

Sverige practices social engineering by tax policy?

...

Some contemporary churchist missionaries I meet and some "foreign aid" organizations I see in the news are "teaching English" as an integral part of their "conversion" work abroad.

Learning an unfamiliar language can thus become a training exercise in how to alienate oneself from local reality.

It's acculturation by "language teaching", a softer version of the Canadian "residential schools" and U.S. "boarding schools" confining First Nations children.

It's preferable and better for all concerned, and the world at large, if language classes only involve a sharing of information and ideas about foreign but equal cultures, in the process of acquiring a useful tool, i.e. language skills, for communicating different human experiences and cultures honestly and without prejudice.

Literacy, formal education, and language training should be no more than helping people to obtain more facility at seeking and learning to improve human communication, not to wipe out humanity's rich and diverse heritage and ongoing reality.

..

I'm awake and bright when the morning sunlight bursts on the quiet New Year's Day morn.

The morning radio news makes no mention of the celebrations of the previous evening.

Even the big but greatly overpriced stadium event, marking 25 years of Singapura's nation-state status, is not mentioned in the news.

There are stories about eastern Europe but nothing about how many people are on Orchard Road last night. There's no police report on festivity-related injuries, etc.

It's as if nothing happens, just like the throngs on Noël Eve. But it does. I'm at both events.

The prime minister's New Year's message is no more than a statistical list of growth rates in the economy, according to what I hear on the Singapura Broadcasting Corporation.

I live in military-dictatorship-controlled nation-states which have local news. Why is there no local news on SBC? Who is running the news depart-ment?

...

Like Canada, Singapura has a declining population rate and a need for more people, at time of writing.

This helps to explain why I can get a work visa so quickly and without any fuss right here.
There's an overall 10% decline in Singapura's birth rate this year alone.

Singapore radio news reports that this is actually a 15% decrease among ethnic Chinese locals with a 5% increase among ethnic Malay locals and a 2% increase among ethnic Tamil locals.

...

România is banning the "communist" party, according to the latest news.

The banning demonstrates România's inexperience in the concept of free expression of opinion.

Improvements don't come from shutting up some people forever.

...In light of the overthrow and execution of the Românian dictator and his spouse last year, I wonder if anyone is drawing parallels with events celebrating France's bicentennial last year.

It's fascinating that eastern Europe's puppet dictators fall on the bicentennial of the French revolution against monarchical dictatorship.

...

A local news report says that Orchard Road is the tenth most expensive shopping street in the world of shoppers.

Given that cities in Sverige, Germany, and the Netherlands, as well as Tokyo, Paris, and New York City must be among the top ten also, number 10 is very high.

Yet I manage to buy meals and other goods along Orchard and its side streets for reasonable prices, eg. a plate of food costs less than $2 (Canadian).

The tourists I see every day coming out of hotels, sitting in hotel cafés, etc. puzzle me. They pay fortunes for a short stay.
I can pay my rent and eat well for a very long time for the same price as their one week's tourist spending.

Is visiting time the only occasion that tourists have for playing boss over people paid less than them?

Is being served instead of a servant (employeed) the real commodity the tourists are purchasing here? That's the meaning of living as a tourist?

Is it an escape, albeit a very short one, from employeed status?

Is it not "getting away from it all", but reserving it all so that the employeed become employers for a little bit of time in an exotic dream setting?

Is it a rebellious dream to make another year of servitude bearable?

...One of the teaching staff I work with here comes to me in tears, ready to resign. After a week off, on vacation in MuangThai, she's smiling, until she returns to employment.

Tourism is the opiate of the employeed.

...

During my first years as a university student there's a book on my required reading list called <u>News from Nowhere</u> in my politics and media course.

The title seems to be a good one to describe reporting in Singapura's local media.

Stories are brought in by international news agencies about what's happening in eastern Europe and the Soviet Union now.

What's appalling is the dearth of background and basic information in the reports, and the excess of opinion without on the scene in depth research, i.e. probing and reporting problems inside the Soviet Union.

There are so many basic reference books in libraries which could help reporters give more complete stories.

News here overuses the words "reportedly" and "seems that", as if the S.U. were some sort of libel case before the courts or a gossip column item.

Editorials' generalizations are built on this shaky vocabulary. News readers, listeners, and watchers need so much historical information to be able to interpret reports.

Is the S.U. just a relic of imperial Russia? Are the old empire's territorial conquests just renamed Soviet Republics?

If so, the U.S.S.R. never really exists? It's just a holdover with new titles under military control using ideological jargon and slogans?

...

A remarkable local media feature is the verbatim reading of local political chiefs' statements and speeches by anchor people during local radio and television news.

There's no opposition reaction, no analysis, no commentary, and no criticism following the chiefs' statements.

The opposition party(ies), if it or they exist, never have a counter or alternative statement reported in the news.

Newspapers report no controversies or problems locally or in ASEAN.

Those kinds of stories only come from foreign settings and events, far away from absolutely content Singapura.

Everyone in Singapura is too busy selling and having fun at the discos to complain? Singapura is perfect? This is what Canada's current prime minister calls unanimity?

Maybe it's just a dying city that never lives, an overseas U.K. theme park.

Singapura's foreign-imposed past and its present behaviour from that past's absolute occupational government is a human tragedy.

At least eastern Europe and the southern Americas have something to look forward to after liberation from their former U.S.-S.U. master empires.

There is no such apparent hope for Singapura.

...

SBC news reports say that the local government is encouraging aging locals to turn in people who are committing food offences.

A "hot line" of the Environment Ministry is ready to hear

reports about unauthorized food sources which are suppling food, as well as reports about dirty food stalls.

One stall is shut down today because of too many "insect violations".

The ministry should patrol the shopping centre area that I find earlier, with its sticky-slippery floors and over-flowing garbage.

Unfortunately, the ministry could find out about a stall I know where the food seller's mother makes the food. Is she authorized?

...

BBC World Service radio reporting on Nippon's current elections provides a good example of poor background information and artificial suspense.

This radio news service produces a 15 minute story on this election, suggesting that the main opposition party is doing very well, i.e. the party in power might be replaced.

Not until the election results come in does BBC mention that the main opposition isn't running enough candidates to win the election.

So there's never a real contest or a chance for the party in power to be removed and replaced.

This is why I sometimes find that news seems like a fill-in-the-blanks test with no correct answers given afterwards.

...

In Brasil, the old military dictators and their local baron allies seem to be using their ill-gotten IMF money to clear land to raise fast food stock in Amazonia and to get more riches such as gold, etc. through garpinheiros and the destruction of more indigenous civilizations.

The indigenous are dying for fast food and gold greed.

...The latest news from Brasil isn't really astounding in the context of indigenous history.

President Sarney legalizes the gold miners' invasion of indigenous living areas rather than helping the Amerinds.

This may not be new. But why repeat a known, avoidable tragic error. History will judge Sarney gravely.

The idea behind Amazonia's "development" is to reduce the indigenous population in Brasil to a minority in their own homeland, as in Canada, the U.S., etc.

Then the bosses running this relocation project tell the indigenous people that they're a declining minority who can't be placed above the majority interests of a "democracy".

Apparently Chuang Hwa does the same thing, turning regional majorities into artificial "minorities" in Tibet and elsewhere.

Large transfers of people from one region to another spreads a region's majority across several regions so that they become a minority in each region, including their own, original region.

They no longer have a core area.

Some anglomaniacs would probably like to try this with Canada's francophones to wipe them out.

Great population growth may be the key factor which saves people in Bharat and Chuang Hwa from the same demise as the indigenous peoples elsewhere - at the hands of the Europeans and their kin abroad.

...

Before leaving Singapura, I note a news item about MuangThai considering a policy requiring all males entering the country to produce a document certifying that they don't have AIDS.

Considering the sexual exploitation of local females by non-local males, the policy is probably already too late.

Non-local males could not only acculturate MuangThai, they could also kill off the local population altogether by carrying in a lethal plague.

...

One SBC newscast uncritically quotes a general talking about preparing for "the battlefields of the future". Very sick.

The general who wants future battlefields, or who perhaps sees them as inevitable due to "human nature", ought to be fired.

Campaigns which present the military's work as fun or sensible are manipulating humans into accepting war as a norm rather than an extreme which only kills people.

Perhaps I'm seeing another aspect of Singapura's acculturation. The little nation-state is infected by the previous 500 years of bellicose European history.

I doubt that "mere" jungle and fishing villages would be the birthplace of a devotion to armed force.

**Melaka:** A Kuala Lumpur newspaper reports that Malaysia's military wants to have camps for local young people to instill them with nationalism.

Nationalism is not a natural human feeling. It has to be instilled.

The Malaysian military's plan is not unique. To me it's like injecting younger people with the AIDS plague.

Both nationalism and AIDS prevent people from living full human lives to their maximum potential. Humans become very sick and prematurely dead.

I guess the military fears that nationalism will decline and thus end war, i.e. the only raison d'être of the military everywhere. Human unity is the military's nemesis.

**Penang/Butterworth:** I see an English-language newscast on a television set in the window of an electrical appliance store. There are also some U.S. fast food outlets.

It's a shame to see robot food and fashion eradicating our pluralistic human heritage.

We do to ourselves what the European occupation forces do to others for nearly 500 years.

We are all like Singapura locals, following our Euro-era programming.

We're also like the computer running an empty house routinely after its residents are long dead, as described in Ray Bradbury's book The Martian Chronicles.

**Xiang Giang**: The first outside news to hit me after arriving here is the spectacular show being made of the return of fully-elected government in Brasil.

The show is celebrating the inauguration of Brasil's first directly-elected by universal suffrage president in 29 years.

It's seven years since my Carioca friend Zita and I sit in a Candelária crowd of a million people asking for Direítas Já.

The military disrupt democracy in Brasil for 25 years.

The first president of the Direítas Já era is Fernando Collor de Mello. He's 40 years old.

Of course the news report does not compare this good news with recent events in eastern Europe.

There are no front page headlines about the decline of the U.S. Empire and its dictator puppets in the southern Americas.

The wire service news report also has misinformation regarding the fall of elected government in Brasil 26 years ago.

The report puts in question the "29" year span since the last elections in which the general population could vote directly for the president.

The report says that the president elected 29 years ago was in office for only seven months and he leads to the turmoil which causes the coup 26 years ago.

Three years are missing?

The report also says that this person is the last president of Brasil. That's not true. In fact, João Goulart, Jango is the last president.

The seven month president preceeding Jango is followed by turmoil, but the coup d'état takes place because the military wants to stop land reforms and stabilize the economy.

The military has 20 years without orders from an elected government and ends up forced into some land reforms and destroying Brasil's economy.

Soldiers are trained to follow orders, not to govern.

**Tokyo**: Since my language skills are inadequate to understand the daily television news here, Mariko explains it all to me every day so that I'll know what's going on in Nippon.

This enables me to think about news I might otherwise know nothing about.

In today's news I learn that, despite or because of the conventional majority here, Nippon's divorce rate is very low compared to Canada's, the E.U.'s, and the U.S.A.'s.

About 21% of all marriages end in divorce here. Only Italia has a smaller percentage of divorces.

Maybe Italia's low rate is merely a reflection of the fact that divorce is only very recently legalized there.

I think Nippon's record may be due to the fact that married men and women don't see each other during most of their married lives.

So many males are away at work during most of their waking hours, returning only to sleep and sometimes eat.

So married couples never get to know each other well enough to get divorced. Yet divorce is very easy here. Each partner just marks his/her incan on a form provided by city hall.

...

The U.S. Far East Network (F.E.N.), the U.S. military's radio station in this part of the world, has some U.S. radio networks' news and some U.S. radio plays that are popular during my parents' generation.

But the dominant programme item is the currently-popular version of rock music in the U.S.

Or is rock'n'roll now rap'n'roll?

However, the overall function of the station seems to be to remind U.S. military personnel of their nation-state origin, i.e. their employer.

F.E.N. has no news about local events and attractions in Tokyo.

It's as if the U.S. F.E.N. and military personnel were actually living far from Nippon instead of in the most populous area of this country.

Weather forecasts do report the temperature in Tokyo, presumably at the radio station's location, but only states temperatures in the archaic U.S. measures system, not the world Celsius system used here in Nippon.

The weather conditions are also stated in a similarly nebulous manner. Announcers never say Tokyo.

The illusion is that the announcer and listeners are somewhere in the U.S.A., not Nippon.

News casts are directly from radio networks broadcasting only in the U.S.

So no news of Nippon is reported unless the networks mention some foreign news story involving Nippon. No U.S. F.E.N. announcer ever says, "Here in Japan."

News of Nippon is far away foreign news on the U.S. military radio station located in the vicinity of Tokyo.

Thus military personnel's' minds are never allowed to stray beyond the homeland that they're serving while only physically abroad.

Military bases are well-insulated from the surrounding country's reality Military minds are isolated.

Thus, military personnel are less at risk of becoming like the soldier in <u>All quiet on the western front</u> who sees the common humanity uniting soldiers wearing different uniforms.

Military base life and manoeuvres are the same everywhere "in the world" that military personnel are stationed.

That global sameness unites the armed personnel of one nation-state.

There's no threat of perceiving a common humanity with the "foreigners".

It's much like the "rules" that isolate and unite bureaucrats without uniforms abroad, such as those working at diplomatic posts, trade bureaus, and colonial office branches.

Fraternizing with locals, enemy or not, is discouraged beyond using diplomatic cocktail parties to loosen foreign elite tongues with alcohol, to find out what the other nation-states are up to and what they're not saying through official channels.

I see U.S. military isolationism in Okinawa, where U.S. cars are on used car lots, showing prices only in U.S. dollars.

A couple of year later, I hear about U.S. military isolationism in Europe's U.S. base towns while I'm hitch-hiking through Deutschland for the first time.

My driver points out "secret" missile locations along the way.

A few years later, near a Canadian military base in Europe, Mariko and I find a small town railway station employee counting a wad of Canadian currency.

Is the isolated military base abroad another meaning for the term "no man's land"?

In order to kill and maim efficiently, military personnel must never leave home in their minds.

"The enemy" must always be unknown, unfamiliar, and a distant target, not our human kin hosts abroad.

Even the foreign nation-state government hosting the base must be kept distant, in case the host ever becomes "the enemy".

Generally, a sense of nationalism, i.e. alienation from the broad human family is an essential precondition and a conditioned response for a military servant.

Trust, doubt, love, hate, etc. are derived entirely from uniform types and flags.

Without nation-states there can be no military personnel. Without isolating military personnel abroad, there can almost never be animosity and wars.

Thus the task of the U.S. Far East Network, and similar military broadcasters, is to perpetuate a sense of the illusion of nation-state membership in the minds of military personnel.

Otherwise they would just be absorbed like many newcomers can be in the new learning situations called immigration.

...

Television news does show empty business streets but there are still people working on May Day.

Some people stay home or visit within the city, just like us. The largest assemblage we see is a demonstration.

It has no audience so most of the people who are still in the city must be demonstrating.

There are actually several demonstrations but we see only one. It begins in Hibiya Koen. The crowd seems quite small at first. I count no more than a thousand people.

But when they march through the Ginza there seem to be 5,000 marchers.

They carry placards and shout chants for at least three hours. The throngs are divided into masses of 400 to 500 people, each stopping in turn at every corner.

Thus police can let cross traffic pass at intersections.

Sound trucks emphasize the chants, using loudhailers to broadcast the voices of chant leaders. It's all so well-orchestrated and run in such an orderly fashion.

This long political parade has various themes about current issues. It's a chance to protest all the ill-doings of the world in one shot.

There's no sign of passion, unlike the Hana Bampaku electricity pavilion demonstration I see a couple of days earlier.

The Tokyo demonstrations are a regularly-scheduled, highly-organized, annual, well-coordinated event.

It's just as lacking in spontaneity as partisan marches I see in the news about the same time as my first trip to Nippon.

I walk up the outer staircases of nearby buildings to take aerial view photographs.

When I'm taking discrete photos of the Tokyo crowd from the sidewalk beside them, they smile at me in a friendly manner.

It's a beautiful day for a walk.

...

According to stories in <u>The Japan Times</u> newspaper and an NHK-TV programme that Mariko explains to me, there's growing interest and sympathy for locals who are Korean ethnics.

They are officially considered to be non-local residents of Nippon and must register as aliens.

This is after generations of living in Nippon. In the Canadian context it would mean everyone except indigenous people would have to register as non-locals.

Some of these "Korean" locals-in-fact who are considered non-locals entirely due to their ancestral ethnicity are refusing to register as non-locals when I live in Fukuoka for the first time.

...

A casual visitor to Canada's embassy who reads the latest newspapers and telex reports, as we do today, might easily wonder if I'll have a country to return to if the prime minister of the time remains in power for another two years.

What a disaster that person is in comparison with Pierre Trudeau.

Trudeau's immediate successor makes all the political crazies feel comfortable again, confident that their unilingual and unicultural extremism can impose its minority rule over bilingual, multicultural Canada.

Nova Scotia is ready to join the U.S. Empire. The party-in-power in Columbia (Br.) passes a resolution which rejects the bilingual foundations of Canada.

Without an acceptance of bilingualism, Canada would never be founded in the first place.

Columbia (Br.) would not be accepted into the federation either.

Today, one of the steps necessary for maintaining Canada as a nation-state is clearly to throw out the party-in-power in Columbia (Br.) and put in a pro-pan-Canadian party.

Meanwhile, the Péquists send their leader of the moment to the U.S. and he finally admits that he supports the Canada-U.S. trade agreement because it's a backdoor means of reviving the defunct sovereignty-association scheme of the Péquists and it converts formerly federalists Québecois business people into supporters of dismantling Canada.

The trade agreement with the U.S. is exactly what the Péquists want to support their separatist goals, coupled with the Meech Lake accord's "distinct society" (formerly known as "special status").

Pierre Trudeau successfully rejects "special status" more than 20 years earlier and is subsequently given huge majority governments by Québec's electorate in all elections thereafter.

The current prime minister's successor will have to learn from this history instead of forgetting it.

He's taking Canada back in time to the era of the Commission on Bilingualism and Biculturalism which reports that Canada is in the middle of an historic crisis.

That era is before Pierre Trudeau becomes prime minister and defeats the Péquists by a 60% to 40% Québec referendum vote against sovereignty-association.

Canadian news in the embassy today is taking me back to times past which should only be history now, after 16 years of Pierre Trudeau as prime minister and five years after his retirement. What happened!?

...

Peru is news in Nippon. Local news reports feature interviews in Español with ethnic Japanese Peruvians who are concerned about one of their fellows running for president of Peru.

He's Alberto Fujimori (pronounced Fuhimori in Peru).

His ethnic group fears that if he makes mistakes there could be a reaction against all Japanese ethnics of Peru. Their fears are based on history.

Old photos of anti-Japanese-ethnic Peruvians are shown in the news. Homes and businesses are burned down by extremists.

It's reminiscent of the anti-Chinese riots in Vancouver of long ago.

Japanese ethnic Peruvians are attacked by European ethnic Peruvians during the 1930s/40s war, even though Peru is only marginally involved in those wars and the Japanese ethnics are descendants of people who immigrate to Peru long before that war.

...

Months later, Fujimori is elected president of Peru by 65% of the voters.

This can be an extraordinary event in the context of IMF mega-debt, Nippon-U.S. relations, and the "third" world.

It also makes Peru the most liberal democracy in the Americas.

Before Obama, can you think of any nation-state in the Americas where a non-European ethnic ever gets elected president, with the exception of the African ethnic majority islands in the central part of the Americas?

On one of several major television documentaries I hear some Peruvians saying, in Español that they'll vote for Fujimori because he's already moneyed.

Therefore, they reason, he's not motivated to be corrupt. I hear this before in other elections elsewhere. Is it true?

He's also popular because he's a farmer who understands the rural people's problems, the Peruvians say in the documentary.

He also studies in the U.S. and France. His family is from Kumamoto prefecture.

With Nippon's sympathy and support, not neo-colonialist, I hope Peru can become a model for the "third" world and give the U.S. and E.U. some very heavy competition.

If Nippon bails Peru out of the IMF mess, the U.S.-E.U. could have another Nippon to contend with, but one inhabited by people who know what it's like to be kicked around by the U.S.-E.U. IMF.

When I share these thoughts with Mariko she says that I shouldn't count on the Japanese government to give Peru any special assistance just because Fujimori is of Japanese origin.

Another documentary shows Peruvians of Japanese origin coming here to live and work. They end up bringing their whole families but still feel very homesick for Peru.

The kids have to go to special schools to learn Japanese. They don't seem to like the regular local school system.

...

There are a surprising number of news items about bombings in Nippon. A customs officer is injured when three go off outside his apartment in Osaka.

The news calls it a terrorist bombing. Another bomb is found on the shinkansen track before it can explode.

In other local violence, Nagasaki's mayor is out of hospital. He recovers from the bullet wounds that he receives from a pro-monarchist extremist.

The mayor isn't pro-monarchy. The new emperor of Nippon asks the mayor to be the official host during a monarch visit.

The mayor calls the attempted assassination the work of people against free speech.

The mayor is shot because he says the late emperor, Hiro Hito is part of the cause of the 1930s/40s war when he lets the Tokyo military dictatorship of the times use him instead of opposing the dictatorship.

A related story is about the first elected prime minister of

Hangoo. He's a retired general of the former military dictatorship which finally permitted elections.

He seems to be the leading the first democratically-elected government in the history of the Korean peninsula.

How many people in the "first" world know that the peninsula is under monarchical dictatorship for most of its history; then part of the former Empire of Japan; followed by military dictatorships, north and south, since the 1930s/40s war?

Hangoo is another dictatorship "ally" of the "free" world. North Korea is another dictatorship "enemy" of the "free" world.

The irony gets worse:

The now elected former dictator of Hangoo is coming to Nippon to ask its long democratically-elected government for an apology for the 1930s/40s crimes committed by the former military dictatorship in Tokyo.

News of this visit makes me wonder when the Hangoo military will apologize to Hangoosaram for depriving them of elections since the end of the 1930s/40s wars.

The Hangoo military dictatorship probably uses North Korea and anti-Nippon emotions to divert Hangoosaram attention away from criticizing their home dictators.

As elsewhere, critics of dictatorship are branded "dangerous radicals" and dealt with by riot police in Hangoo.

It's a shame that the Korean civil war after the 1930s/40s wars did not produce democracy anywhere on the Korean peninsula until now. It' a "first" world secret?

...

The Nihon-bashers, the worst of the non-locals who live and prosper in Nippon, get their nonsense printed in <u>The Japan Times</u> again.

Locals' tolerance for this unwarranted abuse impresses me.

Non-locals here should try to imagine what would happen to them elsewhere and realize how lucky they are to be in Nippon.

How many non-local workers in places like the U.S.A. and Europe could publish a regular stream of anti-U.S.A., anti-Europe letters to the editor without facing physical assault, calls for restricting work visas and immigration, and retaliation against complainants by deportation?

The kindness of Nippon to even the worst non-local elements is another example of how fortunate the world is that Nippon does not suffer a European or U.S. occupation for hundreds of years, like so much of the world.

It's good that Nippon doesn't get abused by those occupiers and consequently end up changed for the worse by an army of colonial office personnel who are set on bringing "civilization" to Nippon.

The latest poison pen letter from a malcontent non-local writing to The Japan Times repeats the same old lie that locals "always leave empty bus seats next to" non-locals.

Local passengers in all the public transportation that I use, from Wakkanai to Iriomote, always sit beside me without a blink.

So my experience proves that the "always" of the non-local letter is false.

The trouble with printing nonsense letters is that they can seep into my head.

Every time I see an empty seat beside me in a bus I'm tempted to start thinking, "Please sit here beside me just to prove those non-local morons wrong".

Then a local sits next to me.

The ugliness of too many non-locals can thus almost spoil my tranquility, as usual.

Such non-locals are pressuring me to feel absurdly uncomfortable about the luxury of having two seats to myself in a big city bus.

I have long legs and prefer to have more space in public transportation instead of being cramped by people sitting beside me.

I really don't want anyone to sit next to me in any public transportation anywhere. I would be happy if locals everywhere "always" let me have two seats to myself.

I'm sure that the same non-locals who complain about locals here also grumble in their homelands about overcrowded urban bus service which never provides an empty seat next to any passenger.

The annoying effects I experience due to the unwarranted anti-Nippon complaints of non-locals helps me to better understand how the most gullible and easily influenced "greenhorn" non-local newcomer to Nippon can be misled and fall prey to misinformation by listening to the axe grinding of "old hands" who arrive a few months earlier.

The emptiness of the Nippon-bashers' lies is much bigger than the physical space on a bus seat.

Surely <u>The Japan Times</u> can make better use of its valuable space instead of wasting it by reprinting the same old false statements of some non-locals for years and years.

Given all the lines of print devoted to printing the on-going harping of non-local malcontents, it would not be against free speech to let the ugly non-locals take a rest from trying to proliferate their lies.

When I submit an item to the news media and they don't want to use it, they sometimes say they "already did that story".

Surely this excuse also applies to ad nauseam repetition of the same old nonsense by ugly non-locals.

Besides which, lies make hate and wars easy.

Fortunately, I meet a few non-locals here who are even-handed.

But perhaps these better-adjusted, happier people don't feel any need or fervour to express themselves in print.

Thus perhaps <u>The Japan Times</u> only hears from the moaners and groaners.

Perhaps the Nazis write more letters to the editor than liberal-minded people too.

An editor should know his/her community of letter writers and the broader group too.

An additional problem of the outlandish non-local complainers is that they can poison the locals who are exposed to the abuse.

I know a very friendly younger student in Fukuoka who says that she's studying English to find out "why they hate us" and "why they call us 'yellow monkeys'".

She knows enough English to be able to read the Nipponophobe liars. Less thoughtful locals might not choose the younger student's reasoned approach.

They might just react, responding to perceived hatred with real hatred against all non-locals, including me.

Hate is not a flesh wound. It's a venom which spreads if not given the antidote of truth.

Some of the antidote comes from the more even-handed non-locals who I encounter during my work at Ofuna. They're all from the U.S.

I see them speaking Japanese to locals in the monorail.

This sort of communication can help overcome the printed nonsense.

I roast the turkeys who nay because they are donkeys.

...

There's a N.A.T.O. meeting in Calgary (Alberta) to discuss the future of the U.S.A. led anti-U.S.S.R. military alliance due to the fact that the U.S.S.R. Empire is gone.

Depending on the TV images more than the news reporter's words, I'm most struck by the people attending the meeting rather than the meeting itself.

Choices of war versus peace are being made by a group of people with very specific characteristics, if their socio-economic appearance is significant.

They are all male. They all look as if they're most comfortable in settings where knowing what table utensils to use is the secret to immortality.

These polished-looking people might be called "well-bred" but when we breed our fellow earth lifeforms, a polite term for gen-etic engineering, they end up either beautiful externally and vacuous internally, or they be-come another herd of cattle.

There's something to be said for the "crude" in the word bred's root meaning.

We no longer think of "refined" as being desirable, especially when referring to sugar and other non-nutritious and unhealthy "food".

I'm sure that many of the military officers who lead generations to their deaths are often very well-bred and refined.

The U.K. officers were committing murder, not "friendly fire" when they executed Canadian soldiers suffering from post-traumatic stress in Europe's "first world war".

And who will ever forget "their imperial highnesses" Kaiser Wilhelm and Hiro Hito, or the "royal" visits to Canada when the Europeans need more Canadian cannon fodder in their wars?

No point in wasting all the "best" people?

...

TV news begins showing how Nippon improves during the oil crisis of nearly twenty years earlier through self-discipline and innovation.

Can the later "bean sprout" and "pepper head" generations, named for their flimsy caretaker society lifestyle and unreflective minds, do as well in their times?

These generations are not limited to just one "first" world nation-state.

...

The Canadian constitutional amendment story is moving to the business news columns here in Tokyo, indicating that some investors are worrying about Canada.

It's a shame because the Meech Lake story is really a fraud.

The Constitution Act of eight years earlier is simply a rewrite of the U.K.'s B.N.A. Act with the Canadian Bill of Rights and a Charter of Rights and Freedoms added as well as extra protection for Canada's neglected and abused French language population in the province of New Brunswick, (added by Pierre Trudeau with provincial assent).

The current Québec provincial government is already applying provisions of the constitution which the separatist Péquist government refuses to sign eight years earlier because that party doesn't want Québec to be a part of any document which recognizes that Québec is a founding partner of Canada.

The current Liberal Party government of Québec applies Canada's constitution to support the previous Péquist government's language sineage law when it's ruled illegal by Canada's supreme court.

The Péquist law prohibits and/or restricts the use of more than one language in business signage.

The law is a backlash against the long-term attempts of anglomaniacs in Québec to wipe out Canada's French language by submerging francophones in English-only advertising everywhere in Canada.

The use of the constitution by the current Québec government to prop up an ill-conceived backlash law is de facto evidence that Québec is in the constitution already, despite the separatists' attempts to portray Québec as "left out".

In fact, the Péquists left only themselves out of Canada. Québecois already defeat the Péquist separatist referendum and throw the Péquists out of office.

That clearly means Québecois do not choose to be left out of Canada.

Unfortunately, the first prime minister of Canada after Pierre Trudeau is receiving advice from Péquist member advisors in Ottawa, i.e. people who are left out.

The prime minister is persuaded to accept the separatist losers' position that Québec is "left out".

So he reverts to the long defunct and defeated P.C. Party election platform of 20 years earlier that Canada is "deux nations".

The prime minister is behaving as if the Péquists win the referendum and the provincial election. In the real world, the Péquists lose both.

There is no reason to listen to their advice. They aren't credible advisors for anyone aspiring to serve as Canada's prime minister.

The current prime minister should not turn Péquist loses into victories by pursuing ideas rejected by the Québec and national electorate.

Why listen to advisors unwilling to accept the democratic decisions of Québecois?

Canada's prime minister must be stupid. Is he vying for the title "Last Prime Minister of Canada", a low budget remake of the Chinese classic "Last Emperor of China"?

Will the U.S. rename Canada "Manchukuo West" when it comes to collect the natural resources?

It shouldn't be a surprise anyone that the prime minister's chief advisor, a long-time card carrying member of the Péquist party is now resigning and declaring himself a pro-separatist member of the parliament of Canada.

But the prime minister is surprised.

The Péquist policy during its referendum ten years earlier is that the party will elect separatists to Canada's parliament if the referendum goes pro-Péquist separatism.

That doesn't happen because they lose the referendum.

But the current prime minster grants party affiliation to Péquists anyway and appoints one of them his key constitutional advisor.

The current prime minister rushes through a sovereignty-association trade deal with the U.S. and pushes for Péquist-friendly constitutional amendments by warning of dire consequences if his policies are not put into effect.

Now I know who that the consequences are dire for the prime minister, not Canada.

He single-handedly puts Canada in peril in a way that not even the Péquists would dream is possible.

He promotes sovereignty-association and "deux nations" as if he were a Péquist.

To their credit, unlike the Canadian prime minister, the Péquists want a smooth, stable dismantling of Canada so that they can escape blame for the economic hardships resulting from the sudden break up of Canada which the current prime minister's ineptitude is threatening to cause.

Without Québec there is no Canada.

The mediocre premiers of many provinces would soon find out what it's like to be one sparsely-populated state in a nation-state of more than 50 states which are vying for attention from Washington, D.C., the U.S. capital city.

D.C. would probably wisely do what the founders of Canada should do at the outset, starting in 1867.

D.C. would cut up the oversized, underpopulated former Canadian provinces into small states and then hold land rushes to settle the large tracts of rich land with loyal U.S. citizens.

Ontario and Québec might escape this U.S.-ruled outcome, hanging on as little nation-states much like Paraguay in relation to Brasil and Argentina, while attached to the U.S. ally and master.

The Maritimes could choose masters among Ontario, Québec, and the U.S.A.

...

The U.S.F.E.N. military radio, much closer to the northern Americas than its host soil in Nippon, actually mentions the Canadian situation in an early morning news broadcast.

The station says there'll be a meeting on constitutional reform.

Another day, evening this time, there's a report from Ottawa saying that six days of meetings result in an agreement among the ten provinces and federal government.

Just before the agreement is reached, the U.S. F.E.N. carries two commentaries on the situation.

One is from a commercial broadcaster. The other is from the excellent U.S. National Public Radio network.

The commercial commentary gives a serious description of how the U.S. can profit from Canada's demise by absorbing the remains.

The NPR commentary on "All Things Considered" is a satirical look at the same demise and how the U.S. would only take the most valuable pieces of Canada, leaving the rest to other nation-states, such as Ireland.

Both the commercial and NPR commentaries and the news reports present the constitutional meetings and amendments as being crucial to the existence of Canada.

They say that if there's no agreement, there'll be no Canada.

These reflect the current prime minister's version of "dire consequences".

Subsequent news says that the six-day agreement falls apart. This brief story is the end of news about Canada on U.S. armed forces radio. Is Canada dead?

According to telex summaries of news stories directly from Canadian news organizations, the six-day agreement which changes Meech Lake fails due to the prime minister's manipulation of events and the long-unresolved grievances of pre-European era residents of Canada.

The current prime minister tells Canadian reporters that he deliberately plans the six-day crisis meetings about a month before they happen.

He says he wants to force the provincial premiers to agree by making them believe that if they don't agree the nation-state will collapse.

The prime minister's confession to plotting causes many to turn against the six-day agreement because he's playing a game with the future of Canada.

The indigenous peoples of Canada are not part of the six-day meetings. Nor are they part of Meech Lake or the original agreement founding Canada.

So they finally strike back. They stop both the prime minister and the six-day agreement.

Since the European era invaders do everything that they can to destroy indigenous civilizations, and fail, it would be poetic justice if the indigenous people of today actually "destroy" the European era created nation-state of Canada by stopping the six-day agreement.

Meech Lake and the six-day agreement are just further examples of creating European era style documents which the indigenous people are expected to just accept, like the old, unrespected, broken treaties and agreements.

In Québec, which is the supposed reason behind Meech Lake and the six-day agreement, public opinion polls show that a majority of the population or a plurality, depending on the poll and question, are in favour of retaining the present Canadian relationship among the ten provinces as described in the Constitution Act of eight years earlier, if Meech fails.

The May 1 issue of Actualité, the Québec francophone magazine reports one poll showing pro-separatism at 27%, "sovereignty-association" at 27%, and the present Canadian federation at 31%.

About 8% want Québec to become a U.S. state.

This poll can be interpreted as saying that 69% of the people are against Canada as it is today.

Thus a great majority want change. That seems to be

healthy. A society opposed to change will be changed from the outside.

But there's no unity in Québec, no accord on the kind of change that's needed. So long as there's no agreement within the province it can't move in any direction.

But disagreement is the basis of discussion, debate, and maybe better ideas than the European panacea of making yet another nation-state to divide humanity. The panacea is just quackery.

The Meech Lake accord and six-days of meetings succeed only if they're intended to distract attention away from the Liberal Party leadership convention.

Maybe this is why the current prime minister plans the crisis a month in advance, to coincide with the convention, instead of negotiating calmly earlier.

It's part of the same strategy as having his members of parliament read newspaper articles out loud during regular debates so that the parliamentary television station won't show Pierre Trudeau coming out of retirement from politics to criticize Meech Lake.

After finally listening to Trudeau's presentation, I conclude that if it were widely broadcast in its entirety three years earlier, public pressure would have ended the Meech amendment at that time.

The current prime minister appears on national television to "apologize to Québec" because his Meech amendment fails.

He says he'll try a new approach. I suggest resigning.

Elijah Harper, an indigenous member of Manitoba's provincial legislature is being celebrated in Canada as the one person who stops Meech plus six.

He does so by simply holding up a feather and saying "No."

In this way he prevents "unanimous consent" for introducing "new business" which in this case means ratifying the Meech amendment.

Harper reminds me of Juruna, an indigenous senator in Brasilia. When I'm living in Rio de Janeiro he helps to resolve the indigenous land dispute in Matto Grosso.

He's born in an isolated area and doesn't meet anyone from outside his community until he's well on the way to adulthood.

Elijah Harper is also from an isolated area.

The word isolated is perhaps misused to describe both the birthplaces of Juruna and Elijah Harper.

They're born where humans can still experience the realities of living on earth rather than in the isolated incubator society urban centres.

People born in those centres are the ones who are isolated from life on earth.

Perhaps the childhood experiences of Juruna and Elijah Harper make their judgement better than politicians who cause the Matto Grosso and Meech plus six problems.

These thoughts take me back to the pages of <u>A Sketch of Terrian History</u> that I write in the southern Americas:

"Humanity's future depends on learning from the example and leadership of the people who are most advanced in improving the likelihood of human survival and fruition on earth... Whenever nations and form settlements are weakest, the native people are strongest."

With all the strange, hate-mongering, i.e. nationalistic groups forming in Canada in recent years, such as the "Reform" Party, APEC, CORE, and the old Péquist separatist wing revivalists, I have other thoughts of Brasil.

During my time in Rio, as the military dictatorship destroyed economy becomes worse and Brasileiros become more upset about it, movie theatres begin showing a public service film to remind locals of the fruits of crisis.

The film shows how Deutschland goes on the path of self-destruction by choosing the hate-based Nazis to help

Deutschland out of its crisis of nearly sixty years before time of writing.

By deliberately creating an artificial crisis, the current prime minister of Canada is bolstering the hate-mongers and putting Canada at risk in a way that I don't see at any time before in Canada during my lifetime.

Canada is a coalition of minorities. There is no majority group. Political parties reflect the diversity.

So creating a crisis which bolsters hate-mongers creates the risk that a major political party might have to depend on one of the hate-monger groups to form a government.

The disaster of this kind of situation is evident in places like Yisra'el, where religionist extremists can manipulate larger parties.

A government head who boasts of creating an artificial crisis and planning it a month in advance is not fit to serve.

The latest of the strange polls showing this bizarrely ignorant negative feeling gives the current prime minster 65% of public support in Québec despite the Meech failure.

Sovereignty-association, alias "free trade" with the U.S. gets 62% support, despite U.S. firms closing shop in Canada to "rationalize" by expanding their U.S. locations.

It's "not because of free trade" the U.S. firms say.

Maybe we can conclude that the 40% who vote against Canada in the Péquist referendum of ten years before Meech are the backbone of both poll results.

The current prime minister makes sovereignty-association easier.

So the real numbers, excluding the 40%, are 25% pro-prime-minister and 22% pro-free-trade?

...

In the midst of the Meech Lake farce, there's another embarrassment for the current prime minister.

Gorby arrives from the S.U. for a visit to Canada. <u>The Japan Times</u> has a front page photo of him with the current Canadian prime minister.

The S.U. also has unity problems, so the newspaper photo is a portrait of the heads of two federations in trouble, one through leadership and the other through stupidity (Canada).

After Gorby returns to Moscow, the news says that he's worried about "nationalists" and "separatists" in Europe. Join the club. These are our common enemies as humans.

...

Argentina's President Menem and Brasil's President Collor are arranging a Brasil-Argentina common market. It's to go into effect four years from this writing.

These two leaders look so young compared with President Alfonsin, General Figuereido, and Presidents Neves and Sarney.

The generals will be hard-pressed to get their dirty fingers into such a non-national organization.

...

NHK news shows a map of Canada with a dot at Vancouver with the big letters "APEC" over it. I cringe. Have the anglomaniacs staged a coup d'état unilingually? Fortunately not.

APEC is simply a meeting of some international trade experts who are sipping while chattering in a number of languages over the eroding cliffs of the university endowment lands at U.B.C.

Security agents in suits must be there to keep away curious nudists from Wreck Beach.

...

Some anglophones are obstinately or aggressively unilingual in extreme fringe groups such as APEC (not the one meeting Vancouver).

They bizarrely view themselves as oppressed anglophones in a world of anglophone minority linguistic world rule.

In great contrast, locals of very enlightened Nippon accept and enthusiastically pursue language learning that goes beyond the eight daily television and radio language courses provided by the NHK broadcasting organization.

I hear French, Arabic, and Russian in the news, with subtitles in Japanese.

That's in the regular daily news programmes, not just in documentaries or special broadcasts.

...

A golf course development in Canada is now gaining international interest, and not in the sports reports. Even the U.S. F.E.N. (armed forces) radio station mentions it.

The Canadian minister responsible for First Nations makes a statement about it.

The story barely attracts my attention. It has something to do with the Kayen'kehà:ka First Nation being opposed to cutting down trees for a golf course.

I wonder why this is in the international news, particularly on the U.S.F.E.N.

Sounds like a simple matter for a public meeting at a town hall to resolve.

If the Kayen'kehà:ka want to leave the forest uncut, more power to them. There are lots of places to build golf courses in Canada's ten million square kilometres.

...

The land dispute centres around Oka. I'm surprised when it becomes the centre of a military standoff against the Kayen'kehà:ka.

Oka is a cheese village to me. That's all I know of it when my Montréal friend Jennifer takes me there in years past.

...

News stories report the alleged involvement of Kadhafi, the unelected head of Libyia in a bizarre "Islamic" coup d'état attempt in Trinidad.

It sounds like a post-Cold-War problem based on religious pretence.

Are we going back to religious wars?

...

'Irāq's Al-Kuwayt situation gets more news reporting every day. First the U.S. president is talking about principles. Then someone from 'Irāq speaks of principles.

So humans are threatened by principles? Maybe principles should be eliminated by treaty.

...

A news report on the 'Irāq vs. Al-Kuwayt situation shows people in white gowns bathed in very Scottish-sounding bagpipes.

Watching this makes me think again that the current sudden U.S.-S.U. friendship originates in mutual awareness of potential common enemies, their Frankenstein's monster military dictatorships around the world.

Perhaps the S.U. and U.S. realize and identify some growing threats among their monsters, such as the U.S. bellicose military dictatorship running 'Irāq, which seems to be getting out of control.

This situation is aggravated by propaganda. 'Irāqis must be becoming as well propagandized as the U.K. and Argentinian citizenry during la guerra de las Malvinas, eight years earlier.

Propaganda has the ironic effect of making people suffering from dictators become supporters of those dictators against the "outside agitators" who put and keep the dictators in power, i.e. the U.S. and S.U. Empires.

...

A U.N. vote to permit military intervention against 'Irāqi forces in Al-Kuwayt passes, despite the 'Irāqi dictator's latest TV show.

I see excerpts of his show on NHK-TV News.

It looks like the old Deutschland dictator or current U.K. prime minister receiving a bouquet of flowers from little girls while taking a break from the war planning meetings.

Are they all using the same media advisors and production companies?

...

Getting ready to leave Tokyo, I begin clearing up the collection of miscellaneous papers that pile up everywhere that I explore.

In the process, I begin reviewing old newspapers dating from before the Oka golf course crisis and 'Irāq's invasion of Al-Kuwayt. Facts and events intrigue me.

The Japan Times reports, five months before 'Iraq invades Al-Kuwayt, that a Canadian-born U.S. arms dealer is shot dead in Brussels (Belgium).

The Times of London (U.K.) claims that the Canadian designs a giant gun for Iraq.

I wonder if it's like the one the Allies of the 1930s/40s wars say they find in Deutschland at the end of that warfare.

Four months before Al-Kuwayt is invaded, Arab states unite behind the 'Iraqi dictator because they think that the U.K. is bullying him due to an alleged weapons muggling plot to take the giant gun components into 'Irāq.

The person chairing the U.K. foreign affairs committee then publishes a commentary comparing the 'Irāqi dictator to 1930s dictators and accusing Arab leaders of appeasing him.

Again, this is four months before 'Iraq invades Al-Kuwayt.

The U.K. official also says that the 'Irāqi dictator is trying to prove his worth after the long war of attrition against Īrān.

At the same time, The Japan Times says Al-Kuwayt's population is 1.8 million and that 60% of them are non-local workers and their families.

So Al-Kuwayt hardly exists? There are fewer Al-Kuwayti locals than the population of Vancouver (Columbia (Br.) at time of writing.

Meanwhile, oil prices drop to about $17 per barrel and OPEC, a club for most of the world's oil producing nation-states, considers production cuts to raise the price.

Months later, 'Irāq's invasion of Al-Kuwayt solves these

problems. Uncertainty and crisis boosts the oil prices.

So is the 'Irāq-Al-Kuwayt situation all about eliminating a weapon shipment and raising oil prices?

But news pictures showing 'Irāq troops looting Al-Kuwayt buildings provide another reason for the invasion.

All that the 'Irāqi dictator seems to want is luxury consumer goods, eg. home video tape recorders, television sets, etc.

Wouldn't it be easier to hire looters from troubled U.S. cities instead of invading Al-Kuwayt with troops?

Could it be that the U.K. prime minister is up to her old tricks, baiting another "third" world dictator, as in la guerra de Las Malvinas?

Does she set up the 'Irāqi dictator's invasion this time so that she can win another election campaign?

Both the old military regime in Buenos Aires and the 'Irāqi dictator may have been goaded and tricked into believing that they could save themselves by making quick, successful military strikes against neighbouring places and that no one would contest the prizes.

But surprise! Las Malvinas and Al-Kuwayt are traps sprung by equally desperate partisans running elected governments fearing electoral defeat.

So the Al-Kuwayt situation is really about the U.K. poll tax? Success in war can erase that from voters' memories?

Of course the U.S. president is also sagging low in the public opinion polls. Beating up a dictator can help in the next U.S. election too?

He claims that 'Irāqi troops are "throwing babies out of incubators" in Al-Kuwayt.

It sounds like a war crime but, after the war, U.S. journalists discover it never happens, just like the Gulf of Tonkin incident in Việt Nam.

Months before Oka too, a news item reports that there is shooting in Kayen'kehà:ka First

Nation territory. But the problem isn't golf. It's casinos.

The Canadian government asks the U.S. for help in stopping Kayen'kehà:kas from shooting each other because they're split about whether or not to have casinos.

A Kayen'kehà:ka chief "pleaded with" the governor of New York State to send in the U.S. national guard military force.

Does the casino war spill over into the golf course dispute? Or does the golf forest unite the casino belligerents?

Are some parties to the golf dispute trying to confuse the forest with the casinos?

Thus the gulf and golf situations tell me that I have to read old newspapers to know what's going on today. That's taught in journalism courses and at the papers too.

...

There are 709 people in Nippon who are 100 or more years old. Tokyo has 297 of them. The oldest known is 112.

Many are on the TV news today. Some could still see, hear, read, and talk.

...

A U.K. BBC-TV news report carried by local television describes Rio's favelas as "a no-man's land where only groups of heavily-armed police dare enter".

That must make me a daring commando guerilla.

I walk into many favelas with Doca and Zita. We aren't hopelessly outnumbered by armed assailants.

In fact I feel greater safety and community in favelas than in conventional residential and commercial areas.

Maybe the reporter doesn't intend to distort reality but every error in reporting reality has profound and dire consequences for interhuman relations and communications.

Most of the world's television viewers only know the outside world through their television screen, computer screen, or tourist industry packaging.

So these viewers have no way of knowing what is fact and accurate versus what is fiction or error in TV news and internet reporting about faraway places.

Most screen thumbers and viewers in the world never set foot inside a favela.

So all of the misinformation put into their heads by television ant internet reports can easily lead them to make erroneous decisions and judgements.

In an electorate-directed form of government, the results can be very bad for everyone. The elected politicians determine foreign policy.

The government of the screen thumbers and viewers might not question or criticize an armed police assault on a Rio favela.

So a person living in a favela can end up getting murdered by police for repairing the roof of a house. I see this person's children in one Rio favela.

...

NHK's evening news is giving lengthy reports about carbon dioxide and other air poisoning by cars and factories.

I'm impressed by this reporting all week. There's also a special about the global artificially-induced environmental problems.

In the special, one of the U.K.'s junior monarchs reads script about environmental destruction threatening earth life, especially forests.

The narrator says that Europeans of the past refer to northern Africa as "the granary of Europe". Now it's called the Sahara Desert.

The narrator also says that the current empires do the same negative things as the former ones, but much more quickly and on a much larger scale than during the European era.

This includes turning fertile land into desert.

I guess that modern technology permits us to apply European era perspectives of the world more efficiently.

I'm glad that someone representing today's vestige of monarchical dictatorship is finally reading something valuable instead of just fiddling around while the Amazon burns.

...

Typhoon 20 just blows or falls through, bringing only steady rain when it arrives here. People abroad tell me that I'm in the middle of a big storm, according to their news.

What the foreign news people call Toky-o instead of To-kyo when reporting from abroad is a much vaster area than the huge city.

They refer to the entire Kanto Plain as Tokyo.

...

I see a Shinto priest in the news who is apparently closing the mountain climbing season with a prayer. So when I call an information office I'm told that climbing is now illegal.

I reply that when I'm 19 I see climbers on Mt. Fuji during the illegal season. I'm one of them.

The information clerk tells me that Mt. Fuji is only open to climbers for two months each year. She says, that during the other months it is "against the law" to climb Fuji.

When I sound surprised she says that she works for an official government office and can only speak officially.

If I want unofficial information I'd have to ask another source.

How many local and non-local people are "officially" criminals in Nippon over the years before and since my first visit here?

I can see good reasons why the government would to want to restrict the climbing season, such as safety and the complications of rescuing stranded climbers.

Equally true is that the unpredictable nature of weather around a mountain summit could be hazardous both in season and out of season.

You never know in the mountains, as I always caution my Carioca friend Zita in the Andes.

Even comprehending the good reasons for closure and caution, I can't help finding the idea of an "illegal" Fuji-sama quite amusing.

As Mariko and I ride the trains from early to mid-morning en route from Tokyo to Shizuoka, I'm imagining the news headlines if we are apprehended by authorities on Fuji: "Canadian arrested for illegal climb".

It would be quite an embarrassing publicity stunt for a headline seeker, which I am not.

If arrested, I would write and file the story myself, including my confession of my previous, undetected offence when I'm 19.

Further headline: "A life of crime revealed!"

The fee I receive from the news agencies might pay our train fare and fines.

I might be able to plea bargain, providing the police with the names and addresses of some accomplices from my 19 year old's offence.

By testifying against my old friends and fellow-traveller illegal climbers I could see them extradited for illegal mountain climbing.

I'm sure they'd enjoy the free trip to Nippon and get suspended sentences due to their youth and the fact that it's just a first offence for each of them.

Since the age of majority is 20 in Nippon, those who are 19 at the time, like me, would be tried in juvenile court.

During the trial my Kelowna friend Mel could play pachinko and I could find out if Cathy is still an adventurous campfire scout.

Since I don't climb all the way to the summit, as Cathy says she does at the time, I might be considered only a minor accomplice who qualifies for a plea deal.

I think of the dragnet of local armed police that must now be surrounding and patrolling Fuji-sama to deter or capture illegal climbers.

If Mariko and I can make it through the police cordon and

perhaps security sensors, will we be hailed down by a police helicopter?

Has Fuji-sama become like the U.S-Mexico border?

I decide to risk it to meet my objective. Hundreds of locals and non-locals are at Fuji-sama. We join the ragtag band of outlaw climbers.

Some who climb only a short distance are pulling and carrying along their children to the holy mountain, encouraging juvenile delinquency.

What a defiant, lawless people, the Japanese! They're setting such a bad example for non-locals.

There are Swiss, U.S., Saskatoon, Korean, and Brazilian lawbreakers plodding laboriously high, flaunting the law with every hard pace, and then joyfully and remorselessly scrambling back.

…

Every night for the past few weeks, NHK News is telling the same story. It's the same message as the hippies try to get across many years before.

It's also the same message that is the centre of my Terrian living.

The message is "change lifestyles".

Every time that I have a newcomer experience somewhere in the world I have to change lifestyles, i.e. daily behaviours.

All human lifestyles and endeavours should be evaluated and altered to make our planetary life impacts positive ones instead of des-tructive ones.

In this evaluation, we shouldn't be so pretentious as to believe that we're "saving earth". We're not earth and earth isn't us.

The earth doesn't depend on us to survive. We depend on it.

Earth is neutral toward us and all other lifeforms.

The planet has the same consciousness of us as we have of the molecular particles which make up our bodies.

For Earth, lifeforms bounce around, come and go unperceived in daily rotation.

To save ourselves, we need to start trying to improve our behaviours in a manner which contributes to environmental conditions not detrimental to life as we know it on earth.

In other words, we need to consciously try not to eliminate ourselves through ignorance or blind, stubborn devotion to the self-destructive behaviours that we express in lifestyles.

A great deal of information is available but it's ignored, denied, or not made widely enough available to people throughout the globe.

So self-destructive lifestyles continue.

Earth sciences might say it doesn't matter. This planet is likely to eventually become uninhabitable for the current lifeforms no matter how we behave.

If the star "Sun" suddenly goes supernova, no change in behaviour can help us or save us. But meanwhile, let's follow the advise of NHK News. Change or die.

...

A tremor hits the city just before a regular newscast is about to go on the air.

The newscast begins with a quake report, complete with a chart showing the magnitude registered in each part of the city. Incredible.

The big quake that Tokyo is awaiting with some anguish is something discussed with a planned response ready.

But the response plan isn't a de-urbanization scheme to save many thousands or millions from sure death and debilitating injuries.

Apparently no planner in the many decades since the last big quake is contemplating simply dismantling the city and dispersing the twelve million people now sitting on top of a certain disaster area.

During the last big quake Tokyo is a much smaller city than it is today, but the casualties aren't a small number.

Removing Tokyo could be more readily conceived and accomplished if there were a general consensus that urban centres and money economies in themselves are unsuitable for human life.

But even without such a realization, it ought to be evident that letting a population centre continue to locate and grow on a known disaster spot is criminal negligence, a real sword of Damocles in plain view of all.

**Kathmandu**: A lot of well-deserved bad publicity should focus on the elite here in all international news media reports.

No wonder some people "rioted" for democratic reforms this year, as The Japan Times reports when I'm in Tokyo.

I'm surprised that a French Revolution scenario is not occurring. If this situation is also related to the IMF, it's all the more scandalous.

...

The Rising Nepal daily English language newspaper has many long and detailed reports for a publication in a land without elected government and without an equitable sharing of wealth.

An item which particularly catches my interest is about tiny batteries that are being developed for electric cars.

Another story that intrigues me is about a major electric company that I almost work for in Nippon.

The company is buying a major U.S. Hollywood movie making studio.

Knowing some of the cardboard television productions of the U.S. company, I hope for the best.

The Japanese company can give them an infusion of stimulating imagination and creativity. They can only get better, not worse.

**Dhaka**: Ironically, since the beginning of emergency measures here, only the U.K.'s BBC World radio news broadcasts tell locals what is happening in their own country and in the world in general.

I honestly see no evidence of disturbances here so far. I'm unhindered by curfews or blockades even during my overnight hotel stop in Dhaka before going to Nepal.

I have a sense of flying into the calm centre of a storm, just as when I fly into Buenos Aires during the war of Las Malvinas eight years earlier.

Will I visit Baghdad in the early new year before the crowds and legions arrive?

**Cox's Bazaar:** During the latter part of the night a sound truck passes, repeatedly blaring out a recorded message. Another sound message vehicle passes once this morning.

People tell me that "the dictator is gone" and elections are going to be held soon.

But even this news only brings 30 to 40 people into the streets to parade back and forth. There is no visible, great outpouring of emotion in this town.

Maybe only the elite politicos are involved and interested. A truck driver the previous day tells me something about "rich people always" but not the 50 Taka wage earners.

That sum in the local currency is little more than one U.S. dollar.

Maybe only the grass roots effects of the change in regime will bring most consciences to a state of celebration.

Later I note 200 to 300 people walking, but men only. Will women vote? How far away is democracy?

I see only one small truck of armed military passing me in the streets here. En route to Chittagong I see two larger troop trucks en route somewhere.

Now that the dictator is gone, I can mail this letter from inside the country instead of in another land.

**Chittagong**: The hotel manager shows me the first newspaper to be published in the past eight days.

It's just out. I buy a copy of the historic edition of one page and hand-soiling ink.

Large photos of the two women opposition party leaders are featured with their speeches calling for calm now that they have won.

It seems that the U.K. and Nippon governments are helpful by cutting aid to force the local government to reform itself.

It's probably a continuation of the global cleanup of the mess left by U.S. C.I.A. and S.U. K.G.B. meddling in the southern Americas, eastern Europe, and elsewhere.

What a great day to arrive here. The mood is so good. I feel safe, relaxed, and welcome, but I still keep my eyes open.

...

There's a bit of non-local news on my mind in the bus.

The local English language newspaper says the generals in Buenos Aires try another coup d'état against the elected government.

The U.S. C.I.A. must be busy making sure that the generals fail. The coup is attempted on the eve of a state visit by the U.S. president.

The generals should know that the U.S. glasnost means generals are out for good.

You can't tear down Berlin's wall and then let the generals slither back elsewhere.

**Sealdah**: I look around carefully. I observe a kiosk selling only books, magazines, and newspapers.

There's an older man buying an English language magazine. That's his only reason for being here.

He's going about his daily routine, not hanging around the station looking for money or other trouble. I approach him. He not only puts me on public transport and tells me when to get off, he also tells me the fares.

I thus have just enough information and cash ready to look as if I already know the system and how to get where I'm going.

This type of knowledge can help to render an otherwise new arrival invisible.

Thus s/he may create enough doubt in the minds of all variety of potential exploiters to cause them to keep their distance and to look for easier prey.

**Kolkata**: The blatant disinterest of the local elite in the experiences of most locals is clear from just reading the daily news that the elite publishes.

The local English language newspapers are written in highly elitist language, in overly effete style, using bookish vocabulary.

Of course only the elite interests are covered in news stories. There are no inter-views with beggars. I see no feature stories about making Kolkata a liveable city for all.

I wonder what happens to the strongly assertive, convinced, "civilized leaders" of Bharat who I meet among foreign university students in Canada.

Are they cloistered away in some cushy civil service jobs in the capital city?

**Chowringhee**: Visiting Lucknow could be a real riot. Newspaper front pages report all sorts of conflicts in the region, along with curfews and enforcement.

I'm heading into one of the areas hit by the marauding religious fanatic currently plaguing Bharat.

**New Delhi**: I meet a Sikh who tells me that the moneyed local elite portray local uprisings in the news as sectarian conflict, but that's just to deceive the outside world and to keep the elite in power.

I think that there are religionist fanatics, nationalists, etc. but I'm not impressed with the local elite's apparent behaviour.

They're not intellectuals in simple clothing who are walking across Bharat, like Mahatma Gandhi.

They don't want to gain power by experiencing material poverty first hand.

Trains show the local elite's order. Non-elite locals get the slowest trains with a cattle car environment. Only the elite have trains with a no nicotine car option.

**Kotah**: News tells me the latest about the unrest, now in Hyderabad or Punjab. Are these the seeds of a revolution against the callous ruling elite?

...

Local newspapers make little reference to non-Bharat events. One day only the S.U. foreign minister's unfortunate resignation makes the papers.

**Hyderabad**: The elite are, as one local says to me, only thinking about themselves. Shame.

They own cake factories and have never heard of Marie Antoinette? Coincidental irony: Today's newspaper says a bakery strike is causing a cake shortage in Kolkata.

**Adelaide**: At I shop I join clusters of locals who are stopping to watch bits of constant news coverage about Iraq, coming from U.S. television networks, not Australian ones.

I see the U.S. president's face smiling as I pass an Adelaide fast food café's TV set. I see the Iraqi dictator smiling elsewhere. The prospect of war makes them happy?

...

A news programme I see one evening speculates about the probability of war breaking out.

Instead of being a grave consideration, the broadcast sounds like a pre-game show for a football game.

But the latest U.S. <u>New York Times</u> and CBS News public opinion poll shows that about 65% of the generation of U.S.ers who take the brunt of the 1930s/40s war are opposed to having a war with Iraq.

The same poll shows that most supporters of war are people in the U.S. who are too young to remember any war.

I wonder if the U.S. news editors aren't voluntarily self-censoring to prevent another U.S. entanglement like southeastern Asia.

But there are reports about anti-war demonstrations in the U.S. which seem perennial whenever the U.S. itself is involved.

U.S. anti-war demonstrators are noticeable by their absence when it's "someone else's war".

**Waikerie**: Australia Day brings news about local identity. Some locals say that the image of Australia portrayed abroad isn't entirely accurate.

But then at least Australians do have an image abroad, unlike Canadians, despite what I write to the Spicer Commission.

...

It must be difficult to tell an accurate local story abroad. Local TV networks seem to be branches of U.S. networks' news operations.

I also notice that TV antennas in Australia are so tall that I mistake them for ham radio towers.

...

A referendum in South Australia State is to decide electoral reforms including the idea of creating electoral districts which are all equal in population.

To maintain this equality, districts would be automatically adjusted between elections.

Despite the advertising surrounding the referendum, news from elsewhere is taking locals' attention away from the important vote.

...

In conversation and television news reports, people in Australia call themselves "locals". The national government is called "The Commonwealth".

...

ABC News (Australian Broadcasting Company) reports public opinion survey results indicating that only 35% of local married couples don't fight.

The 65% who do fight are primarily arguing about issues of money and children.

Logically then, the happy couple has neither money nor children?

Sexuality in conversations and interactions that I observe seem to be far from an adult area of life.

...

Both local and U.K. BBC News readers have trouble pronouncing Al-Kuwayt. They say "Q-wait" in error. Or are they talking about billiards, saying "cue weight"?

Fortunately Kuwait never existed, the Iraqi dictator says. So what's to mispronounce?

...

Local television's prepackaged version of the U.S. C.B.S. News magazine "60 Minutes" carries an interview with some creep who arms the Iraqi dictator.

The arms pusher says, "Some people lose blood, some make money."

He adds the typical apologist's line used to excuse all dastardly behaviours, saying, "If I didn't do it, someone else would."

This thug sells uniforms with letters of reference from a publicly-disgraced former U.S. vice-president and his publicly-disgraced attorney general.

The work of this JFK-nemesis administration in international affairs can thus be long remembered for its contribution to world peace.

The wild card in the southwest Asian conflict seems to be the S.U. military versus Gorby. The U.S. better wrap it all up fast so they can help Gorby stay in power.

Of course the S.U. has so many separatists now that any military takeover in Moscow would likely create a multi-front civil war defying even the military.

Also, the cost per day of the arms of this "third" world war could feed all the people lining up for food in Moscow and reduce the IMF debts.

Is anyone in the news media talking about these types of alternative spending?

The last time that the U.S. was in a war, in southeastern Asia, critics contrasted spending on peaceful outer space research with social needs.

Space research budgets were cut drastically. How about doing the same with war budgets now for the same reason?

In Sydney some mosques and synagogues are bombed by local crazies reacting to the "third" world war.

Why are some protesters complaining about Yisra'el in the context of this war?

I hope this war can be wrapped up within the next 15 days. I'll soon be leaving Australia and don't want to face the added hassle of wartime security at the borders.

On the other hand, the associated fear of travel could make my path easier.

There will be a smaller number of non-local travellers. Accommodation and transportation could be less crowded.

...

I hope that leaving Australia won't be difficult. News reports say the people who refuel aircraft are shutting down all the airports.

...

Local news is reporting there's an overabundance of pickers in Victoria State due to an influx of unemployed people from other types of jobs.

It's a recession period in Australia as it is in other parts of the world.

A truck driver of Italian origin says he has to struggle against discrimination in Australia, so he's sceptical about anti-Japanese racist English language news reporting which claims that non-locals in Nippon are badly treated.

He says he always finds people from Nippon friendly and kind. I reassure him that non-locals have a great life in Nippon.

"Journalists" duped by gringo malcontents aren't doing any serious reporting or investigating.

It's all inductive unreasoning to find any indication that Nippon-bashers are correct.

Of course such mythology can also help preserve Nippon by warding off people who are unhappy everywhere.

**Darwin**: Today's news says that every night more than 200 millimetres of rain is hitting the part of Australia that I just leave.

"The wet" is moving south for the year. Helicopters are taking emergency food supplies south too. Some evacuations are being considered.

Those pesky flies (musca vetustissima) are multiplying by the thousands daily.

...

The temperature in London (U.K.) is a big story in local news. It's -12°C. A routine -27°C somewhere in Canada goes unreported.

...

I find a Canadian newspaper in the public library and discover there's a constitutional committee in Ontario. I start writing a letter for it.

The newspaper also reports another incidence of the atrocious legacy of the European era - preventing us from knowing part of our past.

The former racist European ethnic minority dictatorship of Zimbabwe is the culpable one in this particular case.

The dictatorship won't accept the fact that a past great civilization exists in what is now Zimbabwe before the European invasions.

Archaeologists of long ago and today find that Zimbabwe has a huge walled city.

The great wall stands throughout the European era and continues to stand today. Europeans pretend it's not there?

Here's another example of how the European era retards human progress by preventing humans from knowing their own, true past.

**Xiang Giang**: Reporting the U.S. bombings in southwestern Asia, news reporters compare them with a fireworks display.

It sounds atrocious when news reporters compare the beautiful light shows of peace with the gruesome missiles of death shattering the air of the "third" world war in Iraq.

News reports should choose some more appropriate comparison.

...

A news bulletin on Lunar New Year's Eve says Iraq is ending the "third" world war.

I imagine military arms sellers congratulating themselves on enabling a quick, minimum human casualties war. It's like a gun that only kills the person who fires it.

Computerized war devices take us back to a time when professional armies fought on battle fields while civilians carry on their routines unmolested.

The winner might change little, perhaps using the same bureaucrats as before the battles to collect taxes and perform other functions.

But the merchants of death and disfigurement still have to wait a bit until things cool down and perhaps boast about their deadly products during post-war sales campaigns.

Perhaps the airports can return to less rigid security measures now that the battles are over.

In the last few flights I find soldiers with machine guns at every airport except Darwin and Brunei.

I hope someone from the U.S. television networks will start helping U.S. military spokespeople learn how to use ordinary language instead of George Orwellian Newspeak.

Soldier gibberish jargon requires subtitled screens.

When the U.S. military speaks it uses terms such as KIA. KIA stands for killed in action.

In ordinary, straightforward, simple language, that means dead.

A better approach would be to name each of the dead, telling reporters "Bill Jones of Smithtown is dead today because we decided to solve this dispute through warfare."

...

A newspaper article published in this region surprises me with the information it presents about the annual Carnaval in Rio de Janeiro.

The article mentions that the performers in the desfiles are favelados and perform for free. They are volunteers. I learn that in Rio.

While they bring in the non-local visitors and their money, the tourist industry elites pocket the hundreds of U.S. dollars which each tourist takes to Brasil.

Each tourist spends lots of money just to sit and idly watch the "poor" "ignorant" people dance for free. The moneyless smile and sweat.

They keep smiling, even if they're "in debt" to the banks of the idle sitters. Some of the "poor" don't dance. They offend the tourists by robbing them.

But who are the real victims of economic crime?

Tourists should stay home and deposit their overseas holiday funds directly into their banks to the credit of Brasil's IMF account.

At Carnaval this year the satire apparently emphasizes the "third" world war, fires destroying Amazonia, etc.

Meanwhile in Nippon, "Chocolate Day" has people sending chocolates to the Iraq and U.S. heads of state.

**Shanghai**: I'm thinking of Gorby's perestroika, his restructuring of the Soviet Union in the context of news reports about a famine in Moscow.

What a contrast with the plentiful food and incredible burst of stylishness, colour, and generally greater strides in material wealth in Chuang Hwa since my first time here, four years earlier.

I wonder if the real reformers are in Beijing. The stodgy are too entrenched in Moscow to keep up.

...

Local television in Nanjing shows U.S. tanks rolling and firing in Kuwait.

The China Daily newspaper has interesting war stories, including one about how the "third" is paying for the war with hunger.

The war arms spending could be helping millions to eat.

The U.S. C.N.N. news images are used in Chinese television news. I see happy looking U.S. soldiers and their president back in Washington (D.C.)

A caption in English reads, "Toward peace in the Gulf". So the "third" world war is almost over?

The U.S.ers are going to be very prideful until they get the bill.

Will the all-volunteer, dominantly African-U.S.er and unmoneyed U.S.er armed forces get as much praise as the weapons technology is getting?

In the lobby of a large Beijing hotel I read that the war is over. It lasts about a month and a half? No war should be any longer.

There are no front page stories about casualties or costs in the Chinese or U.S. news that I see and understand.

The full economic consequences have yet to be known, although the government of Jordan says the war cost about $US8 billion.

That's eight return trips to the moon using technology available 20 year before this war.

Nippon is contributing $US9 billion, which is supposed to be used as reconstruction aid. But the U.S. will decide how to use the money.

Jordan's monarchical dictator gives a postscript of the war on television subtitled in English.

I agree with his view that the very long Palestine-Yisra'el dis-pute needs to be settled. It causes so much violence against so many people for so long.

...

...Sorry to hear that Muang-Thai has a coup d'état. The U.S.-S.U. allies must be too busy to stop this tragic reversal of current world trends.

The Muang Thai military must be very bad since I see none of the material economic deterioration which would normally be used by military offenders to destroy governments.

All the new developments I see around Bangkok give me the impression that there's a material boom in MuangThai, at least for the moneyed people who are usually financing and collaborators in military coups and dictatorships.

I hope the U.S.-S.U. allies aren't too tired after their "third" world war to make an example of the Muang Thai military dictators.

Surely the U.S. isn't happy that the inherently incompetent and corrupt form of government called military dictatorship is very unlikely to combat its natural and equally criminal allies, the drug industry.

Unlike the U.K. invaders during the old monarchical dictatorship in Chuang Hwa, the U.S. surely doesn't want to be on the drug dealers' side in today's Opium War?

...

A London (U.K.) newspaper I see here reports that Gorby's referendum to restructure the CCCP wins by 70% of the vote.

But the newspaper says this means he loses.

What's the theory behind this new political arithmetic?

...

In the aftermath of the "third" world war, news reports say that ethnic and minority religious groups in Iraq are being protected militarily by US-UN allies.

Reflecting on this situation I wonder if followers of the Jewish religion would have the same protection in Deutschland prior to the 1930s/40s wars if there been day and night live news reporting from Deutschland in that era through some sort of international television system.

Exposing and guarding against attacks on humans by nation-states can help us all.

Discrimination and other forms of maltreatment of the human community make the world unpleasant for everyone.

The attacking of human groups tends to reinforce the myth that nationalism brings happiness.

So every group decides that it can't survive and flourish without a nation-state that's exclusively for its group.

But in reality, just because you are maltreated or unhappy does not mean that you have to isolate yourself by creating yet another nation dividing humanity.

Barricading the doors blocks the persons inside just as much as the persons outside. Nation-making is an easy way out dead end street.

After the warring states within Chuang Hwa, Nippon, and Europe killed each others' people to secure their borders for nationalism, they realize that they're better off united in multi-group structures instead of divided into uni-group units.

Eventually, on a larger scale, even the idea of a United Nations Organization makes sense.

No nation-state wants to be excluded from this non-nationalist, all-inclusive human group.

**Montréal**: Montréal seems to have more Canadian flags than I ever see here since Expo-Centennial Year.

Only provincial flags are dominant during the years of separatist government. Is the switch back to the maple leaf a sign of real sentiments?

Contradicting our observations as residents of Montréal, a CBC-TV news reporter in this province claims it's hard to find a Canadian flag here.

He already wears glasses. Don't they work?

...

**Toronto**: Sections of the Toronto Star newspaper proudly declare themselves "printed entirely on recycled paper". More logging jobs are lost while life on earth is extended.

Which do we prefer, jobs or life?

...

The worst news I see since arriving in Canada is that victims of employment-based society are shouting racist chants in Montréal.

Like some ignorant group of thirty years earlier, the frustrated shout, "white power", i.e. supremacy for the European faces.

This too is part of our European era heritage which says that all non-European civilizations and people are inferior.

Untenable world views are also a result when job training supplants a liberal education.

Being a money-ruled, employeed person is such a priority that human communication is "impractical", off the curriculum.

The "jobs-jobs-jobs" inanity of the conservatives of the moment is a slogan plugging the ears and blocking all thought.

It's revitalizing the "biological nationalism" which Laurier so passionately condemned.

The employed street gang even attacks television cameras like the thugs of dictatorship do in other settings and eras.

Canada's immigration department, apparently always ready to bow to racism and extremism, is cutting the number of people from Africa and the southern Americas who will be admitted.

I'm substantially impressed by the multiplicity of languages and colours of people who do manage to get through Canada's immigration barrier and who I see in every street car, bus, and subway compartment in Toronto.

This variety among Canadians is amazing compared with the Toronto I travel widely through during my original four years of living here and even my more recent life here with Mariko.

The current immigration ministry's pillars are money entry, indentured labour servantism, and nepotism.

It may be bureaucratically neat and it panders to nationalistic fools who are conned into job-based entry politics.

But no country the size of Canada, with all its resources, in this era of desperation borne of minority greed, can ever hope to survive under such immigration meanness.

...

Mariko and I find ourselves sitting next to Keith Spicer in front of televisions news cameras at Toronto City Hall. We just happen to be there during a small group session of Citizen's Forum on Canada's Future.

I'm glancing at a television screen at the right moment and notice that this meeting is happening. That brings us here.

The Forum is part of the aftermath of the failure of the Meech Lake Accord.

Keith Spicer is responsible for the Forum.

He's Canada's first Official Languages Commissioner and then refers to the former anglophone minority rulers of Québec as "Westmount Rhodesians".

Westmount is a moneyed area of Montréal then inhabited by anglophone minority rulers.

I write up a submission for Spicer and another one in French for the Bélanger-Campeau commission set up by the Québec provincial government.

My writings are constructive, positive, and pro-Canadian unity.

If anyone asks me how I feel to be in Canada, I have to say that from my outside world perspective I get the impression that most of this nation-state is suicidal.

But Mariko and I only come to Toronto City Hall to observe and listen to what locals have to say about post-Meech Canada.

I have nothing to add to what I write to Spicer earlier.

Even if I want to repeat myself or add something I find myself wordless. I'm so surprised to being sitting next to Spicer that I am strangely shy and amazed.

I am in awe of Spicer and unwilling to speak in the presence of a person who impresses me so much.

Mariko knows my willingness to talk around the world about Canada's situation. But now I'm leaving it to Mariko to convey my words for me, and more.

We're signed-in as participants, but only Mariko participates.

It's a strange experience for her because she's being identified as a new Canadian and gets questions according to this false impression.

As a non-Canadian, this makes her feel uncomfortable, knowing that her views aren't supposed to be a part of an internal political meeting in Canada.

She knows that I consider myself strictly an outside observer and a learner when I'm outside of Canada and that I know I lack the profound knowledge and competency to offer advice on local matters everywhere I go overseas.

So Mariko keeps her remarks general.

When the television news crew shows up and makes some video of the three of us sitting together, Mariko and I both keep our mouths shut, leaving centre stage to Keith.

Unfortunately, the session is competing with a warm, sunny day. So only a few hundred participants are here.

What impresses me is that the apparently relatively elite-heavy groups are expressing many of the thoughts about Canada that I'm writing outside the country.

I'm even more impressed with the positive attitude and great enthusiasm being expressed about having one united country, one that's completely bilingual everywhere and multicultural too.

These are the heirs of Pierre Trudeau.

...

Moderate, "Red Tory" conservative Joe Clark gets called a "traitor" in Columbia (Br.) because he listens to and negotiates with a variety of people instead of embracing the most narrow of provincialist views.

I write a humourous letter to a Vancouver newspaper in Clark's defence, but the paper may be afraid to print it.

How intellectually oppressive and vacuous Columbia (Br.) must be with a noirceur much grander than Duplessis in Québec, if the province is unable to produce the likes of Pelletier, Trudeau, and Cité Libre.

**Edmonton**: In the news I see another consequence of the past few years of conservatives controlling government. Many hospitals in Canada have medical staff and equipment shortages.

Patients are being treated in hallways instead of rooms. The conservatives call it "a balanced budget".

In reality it's an off-balanced government. The inanity of government by ledger sheet is clear.

A caretaker society can't be run by balancing numbers, no matter who is elected. Disabled by caretaker society, people aren't prepared to deal with budgets.

...

On the way to Toronto I hear Canadian and U.S. newscasters talking about a volcano which is currently erupting in Nippon.

The newscasters call the volcano Mt. Unzen but they pronounce the "Un" like the French "un" instead of "une".

CBC mentions that the volcano is on Kyushu Island but pronounces Kyushu as Keyeshu. It's "cue shoe".

A U.S. national television network host says that Kyushu is "an island near Japan".

As retired U.S. newscaster Walter Cronkite says at the current Banff media conference, news people are lacking when they only know one language.

A serious factual account of the volcano story would report that Fugendake, Mt. Fugen is erupting. It's near Shimabara in Nagasaki Prefecture on Kyushu Island in Nippon

If a big news organization can't afford multilingual staff it could at least pay someone to translate the news feed coming from the Japanese television networks and get the locations and pronunciation of place names right.

Otherwise, all news that I'm now hearing from Canadian and U.S. news services is suspect. It seems to be flawed and fictional storytelling.

With all the myths of my parental homeland, the "first"

world, myths that are broken by my experiences around the planet, why am I still surprised by the "developed" ignorance?

**Québec City**: The news reports that two immigration ministry employees in Winnipeg are getting fired. Could they be the ones Mariko and I encounter at Emerson?

I wouldn't be surprised. I can only hope.

Meanwhile, Amnesty International has words about the Emerson duo's police brethren in Austria. The organization is putting Austrian police on its bad list for arbitrary detention.

We see that problem first hand a short while ago. Every person in uniform in the street demands our passports.

...

Our "first" world schooling and news services rarely mention anything truly global or any details of the practical realities beyond our enclaves, at time of writing and before.

If the elite among the "developed" elite know any of the details, they don't bother to help spread them around or emphasize their importance.

How many schooled people in the "first" world can answer the following basic questions about some essential global realities?

What percentage of the earth's water is potable? What are the overall human poverty, mortality, and nutrition rates?

Our partial, restricted "first" world perspective makes our vision of yesterday, today, and tomorrow grossly distorted and inadequate.

We "first" worlders lack the interest in and information about the rest of the world to enable us to declare ourselves "developed" or "world leaders".

...

A CBC-TV news report points out, for a fleeting moment, that violence and poverty experiences, which are sent abroad by "developed" world arms exporters, return to the "first" world in the form of violence and poverty among immigrant youth gangs.

They flee their homes and come to the "first" world as refugees. They come from places such as Northern Ireland, Lebanon, Vietnam, etc.

The arms exports' effects are coming back to deal poetic justice to the arms exporting societies.

But the actual people exporting arms, uncontrolled and unregulated by the majority of people in the "first" world are not worried.

The arms dealers have the best guarded homes. They're as safe as IMF bankers.

...

The news media is giving IMF "debtors" a lower rate of interest. The IMF's southern loan sharking all but vanishes from the news reports in the past few years.

But now everyone in the world is paying the IMF, in the form of service charges and lower interest rates on bank accounts and other investments.

How many "first" worlders are auditing the situation? How many are seeing what's in the balance?

Most "first" worlders are too busy with routine "responsibilities" to take account of anything beyond.

If they have time to pay attention, it's only during the few moments of a daily television news summary they see five days out of seven.

Ten years after the huge "third" world debt crisis is reported widely in the news, there's still little awareness of the origins of the debt.

"First" worlders are largely unaware of the fact that the "first" world is the cause of the original, "third" world debt crisis that is now a "first" world crisis.

...

In Nippon, regular evening newscasts interrupt and preempt baseball games, unless the most popular team in the country is playing.

But in Canada, no vital news, information, emergency, crisis, or disaster takes precedence over hockey game broadcasts.

The hockey arenas would be vaporized in a thermonuclear war before fans could be informed.

NHL teams now include ones in climates of the U.S. south where there is never ice or snow and yet the hockey season goes on for at least eight months every year.

Although there are television channels devoted exclusively to sports and showing all the games each season, the regular CBC-TV network also carries the games once a week.

That's all right until the hockey semi-final and final playoffs begin. Then all the regular CBC programmes must end their season.

Hockey isn't scheduled and interrupted to permit the airing of the regular, daily, 20-minute national television news report.

It's delayed by hockey until most non-hockey viewers are asleep for the night.

...

CBC Newsworld, the relatively new all-news television network and the first of its kind in Canada, at time of writing, mesmerizes the viewer in his/her own northern hemisphere, mid-latitude perspective of the world.

It can't be mere coincidence that the network has a name strongly resembling that of a theme park. It later changes to a name that sounds like an affiliate of a U.S. network.

But Newsworld does represent the best of its genre.

I suggest what I see at Newsworld during its first months of existence, long before the network is born.

I write to the CRTC during its early years, suggesting that a Canadian TV network broadcast daily local news from across the country to viewers across the country.

That would make experiences like my Labrador viewing of a Vancouver local news show a regular part of everyday life for Canadians, enabling them to see what's going on throughout Canada.

This daily exposure to local Canada everywhere could make Canadians feel closer and become more understanding of each other on a daily basis.

CBC Newsworld takes a first, albeit short-lived step in this direction.

The network start out by having a regular daily segment which checks in with local CBC newsrooms at stations across Canada.

This should help to accomplish what I suggest.

Unfortunately, instead of featuring local news, the local newsrooms merely tell CBC Newsworld about the big national or international stories they are covering.

This is probably why Newsworld abandons the local segment.

Do local CBC newsrooms have the impression that they must show off their awareness of "big news", or are local anchors and reporters auditioning for network jobs?

Perhaps this failure to show local news on Newsworld also makes it easier for a post-Pierre-Trudeau government to reduce funding for CBC, contributing to eliminating some local CBC newscasts.

Much later, cable companies enable subscribers paying for more expensive "packages" to watch almost any local TV channel and regional network news in Canada.

But such "packages" contain such an abundance of channels that viewers I know are unaware of their access to local news from anywhere in Canada.

At the same time, since there are seven time zones in Canada and each local and regional channel and network caters only to their local time zone, local news plays during the working hours and sleeping times of far away Canadians.

Thus my concept of access to all local news from and to everywhere in Canada has yet to be accomplished at times of day convenient to all Canadians.

This won't change until Sandi Renaldo starts an early evening national news broadcast on CTV that all Canadians can watch without losing sleep.

...

The U.S. TV news programme, "Sixty Minutes" has a segment recently with a self-righteous, indignation-style interview asking, "You mean Moscow dictates movie ticket prices in Lithuania?"

So what?

The "Sixty Minutes" correspondent from Canada, Morley Safer needs to tell his co-workers that Hollywood controls the film distribution, pricing, and content of most television and movies in Canada.

This includes U.S. movie distributors who are fighting with Québec over whether or not to show movies dubbed in French instead of English-only versions.

So send a correspondent to Canada for this bigger story.

(Some years later, during my first visit to the city of Mos-cow, I find first-run Hollywood movie tickets there much cheaper than in Canada. I just have to learn Russian to understand the dubbed voices.)

...

As Maurice Strong says in a recent CBC-TV news interview, the "first" world has to learn how to live well simply.

My lifestyle is therefore at least ten years ahead of my "first" world born contem-poraries.

I can only set one example by my way of living during my forays into the "first" world.

I live with about one-seventh of the average income in Canada.

I'm in better health, eat better, and am more mobile and free in my daily and longer-term choices than most people with far more money than I have.

I can be more creative, adventurous, spontaneous, happier, more fulfilled, less stressed, more ambitious, more productive, etc. than the most money-ed people in Canada.

I conclude that more income has no value.

I need no money from government programmes of any kind to do as I please.

Why is it apparently so difficult for most "developed" worlders to act so intelligently? With all their material wealth...

**Santa Ana to Guaymas**: We see little out the windows while our bus driver struggles to fight the 100 km/hr head winds trying to push us backwards.

We must be pressing forward very hard to move at all. Wind-driven rains batter our windshield.

Arriving in Guaymas we step out of the bus and stand on the shores of cyclone-flooded streets. Locals say we miss the big storm.

Since we're not following the news, we are unaware that this is Hurricane Andrew, a huge storm causing major damage in the region.

**Mexico City**: Local newspapers say that Mexico is becoming the key pin in trade in the Americas.

This nation-state has a trade agreement with the central Americas as well as one with Canada and the U.S.

This is supposed to mean that economic power is growing here, but for what small percentage of the local population?

The Mexican government appears to perceive itself as replacing Canada and the U.S. as the moneyed nation-state in the northern Americas.

But will the money be as well distributed here as in the northern countries?

The Mexican cities that we see up until now suggest that there's no local history of creating a general wealth instead of just elite money in Mexico, since at least the European era.

...

A visitor I meet from Austin (Texas) talks about a "world culture" which he says exists everywhere. He calls English "the world language".

He sees himself as "avant garde". I see him as a myopic

apologist for monolithic UK-US Empiremania.

He supports his "world culture" assertion by saying that even in apparently remote areas of Mexico people are watching the USCNN television news channel and finding out what's happening in the U.S.A.

Sure, the elite everywhere cluster around the same kind of illusions.  Some of the elite that I meet in Rio de Janeiro flock to U.S. amusement parks like commercial Meccas.

I refute the "world culture" perspective as an elitist, U.S.-centric view of the world.  It blatantly misses a vast world of events and cultures.

I tell the Austin person about Robert, the person from Scotland who we meet in Barcelona who says that the English business is "one of the last vestiges of colonialism".

...

Local news indicates that the current U.S. president is suffering from gulf justice.

What he gains in popularity by military success in the "third" world war of the Persian Gulf, he loses by failing to provide rapid and adequate help to his fellow citizens after the hurricane we edge past hits the Gulf of Mexico during the past couple of weeks.

**Cancun**: The tourist industry is having a money lust frenzy here.

It shows how cruel and negative it is to release people from employed captivity for only a few weeks each year.

They can do nothing except pay more money for less than they do at home, and contribute to destroying local economies, cultures, and natural surroundings through the tourist industry.

Cancun is a clear indictment of the tourist industry.

Apparently so are Acapulco's beaches, which are now so polluted that even Mexico City newspapers say they're unhealthful for human swimming.

The fish must already be dead.

But like Cancun, maybe tourists still flock in like sheep.

**Fort de France**: Watching the television news broadcast with me one night, a local complains out loud in French, "Europe-Europe-Europe! Isn't there any other news in the world?"

I reply, "It's been that way for 500 years." The Afro-French viewer agrees.

News of the Americas depends on what the newsroom in Paris thinks deserves national attention in a news broadcast for France and the rest of francophone Europe, not Martinique.

In Fort de France, news of the nearby and neighbouring countries of the Americas, and larger ones such as Canada and the U.S., is filtered through European editors' eyes.

Southern Americas? Never heard of them.

Consequently, when there is news of countries in the Americas, the stories have a distant tone and emphasis. It's buried in the European news and mentioned in passing.

Not even Canada's French-language television news programme is not showing in our TV lounge. (This is before TV5?)

So there's almost no word of the referendum on the proposed constitutional amendments in Canada until two days before the vote.

Even the overwhelming influence of USCNN and other media is muffled in Martinique's local news broadcast.

The local newspaper in Fort de France is only reporting voter turnout the day after the U.S. elections.

The paper must have a deadline for new stories that's based on the time zone in France.

But then Singapura locals behave as if they're living in the U.K. social milieu of 100 years ago.

So the news time lag here doesn't seem that bad. Just call it a daily version of auto-acculturation.

The filtered news in Fort de France also reminds me of the

U.S. military radio news in Tokyo, which doesn't mention Japanese news if it's not considered important to U.S. news editors in the U.S.

...

While there's rare mention of anything north of Martinique in the news, including the current U.S. presidential election, it's amazing how much coverage is being given to Europe's current cannibalism war in what was Yugoslavia.

Children there "are starving" but Sudan's children go unmentioned. Where is that "world culture" that the Texan talks about in Mexico? Made in USA.

Sadly, news is no less "developed"-centric than any other "first" world based phenomena.

The largest, most powerful, and omnipresent main stream news organizations collect what the "developed" decide is newsworthy, before AlJazeera.

The "third" world is only newsworthy sporadically, as a contrast, scene of tragedy, or imitator struggling to pass the initiation tests of the "first" worlder street gang.

There's no "third" world news agency flooding the "developed" minds with alternative perspectives and definitions of newsworthy.

At best, there are only the European-type nation-states' censored copies of "developed" news-telling models.

The "first" worlders can have peace of mind, secure in the knowledge that they alone tell "the world" news.

I think of the "first" world reporters talking about air pollution and dirt in Rio de Janeiro during the recent environmental conference there.

But other "first" world reporters, during the same year, make no mention of the extremely visible air pollution and dog feces in Barcelona during the Olympic games there.

When the same games are held in Mexico City a few years earlier, there's extensive reporting on the impact of air pollution on athletes.

There's much talk of breathing problems in the "third" world city.

Apparently a problem can be left out of news reports if it occurs in the "first" but not the "third" world.

The setting determines the news coverage, rather than the news itself.

...

The E.U. news in Martinique makes little reference to trans-Americas demonstrations against the celebration of the start of the European era, when Colon invades Guanahani.

...

Channelling television news through Europe doesn't help to dispel the strange identification with far away Europe in Martinique.

...

It's not the first time that an item in the news sends us out looking for information or exploring territory. Why would Martinique be any different?

The two overseas Radio France television stations available here via ordinary antenna carry about an hour of local news per day.

One night they mention that there's about to be a special, live broadcast from somewhere in Fort de France called "Texaco".

I ask one of the locals sitting with me in the television room how to find "Texaco". His explanation sends Mariko and me out into the streets. We're very close to "Texaco".

It's exactly where we walk through a few days earlier while seeking a shoreline route.

We go to Texaco tonight to see what the news bills as a musical show that will also feature Patrick Chamoiseau, an author who writes a novel based on the Texaco neighbourhood's history.

He later wins France's major literary award, Prix Goncourt, for his book <u>Texaco</u>.

Our walk covers both geographic and developmental territory. We're following the path that illustrates Texaco's community history. It's like a favela becoming a town.

But the maturing of such communities tends to be put under harsh spotlights.

Sometimes they accompany news crews sent to uncover the "social ills" mythically attributed exclusively too this particular type of community.

Sometimes the spotlights accompany bulldozers sent by governments wanting to eradicate an "unauthorized", unconventional model of community-building and to clear the site for other uses.

So it's all the more marvellous to find Texaco's streets floodlit so that television cameras can help residents rejoice at their accomplishments in community development.

The cameras focus on smiling people who are happy and proud to be living in the neighbourhood that they and their predecessors create and maintain.

We see people chatting and watching their homes on a big screen projection of the live television broadcast. Others are barbecuing chicken.

The images of Texaco are interspersed with on-site interviews with people sitting on chairs arranged in a circle and on-site musical performances with costumed dancers and singers.

I'm thinking that this could be Brasil's TVE (educational television system) covering a favela in Rio.

What a way to encourage community development. Make such a parallel settlement into a TV news star.

...

At time of writing, about 53,000 of Martinique's 300,000 or so population lives in Texaco-like favelas, called "communauté populaire".

That's more than 17% of the people here.

I read that about eight million people live in poverty in Europe. Martinique, a "departement" of France, i.e. Europe, is included in that number?

If the communautés populaires are considered poverty, then poverty takes up a much larger percentage of the population here than in Europe.

Martinique's communautés popu-laires are characterized by high unemployment, i.e. non-employeed-dependent, versus non-dependent living.

But a local news report mentions that Lamentin, a conventional town by the airport, has 30% unemployment.

...

Paris newspapers are calling Texaco author Chamoiseau the writer who expresses Creole reality.

But Creole undergoes changes in reality over the past several hundred years.

Now the term seems to be used to describe a type of language or group of languages.

But there is an apparent lack of recognition of the language or languages, even though there are French Creole dictionaries. Some academics describe French, Italian, Spanish, and Portuguese as Creole of Latin.

As I discover some days ago, in an earlier era people like Napoléon's Josephine are called Creole, i.e. overseas born French.

In effect, any people of non-First-Nations origin who are living in the Americas could be considered Creole in both a language and cultural transplant sense.

Here, First Nations of eastern Asian origin would also be Creole of sorts. Perhaps most people in the Americas could be called Creole.

...

While the extreme nationalists called Nazis, now neo-Nazis roam over the U.S., U.K., France, and Canada, the news reports focus on Deutschland.

Why the selective attention – because Nazism is founded in Deutschland?

But during the same years that Nazis rule there and long before, people of African origin are being lynched in the U.S.A.

We have to be on alert for hate-mongers of the nationalist-racist variety everywhere, not just in Deutschland.

...

It looks wet on the Fort de France runway showing in the news. Tents and food services are being set up for the airport occupation group.

Initial television news reports from Paris show nothing from here but much about agriculture industry protests in mainland France.

Farmers there are angry because the U.S. claims they have unfair agricultural subsidies from the French government and the U.S. demands that France remove the subsidies.

U.S. commercial food and drink symbols are being attacked rather than diplomatic offices.

The U.S. sugary mud-coloured soft drink and the fast junk food chains are targets. So their management is expressing sympathy with farmers.

Management says that the products they sell in France are made using French-grown ingredients. What a waste of good products!

In Martinique, U.S. fast junk food outlets close down and put up signs favouring the banana growers protesting here.

My initial reaction is that opposing the U.S. export of unhealthy, junk food is good. Sure. End the pop and slop industry. Up with nutrition.

The strike is all about a healthy type of food, bananas.

One local newsletter reports that the production cost per kilo is more than 20 times the retail price that Mariko and I pay for bananas in faraway Québec City during the great snows of winter.

Martinique bananas are clearly not a wise choice for an export crop.

...

For all my learning here, I remain unaware of Frantz Fanon until almost our final day in Fort de France. Fanon is a political writer from here.

I don't recall ever seeing any of his writings appearing on any of my reading lists during four years of studying political science at university.

How appalling that my schooling tells me nothing of Fanon or any other Afro-Americas or African authors.

During my schooling and later formal education, I only learn about people with black skin pigmentation from U.S. television news.

They're people just trying to gain the ordinary, commonplace rights of sitting where they choose in classrooms, eateries, and buses.

None of my schooling or the news I get reveals that any Africans or people of African origin are authors or intellectuals.

What poor "first" world education and information services I have in my life!

Only in Martinique do I finally learn about Fanon. He applies his skills as a psychiatrist to the study of what I call auto-acculturation.

**New York City**: Some homeless people are selling their own newspaper in subway cars. When I first see it, I wonder if it's for real or just a non-homeless people scam.

But youth hostel staff tell me that the paper is an authentic means of support for many homeless people here.

...

From the criticism of Bill Clinton that I already read in the major U.S. newspapers, before he's actually sworn in to office, I wonder if editorial writers don't already have negative comments on his first term of office ready before he becomes U.S. president.

Of course reading about how much the inaugural events will cost, I think the money could be better used for social programmes.

Clinton could give his speech in a soup kitchen. It would have to be good there. The hungry and homeless are a tough audience to please.

**D.C.**: I'm in front of the U.S. capital, a long way from the new U.S. president who is smaller than a pin from my vantage point.

U.S. locals only come here to listen to Clinton, no one else. He has much riding on his words thanks to local news editors' advice in the previous days' newspapers.

...

Newspapers covering Clinton's speech all have the same quote in their headlines. "This is our time. Embrace it."

I don't even notice those words when I listen to the speech. There are much better quotes with deeper messages.

The headlines are based on a printed news release of the speech?

It's not just a new generation taking the U.S. presidency.

It's a generation that reputedly wants and demands change in its younger days, then becomes stagnant and conservative under yuppiedom. And now?

**Atlanta**: I suddenly realize that I'm at the headquarters of the USCNN news company.

It's free to look around the lobby but a close-up look is only available to people who pay a relatively expensive fee.

Of course only paying subscribers to cable TV have access to the USCNN on television. It's pay-per-view news. If you can't pay, you get no news.

You can't find an abandoned or discarded TV newscast somewhere, like a newspaper left on a park bench.

**Saskatoon:**...Heterosexuals have molested a child near here and murdered a young woman in St. Catharines, Ontario, according to recent news stories.

Why is no one saying that heterosexuals are not fit for day care jobs or church ministers' jobs? Why is ignorance not calling for lynch mobs now, against heterosexuals?

...

Without a television, all my news comes through radio. It seems to have more news and details.

I listen to the news in both French and English on local radio stations here every day.

There is quite a bit of background sound to set the scene of stories. Great effort is made to keep me paying attention and listening.

It is not just noise to catch my ears so that I will sit down passively in front of the radio.

Radio requires listening, not just hearing. In contrast, television just requires sight and viewers can only look at what is fitting into the camera lens.

Radio forces the mind to concentrate and create visual images to describe what radio does not show.

Even when radio gives a detailed verbal description, different listeners will see different images in their minds.

TV not only requires less imagination from its audience, it also reduces the quality and content of writing.

On television, there is only caption writing now, in the form of story intros, sound bites, and nondescript dialogues, in most programming.

The visual message is supposed to tell the details of the story. Wordsmithing becomes little more than making fillers and pauses between action scenes.

Pointing a camera can set a scene, see farther than the naked eye, create impressions of action, debate, beauty, tragedy, etc.

But the use of the camera still lags behind the use of words, except in exceptionally good motion pictures. Of course they require excellence in writing and acting too.

...

...When Mariko gets here, we happen to find a good used television at a garage sale down the lane. We watch news and other shows that interest us when we have time, but we still continue to listen to the radio.

...

...The early success of the new immigration-police-spy ministry is soon in the news. The ministry apprehends a Montréalais at the airport when he returns from a visit outside Canada.

He's detained when immigration personnel find he has a traffic violation.

Having captured such a dangerous criminal, immigration immediately hands him over to the local police.

The police take him straight to jail. He objects to this unusual, special treatment for a traffic violation. Police respond by hitting him in the chest.

He dies.

...

As I watch school children listening to the 20 year old guide at the Diefenbaker Centre, I wonder if they're the first generation of Canadians to learn that our past is actually so bleak, even in recent times.

I see this within the context of recent news reports about anti-immigration laws in Europe in general, and neo-Nazi mobs attacking Turkish workers in Germany.

These stories already remind me of the Vancouver anglos' anti-Asian riots that attack the people who build the trans-Canada railway that make Columbia (Br.) part of Canada.

If Canadians don't know their own history, good and bad, neo-Nazis can continue to easily find minds fertile for planting the anti-foreigner line and anti-immigration politics of today.

Canadian news reports show it in stories about racist people and events in Montréal, Vancouver, and in stories about the candidates and supporters of an Alberta-based national political party, which says it wants to halt all immigration to Canada, for an indefinite length of time.

...

...How does the recent news of a politico's pre-meditated attempted murder of an international tennis player get categorized as sports-provoked violence rather than a criminal act?

...Recent, murderous acts committed by soccer fans from Liverpool, United Kingdom, should put an end to the false stereotype that football violence is committed by "latinos".

Or the term has to be redefined, to mean people from southern England?

...

I read a 1928 book about Riel written by William Davidson, founder of the Calgary Albertan newspaper. It's published just a few decades after Louis is executed.

Someone who is in his/her 20s the year of Louis's execution would be in her/his 60s when the book is written.

So Davidson's book is finished not long before all the witnesses to the times are dead.

Davidson interviews people who actually meet Louis, such as his captor and the last surviving juror from Louis' trial in Regina.

The book is called Louis Riel 1844-1885.

It's amazing to learn that most of Louis' image during his lifetime is based on the tales of escaped criminals from Manitoba, the propaganda of a racist group in Ontario, and sloppy, fictional journalism.

...

Saskatoon seems to have far fewer mosquitoes than Regina. So, it's hard to believe when the news reports an overnight mosquito count of 23,700 at mid-summer.

That's a new record. The previous record is 3,000, ten years earlier.

We encounter none while walking along the riverside pathways by the Bessborough.

But some grassy areas in our neighbourhood park become small clouds of thirsty white mosquitoes if we walk there. So we run instead, or avoid that route now.

...

...A studious older person working at a Region museum tells us that he has a bad start in formal schooling.

He's abused in the notorious church orphanages that are in the news in Canada now.

He says the country boys and First Nations boys at his orphanage are the most trusting and so the most abused.

Not all the boys are orphans. But they all have to be signed out to leave the institution, even temporarily. Some of them are trapped for years, he says.

CBC-TV does a movie about the First Nations children who are kidnapped by the Canadian government and held prisoners in church residential schools.

...

Although this is a small city, we don't find out about some events until we hear about them later, in the local news reports.

One afternoon we're walking home along the main street and find a stage set up.

Later on we pass the same area and find many downtown blocks are barricaded and full of pedestrians.

Every parking spot has a classic car parked in it. This is the annual "Cruise night". We see no ships.

...

According to CBC News today, only 11% of Canadians have one university degree. Far fewer have more than one.

Only 15% of Canadians have an income exceeding $40,000 per year.

These facts of minority rule are the real expenses being paid for by the lives of too many Canadians as well as 80% of the human population.

...

Local post-secondary school students may join me abroad after they complete their studies.

I see them interviewed in the news, during an event where they learn about future work opportunities.

They talk of going abroad to seek their fortunes, not staying in Canada. Too bad. The population will age and decline faster than predicted.

But that's what happens when a big land is managed like a small land, in trade, immigration, and official languages practices.

At time of writing, the Canadian government is isolating Canada, instead of seeking broader horizons.

The government isolates francophones in one province; isolates the country to one overwhelming trade deal partner; and, cuts the country off from the non-moneyed, non-family immigrants.

What Canada really needs, if it is not to disappear altogether, is pan-Canadian expansion of bilingualism, especially through French language education for anglophones so they will no longer be handicapped unilinguals in a bilingual country and multilingual world.

...

I work for the government on election day for the first time in more than a decade.

I'm a district returning officer, making sure that voting is carried out honestly and that the ballots are counted correctly.

I also have the power to issue a warrant for someone's arrest. The warrant is in my kit.

The last time I do this type of job I'm in Toronto.

I work as a poll clerk and a clerk in a chief returning office during previous elections, federal and provincial, since I turn 19.

In Saskatoon three candidates come by to say hello to all the district returning officers and poll clerks. I never see that before, anywhere.

Television cameras and a newspaper photographer also show up. That's another first for me. I don't see their shots.

The election is almost over across Canada by the time I leave the polling station.

...

This day's news broadcasts images, taped by a Canadian camera operator, are showing a dead U.S. pilot's body being abused gleefully by some people in Somalia.

The joy is incomprehensible. The pilot is part of a United Nations force sent to ensure that food supplies can be delivered to children starving to death in Somalia.

The glee is anti-U.S., having nothing to do with the dead man or the starvation.

He's not in Somalia to kill, but to protect food supplies.

He's not slain by a weaker adversary, but by arms produced overseas, maybe by the same company that manufactures the pilot's crashing and burning helicopter.

The arms are equally foreign to Somalia.

To this minimal extent the weapons supporters are correct. Their use does depend on the user.

Killing is no cause for joy. Death is no cause for anger.

The news report dilutes the perception of events to this:

1. The joyous feeling of killing an armed invader.

2. The angry feeling of being murdered by people they want to help stay alive.

Maybe, in fact, the armed invaders are just trying to help and the helicopter is shot down by people wanting to stop the food supplies.

In more general, "first"-"third" world relations, the news images send a more disturbing message for the "first" world.

The news story shows the "first" worlder is vulnerable to the "third". Television brings a direct, immediate image of the vulnerability.

This is very new. There's no live, 24 hour television news coverage of France and the U.S. being ejected from Algeria and Viet Nam respectively.

Today's immediate news coverage has no time lag to cushion the blow or to allow government censors to easily alter it.

In effect, the "first" world could be blown over by a newscast, any hour, on the hour.

We "first" worlders see ourselves dragged like a corpse from the wreckage of our world, defenceless against the "inferior" by implication.

Since most of us believe that we can only live as we currently live, and therefore we can only help others by sending food, they must be inferior because they live differently and thus depend on us to send them food.

It's entirely their fault, not ours.

Our greedy, wasteful, polluting, materialistic lifestyle and way of life can't be wrong.

Our definition of progress and our use of technology can't be wrong.

Such denial in the face of the death won't bring the pilot back to life.

Nor is the "first" world illusion of "superiority" likely to salvage or revive the "first" world.

The S.U. has already fallen. How long will it be before the other boot falls, the one that has been holding down most of the world's population?

...

I hear a television commentator saying, "There will always be a third world."

So the 20% are destined to rule over the 80% forever?

He goes on to say that the 80% don't seem to have the diseases of the 20% because the "third" world has poor statistics.

So we can forget about "first" world scientific researchers who appear in the news saying that our diseases, such as breast, stomach, and lung cancer are a product of our "first" world society?

Why do we assume that we can cure our sick society by pretending it's not sick?

We are out of touch with reality. That's the fatal illness of the "first" world and its predecessor in the European era.

**Québec City**: Local news says Hydro Québec is warning that electricity use is reaching the maximum capacity for power not sold to New York State (U.S.A.)

So local customers are being asked to use Noël lights sparingly.

...By the end of the first month of the new year, Hydro reports a record peak in power consumption. First thing in the morning one day, 30,500 kilowatt hours are in use.

...The severest winter days in 30 years in more than 90% of Canada are rendering some buildings unliveable.

Tenants are being evacuated due to burst pipes, furnaces destroyed by overwork, and fires. Our apartment building holds out fine.

When the heating stops working in one Lévis apartment building, the owner declares that he's no longer the owner. SRC radio's morning news reports his name.

...

One night the Anik communications satellites have a problem.

We lose most of the CBC News in English and Le Téléjournal in French, missing all their international stories.

Our increasing dependence on satellites means that if all the satellites go off, we'll lose all communications beyond short distances.

So the range of interhuman communication could be reduced to the way it is before underwater cables and microwaves.

...

A local business group is pushing a bid to make Québec City the site of a future Winter Olympic Games, nine years from time of writing.

The group is trying to play on local pride and claiming that the games will be entirely privately funded.

That means the group will pay for everything? That would be a first among elite groups boosting games around the world.

Local CBC and SRC television news show the main rival in the U.S.

It already has all the facilities built and paid for because it begins preparing for an earlier bid that it loses to Nagano, Nippon.

Unlike the U.S. city, Québec City's facilities for the winter Olympic games are practically non-existent.

The hockey stadium is also not up to the standards of the Canada-U.S. National Hockey League.

An Olympic quality stadium could save the local hockey franchise. Is the Olympic bid about Olympics or the NHL?

The ski run plans are so controversial that local promoters say they'll use a Calgary run for the events.

Since Calgary is thousands of kilometres west of here, the organizers are obviously not separatists.

The mayor of Calgary is invited here to boost the Québec City bid.

...

News stories feature mobs of nicotine addicts clamouring to buy tax free nicotine supplies that the nicotine producers are marketing through Ganienkeh merchants.

The Québec government just gives up and lowers the taxes.

Ontario has to do the same and provinces in surrounding regions do what they can to prevent interprovincial smuggling.

The governments seem to think that it's better to collect some taxes than no taxes.

There are also provincial elections coming, which means no party wants the nicotine addicts to be angry voters.

But why not just set up customs posts on the borders of the Ganienkeh lands, search non-First Nations' vehicles for contraband, and charge taxes routinely, the way customs do at the Canada-U.S. border?

It's First Nations sovereignty-association with Québec?

...

As March begins, spring madness hits Montréal. News reports say someone steals a set of bagpipes. Police should check the mental hospitals for suspects first.

Who would be crazy enough to steal what amounts to a bunch of tubes stuck in a cloth vacuum cleaner bag to make noises like rusty old water pipes?

...

Various student friends of Mariko come over to sample my pancakes and pizza during our last months in Quebec City. Most of these visitors are from Nippon.

There are a couple of exceptions, including two from the Fraserview area of Vancouver. One says she doesn't find Vancouver particularly friendly.

The other says "everyone" has a car and "no one" can walk because of the air pollution.

These are the words of the Vancouver people, not me.

They're sisters from a family of seven or eight, and the first people I ever meet from there who are not local chauvinists.

...Days later, a news report confirms their comments on air pollution. The report says Vancouver risks becoming like Los Angeles or Mexico City within five years.

There needs to be a crackdown on cars, which cause 80% of Vancouver's pollution.

If Vancouver is so beautiful, why rush by in cars?

Why is Vancouver planned around cars instead of pedestrians?

Why do new housing areas have no pathways, (which don't have to be concrete sidewalks)?

Why is there such widespread servitude to cars, polluting with toxic gas, raising health hazards, lowering the standard of health, eliminating walking almost altogether, thus further lowering health standards and increasing health care costs?

My paternal grandad used to walk across the city when he was in his 80s, counteracting his nicotine addiction.

Now 70 year olds are in worse health and strapped into their wheelchair cars.

By the time I'm 70, most of my generation will be dead from enfeeblement. The hobby exercise gyms won't save them.

In mid-sentence I realize that during my first visit to Toronto, just after my first university graduation, the downtown view is pollution-free.

From the top floors of Toronto downtown area buildings I see no brown air. Likewise ten years later.

But during both years in Toronto the city has more people than Vancouver has now.

Is the city's air clean due to the winds across Lake Ontario and the lack of mountains, plus the wonderful TTC subway, street car, and bus system?

...

The solar eclipse is 80% here, centred somewhere in the middle of the U.S.

Only the local, French-language television stations show the eclipse as it happens during regular programmes, in the corner of the screen.

The CBC/SRC networks have no coverage except during their evening newscasts.

The stations covering the event have shots taken from four different perspectives, two in Montréal and Quebec and two in the U.S.

It's overcast here until the eclipse begins. But clouds drift across, raining briefly, just before full eclipse.

We take a walk just before and during full eclipse but take great care not to look in the direction of the sun.

We don't notice any great difference in daylight, lighting of objects, or sky colour with our backs to the sun.

...

A few thousand people are affected by the power outage. But there's little reference to it in the news.

Nobody says, "Go knock on your neighbours' door to see if they're all right and to find out if they need to put food in your fridge."

Those who have the ability to act positively remain inert. It's the "first" world mentality.

Our building is completely dark. The power is out and remains out for half a day. But our fridge doesn't defrost so everything is all right.

**Montréal-Paris**: I'm learning to master the temperamental video screen services aboard this plane, finally getting to the news report headlines during the last air borne hours of the voyage.

The top story is making me suddenly alert. It says that "giant" Pierre Trudeau is dead, another victim of prostate cancer and Parkinson's disease a few days short of his 81st birthday.

I know Pierre is ill for months, but I'm still quietened when I read the news on the airline screen.

At Canada's embassy in Paris I'm writing, "C'est grâce à lui que je suis ici, en train de profiter de la joie de vivre dans les deux langues officielles. Si jamais il y avait un autre grand canadien comme lui, le Canada aura de la chance."

**Malmö**: Jan's telling me that during his schooling, any English usage that's not broadcast by the U.K.'s BBC radio and television is forbidden.

So now Jan finds BBC clear, but the U.S. cable network news is too fast. I'm listening to that U.S. network on his television and agreeing with Jan. It's fast.

The U.S. network has to be short, fast, and limited to U.S. interests to make more time for commercials.

BBC is lacking in such restrictive, money-centred news values and judgement. So BBC news can be clearer and more comprehensive.

SKY-TV, a U.K. commercial station isn't covering "the world" like the BBC.

SKY is mentioning the world and the U.K. floods, but making no mention of mainland European floods and flood threats.

Fortunately, Jan and Eva aren't limiting themselves to English or any of these stations while watching television.

**Stockholm**: Before doing anything else here, we're finding ourselves walking in front of the Canadian embassy close to the train station.

We're going in to scan the multiple page newspaper stories about Pierre Trudeau, his impact, and his state funeral.

"If Trudeau is dead, Canada is dead." one person comments. I think it dies before Pierre does.

...

Svenska television commercials are providing us with very humorous and colourful relief from an often black and white fade to gray programme schedule.

In Norway, the situation's looking similar, with black and grey dressed morning news show hosts appearing to be in mourning. It's the mourning news show?

Even the sportscaster is wearing a black blazer over a grey turtleneck, forever putting to rest the stereotypical image of the loudly dressed sports announcer.

There's no colour commentary being added to this sports news.

Lively, awakening broadcasting it is not. No audience is

being jolted out of its sleep and rushed out the door to work.

Both male and female announcers share the colourless casting.

Store mannequins are displaying much brighter shades for women's clothing. But men's stores are pushing the deadliest hues of dark shadows.

Maybe it's the vampire look in vogue this fall of the House of Usher. These pale faces lurching in the northern streets are actually vampires?

Or are we just seeing the Adams-Family-look catching on with the approach of Hallowe'en, which seems to be a big highlight of the season in these parts. No surprise?

**Shrewsbury**: This town is one of the flooding centres we're seeing in the news since first arriving in Paris several weeks ago.

Although centre town is on a steep hill, the riversides are lowlands. A town map shows the problem causing the flood. Shrewsbury is in the middle of a long curve in the river.

Centertown should be an island in the middle of an oxbow lake formed naturally by the river shortening its path instead of meandering the long way around.

The river is still nearly bursting at the banks when we get to town. Nearby houses are having their cellars drained. The local abbey is closed for repairs.

Some very modest bed and breakfast places near the abbey are suspiciously expensive in these post flood days.

We very few and rare visitors to the disaster site are paying for the damages? The tourist industry isn't hungry after the diluvial drought?

...

News reports are saying that U.K. tourism is declining, no doubt due to the extremely overpriced accommodation and much overvalued local currency.

But problems in agriculture are taking the blame. The livestock business is also being wiped out by the mad cow and hoof and mouth diseases.

...

In related news: The U.K. is delaying its parliamentary elections until the cattle crisis subsides. Bull shortage?

**Venezia**: The news flash that's arriving only now on the front pages of Italia's G7 newspapers and in the television features is that second hand smoke is a health hazard.

It's only 25 years since that's news is reported in Canada. But then ancient U.S. television shows are also big here now.

**Castelfranco**: We can see a U.S. military TV station here. Once in a while, it's showing printed headlines on screen, helping us to fill in the big gaps in our understanding of the news in Italian.

We're finding out that the celebrated and extremely expensive U.S. military technology isn't working very well.

Instead of using its fortune to provide better, universally accessible education, health care, and freedom from poverty, the U.S. is squandering vast sums on defective killing forces.

Avoiding an accidental nuclear holocaust during the very long, wasteful, and destructive Cold War seems all the more miraculous.

Only the Soviet Union's weaponry is saving us all from the last world war?

U.S. weaponry and military preparedness is becoming notoriously infamous for malfunctioning or missing the targets.

The U.S. forces are accidentally hitting passenger trains and buses, destroying the embassy of Chuang Hwa, sinking a training ship from Nippon by surfacing a submarine under it, and letting a plane stray over Chuang Hwa and bump into a plane from there.

The U.S. is refusing to apologize to Chuang Hwa for the straying plane, saying that the U.S. spy plane isn't a spy plane. It's just a plane left on auto pilot.

The auto pilot and passengers enjoying the uninvited visit over Chuang Hwa's air space aren't noticing there's a Chuang Hwa plane flying right alongside.

Of course not. Military fiction is stranger than fiction. U.S. public opinion is supporting their government's refusal to apologize.

The U.S. is the last of the superstupidpowers.

So much of the military TV channel's schedule isn't being devoted to reporting flaws in the military itself.

But more hours of military TV seems to be going to cartoons and sports, plus anti-drug advertising.

So the military's numerous and forever recurring mistakes are coming from watching too many cartoons and taking too many drugs?

The U.S. military presence isn't restricted to the TV station. A regular Italian channel is featuring an Italian air force officer in full uniform giving the weather forecast.

...

We're finding out just how difficult it is to understand the news in Italian, despite our French language skills and my experience with Portuguese and Spanish.

We're guessing the news in Italian most of the time. A visual image of older people is being followed by one of a major looking drug bust by the police.

So we should be concluding that older people are selling drugs in Italia? Aha! They deal to U.S. soldiers?

Unfortunately, too many of the local television shows we're seeing here aren't demanding any language skills or any intelligence at all.

They're TV for air heads, like the U.S. game shows and moronic emissions showing too often in Brasil and Nippon.

Only the long news shows are partially compensating for junk TV in the G7's Italia.

**Paris**: <u>Le Monde</u> is reporting U.S. population growth, despite the U.S. "Berlin Wall style" southern border.

I'm calling that border the same thing in Miyazaki, after seeing a CBC documentary on the subject.

The Paris newspaper says the U.S. is still receiving about two-thirds of its illegal immigrants from Mexico. Hispanics now outnumber Anglos in California.

While I'm living in Rio de Janeiro, I read predictions about the dominance of Español in the U.S. that's then expected to occur in the early 2000s, by Europe's calendar.

California, Florida, and Texas are already more advanced along that road.

When this prediction is made, there are about 823 million people living in the Americas as a whole, thus approaching the population of Chuang Hwa.

Most people in the Americas, about 511,578,094 at the time of the prediction, are not living in Canada or the U.S.

So the non-Hispanics, non-lusophones are a minority. So how could the U.S. dominate the region if it weren't for the arms and dollar religionisms?

I'm remembering a pavilion guide at Bampaku, Osaka's World Expo in Showa 45, who is telling me that she's studying Español due to Nip-pon's future trade with the southern Americas.

It's like a line from a movie saying that leaders in Nippon aren't just planning for the next quarter financial year, they're planning for the next quarter century.

...

One news commentary is talking about the impact of the current cool weather on Europe's economy, especially on the agriculture business.

I'm thinking of the potato famine in Ireland and the climate change pushing the ancient Vikings to relocate. So the current weather might start driving more emigration.

Will they go to Canada and the "third" world?

Will the cloud, rain, and prolonged cabin fever drive up depression and crime?

Will France become a tourist Mecca for rain-loving Vancouverites?

It's Europe's biggest rainfall in 100 years.

...

News here is showing the Canadian prime minister and Mexican president in Québec City at the Americas free trade meeting.

Continuing reports are making it clear that Québec City is looking more and more like a police state while preparing to host the latest G7 meeting.

Québec City is defending itself against dissent and possibly violent demonstrations with a vigilance exceeding the October Crisis of 31 years earlier.

The streets of Québec City are full of soldiers then, guarding government buildings and politicians.

They're not as numerous or widespread as the massive riot squad police presence of the present time of writing.

So demonstrators are more dangerous than the defunct FLQ terrorists?

Old Québec City is surrounded by a three metre high wire fence and 6,000 extra police.

On European television news, frightened Québec City small business people are shown boarding up their store fronts.

This is all being done without the old War Measures Act of the October Crisis and newer national emergency law replacing it after the October Crisis.

Are the G7, the silent partners of past military dictatorships and current ones in places such as Algeria and Myanmar, now starting to apply the same decisive, dictatorial power-holding techniques in the G7 itself, after testing them out in the "third" world?

Subsequent reports from Québec City are showing the wire wall being torn down by demonstrators.

Another scene is showing water cannons blasting demonstrators holding up a Canadian flag at the fence and then fighting with riot gear police.

News reporters are calling the riot squad "la police militaire".

It's making me nostalgic for living in Rio de Janeiro 16 years earlier, watching the news on Rede Manchette, and seeing the military dictators in Warsaw and Santiago doing their precision water cannon routines simultaneously against pro-democracy demonstrators.

Ironically, today's news is playing a clip of the Canadian prime minister saying that free trade in the Americas has to be tied to democracy.

After playing this clip, the news reader is saying that the prime minister's words are quite a contrast with what's happening at the same time in the streets of Québec City.

Then the news is running the video of water cannons firing on the crowds.

The official explanation of the trashing of democratic freedom of speech by the Canadian government is that demonstrations in Seattle turn out violent a year earlier.

So if there's a violent demonstration somewhere else, repressive police state tactics are legitimate everywhere else?

So drawing this situation to its logical conclusion, if all demonstrations being planned from now on are going to be greeted with such tactics and precautions, free speech itself can eventually be perceived as a security threat requiring security action by all the nation-states.

Pierre Trudeau would be opposing it if he were still alive.

He's the prime minister telling a huge, noisy, outdoor demonstration on parliament hill to let the U.S. president speak during his visit to Ottawa a couple of decades earlier.

He's not calling in the police to keep the anti-U.S. demonstrators far away from parliament hill.

...

Reports of the Québec City conference are reminding me of something I'm learning back at the Carleton University School of Journalism in Ottawa (Ontario).

One of the profs is telling us about a reporter sent to city hall to cover the mayor's speech.

Returning to the newspaper office later, the reporter says, "Sorry, there's no story on the speech. The mayor was shot."

Québec conference reports are showing the participants and results. There are shots of demonstrators and police sparing in the streets.

But the ideas of the demonstrators are not being reported in the newscasts we're seeing. There are no interviews of depth and no debates being shown.

So it's not newsworthy to say that the largest corporations, which are the world's biggest economies, are demanding minimum costs, wages, working conditions, and environmental standards in return for providing employment and investment.

So the nation-states can't sign minimal environmental clean-up accords such as the one written in Kyoto.

...

**Strasbourg**: Newspapers and television weather reports are reporting the endless rains of the past six months, including most of our time in the EU. They are months of flooding and spreading cattle diseases.

The low and high temperatures are 0°C and 7°C to 12°C during our visit.

...

France Soir mentions in passing that six months of rain could be part of a drastic weather and climate change coming from global warming.

So, the newspaper is concluding that everyone is going to have to change lifestyles.

Of course the story is strongly implying that only the "first" world can be leading the changes.

After seeing this story about the need for changing lifestyles, Mariko's telling me to look around. She's saying that we're the only ones changing our lifestyles.

We're the only ones walking on the narrow sidewalks beside all these noisy motor vehicles which are coating all the green surroundings and us with their toxic exhaust fumes.

If their world runs out of gas, what will they do?

What fuel will generate electricity for maintaining and continuing their wasteful lifestyles for the fast growing number of older people in the aging, declining populations of most of the G7?

I'm looking around and wondering about the car people's chances of surviving their present lifestyles.

We're walking about six hours during our first day in this city. During the last part of our walk we're carrying six kilos of food supplies.

I'm saying that dinosaurs are here for tens of millions of years and their remains are still creating the fuel for the present lifestyles.

So dinosaurs are still ruling the world.

Apparently it takes an enormous natural disaster to wipe out the dinosaurs. We're the natural disaster wiping ourselves out.

The earth's dinosaur-based fuel supply could last longer than us. So the dinosaurs' remains would outlast ours, in the interior of the earth.

Their impression and impact on this planet remains much deeper than ours. They're still part of the earth, not temporary, surface roamers and scourers like us.

**London**: Local news is telling us that since the government's sale of its railway to a private company, there are numerous problems with maintenance, and some bad accidents.

Our train from Dover to London is being held up along the way by a "train under investigation" on the line ahead. No one is translating this nebulous phrase to us.

**Walsham le Willows**: After I mention the current news stories about the U.K. monarchy losing its appeal to locals, old Colin acknowledges the news but then lists the names of each descendant of the current U.K. monarch who he says will inevitably succeed her.

Since I prefer democracy to monarchy I find his absolute believer religionist determinism baffling. Such beliefs are the domain and underpinning of absolute dictatorships.

...

At one point I'm mentioning seeing a news story about people demonstrating against what they're calling capitalism.

Old Colin is replying that he's a capitalist and I'm an idealist.

But I'm not expressing any opinion about the demonstrators. I'm just relaying what they're saying and not what I'm saying.

...

Television news here is reporting fears of rioting during a London summit after the battling in Seattle and Québec City.

When the London summit ends without any problems, the news says that the police successfully prevent violence.

BBC and other reporters broadcasting "live" from the summit area are taking great pains to provide colour and in depth coverage by giving TV viewers complete details of where demonstrators have to urinate while being cordoned off by the police.

There are no long interviews, no debates, and no positions aired. It's a story about crowd control techniques and preventing demonstrators from being heard.

Why there are any demonstrators there at all is a total mystery to the television news audience. It's a huge unanswered question in the news story.

It's a huge unanswered question that reporters apparently are not interested in asking.

So television news watchers are left with only one conclusion: Demonstrators must be just a bunch of troublemakers who have nothing to say.

Otherwise a professional journalist would be reporting what the demonstrators are trying to say.

Organizing a demonstration for the police to corral and for a swarm of reporters not to bother covering is a waste of time. Fade to black. Go to commercial. Please!

...

Whatever happens to the effective protests bringing about positive changes, such as those of Gandhi and Martin Luther King? I mean non-violent civil disobedience.

Violence is getting news now, as it is then. People in uniform-like, bad ninja-like, black shirts, pants, and masks are throwing stones at windows and at riot gear police.

It's making the news, leaving no time for issues, debates, or talk.

The picture is one of rational society taking a last stand, putting up a final line of defence, a Hadrian/Great Wall against violent overthrow of elected government.

In fact societies are irrational, spotlighting their irrational counterparts instead of recognizing them as equals, instead of dealing with reality by discussion and action.

In this picture, the U.S. would still be a haven for segregation and still fighting in Viet Nam.

**Doseley**: The U.K. prime minister is calling a national election, after delaying it due to the cattle diseases. A newspaper headline reports: "PM names election day."

He may as well be naming it after himself, since the opposition party is virtually conceding the election before the vote is called.

Back in Walsham, Colin is telling me that the election is already won before it's called. Delaying the election day is just prolonging the agony of defeat for the opposition.

Opening public opinion polls are showing the Labour Party has 51% support, the Cons have thirty something percentage points, and the Liberal Democrats are following with more than 20%.

No one is expecting the prime minister to suffer the same fate as party leaders with exactly the same big opening day lead who lose in Canadian general elections, Turner and Campbell.

...

We're watching a string of different newscasts each night thanks to my ongoing curiosity about how news is covered in different places and during the current U.K. election.

It's amazing to see the Cons are running against the U.K.'s future as part of its European homeland. It's separatism, a position without a future anywhere.

My news-watching is favouring a white haired news host named Jon on Channel 5, which is not BBC.

The station is also featuring an exposé on how public opinion polling is deliberately being manipulated to change voter perceptions and balloting.

Channel 5's U.S. guest is calling this polling approach a "message poll".

Message polls are being designed to select popular key words and then put them into politicians' mouths' and party propaganda to swing votes.

Never heard of it. But I can see it as a logical conclusion of non-direct democracy political systems, such as the parliamentary system.

Indirect systems are dedicating themselves to self-preservation by always trying to persuade most people not to try to govern their own lives.

Indirect systems make representatives look as if they're just as good as having a direct democracy. It's not the same.

...

Public opinion poll results are being shown in the news weekly, but there's little change aside from improvements in the Lib-Dem standings.

During television interviews, TV interviewers and party leaders are calling each other by their first names in some cases.

...

What election? There are local and national elections today, but we're not seeing any signs of polling stations while walking in mid-village Doseley, Madeley, and Dawley.

BBC-TV says there are 60 million potential voters choosing among 3,318 candidates and 74 political parties running in this election.

There are 659 seats in parliament and many other local government posts being filled.

On election night, the polling station at Sunderland is trying to keep its record of being the first station in the U.K. to finish counting the ballots.

In the previous election, it takes 45 minutes to count.

Unlike the U.S., they aren't using voting machines here. So it doesn't take weeks to find out who's getting elected as it did during last year's U.S. presidential election.

Small white trucks are carrying ballot boxes to red-shirted runners who are rushing to carry the boxes into a big, empty building, where counters are dumping out the ballots and tallying the votes.

But outside of Sunderland the counting is much slower. Two hours after the polling stations close there are only 12 parliamentary seats decided.

They're all Labour seats in the cities.

At 10 p.m., the BBC and ITV exit polls are showing a landslide victory for Labour with about the same seat results as four years ago.

The Lib-Dems have more seats but the same percentage of votes as last time. The cons are winning 1% more votes than in the previous election.

In the exit polls, Labour is getting a total number of seats ranging from 408 to 417. That's a 157 to 175 seat majority.

The cons are getting 157 to 175 seats. The Lib-Dems are getting 44 to 58 seats.

Other parties and independents are ending up with 30 seats.

The three other U.K. television networks that we can see using our antenna reception are broadcasting only their regular shows until the regular newscasts time.

The actual results are not ready until the following evening. Labour is getting a 167 seat majority, winning 413 seats.

The cons are getting 166 seats. Lib-Dems are taking 52 seats. Others are getting 28 seats.

This election is resulting in the biggest majority and the smallest voter turnout in 83 years. About 59% of eligible voters cast their ballots.

So the parties are getting seats based on small fractions of the total possible votes if every voter actually voted.

Labour is taking 25% of all possible votes. The cons are getting 19 % of the votes that could be cast. Lib-Dems are receiving 11%. Others are totalling 6%.

The tiny percentage of eligible votes cast for each party is further evidence that representative government is not democracy and that plebiscites on policies and on everything is a better system.

It's a non-confidence vote in the U.K. electoral system.

But by voting Labour, UKers are at least saving the EU from separatism.

...

Local news is reporting that obesity is causing a large percentage of the cancer cases here.

Among the seven to 11 year old kids in the U.K., about 20 per cent are overweight. One in nine is obese.

...

BBC-TV's morning news show is mentioning that France is benefiting from its new shorter week employment system.

The employeed now have three days out of seven away from the job. France is abandoning the seven day work week.

But my parents are working a 35-hour work week and getting only two days off a week about 20 years before France's change.

They also get a long weekend every month on top of the statutory ones.

So what's happening now in France isn't particularly surprising for me.

The current innovation is demanding that the employeed pack their 35 hours of work into four days instead of five.

It seems as if the employeed are making up for days off, as in Nippon, by doing extra work and hours between days off.

My parents don't do so and are under no pressure to do so.

Making up for time off means increasing stress and pressure. It's unlike my calls for devoting the prime lifetime years to the person living them.

As BBC host Jeremy says, "When we're lying on our death beds, we're not going to be saying, "I wish I'd spent more time at (my place of employment)."

It's better to be doing our work, not being employeed, and then not dying in bed.

...

Aside from a Canadian newspaper baron changing his citizenship so that he can become a U.K. "Lord", the only word of Canada reaching here is that the Montréal police are escorting thousands of Montréalais/aises nu(e)s, so they can pose for a mass photo par terre au naturel in an area of the city which appears to be in front of Place des Arts.

The mass of models is posing for a U.S. photographer who the police are arresting in the U.S. for shooting the same kind of pictures in that country.

Montréal has to be warmer than Doseley, or the models are shivering. Yet this month in the U.K. is being described as the hottest May in 100 years.

Sure it's mainly sunny, but the temperature doesn't exceed 25°C Celsius and then for only a few days. It's a cold 100 years?

There's also news of an earthquake in Cornwall, registering 3.5 on the Richter scale. It's a minor rumble in Nippon.

**Kiyotake**: We're watching one of Sigourney Weaver's "Alien" movies, seeing the invincible aliens finally destroyed again.

Then I'm switching the TV back to NHK and seeing a shot of one of the New York City World Trade Centre buildings on fire.

It looks like another film, a disaster movie. I'm wondering how anyone can escape from such a high tower.

I'm thinking of the old movie "Towering Inferno" and how the firefighters' ladders aren't long enough to reach the higher floors.

I don't know how anyone is going to escape. Are those windows falling out, or people?

I'm thinking that the buildings will burn so much that they'll have to be abandoned and torn down.

Then the buildings start collapsing. It's surprising, yet I know it's going to happen. Maybe this is the aftereffect of the science fiction horror movie we just finish watching.

I'm seeing a plot line instead of the reality on the screen.

The TV screen says "live", so this is happening now, nighttime here and morning in New York City. It's real, not a movie.

The story isn't just a fire. It's another terrorist attack. The same buildings are attacked by some bomber in the basement a few years ago.

I'm realizing the significance of the time of day there. The poor people inside the building must be just starting their day at their jobs.

With all the spies and security systems, how could such an attack succeed?

Then the news is showing U.S. military headquarters in Washington, D.C., a building called "The Pentagon" because of its geometric shape.

Another terrorist attack is happening there.

I keep writing about the mortality of empires, how they all fall eventually despite the false sense of security of the present imperial era, even after the Soviet Empire falls.

But this dramatic, sudden fall of the financial and military centres of the U.S. is surprising me too.

It's a severe shock for the conservative era which confidently sees the world as U.S. owned, controlled, and operated since the disappearance of the S.U.

My first thought is that the attacks are conducted by people from the southern Americas to retaliate against U.S. support for and alliances with nasty military dictatorships there.

But I'm wrong, the terrorists are former U.S. allies against the Soviet invasion of Afghanistan.

Only a mentally ill person could plan and carry out such an attack, even if the whole world were angry with the U.S. Empire.

But mental illness seems to be a prerequisite for all war. Healthy minds don't rationally decide to kill other healthy minds.

The U.S. attacks have implications which aren't good for the immigration border control procedures, human migration, and civil liberties.

Insane attacks are used as excuses for police states, just like the Reichstag fire in Deutschland.

To protect only themselves, Cons make our lives harder.

...

News of planning for a back-up U.S. government, to keep public utilities running in case of an emergency, apparently dates back 39 years before the terrorist strikes, to the Cold War's fears of a nuclear arms catastrophy.

Why are they activating the plans now, after not doing so during the peak tension years of the Cold War?

Conspiracy theorists might speculate that this is the push to completely turn over the

U.S. to an unelected government, the final stage of the JFK assassination programme.

...

In the sudden flurry of news reporting about Argentina, a largely forgotten country since the return of elected government, I'm finally learning why the currencies of Brasil and Argentina are so overvalued when we're visiting there seven years earlier.

I'm finally being told why those currencies suddenly become more valuable than Nippon's yen in terms of U.S. dollar exchange rates.

It's all based on money coming from foreign investors using U.S. dollars.

Investors are pumping up local currencies so they won't lose any money on their investments.

Foreign investors' money is being pulled out at time of writing, leaving Argentina and Brasil at the mercy of the IMF again and returning their currencies to the real world.

Maybe our plans for returning to the south very soon are perfect timing, in terms of costs.

...

One good thing coming from all the news reporting about Afghanistan is that I'm learning that the first day of northern hemisphere spring there is Afghanistan's New Year.

When I'm writing the original <u>A Sketch of Terrian History</u> I'm saying that the year should start with spring, the beginning of new life, not in the dead of winter.

...

On the first day of spring, the news is reporting winds blowing up to 126 kilometres per hour between Tokyo and Hokkaido.

The winds are blowing dust from the Yellow River in Chuang Hwa. It's reducing visibility to 3 kilometres in Fukuoka and to 1 kilometre in Seoul.

Many flights are being cancelled. But a few days later we're taking off with no difficulty.

...

Trying to improve the world is better than sitting in the parlour and trivializing all the world's problems, and sitting as a passive audience to news media that are trivializing all the world's problems by squeezing them in between the commercials and the sports reports.

Everybody's talking about the world, but nobody's doing anything about it.

**Quito**: TV news says the pace of national inflation is slowing to 49 per cent.

Prices inflate in U.S. dollars now, since Ecuador discards its own currency, further enriching the local elite by overvaluing the former currency to make U.S. dollars cheaper for them to buy, hoard, and take abroad.

Today's inflation rate makes the buying power of the U.S. dollar go down 49 per cent in Ecuador.

It's unique in my experience. Today's $1 item will soon cost $1.49. Imagine that in U.S. dollars in the U.S.

In Ecuador, using the U.S. currency instead of a local one means cheap prices are exchanged for expensive ones.

...

A local newspaper devotes its front page to a photo of the U.S. dollar, with the caption: "Yes, there is a way out of dollarization".

Another newspaper front page story reveals how to retreat from the U.S. dollar. When money moves are so well known, the plans of the elite are already well underway.

A non-dollar currency will return after the presidential elections or after OCP (oil pipeline) is completed?

A report on the impact of "dolorizacion" one night on Canal Ocho television features interviews with street merchants and factory owners in Ecuador and bordering areas of Colombia and Peru.

The programme compares prices on specific basic items, such as rice, eggs, bread, cooking oil, and shirts.

A 40 cent shirt in Colombia is $4 in Ecuador.

Prices in Colombia are already less than Ecuador before dolorizacion, but now most Colombian prices are 14% less.

Peru's prices are 25% less, according to the programme.

The price difference percentages are based on comparing "canastas", i.e. shopping baskets.

Some of the comparisons made differ from our shopping experiences in Quito. It depends on where you shop.

But it's not surprising that exports and tourism are declining in Ecuador under dolorizacion.

La bête, our landlord says that without that revenue there are no U.S. dollars coming into the country. So Ecuador ends up with no national currency.

The IMF rules.

The news programme also mentions that 79% of the people in Ecuador live in poverty. Others are destitute.

Newspaper front pages and some information for the upcoming presidential elections say that corruption is a big problem.

Local Norma says that foreign employees of petroleum companies get paid US$96,000 to US$120.000 per year.

She also says the salary of the president of Ecuador is US$120,000 and a law forbids paying anyone any more. But the law isn't applied.

La bête says the moneyed sell their Sucres at 15,000 to the U.S. dollar, then reset the exchange rate to 25,000 per U.S. dollar a few days later. Talk about insider trading.

All the talk of government corruption here gets me talking about dictator General Stroessner's Paraguay again and recent charges of corruption against Canadian cabinet ministers in Ottawa.

It really might be the best time to buy Canadian citizenship, before the prices go up.

...

...

There's a U.S. politician in the news called "Traficante". It's the same as the Español word used in the news to describe drug dealers.

**Cumbaya**: A person can pass a lifetime in Cumbaya's fortress living area without knowing what country s/he's living in, passing every day in front of thick screens.

There's a computer screen for the U.S. Internet system.

Non-locals use it for keeping in touch with everywhere except the here and now, and for keeping in touch with everyone except the human masses outside the gates of Cumbaya.

There's cable television for viewing the three main U.S. commercial networks and the U.S. cable television news station, as if Cumbaya were in New Jersey, (i.e. a place near New York City).

Cumbaya is like the foreign elite ghettos in Ballard's book Empire of the Sun or in Snow's book Red Star Over China.

Off in the distance, the mountains and surrounding scenery look like a real paradise, a rich land that's impoverished only by the moneyed elites from home and abroad.

**Quito**: Canada's conservative news magazine, Macleans does a story on the ENCANA OCP storm. It's about an oil pipeline being built here by a Canadian company.

Craig, a Canadian engineer working for ENCANA here, says that he's shocked by what he calls factual errors.

The pipeline goes through 160 kilometres of rainforest, Macleans says.

Craig says the pipeline goes through 1.6 kilometres of cloud forest, nothing else, and the land there is only fields.

Macleans says a baby is killed in an anti-pipeline demonstration. Craig says the demonstration is against privatization and the electric company, not AEC.

**Cuenca**: Just before entering the city, a passenger leaving the bus catches my attention. There's a revolver handle sticking out of the back of his pants.

The next day's news might explain why. It reports that this bus company is attacked by thieves more than once lately.

**Lima**: Waiting for our hostal room to be cleaned one day, we see a bit of news in French on TV5 on the front desk television set.

The news is showing a summit meeting in Johannesburg. A reporter is calling it the world's most dangerous city. He doesn't know New York City?

The news item also says that half of the world's population has a daily income of $2 U.S.

So, without deducting any money for housing, food, or clothing, half the world's population has to pay 500 days income to apply to immigrate to Canada. To be specific:

$1,000 U.S. is about $1,500 Canadian at time of writing foreign exchange currency rates. That's how much the Canadian government charges immigrants to Canada.

That's 562 days of total gross income for half of the world's population. It takes another 500 days gross income purchase an airline ticket to Canada.

An additional 11,250 days of gross income is required to show the officially deemed sufficient funds necessary for setting up residency during the first year in Canada.

A person has to save the equivalent of 34 years of gross annual income to immigrate to Canada.

That's only possible if the person saves 50% of his/her gross annual income for 68 years, after starting work at age 18, and if s/he lives to be more than 86 years old.

At that age s/he can finally immigrate to Canada.

But realistically, to save that much money a person would have to work more than one hundred years at $2 per day.

Thus, Canada's immigration policy automatically and completely prevents half the human population from ever immigrating to Canada.

More than 3 billion people are excluded by Canadian immigration fees, no matter how much good the economically excluded might do for Canada.

...

El Mercurio newspaper's ornate towers and golden decorated doors are facing a lineup of older men one day as we pass.

Their old backs are bending over. Their looking intently and talking together with pens in hand.

They're writing letters on photocopies and originals of the daily paper's crossword puzzle. Sometimes they confirm words together.

First I think the photocopies are answers for sale to win a prize. But then I see other people filling in blank photocopies, perhaps as rough drafts.

...

Three gringos in Quito swear to me that Ecuador is the number one country in the world for corruption.

But here in Lima the Español version of a US cable television news network reports that Transparency International shows Ecuador is either the 68th or 86th in the list of corrupt countries.

It's not number one.

The absolute certainty of gringos is the same as when I'm first in Fukuoka. They never learn anything true? They get everything wrong everywhere?

...

One local morning newspaper I notice today has a small item saying that the U.S. is on maximum alert today, fearing a repeat of the financial and military headquarters attacks.

The Canadian version of a major site of the U.S. Internet system says <u>that</u> tragedy "changed the world".

But my impression is that if you don't change the world in a positive sense, it will change you. That's what happens to the U.S.

The world will change and change you more than you change it.

...

The good news from Canada is that the Péquists are running third in the public opinion polls behind the Liberals and the newest party of Mario Dumont.

The quick rise of Dumont is being attributed to his youth. He's the former leader of the Young Liberals under Robert Bourassa.

He quit that party a few years ago to join an older politician who founds an alternative party to eliminate polar voting, federalist vs. separatist.

He wants to give voters another option, an alternative to having no choice but to vote separatist just to oust the Liberals from office and vice versa.

Dumont's success means stable politics is returning to Québec for the first time in 30 years, instead of frantic yo-yo politics which only retard the province and do nothing to help its people.

But I have no idea what Mario represents.

...

News of the former Peruano president, Fujimore is not good. One of the police talking to us back in the park in Sullana has no good words for the former leader.

Here there are stories coming out about his alliance with the military against guerrillas, causing many innocent people to be kidnapped and tortured.

That's what the military does best?

Fujimore's regime is also infamous for its financial corruption.

A key figure in the government is caught on video a few years ago accepting a table top covered with piles of U.S. currency.

The sum that Fujimore takes with him to Nippon is substantial but as yet uncounted.

It's difficult for locals to understand why Nippon is not returning Fujimore to face criminal charges in Peru.

The official excuse is that Fujimore is a citizen of Nippon, and thus exempt from extradition. How does he become Peru's president if he's Japanese, not Peruano?

There is also apparently no extradition treaty between Peru and Nippon.

I tell Benni, who works at the front desk of a Lima hotel, that people in Nippon are unaware of Fujimore's crimes. If they were, the government would be forced to return him to Peru for trial.

Benni says people can find out about Fujimore if they want to know. My pleading ignorance for people in Nippon is not an acceptable excuse.

I could say the same thing about people throughout the G7/8 who are not bothering to act to abolish their minority rule behaviours.

[Years later, after running as an unsuccessful candidate in Nippon's elections, Fujimore returns to Peru and is sentenced to imprisonment. Eventually, he's released due to failing health.]

...

**Frederick**: All news television stations in the area are so obsessed with the sniper here that they neglect to mention hundreds of hostages in a Moscow theatre and the assassination of a politician in Nippon.

We find out about this news on the U.S. Internet system and during a delayed news broadcast from Nippon that's shown on the international news programme of a cable television company's community station.

But local news is important to us because we're in the sniper target areas daily. He's captured 8 kilometres from where we're staying.

**Québec City**: After Hallowe'en, the snow goes and comes, the air warms and cools, ranging from +7°C to -3°C.

Some people express their surprise in the news, about a sudden snow storm of more than 30 centimetres that is predicted and forewarned two days in advance.

This is Canada.

"It's snowing, but it's only autumn!" someone exclaims in passing.

But this is November and this isn't really winter weather. Some leaves perch in the flakes like feathers on a browning dove.

This snow story reminds me of one that appears on page one of Toronto's <u>Globe and Mail</u> at least two years in a row.

When a mid-October snow storm hits the area between Barrie and Toronto, the paper leads with the same front page headline:

"Surprise storm hits". How can it be a surprise when it hits two year in a row?

...

A couple of Canadian public figures have to scurry around apologizing to the U.S. for being too honest about their reactions to the foolish and unfriendly role of the U.S. in the world.

Both figures are apologizing for joking, but they get the attention of the U.S. cable news entertainment television channel.

The mindless discussion and debate on that channel only emphasizes the verity of the joking.

One of the Canadian public figures calls the current U.S. president a "moron".

(She's later a guest on a Canadian comedy TV show and makes fun of him without using that word.)

An article in a Québec City French-language daily paper argues that the moron tag has a real semantic basis in the U.S. president's reality, or lack thereof.

This is why he is known as U.S. president moron in <u>Terrian Journals</u>.

...

Large crowds are gathering in many parts of the northern

world, including Québec City, to demonstrate against U.S. president moron.

The anti-war movement is being revived, if only for weekends, with demonstrations larger than any since the U.S. fights in southeast Asia 40 years earlier.

Many of today's demonstrators say they're taking to the streets for the first time in their lives, and not just the youngest ones.

I'm almost in the streets myself. That would be a first. I never take part in any demonstrations in this part of the world, and only one elsewhere.

I'm one of the million people at a Direítas Jà demonstration in Rio de Janeiro 19 years earlier. But I'm only an observer in the midst of it.

Trudeau's surviving sons, Justin and Sacha are part of the anti-war protest in Montréal.

SRC's news channel, RDI is the only station with reporters in the crowds reporting live and direct all the time, without interruption, non-stop, all day during every demonstration in the major cities of Québec and Ontario.

RDI also shows demonstrations in Europe, Nippon, Australia, and the U.S. Some of the biggest demonstrations are in London, U.K.

The U.S. cable news channel has reports from demonstrations now and again, but then switches back to their studios, saying things like, "Of course there's another side to this story."

Since when is broadcasting the official propaganda and position of U.S. president moron the criterion for objective reporting?

There is no equal time consideration. Most of that TV station's reporting is only the pro-war side against the demonstrators.

While U.S. president moron and the demonstrators against him are dominating the news, the rest of the world is virtually ignored or given passing mention in the news.

Stories of new famine, accelerating environmental deterioration, warfare in Africa, and events in the southern Americas are happening but hardly noticed.

The U.S. wars are a diversion?

...

The Péquist premier during the U.S. invasion of Iraq is very dishonestly saying that only Québec is strongly against the war and the rest of Canada supports the war.

He denies all the news coverage of RDI? It's a desperation act to save his party from defeat in the upcoming provincial elections?

His main election promise is to erase Canada by two years from now.

A pro-U.S.-war splinter group in Ottawa is helping the Péquists. The group says only Québec is keeping Canada from supporting the U.S. war.

The first casualty of war really is the truth.

After much wobbling, the party in power finally sides with the United Nations, especially France, Germany, and Russia, instead of the U.S. They won't invade Iraq.

...

Fortunately, the U.S. war does not appear to be as bad as the U.S. news reports expect in background stories about the U.S. military's plans.

Those plans call for hundreds of bombs to be unleashed on Baghdad during the first few days of the attack.

The military claims that civilian casualties would be minimal because the bombs would be carefully targeted to hit only military objectives.

But hundreds of bombs hitting a smaller city like Baghdad, about the size of Fukuoka, could not help but kill hundreds of thousands of civilians.

Even if the civilian deaths are far fewer than expected, the U.S. war is going to cost hundreds of billions of U.S. dollars.

Twelve years before this war, the U.S. spends half a billion dollars a day for its war in the gulf, the same cost as sending one spacecraft with three astronauts to the moon thirty years earlier.

With the Iraq war money, the U.S. could have the world's best public health care system, the one that private insurance companies block in the U.S. when Hilary Clinton tries to create one.

While the U.S. spends hundreds of billions on war, millions of U.S. citizens will continue to go without health care because they can't afford the costs of private companies' health care insurance.

While the U.S. is going deeper into debt for military spending alone, the news mentions that 28 million people are starving today in Ethiopia.

The war money could feed them all like kings.

The U.S. changes its objectives for this war a couple of times, saying anything to justify it.

After being embarrassed at the U.N. Security Council, the U.S. says it's going into Iraq to liberate Iraqis and to rid the world of a dangerous dictator.

**Van Couverden Airport**: Many passengers are doing nothing more than involuntarily staring at TV monitors strategically placed in front of their tired eyes, in rows of welded down waiting room seats.

Despite the 500 channel TV universe, passengers are obliged to watch a steady diet of US-only cable news station paranoia about terrorists hiding under every bed.

While I'm waiting at Vancouver's airport, there's no chance of watching the calmer CBC Newsworld, RDI, CTV Newsnet, or LCN.

A CBC news report talks of G7/8 powers losing control around the world as small arms action grows in all the streets elsewhere.

...

At time of writing, Brasil's population grows to about 160 million people since I first arrive there.

About 54 million live in favelas, according to LCN, Canada's privately-owned francophone television news network.

So about 34% of the people in Brasil are now favelados.

Eight years earlier, my Carioca friend Zita is already warning us about arms in the favelas of Rio.

At time of writing Brasil just elects a new president, Lula. He's considered a radical choice by some people twenty years earlier, like Mitterrand in France before he becomes president.

But some of the elite who I meet in Brasil at that time are considering voting for him as the next step, after electing Brizola in the first entirely free gubernatorial elections since the coup d'état of 18 year earlier.

...

At the beginning of what becomes <u>Terrian Journals</u>, during my first months in Brasil the military dictatorship permits gubernatorial and other elections.

In Rio de Janeiro the results arrive slowly.

One television network news broadcast deliberately delays reporting the victory of the non-military-inclined candidate for governor of Rio, while others are declaring him winner. That's Brizola.

Today, tens of years and many elections later, the results of the direct presidential elections in Brasil are being counted and reported very rapidly.

Polls close at 5 p.m. (Brasil time) and the results are reported very quickly. Within three hours more than 79% of the ballots are counted.

Within four hours the leading candidate almost reaches the percentage of votes necessary to win the election in the first round, which would eliminate the need for a run-off vote.

The relative closeness of the vote count, ranging from one to five percent (more than 5 million votes) in this early counting, surprises me because news reports pre-election public opinion polls with a widening lead for the leading candidate, Lula.

He's returning to politics, like Joe Biden in the U.S., because an incompetent and foolish person becomes president after Lula retires from politics.

The departing president of Brasil, like his model Punchline in the U.S., denies climate change, COVID-19, and his electoral defeat.

Consequently, there are a multitude of preventable deaths and surviving virus victims with long-term aftereffects.

In the absence of decisive action against the destruction of the planetary human life-support system, climate change accelerates and worsens.

Mob violence in Brasilia, egged on by the defeated candidate also copies post-election violence at the U.S. capital.

...

**Miyazaki**: An opinion article in the English language edition of The Japan Times, written by the head of the United Nations University in Tokyo, attracts my attention.

The article is titled, "Politics of human migrations". It starts by saying that 20% of Canadian workers are born outside of Canada.

I write to the person who writes the item, but get no acknowledgement or reply. Ignoring letters must be a perk of the elite job.

After a paragraph thanking him for writing his article, this is what I write to him:

Given the strong evidence supporting migration in your article, and the unpleasant consequences of opposing the historic, long-term natural flow of humans around the globe, it's surprising that G8 nation-state leaders are not taking the initiative in educating themselves, the elite, and the majority of their people, while they still have the opportunity to help mould the future.

...

News reports say Tokyo is having an unusually cool summer. The weather is "unusual" everywhere I go while writing Terrian Journals.

Miyazaki is having some refreshingly cooler days too.

After a cool, rainy spring, summer fluctuates to a cool 23°C in mid-July. It rains for more than 10 days. But most days are more than 30°C.

There are some more amazingly cooler days of 24°C the following month, normally the hottest time of year.

...

As usual, I'm here for the elections, just as I am in so many other countries during these Terrian Journals.

Nippon's prime minister goes through a pre-election publicity stunt about challenges to his leadership of the party-in-power.

Despite loud-mouthed challenges, his leadership is reinstated by a landslide at the party convention.

After focusing news media attention on his party and his overwhelming support as leader, it's time to call an election. What a happy coincidence for the party-in-power.

He also decides to show that he's trying to get rid of the oldsters who always dominate his party.

The ancient politicians rule from the back rooms as if they're part of the old regimes in the CCCP and Chuang Hwa.

Two members of parliament in their 80s, key leaders in party affairs and former prime ministers, are asked to retire. One of them is Nakasone, the former prime minister.

He's still there!

I'm only impressed by the proportional representation system that is part of Nippon's politics. It's a system that's sorely needed in Canada's federal and provincial parliaments.

In the current lower house elections of Nippon, there are 300 seats filled by voting in geographically-based electoral districts. The remaining 180 seats are decided by proportional representation voting.

Proportional representation in Canada would prevent the nutty splinter parties in federal politics, such as Alberta's American Alliance and Québec's Blocheads, from having many more seats than their votes merit.

Alberta and Québec members of parliament would represent a far broader and more varied cross section of political opinion in those provinces, instead of giving too many kooks too big a voice in making decisions for Canadians.

The only flaw in the proportional representation system used in Nippon is that a candidate can lose a riding but win a proportional seat.

...

A couple, him 41 and her 45, decide to have a royal wedding reception and turn it into a fundraiser.

The couple makes the news because they're bigger fakers than most monarchs. They're pretending to be relatives of the monarchs in Nippon.

They send out invitations, dress royally, and collect 12 million yen in gift money.

Unfortunately for the couple, there event is considered fraud. They're arrested and charged for that crime.

...

According to the U.S. ABC News broadcast of Canadian Peter Jennings, the office of U.S. president moron modifies reports from the U.S. EPA (Environmental Protection Agency) about problems needing attention.

All reference in the reports to "global warming" and the need to do something about it are eliminated and replaced with the phrase, "climate change needs more study",

(Ironically, climate change sticks and is more appropriate.)

...

Nuclear weapons are only the best known and most obvious enemies of the environment and all life.

While public attention focuses on nuclear weapons, the environmental costs of non-nuclear weapons go unnoticed, unreported, unrecorded, and unremedied.

News stories about 23 years of bombing and megabombing in south-western Asia fail to mention the bombs' impact on seismic plates in this region known for tragic earthquakes.

All types of bombs are bad for the environment.

...

Television reporters in Nippon, Hangoo, and Iraq equate cars to development and progress.

North Korea's economic problems are said to be evident due to the absence of cars.

Iraq's improvement and economic advancement under the U.S. military occupation is shown by more cars.

So pollution, toxic fumes health hazards are measures of improvement. Really!?

**Gatineau**: Canada's prime minister calls an election. He walks across the street from his official residence to the park and strolls quickly to where we await, beside the news media camping in front of the Rideau Hall building.

Security guards protecting the prime minister get surrounded by the general public who are enjoying the day, picnicking like us or playing ball in the gardens.

It's a democratic experience, a democracy walk.

We're standing in the crowd and alongside it when this news event occurs.

Somehow, in the jailkeeper society, we can still step over the rope barrier and approach both the political and media elite in Canada. It's hope.

This is Paul Martin. The next prime minister is surrounded by body guards.

...

My would-be Canada Day contribution to a major Canadian newspaper in Toronto never appears because the person I offer it to a month and a half in advance doesn't get around to saying it doesn't arrive at the paper until it's too late to re-send it.

She waits until Canada Day eve.

She fails to reply to my resends and messages until it's too late, after I call her collect. Then she says the paper has to make other arrangements.

Of course it does not. So much for communicating inside the communications media.

Meanwhile, I get two cash offers for my writing, subject to acceptance, from two small weekly papers in Florida, both apologizing for their small offers because they too are small.

But they do want my items, the ones I describe as inspired by Mike Collins of the Apollo 11 lunar landing crew of 35 years earlier.

The items are my way of introducing some Terrian Journals

concepts and planting some interest in my writing abroad.

One of these papers also makes a last minute request for the items I already send it well in advance.

But after reading my articles they turn them down on the grounds that they don't include an interview with the astronaut. I make no claim that there'll be an interview.

Besides, if I had an interview, I wouldn't be offering it to small papers with little ability to pay. I'd be asking for a big sum from a big newspaper.

The editors of the small papers must be stupid or they assume that I am.

...

I'm also working on publishing Terrian Journals as a syndicated column.

It's an interesting exercise in rewriting some of the earliest Terrian Journals and a sampling of more recent ones.

It's another opportunity to spread my ideas and help to awaken the sleeping G8 citizenry.

The Internet makes it easier and saves me a fortune in paper, envelopes, and postage.

But the editor of one large daily newspaper corporation says that he and most editors prefer writing submissions on paper, not via e-mail.

When I write back advocating using the latest technology he relents, but still only sends a flattering form letter by e-mail to say he won't accept my syndicated column.

Initially, I send my proposal to mainly weekly community newspapers.

I write personalized letters to certain editors in towns in Canada, the U.K., the U.S., and

Australia, places that I know in passing as a visitor or resident.

Two Canadians reply within a day or two.

I find one while checking e-mail at Arctic College and Iqaluit public library. They enjoy my work but only want local material.

I also approach a Canadian syndicate which likes my writing. But it can't find enough papers to make money on my work. Poor baby.

Another says its publications are "intensely" local. Forget the outside world altogether?

A bimonthly Ottawa paper devoted to peace and the environment publishes a couple of Terrian Journals items that I send to a newspaper in Nippon some months earlier.

Just before sending out backup messages and a general form message, I catch part of a documentary about syndicating comics.

The Superman series, drawn by Canadian Joe Shuster, is rejected by every newspaper in the U.S. before it becomes the premier launching vehicle of a new genre called comic books.

I use that fact to introduce my next mailings.

...

A well-known U.S. news magazine television show is finally catching up with concepts I'm writing long ago in the original Terrian Journals.

The show is interviewing someone who says it's a good idea for younger people to get out of employment for ten years and then return as if there were no gap in their employment.

...

For the "first" world, "third" world life, both at home and abroad, is remote, abstract news.

It can be switched off at the viewers' discretion if the information appears offensive or troubling to "first" worlder children of all ages.

This writing item is inspired by observing reactions to ambulances carrying injured people in the "first" vs. "third" world.

In the "first" world, bystanders watch ambulances from a safe distance, feeling uncomfortable about the unpleasant sight and leaving the work of helping strangers to professionals only, people paid to help people for a living.

In Palestine, as shown in TV news, bystanders seeing an ambulance unloading the injured run alongside stretchers, helping rush them into the hospital.

It's an activist demonstration of valuing life, not a "first" world, theoretical generalization about valuing life.

I can only add that the elite everywhere don't seem to value life anywhere, except their own.

**Miyazaki**: G7/8 and associate state news stories about the current Sumatra tsunami concentrate on the personal human tragedy of the few individual tourists, not the locals.

Huge numbers of local deaths and casualties are only reported as big numbers, like other "third" world tragedies.

Annual disasters in non-tourist spots, at least spots not favoured by tourists from the G8 and associates, are always reserved to news coverage with titles such as "in other news" and "around the world in 60 seconds".

That's just before the special feature report about flipping the world's biggest pancake or on winter clothing to keep dogs and cats warm.

All this "news" is in the "first" world of course.

Human life has so little value in the G8? Or just "third"

world life has so little value in the G8?

My only other lesson from the loss of a quarter of a million non-tourist, non-G8-and-associate-state lives is the need to evacuate threatened people everywhere.

I don't mean the G8 tourists.

...

Many people are sending tonnes of aid in the form of food to people in areas where the Sumatra earthquake and tsunami hit.

The news reports I see show some food having little food value or nutrition.

Senders are perhaps assuming that disaster victims need sugary cookies to give them quick energy to bury the dead, care for the injured, repair the damage, rebuild their homes, and reopen tourist resorts?

Mariko tells me about a specific news story related to foreign victims and aid. The story is in Japanese, broadcast on NHK.

Unfortunately, she only hears the story once and only partially. To date, I'm unable to confirm the details. This is how I feel about the story as I know it.

Having mourned the tourists from the "first" world and having sent aid such as butter cookies to the surviving locals of the "third", the "first" tourists' families are now suing the "third" for "not warning" the "first" tourists in advance about the tsunami.

Is this a new "first" world strategy to keep the majority of the world population under "first" worlder dominance?

The "first" worlders can waste the energies and money of the "third" in the law courts and in paying compensation to the "first".

...

Global warming is already reducing world food supplies, according to NHK news reports.

Warmer temperatures are preventing apple trees from producing fruit and reducing the number of eggs that hens are laying.

...

In Nippon, a place of very long term planning, the monarchists are already worrying about who will be the successor of the current emperor's successor.

These worriers have nothing else to do in their lives?

The complication is that here, as in many other monarchies around Europe, there's a traditional restriction against women.

Only males are legally (regally speaking) entitled and permitted to become chiefs, i.e. kings.

But none of the emperor's grandchildren are males. They're all females.

News reports say the pressure to bear a male child is causing greater stress to the wife of the current emperor's oldest son and successor.

Before marrying the emperor's son and heir, she gives up her career as a leading bureaucrat in Nippon's foreign affairs department.

She's getting some relief from constitutional experts and public opinion, which favours a female heir.

News reports show examples of female monarchs elsewhere, such as the U.K.'s queen.

The irony is that Nippon invents female monarchs long ago. According to legend, Nippon's first monarch is an empress.

It's also a distant issue.

The current emperor's granddaughter is unlikely to become the monarch for another 20 to 30 years, if there are monarchs anywhere in the world then.

More than a year later, a younger prince has the imperial family's first male baby. It replaces the granddaughter as the eventual heir.

Male sovereignty is preserved and all talk of sexual equality comes to an abrupt halt. Aren't men lovely! Aren't men radiant!

...

Another NHK story, one I have yet to confirm, is about the U.K. in the context of this made-in-U.S.A. age of terror, when the caretaker society is turning into the jailkeeper society.

The jailkeeper society is getting more deeply entrenched.

The U.K. is thus aligning and allying itself with Euroreligionism's beliefs in "the fall of man", i.e. we are all guilty at birth.

According to this religionism, our crime is being born human and then showing no remorse for it.

Our punishment is apparently the eternal damnation of spending our lives confined in the nation-states, to control our "bad by nature" behaviour.

The U.K. parliament has decided it's all right to implant GPS (global positioning satellite) sensors in the bodies of any person suspected of terrorism who is released because of insufficient evidence to lay criminal charges or to prosecute the suspect(s).

So bye-bye legal system, as in the film "Pra Frente Brasil". Anyone can be treated like a criminal, even completely innocent people. They're not criminals "yet".

Under the old rules, these GPS-implanted people would have

to be arrested for committing a crime, legally charged with the crime, considered innocent until proven guilty, and finally tried and convicted of committing the crime before the nation-state could do anything to them.

Once convicted, they would be sentenced by a judge. Then they would be put in a jail or prison for a fixed term, which could be altered or unaltered later on.

People found guilty of a crime would never be implanted with anything.

If their crimes were minor, they could face restrictions on their movements.

Those restrictions could be enforced by obliging them to wear a wrist or ankle bracelet tracking device.

It would verify that the convicted never go outside of a specific geographic location.

Under the new rules, the nation-state can go straight to the last step, making sure the uncharged, untried, and unconvicted suspect never moves beyond a specific geographic location.

The U.K. legal system is based on creating precedents, i.e. current decisions are based on past decisions, ad infinitum.

So, if a court decides that implants are legal for terror suspects now, it's creating a legal precedent for putting implants inside any and all suspects of all crimes in the future.

Extend this precedent to any behaviour considered "suspicious" because and only because it is uncommon or unconventional. "Report all suspicious behaviour."

The result is the ultimate police state legal system.

Forget the minor disruptions of the anti-communist witch hunts in the U.S. during the Cold War.

Forget the minor disruptions of the Inquisitions during the European era.

Forget all the holocausts and genocides of the past.

They're just mild temporary problems compared with a permanent change in the way the U.K. legal system and similar systems could eventually treat all suspects, all non-conformists, all unconventional people, all writers, all artists, and all imaginative, creative, questioning, unorthodox, rebellious people, and anyone else making vital contributions to human progress.

...

Japan Post's banking section is so good that it's overflowing with money from depositors. They run to Japan Post due to bad news reports about the private banks.

So why is the government of Nippon now intent on abandoning Japan Post and turning the postal service into a non-government, non-public-owned entity?

Why meddle with perfection?

The reason given: to make it a profitable banking institution. But if Japan Post's banking section becomes a private company it might have the same problems as the other private banks. Bad idea.

...

Nippon has the longest life expectancy in the world, 82 years at time of writing.

...

Yamanashi Prefecture records the highest temperature so far this year, 30°C, just as the cher-ry blossom season is peaking.

It's amazing, completely out of season. Fukuoka hits 24°C the next day.

...

Somewhere in Nippon, (I miss the place name), the pollen is so thick that firefighters are called in to find out whether there's actually a forest fire.

...

In Europe, Pope John-Paul II finally dies at 84, after 27 years in the job. He travels a lot, does some good, but fails to support women's rights. I glimpse him in Djakarta.

...

Chuang Hwa–Nippon relations are in the news. There are anti-Nippon demonstrations in Chuanga Hwa. Why?

There's anger about rocks, a chair, history, and nothing at all.

Chuang Hwa and Nippon both want the same tiny chunks of unsubmerged rock sticking out of the ocean. Nippon wants a permanent seat on the U.N. Security Council.

Chuang Hwa still holds a grudge against Nippon for a war ending 60 years earlier. Yet Nippon allies with the U.S., the nation-state that atomic bombs Nippon.

Chuang Hwa demonstrators know almost none of the above.

None are old enough to even remember the year of my first steps into Chuang Hwa, long after the big war of Mao's time.

The demonstrators are too young to know and probably not descended directly from any of the victims of the massacres by Nippon's long gone imperial forces in Chuang Hwa.

People shouting in the streets of Chuang Hwa today are nothing like the Madres de Mayo at Buenos Aires' Casa Rosa, risking their lives against a ruthless military dictatorship in the past.

The Chuang Hwa demonstrators are not survivors of Tienanmen Square.

So the Chuang Hwa dictators must be simply using state-organized demonstrations to convey a message directly to Nippon's youngest generation, who also don't know their nation-state's past ill deeds of long before their birth.

...

I see an item in the news, write to someone I don't know, get a reply, and change plans about what I'll do next.

My life truly depends on what's in the news and what I get in the mail.

**Jasper**: Nelson Mandela is featured in a world anti-poverty campaign television commercial.

A large letter message says eight million people will die of extreme poverty each year around the world.

Then the local news comes on again, calling the death of eight horses in Calgary a tragedy.

**Van Couverden**: News of Enoch Powell, the U.K.'s Le Pen of years past, tells me there's much abuse directed against U.K. newcomers with family roots in Pakistan and Jamaica for many years.

So it shouldn't surprise anyone if the young U.K.ers who bomb public transit in London are of Pakistani and Jamaican origin.

They come from families of people who are made to feel unwelcome, unhappy, and undesirable in their adopted homeland.

Their ancestors' homelands are invaded and occupied by the U.K. too. They are forced into subservience at home.

The world eventually responds to abuse from all empires in all times.

Surely the long defunct U.K.'s empire and its misdeeds, including more recent ones alluded to in my dad's letters from Bharat, along with the behaviours of the U.K. society for generations toward newcomers, don't make Londoners "innocent victims" of bombers any more than their U.S. heirs and successors.

...

My own delusions about being a person of great value and worth when I first step into the southern Americas is evidently a widely-shared delusion in the G7/8 and associate states news media.

G7/8 news reporters, editors, publishers, and broadcasters apparently share the inflated, G7/8 value that I give myself.

Everyone from the G7/8 is given similar importance, and the status and treatment going with that kind of group egoism.

The 50 dead and 700 injured in the London bombings are treated the same way as I expect to be treated when I set out for the southern Americas for the first time.

The London victims receive extensive, extended news coverage, including interviews with witnesses, victims' friends and families.

The lost and wounded are "much-loved, special, fine, innocent human beings" who are "cruelly and horribly" murdered and maimed.

Meanwhile, "in other news", "third" world victims of equal and worse violence remain unnamed, unnumbered, and only mentioned in passing when time permits during news broadcasts.

"Third" world tragic deaths are so low in priority, so common, and so frequent that witnesses and survivors are rarely if ever mentioned or interviewed.

If they expect to get attention in the news they must also

speak a widely-known European language, or there must be a voice-over interpreter who is easily available at the scene of events.

At time of writing, annual floods in Chuang Hwa, Bangladesh, and Bharat with dead and homeless numbering in the hundreds of thousands are merely numbers spoken while showing a few scenes, if any, spliced in from local TV news pictures there.

After these brief items, which are no more extensive than superficial and superfluous fillers, the G7/8 news readers carry on as if nothing happens, saying, "In other news…" again, or, "Closer to home…"

Meanwhile, the annual hurricanes in the southern U.S. get top headlines, lead story treatment, and extensive live reports from the scene describing every minute detail for many, many days, with follow-ups and special broadcasts.

These reports tell us about the "terrible, tragic" loss of family homes, luxury housing, and exclusive resorts.

The victims look dismayed and weep in front of the cameras, as they solemnly declare, "We lost everything!" "My G.I. Joe (doll) collection is gone!"

Oh, those poor affluent people; those wretched of the earth millionaires!

Think about what the big insurance companies must be going through in times such as these!

So many preachers will be saying, "Let us remember them in our prayers."

How will they ever survive the hardship! What tough times they will they have to endure!

It may take them as long as one or two years to get back on their feet, to replace the flat screen televisions and computers, to refill their two and three car garages.

Many will have to use their private health insurance plans to pay for private visits to psychologists.

There will be new support groups to organize.

Oh, does this tragedy have no limits!

Perhaps this is a news reporting story where truth and sarcasm truly meet.

After this very brief, barely respectable moment of silence for the losses of the moneyed, the "first" worlders carry on, merrily living on with the underlying belief that ignorance of the outside world is bliss.

In contrast, the unmoneyed vic-tims of U.S. hurricanes are of little consequence, except for gawking, temporary attention, and passing rhetoric.

So many authentically poor people are abandoned, dying of hunger and thirst while pleading, weeping, and shouting "HELP" into the lenses of television news cameras.

The news people bring no water to help?

More than 100,000 unmoneyed refugees are rotting in a domed (doomed) "super" stadium with clogged toilets and a broken air circulating system.

They have no food and water for nearly five days – turning to looting, guns everywhere, police overwhelmed, unmoneyed screaming into an abundant number of TV cameras – begging for help.

Results: U.S. emperor moron flies over and lands outside the city, hugging and comforting luxury home and resort owners.

This is perhaps and almost surely the beginning of the first massive popular insurrection in U.S. history?

Eventually the desperate U.S. home grown refugees attract too much attention in the news, so they are whisked away in charter buses and dispersed across the land.

Once dispersed they become too small and insignificant in numbers to merit any further mention in the daily news.

They're taken to widespread shelters including another big sports stadium far away from the hurricane site, where they can be left until the news coverage dies out.

Then they can be put out in the streets to fend for themselves, to be ignored and forgotten, just like their counterparts in the foreign "third" world.

When ratings drop, the news reporters pack up and are sent to the next big story.

About 1,000 people are killed in the U.S. hurricane but more than 26,000 are killed in Kashmir's earthquake this same year.

Remember the Indonesian Sumatra tsunami story? It's a big news event only because a few G7/8 tourists are killed.

When the major quake strikes Kashmir, a short time after the U.S. hurricane, there's also lots of news, for a while.

The "first" world newsrooms are probably shamed into covering the Kashmir story because it happens so soon after the U.S. hurricane.

Normally, only affluent, "first" worlder victims of natural disasters and the offensive reality of rare and sensational "first" world events, such as the London Olympic bombings, intrude to shock in "first" worlders' news reports.

Apart from these anomalies, the "values" of the "first" worlders can remain little and small.

The London bombings shock and awe but don't profoundly stun the lifelong stunned "first" worlder.

...

The story of the latest world humanitarian crisis will eventu-ally disappear from the daily news, as the short, limited attention span of the news media expires.

The news editors and publishers get bored with covering one story for more than a couple of days.

Then the news gatekeepers reassign their reporters to move on to the next big, breaking* news story. (*Coverage of old stories is broken by new ones.)

The lack of substantial change and improvement in the general world situation for the majority of humanity indicates that most "first" worlders, especially the cocooning full time mothers, are not developing an effective consciousness of the outside world.

"First" worlders are not getting more stimulated, motivated, or catalysed into positive and decisive action due to a growing bad conscience about the state of the world.

What little they know of the world is coming from casually following news stories and making token charitable contributions.

This lack of consciousness and lack of enduring conscience is particularly apparent in full time mothers.

They can't cope with anything that might place a bigger burden on their lives than their own children.

The outside world cannot be permitted to intrude upon or interfere with the childcare world at home.

This is the most significant, all absorbing and all effacing global tragedy of full-time mothers' second childhood.

...

A Canadian television news report says that toxic exhaust fumes from cars now kill thousands of people every year in the Greater Toronto Area.

This report includes an interview with a car driver who seems to reflect and sum up the true G7/8/"first" worlder public attitude and action/reaction to human and world problems in general.

Here's my undistorted, factual paraphrase of the TV news interview:

News Reporter (asking car driver questions): "Did you know that smog from car exhaust fumes kills thousands of people in the GTA every year?"

Car Driver: "No."

News Reporter: "Now that you know that, will you stop driving your car tomorrow, to save lives?"

Car Driver: "Sure." (Then, as he's driving off he says,) "I'm just kidding. I'll be driving tomorrow."

So the "first" worlders are also "just kidding" about their concern for the rest of the world, inside and outside?

Life must be cheap. It must have a very low value in the "first" world.

Like the Toronto driver in the news, the fuel addicts care about no one.

The fuel price rises inflate all the other prices too, making all living costs go up, increasing poverty and hunger everywhere.

But drivers' loudest complaints are about rising fuel prices, not the plight of people who can't even afford to buy vehicles and who must always worry about food and shelter.

Driving motor vehicles using petroleum products is a substance abuse problem and a crime against humanity.

It's abusing yourself along with everyone and everything around you with petroleum as a non-medical drug.

Considering the "first" world's priorities, "values", and disinterest in the rest of the world, where 80% of humanity live, no wonder some people might turn to violence against the "first" worlders without any remorse.

...

At time of writing, the new Arab language news networks, such as Aljazeera, are beginning to fill a news gaps for the multitudes with this language skill.

But, for a very long time billions of other people in the "third" world have no such voice to fill gaps and to counter the single (empire) perspective news of events.

Aljazeera's next move is to start an English-language news network to broaden the perspectives of anglophone "first" worlders.

Of course the "freedom-of-speech" preaching G7/8 nation-states want to discredit and restrict access to this alternative news service.

But Aljazeera hires respected veteran news people, such as the U.K.'s David Frost.

**Buenos Aires**: We watch Kobe burning from Buenos Aires, on a local television news station, after the Great Kansei Earthquake. Our visit to Argentina is about to end.

The broadcast is in Spanish, but there's also a report from an English-language station in Germany. The German announcer says, "No looting is reported."

Of course not. It would never happen in Nippon.

The German news service must be imagining what would happen in the U.S. or Europe, with their imperial history of invading and looting around the world.

After a category 4 hurricane destroys Nouvelle-Orléans (U.S.A.), starving survivors don't even have water to drink.

The aftermath of disaster in Nippon is quite different.

In Niigata, news is showing supermarkets handing out free water and food to people shaken from their homes.

At least one convenience store chain is delivering truckloads of food supplies free of charge to shelters, etc. in Niigata.

Thus, in a generous, honest culture, looting is unnecessary. Humanity is put ahead of monetary profits.

**Toronto**: The Niigata quake shuts down a car parts company serving Nippon's major motor vehicle manufacturers.

The story is reported in the Toronto local news, saying that Toyotas might be slower getting to Canadian buyers.

All the motor vehicle manufacturers of Nippon depend on the Niigata parts maker. So it's getting top priority in restoring power and water services.

Furthermore, Toyota is sending in 200 of its employees to help the parts maker get back to work.

Altogether, the motor vehicle makers send in 700 of their employees to help out.

That's why the plant is back in service within only seven days, instead of months or years.

**Ottawa**: Canada's history-making news goes virtually unnoticed in Canadian news reports.

Canada becomes the first "first" world G7 nation-state with a "third" world official resident head of state. She's Michaëlle Jean.

She's from a background and lifetime of slavery, hardship, and struggle.

No previous governors, few Canadians, and few "first" worlders alive today have that kind of background.

She knows what it's like to live under rulers much like the absolute monarchs of European history.

She's born in the "third" world under one of the modern blood-thirsty dictators in Haiti, the natural heirs of the old mon-archs.

She arrives in Canada as a real refugee with no material wealth to leave behind. She grows up as the child of a single-parent family, not a diplomat.

She's also not a Euroface, unlike most of her predecessors, and she hasn't lost her identity or a sense of her origins.

She's the first "third" world person in history to become a head of state of a G7/8 country.

Europeans kidnap her ancestors and bring them to the Americas as slaves. It's miraculous that her ancestors live enabling her to be born generations later.

No descendants of the same slaves in the U.S. ever become the U.S. head of state, at time of writing. None are nominated. This is just before Obama.

Michaëlle Jean's first speech in parliament brings her close friends almost to tears. Me too.

But mine are because the "third" world message and lessons that I begin learning in Rio are finally getting a voice in this ignorant zone of the world, the G7/8 and associate states.

Canada's new official head of state is speaking from her heart and saying much for all to know and learn.

It's an opportunity for the "first" worlders to save themselves from themselves.

But news reports are ignoring all this, making me incredulous.

...

News focuses on Remembrance Day in Canada.

It's a day that always touches me. For me it's about the futility of war, the waste of young lives, whether wounded, killed, maimed, or only deprived of years of their youth.

All these consequences are sad. I hold back tears.

Today it's 60 years since the biggest war of the recent past ends, years before I'm born.

It's a celebration finale in sombre memories.

Unfortunately, it's marred by a few ex-soldiers who decide their prejudices against the titular, ceremonial, Canadian head of state take precedence over mourning and remembering.

Twenty-five bigots in veterans' uniforms stand out for TV news crews in a crowd of 25,000 people who are standing ten deep around the war memorial.

(It should be called The Peace Memorial.)

The 25 arrive at the memorial much earlier than everyone else so they can hog a central spot.

Canada's "third" worlder resident official head of state arrives in a government limousine just before the ceremonies begin. Everyone turns to face her.

But one of the 25 shouts, "About face!" which is military dialect for turn around so your back faces frontward.

The same order and act is repeated as Canada's official resident head of state goes to place a wreathe at the base of the monument.

Talking to news reporters later, she says she doesn't notice the 25. Probably not. That's good.

At first I think it's simply annoyingly pitiful. Present day "yellow journalism".

Anglomaniac and Péquist racist dogma and propaganda easily manipulate some older people too.

Then one Canadian news network shows closer details.

A spokesperson for the 25 says they "believe, er know" the governor-general supports the break-up of Canada by "violent separatism".

The spokesperson says the 25 are using the freedom of speech they fought for in battle.

But other war veterans say it's a day for remembering fallen soldiers, not playing politics.

Zoom in further – A younger person, the age of a veteran's grandchild and my dad in war, a youth of maybe 20, says very politely to the 25 near him, "I think this is inappropriate."

A television reporter says that apparently the freedom of speech doesn't apply to the younger person because of what happens next.

One of the 25 says, "If you don't want to be near me, go away! I fought for the right to be here. You didn't!"

This sounds familiar. Military dictators say they're protecting liberty, so anything goes for them alone.

The younger person takes off the symbolic plastic poppy that he's wearing, representing respect for the war dead and other veterans who contribute to wars.

...

I hear former U.S. president Jimmy Carter telling a news

reporter that Venezuela's President Chavez practices a pure form of democracy.

Is that why the U.S. cons and their elite moneyed allies in Venezuela want to overthrow Chavez?

News reports say that in Venezuela today only 5% of the population owns 75 % of all the land. About 83% of the people live below the poverty level.

Chavez wants to fix these prob-lems, to give the majority rule over and access to land and wealth.

That makes him a "dangerous, radical communist" according to the U.S. cons and their elite allies.

So the majority of the world population must be like Chavez.

The cons will need to bomb almost everyone, everywhere, to maintain the "first" world's elite minority world rule.

Democratic majority rule over the world would be "communism"?

Chavez also has a new "wild-eyed radical" policy of requiring Venezuela radio stations to play Venezuelan music 50% of their air time.

U.S. news reports this idea as if it were an extraordinary act.

Nobody in the news rooms knows that Canada creates this policy more than 30 years before Chavez for the same reason as Venezuela. U.S. music is washing out Canada.

Ironically, U.S. music is later dominated by Céline Dion, Shania Twain, K.D. Lang, Alannis Morisette, Avril Lavigne, and other Canadians.

The "wild-eyed radical" policy of Canada made that possible. Otherwise, those famous singers might be unknown today.

**Dyingtown**: When I go to the local newspaper editor to ask about submitting articles, he asks a reporter to interview Mariko and me for a story about our plans here.

The reporter asks a lot of questions, takes our picture, and writes a very friendly story about us. There is only one minor error in fact.

The reporter makes an audio recording of our interview.

The editor also asks me to send him samples of my writing, but never responds when I do.

This is a minor weekly paper editor in a tiny town, not a huge city editor.

The lack of response is typical of almost every small paper I contact in Canada, except for one that requests I send in an item about her town.

I know almost nothing about her town, so I have nothing to write about it. The same applies to Dyingtown.

That doesn't mean I can't cover local events now and again, but not without a reply from the editor.

At least I get a month's free subscription to that paper from the local "Welcome Wagon".

Some far away weekly newspapers reply that they're "intensely local", when I send them my writing for syndication.

Yet I'm sure they do use non-local syndicated features as filler.

**Miyazaki**: A new media company called "Live Door" dominates the news in Nippon, as it does the previous year.

Then it's about a young local entrepreneur with overseas partners seeking to buy up media shares here.

The company is hailed by its head and the party-in-power here as a new way of doing business in Nippon, more bold, daring, and brash.

This annoys the older business people.

This year's news is different. Now "Live Door" is getting exposed for stock market and profit fraud. The head and his associates are going to jail.

The older business people feel much better. The party-in-power is embarrassed.

...

The second biggest news story is about U.S. government stupidity.

Nippon closes its markets to U.S. beef a few years earlier because of mad cow (B.S.E.) contamination of U.S. beef.

The U.S. government negotiates and promises to tightly control all beef shipments to Nippon. So the market re-opens.

The first shipment of U.S. beef violates the agreement.

**Crysler's Farm**: News becomes a means of taking people's minds further away from their humanity whenever it's dominated by the distractions of fluff, features, sports, and commercials.

They work just as effectively as any military drum for an historic battle reenactment. It's all show without the realities of actual war battlefields.

**Ottawa**: Jogjakarta, a place I visit on a few occasions while living in and travelling through Indonesia, is the site of a tragedy somewhat milder than the one hitting Sumatra more than a year ago.

A 6.4 quake hits Jogjakarta, killing more than 6,400 people, injuring many more, and leaving many others homeless, without potable water, and in danger of being infected by disease.

Meanwhile, the local CBC television station in Ottawa features uncritical wedding spending stories in its daily news for several days.

Canadian families are spending $25,000 and more on these social events. The cakes alone cost more than $1,000.

In one feature news report, the TV station reveals, without a blink, that some Canadians pay as much as $600,000 for a wedding.

At the time of this "news" story, that sum is greater than the average cost of a house, even in Van Couverden and Toronto.

One person says her daughter's wedding will cost $100,000.

This mother says, without remorse, smiling with unhidden sentimentality, exuberance, and enthusiasm, "It's worth it!"

I don't make up these stories. Really. She actually says exactly those words. She exclaims them without hesitation.

Does she mean it's worth starvation, disease, and death around the outside world, outside the wedding world?

Of course not. What "first" worlder would be that conscious of world reality?

So the basic question is this: How many injured, sick, and dead people and how many homeless, impoverished lives are the "first" worlders and their excesses worth?

How much longer will the outside world continue to tolerate the "first" world? For some in the "third" world, the limit is already long past.

In the simplest terms, to paraphrase one desk clerk we meet in Lima a few years earlier, people can know what's going on in the outside world if they want to find out.

Then they can act upon it in positive ways.

Apparently, the "first" worlders aren't really interested in doing much beyond passively watching the TV news and documentaries.

Apparently, the "first" worlders aren't interested in doing anything besides dropping some coins and bills into a charity box. That's the most action they want to take.

...

I know it's nothing new, but is the contrast between news of the outside world and the trivial "first" worlder news becoming stronger?

Is the "first" world ignorance, ignoring the entire "third" world getting worse?

I'm noticing it more in Canada during my most recent visits and living as a newcomer experiences.

I'm getting the impression that I could take almost any daily newspaper from almost anywhere in the G7/8, in any language I can read, and find there are more pages devoted to the trivial than to global humanity.

Most reporting, editing, and reading is not being devoted to what humanity's doing, what's happening to it, and what it could attempt and accomplish if the earth's resources were not being mindlessly dominated, exhausted, contaminated, polluted, squandered, and destroyed by the "first" world.

Most radio and television broadcasting fares much worse than newspapers.

Their roles in communication, their signals, and their content grow fainter, more vacuous, and emptier.

Their waves of sounds and images drift into specialties and vagueness, then disappear.

Fewer and fewer people tune in and notice the vanishing waves, until a permanent low tide settles over the terrain once covered by both radio and television.

Newer communications technologies seem to be determined to abandoning communication altogether, while claiming they're improving it.

They're devoted almost entirely to merchandising, advertising, and very idle entertainment.

The only human communication that the newer technologies are carrying are some letters, diary entries, gossip, unsupported opinion, etc., along with prejudices and other dehumanizing messages.

Newspapers, radio, and television are also replicated, with the same results as printing presses and broadcasting media.

Newer technology is a net that the "first" world spins around itself, a cocoon of oblivion instead of a temporary vessel for evolving into a beautiful new life for the whole world to enjoy.

I suppose it's better for the "first" world to go this way, putting itself down gently and quietly like it's own favourite house pet, instead of using the huge arsenal of total world destruction weapons that the G7/8 insanely manufactures and stockpiles for far too many years.

...

Canada's spy agency, CSIS, in co-operation with the Toronto and Ontario police and others, suddenly announces the arrest of 17 people in southern Ontario.

CSIS alleges that the suspects plan to use many tonnes of fertilizer to blow up some famous buildings and attack public transit passengers.

The details, exact targets, etc. are not revealed. With all the new secrecy and "security" laws, we may never know exactly why the arrests take place, or anything about the evidence.

We might only find out about the final results of the trials.

Only the lawyers hired by the 17 are revealing the charges and conditions under which their clients are imprisoned while awaiting trial.

I write the previous paragraph soon after the news of the arrests is reported.

A few days later, when I insert this paragraph, the government imposes a ban on all news reporting of the trials. I'm right in my concerns.

As the police state grows, the secrecy and propaganda increase until no one knows what's going on and anyone can be arrested, tried, and convicted, or secretly imprisoned indefinitely without anyone finding out anything about what's really happening.

People are already being imprisoned, indefinitely and without due process, under Canada's "security certificates".

News reports say the CIA, a major U.S. spy agency, is running secret prisons in various countries.

People who are never charged or tried are being held in a U.S. prison in Guantanamo, Cuba for years.

It reminds me of the old European monarchical dictatorships and modern military dictatorships, which arbitrarily and randomly kidnap, torture, murder, and imprison anyone at whim.

This is not supposed to be a legal activity in a democratically-inclined system of government.

The GTA plot leads to a special Canadian news documentary from Europe.

The programme is puzzling over racism there and asking whether multiculturalism is good or bad.

The reporter says European governments are deciding to implement policies of forced integration (acculturation).

The reporter is unaware that human beings are multicultural? The whole planet is multicultural.

I phone the news department to make some comments. I say I'm wondering why the reporter is surprised about racism in Europe.

I remind him about anti-Pakistani and anti-Jamaican racist politics in the U.K. 35 years earlier.

Then I say that Europe has been trying to "integrate" the world for 700 years.

I list major examples, such as the inquisitions against Jews, Moslems, and non-Catholic Christians, as well as the conquistadores, the crusaders, and the holocaust.

I add that in Canada we create the Indian Act, (to eliminate the First Nations' cultures and languages) and start residential schools (to implement the act).

We also intern people of Ukrainian, Italian, and Japanese origin. We have the Chinese Exclusion laws too.

I conclude by saying that anti-multiculturalism is nothing new in Europe or Canada.

The only difficulty I'm facing is that the newsroom ignores comments that come from people who don't have telephone numbers. I don't have a phone.

So freedom of speech means you have to pay money to a phone company?)

Only the former Canadian "security" minister, Ralph Goodale, defeated in the recent election, seems to allude to the causes of "terrorism" I mention, by making a passing comment about "marginalization" of people inside Canada.

...

News-related interviews and special reports are speculating that "terrorism" is spreading through people using the internet to share information about how to make bombs and how to attack people.

Conclusion- the internet needs to be monitored and controlled by the "security" forces, i.e. secret police.

The same can be said for schools, universities, and books in the public library.

Science courses and books provide information about chemistry, electronics, etc. that can be used in bomb making.

Decades ago news reports say people can learn how to make a nuclear bomb by reading library books.

There are also fiction and non-fiction books about how to commit murders, how to kidnap and torture people, etc.

"Terrorists" could read Sherlock Holmes or the stories of survivors of concentration camps and military dictatorships.

The only way to stop some people from learning about one thing is to stop all people from learning everything.

...

One news story says the 17 "terrorist" suspects in Toronto give up their alleged plans to storm parliament hill because none of them knows much about the national capital.

So they're typical Canadians.

Members of parliament are meeting to talk about how they

can make parliament hill safer, for themselves.

Where do I hear that before? Oh yes, from military dictatorships saying they're "protecting the constitution".

In fact, they're only protecting themselves from the general public.

One Canadian member of parlia-ment, an alleged "liberal" and brother of the current premier of Ontario, seems delirious on television as he decries the current lack of security on parliament hill.

He says he's complaining about it for years.

He's talking about all the things I see as merits on that hill, i.e. anyone can walk up to the parliament buildings, play games on the lawn, read books, picnic, etc.

It's clear evidence that the government and its buildings belong to the citizens, not to a cloistered elite.

So if the government tries to destroy democracy, the public can easily storm the buildings and rescue democracy from would-be dictators.

The same thing goes for the building where the security-obsessed member's brother works in Toronto, along with all the other provincial capitals in Canada.

The paranoid member of parliament seems to want to hamper or block public access to public buildings, i.e. to create a sense of dictatorship in Ottawa, to replace the strong sense of democracy created by open public access to the buildings where elected representatives work.

Frankly, if anyone wants to blow up Canada's parliament buildings and kill all the current members of parliament that act will be murder and destruction of public property.

But it will not destroy Canada's system of government.

The governor-general can call new elections to replace the dead members of parliament. The general public can vote in defiance of the attackers.

The electoral system of Canada doesn't depend on a building, a bureaucracy, or the people we happen to elect to serve us for a few years.

If the government wants to create a fortress system to protect all the buildings it considers important, it has to put the military along the Ottawa River and Rideau Canal.

Parliament hill, ministry headquarters, research facilities, the Museum of Civilization, and at least three G7/8 foreign embassies are located on or near these public waterways.

The prime minister's residence is there too.

They are easy targets, sitting ducks.

So, if parliament hill has to become a fortress, with very restricted public access, the military would also have to fortify and guard all the water-ways.

Rideau Canal and Dows Lake would have to be closed to non-military watercraft.

The yacht club and pleasure craft docks on the Ottawa River would have to be relocated far downstream on the Ottawa River.

The area from Chaudière Falls to a spot many kilometres south of Pointe Gatineau would be a "no sail zone" for non-military watercraft.

All tour boats and pleasure craft would be banned there. Only military gunboats would be allowed to sail within the zone.

There would be sandbags on the water's edge, and in all the

public parklands and walkways beside all of the rivers in Ottawa-Gatineau, and along Rideau Canal.

It would be like the street corners in downtown Buson and Seoul, especially under the former military dictatorship there.

The scenic playground of Ottawa's waterways would become like the beautiful beaches along Hangoo's northwest coast.

The former military dictatorship closes those beaches to the public and puts barriers along the shore, like the ones used by a European nasty regime during the European war that ends more than 60 years earlier.

The Canadian military could put up guard houses and gun emplacements, and position snipers and heavily armed special forces with combat gear along the water's edge in all the forested public parks of Ottawa.

This military presence in Ottawa would be like the one assigned to guard the courthouse during the preliminary hearing of the 17 people arrested in the Toronto area.

It's a good idea for anyone wishing to eliminate all traces of democratically-elected government in Canada.

...

A newspaper headline reads, "North Korea fires missile". Should we anticipate a lawsuit for unjust dismissal?

...

In related news, 42 years after the U.S. surgeon general reports that nicotine delivery systems kill people, and 32 years after governments admit they know about the health hazards of second-hand smoke, Ontario and Quebec are enacting laws prohibiting nicotine smoking inside and in close proximity to all public places.

How many lives would have been saved if the laws existed 32-42 years earlier?

How much public health spending on preventable diseases would have been avoided for 32-42 years?

The main reason for these laws seems to be that nicotine delivery system makers are losing giant lawsuits and paying compensation to governments for increased health care costs and to individuals for causing diseases and deaths.

A law prohibiting exhaust fumes in all public places seems even more appropriate than the anti-nicotine smoke laws.

So do law suits against the manufacturers of air polluting motor vehicle engines and the companies drilling, refining, and selling air polluting motor vehicle fuels.

These will be the next great battles to improve public health and to prevent murder by motor vehicle exhaust fumes.

**Miyazaki**: My logic proves to be sound, but already successfully argued by others in a court of law in Tokyo, ten years before I write.

At that time, people suffering from asthma start just a lawsuit here in Nippon. The judge is now ruling in their favour.

The governor of the Tokyo region is agreeing to pay the victims compensation.

The car makers and national government are also named in the law suit. But they're reluctant to pay the compensation recommended by the judge.

**Ottawa**: Television news reports that a seven year old boy losses both his legs in a water park accident. Negligence charges are pending. We now go live to the park.

A 15 minute report follows. That's half the news cast time. Interviews, analysis, concerns about safety, security laws covering water parks – no angle is missing.

Go to commercial.

In other news, more than 200 people are killed in train bombings in Mumbai (formerly called Bombay), Bharat.

The greatest tragedy is the editorial decision on the news lineup order.

The exposed myth is that people in the "first" world place a higher value on human life than do people in "third" world Bharat. One of "ours" is worth more than 200 of "theirs".

...

While all this is going on, thousands of Canadians are having a great deal of trouble getting evacuated from Lebanon.

The Canadian embassy in Beirut follows its ministry's usual bureaucratic procedures, having people fill out forms instead of simply accepting their passports.

The Canadians are herded into a port area. After waiting for many, very long days outdoors, in the torrid, summer air, they're becoming increasingly frustrated and angry.

Canadian television news reports their very poor situation for days.

The people waiting are interviewed, weeping and sputtering out words of how desperate they are for help from Canada.

Finally some tiny boats take away a few hundred people. Eventually much larger vessels arrive.

The first people to sail find their boat lacks food and water for its journey of more than a day. The toilets aren't functioning and aren't cleaned or repaired.

En route, Yisra'eli military ships delay the boat for hours.

There are no protests from Ottawa about the Yisra'eli delaying efforts. The only complaints come from the Canadians getting evacuated.

They're condemning both Canada and Yisra'el.

The Con prime minister of the day picks up about 80 of them and takes them back to Canada in his government plane. The rest wait for other flights arranged by the government.

Arriving in Canada, the Con prime minister says the evacuated Canadians have a rough trip and don't like it.

Then he adds, "but they're happy to be back in Canada", and not upset the way "some news reports" suggest.

...

Most airline passengers interviewed in news reports, as if they're hand picked by the "security experts", are saying they would rather have "security" than death.

They don't realize they're talking in the synonyms of the "security" lingo.

The yearning and hunger for security is insatiable. Power-hungry consume it. Fear is the best fuel.

Civil and human rights are history, rapidly becoming "luxuries" and things truly of the past.

**Miyazaki**: one grandmother mentioned in the news will do anything to help her daughter.

Her daughter is unable to have a baby due to medical reasons, so grandma becomes the surrogate mother and goes through the pregnancy and delivery for her daughter.

Apparently, this may be illegal, but the legality of the situation is a minor problem compared to the extremes that some parents are willing to go to in order to serve their children.

Why not try letting their children face life on their own feet and solve their own problems instead of leaving them to mommy and daddy?

...

NHK-TV News shows the harvest of an unusually warm autumn, i.e. bumper crops of green peppers and daikon.

Instead of being picked and sold they're being plowed into the ground because the abundance is forcing down food prices.

Less expensive nutritious food is apparently bad for "the economy".

Therefore, what's good for the economy must be the opposite of what's good for human life, i.e. abundant, less expensive food.

I'm waiting for a news editor who will follow this story with one about soup kitchens, starvation, malnutrition, and homeless people begging for food.

Apparently some news editors exclude that human interest approach from the realm of news judgement.

**Gateshead**: A news headlines say, "Extreme weather warning – heavy snow and plummeting temperatures".

BBC news reports "bitterly cold", then forecasts a mere minus 5°C and reports a "severe weather alert" with "blizzards" expected.

I hardly see a skiff here.

In the "hard hit" areas, reporters talk of cancellations and closings.

I look for snow and see fewer flakes than a "mountie bubble" toy and observe cars racing by on clear, black pavement behind BBC reporters declaring the weather disaster.

The devastated areas have daytime temperatures of +5°C and overnight temperatures of -4°C, with about 10-15 cm of snowfall.

All I can do is laugh.

I forward copies of Winnipeg snow photos from our friend Frank to the BBC, so it can explain real winter to the locals.

...

According to Kevin Warwick, a bio-robotics prof we see at a life sciences centre in Nutgate, the U.S. has a "no body bags" war plan that's due to start about 13 years from time of writing.

From then on, the U.S. will use remote controlled robots instead of human soldiers to carry out wars abroad.

I see what's up. The U.S. can slaughter humans overseas by remote control, keep out news reporters by claiming there's too much danger and risk of "accidents" to permit news people into battlegrounds.

It's a new version of censorship policies.

Then U.S. perpetual war ambitions can carry on without U.S. casualties and deaths. So there's no U.S. peace movement to "bring the robots home".

The U.S. finally gets a free hand to kill every non-U.S.er in the world.

[But the U.S. doesn't during its twenty year war in Afghanistan and Iraq, unless you count remote control flying drones.]

...

Today's U.K. news complains of binge drinking and "anti-social" youth behaviour without any reference to the pre-slavery U.K. tradition.

Hochschild's book about that era mentions large scale, widespread, cross-societal drunkenness and corruption, along with violent press gang shootings, beatings, and kidnappings.

The tradition continues.

We see drunks at early evening and more still when there are evening soccer games in NUT.

**Miyazaki**: A new "virtual life" on computer screens enables people to spend their non-employed time in another fantasy world.

During a television news story about this unreal experience, a user of the virtual life programming appears happily clicking while ignoring and pushing further away his real child, who is sitting right beside him.

The child is the clicker's natural, real, biological son. The boy is yearning for real human contact and affection, unlike his father.

This child will become like others? He'll be dehumanized, effectively orphaned by living parents?

...

There are people being forced to take refuge in the internet because they have few other alternatives.

They're homeless.

The TV news shows these new internaut refugees sleeping in internet cafés, i.e. places offering public access computers all night for a fee that is cheaper than staying in a hotel.

The ones that NHK-TV news are showing have mats on the floor in front of the computer screens, enabling internet refugees to stretch out and attempt to sleep under the flashing, flickering lights of the flat screens.

There are 5,400 places like this in Nippon. At least 1,300 unemployed/homeless people are paying 1,000 yen per night to sleep in these places.

About 27% of the screen sleepers are in their 20s and about 23% are in their 50s.

Many say they want to use the computers and internet to find jobs, but there is one major barricade for them.

Since these people are homeless, they have no address to put on the internet job application forms.

An address is a "required field", i.e. compulsory, which means that if a person has no address to put in the electronic application form, the computer software programme will not accept the application form.

So the homeless internet refugees are automatically excluded from getting the more interesting or higher paying jobs.

...

An NHK news report says that there's an annual decrease in carbon emissions of about 463 tonnes in Toyama, and 240 fewer cars on the roads.

Toyama used to be one of the most car-centred places, per capita, in Nippon.

But the new light rapid transit system, along with a widely-held, growing consciousness of the need to eliminate carbon emissions, air pollution, greenhouse gases, and global warming is changing all that.

Older people are being encouraged to stop driving by offering them 20,000 yen in rapid transit credits for surrendering their driver's licenses.

At the same time, used cooking oil from restaurants and homes is being collected and used for fuel, instead of being thrown away.

...

A news story about Nippon's national pension plan is becoming the top news here.

The government loses track of the pension contributions and entitlement of about 50 million people, more than 40% (per cent) of the total population.

Months after this writing, at least 40% of the pension cases remain unresolved.

To make matters worse, people more than 75 years old will be obliged to pay a percentage (15%) of their public health insurance premiums for the first time.

This premium is to be automatically deducted from their pensions. Somehow, this includes people with missing pensions.

This whole situation helps me to recall a story, a year or two earlier, saying that retired people were being asked to accept cuts in their hard-earned pensions from their former employers.

I conclude that waiting for retirement is a waste of a lifetime far beyond what I'm thinking when I write the first words of these <u>Terrian Journals</u> in Rio de Janeiro.

My writings are an understatement.

People who are passing their entire lives in employment and contributing part of their incomes to a pension for old age are finding out that the nation-state government does not know exactly who contributes how much for how many years.

Records show the wrong names, wrong birth dates, etc.

The confusion has something to do with the way pension contributions are made and the record-keeping involved.

Pension contributions are paid through employers, but when an employee changes employers or ceases to be an employee, the record of pension contributions doesn't necessarily follow the employee.

It may be something like the "pension portability" debate in Canada.

So here's yet another good reason for making the most of our lives during our best, prime years, instead of selling those years to employers and hoping we'll live long enough to collect pensions and be healthy enough to enjoy them.

...

Higashi Kokubaru owns a comedy company and previously works as a stand-up comedian for many years before going back to school to study politics.

We see Kokubaru's face everywhere, including television news, national quiz shows, and interview shows.

Caricatures of his gaunt, smiling face and skinny-looking frame cover made-in-Miyazaki products ranging from milk cartons to boxes of cookies.

He has to hold a news conference to explain that using his face in such advertising isn't officially sanctioned and it doesn't indicate that he or the government endorse particular brand names.

...

News reports that the biggest language business establishment in the land is finally getting its comeuppance from the national government and court system.

We hear complaints about this company for a number of years from former customers such as Mariko's childhood friend Hiroko in Osaka.

While we're in Europe this particular LBE loses a supreme court case to a former student. The supreme court says the LBE is violating long-term contract law.

But this story goes back at least five to ten years. The government is receiving complaints from customers for the previous decade.

About 9,000 people complain, including nearly 2,000 one year alone. Five years earlier the government warns the LBE to improve its business practices.

When the story breaks, the government orders the LBE to stop signing long-term contracts for the next six months.

The government also cancels the LBE's privileges under a refund system for customers.

Under the system, customers could receive money from the government for completing a series of language classes covering a minimum length of time.

The LBE even lists itself on the Tokyo Stock Exchange, but the bad legal news puts the stock down 10%.

The bad publicity coming from the court case loss, along with government action against this LBE, is encouraging more customers to come forward to complain and demand refunds from the LBE.

…

There's a news update on the ten year law suit in Tokyo blaming car makers and governments for lung disease.

This case, entering its eleventh year at time of writing, seems to be reaching a settlement.

Although Tokyo promises to pay compensation to lung disease victims a year earlier, the big seven Japanese auto makers are only now making offers to their victims.

The lung disease victims want more than the companies are offering. But a settlement is being reached.

...

News from Toronto shows a jubilant mayor of Toronto and Canada's Health minister glowing with self-congratulations for creating a new air quality measure system, much like the already well-established UV warnings.

A new gauge, great!

Of course people will continue to die from heart and lung diseases caused by motor vehicle exhaust fumes, just as other people will continue to die of skin cancer due to ultra violet solar rays coming through holes in the ozone layer caused by air pollution.

The new gauge is better than nothing, but not much better.

...

Michaëlle Jean, Canada's "third" world official head of state, has three citizenships, but news says she's being pushed to renounce one due to a potential conflict.

As head of the Canadian Armed Forces, Michaëlle Jean should not maintain her French citizenship, critics say. Yet France and Canada both belong to the N.A.T.O. military group.

In related news, Peru's former president Alberto Fujimore is a citizen of Peru and Nippon, which proves favourable to him.

Peru lays criminal charges against him. Nippon's government says he can't be extradited to face trial in Peru because he's a citizen of Nippon.

Yet to become a candidate and president of Peru, he has to be a Peruvian citizen. He's born in Peru, not Nippon.

So Alberto Fujimore has two citizenships, and so he's apparently blatantly violating Nippon's law against "dual nationality". But he is not arrested in Nippon.

Instead, Fujimori returns to the southern Americas because he says he wants to run for president of Peru again.

He's under house arrest in Chile, pending extradition to Peru for trial.

Meanwhile, he's accepting the invitation of a political party in Nippon to be a candidate in Nippon's elections this summer.

To be a candidate in Nippon he has to be a citizen of Nippon. The government of Nippon doesn't challenge his right to become a candidate. His election posters go up.

Nippon news stories about Fujimori describe him as a Japanese-Peruvian who also has Japanese citizenship.

So, in effect, Nippon is breaking its own law by openly permitting Fujimore to have dual citizenship.

But nobody in the government of Nippon is talking about this law-breaking in public.

**Montréal**: Canadian news reports that Canada adopts the U.S. "no fly" list to keep "terrorists" from boarding commercial passenger flights.

As a result, at two different Canadian airports, a seven year old and a ten year old boy already know what it's like to be stopped by the security services (SS) as potential "terrorists".

Today I see the SS giving special attention to another little boy by frisking him while he's standing in line at Trudeau International a few months before this writing.

News from Canada says the seven and ten year old "no-fly" boys eventually get aboard their flights. They both have the same name as an adult on the list.

The list, like all the SS laws, turns the legal system upside down, assuming people are guilty until proven innocent.

The mother of one boy says she's outraged because the airline suggests that she change her child's name to suit the SS, i.e. so his name won't be on the "no-fly" list.

Unfortunately, at least one of the boys' parents and other mere passengers-in-life at the airports are saying they agree with all the SS laws because they're needed to make everyone safe and to protect the "developed", i.e. U.S. Empire way of life.

Are these interviewees afraid that their names might be added to the SS list, for expressing their freedom of speech?

According to the news, people on the no-fly list can be delayed to the point where they miss their flights even if they're found to be innocent.

And there's no possibility of compensation or appeal.

So the era of consumer protection is now officially over? According to <u>The Washington Post</u>, at time of writing, the U.S. "no-fly" list grows from 100,000 people to about 430,000 around the world. At this moment, there are 6 billion people in the world.

The following year, a daily U.S. TV news broadcast says there are 3,400 people on the "no-fly" list and 400,000 on the "watch" list. So there are two lists?

**Miyazaki**: Following a car fire at a London (U.K.) airport, some medical doctors in the U.K. and Australia are arrested under the new S.S. laws.

The doctors are accused of plotting to cause the fire and carrying bombs that don't ignite. The medical profession is joining the list of "terrorist suspects".

One news report says that medical students and practitioners are in a group susceptible to recruitment by "terrorist groups".

Doctors are all potential serial killers?

So now we're all in danger of being attacked by doctors, nurses, and other health workers?

Instead of anaesthetics and scalpels, they're going to start setting fire to us and/or blowing us up?

All patients are now at risk?

In typical, contemporary, pseudo-journalism, too many questions are being left unasked and unanswered in the rush to report what the public manipulators want to say to us.

For instance, since the doctors at London airport are presumably well-educated and literate, why would they not leave a note explaining their actions and why is no one finding anything they write to explain their actions?

Why would medical students and practitioners want to put human life at risk and kill themselves at London's airport?

We are all left to merely speculate.

After many days of news quoting the U.K. government calling the doctors "terrorists", there's finally a story about what the doctors say.

Their plot is a hoax to protest against U.K. participation in the U.S. wars in Iraq and Afghanistan. Anti-war protests and hoaxes are now "terrorism"?

...

Daily news coming from the U.S. shows polluted and crime-ridden cities where there's a very widespread belief that the only real security comes from a citizenry having the right to carry and use guns.

News stories show that the U.S. is the homeland of mass shootings, gang violence, random drive-by shootings, road rage, child molesters, and poverty.

Tens of millions of people are deprived of equality in education and health care before Obamacare reduces that total.

Why would anyone abroad want to embrace this kind of way of life, which declares itself the provider of "freedom" and "democracy"?

Apparently it has nothing to offer except endless war and, if war ever ends, a post-war existence of further suffering, perversion, and random violence.

...

I keep correcting Canadian news programmes, as I do while living in Saskatoon. I speak with a network news editor too.

It's easy to say Kyushu correctly in English. It's cue-shoe.

I get the impression that mispronunciation is a U.S. Empire export.

Car-ow-kay is mangled out of recognition. It's karaoke in Japanese Romaji spelling.

U.S. military stationed in Nippon say car-o-key, locking anglophones out of the correct pronunciation universe. I also hear them say "fukeyokey" for Fukuoka.

...

Niigata has its second big quake in three years, at time of writing.

This time the epicentre is only about 15 metres deep, just offshore, and the force is M6.8 or more at the epicentre. An aftershock of M6 follows within a few hours.

There's a smaller shock in the evening.

The Miyazaki daily newspaper delivers a one page "Extra" at a supermarket where I happen to be shopping.

The headline says two people are dead and 200 are injured. By the next morning, television news reports nine dead and 900 injured.

The toll rises to ten and more than 1,000 the following day.

...

Toronto news calls the Niigata nuclear power facility the largest nuclear plant in the world.

Apparently, a U.S. news service reports radioactive leaks, and that country's government offers to help. But Nippon's government says it doesn't need help.

However, Niigata Prefecture is so concerned that it wants the facility inspected.

The prefecture persuades the nation-state government to invite the International Atomic Energy Commission to send a team of inspectors to Niigata.

The IAEC is usually only in the news in connection with sending inspectors to places such as Iraq before the U.S. war there, and more recently to Iran and North Korea.

...

Well into the final month of summer, news from Chuang Hwa is getting worse.

The biggest problem is the pollution caused by burning coal everywhere and petroleum in motor vehicles.

But the most widely and frequently reported news story is about products made in Chuang Hwa, showing that the news is more concerned about commercial products than the state of the world's environment.

The source of most of these reports is the U.S., where domestic pet food imported from Chuang Hwa is killing dogs and cats.

Getting less mention in U.S. news is suspect food for humans exported by the U.S. to Nippon. This problems adds to the bad U.S. beef exports to Nippon.

Finally, U.S. toy companies say their products are defective and dangerous because they're made in Chuang Hwa. U.S. toy makers have no quality control in their Chuang Hwa factories?

The resulting dent in Chuang Hwa's growth as the world's manufacturing centre is bigger than the dent recently found in a made-in-U.S. space shuttle tile.

More bad news for Chuang Hwa comes from New Zealand.

A random check of clothing imported from Chuang Hwa finds it contains 900 times more formaldehyde, a known carcinogen, than the maximum acceptable health limits of that substance in clothing.

Why is any amount of any carcinogen acceptable in any product from anywhere?

Almost every type of clothing imaginable, ranging from the very expensive to the relatively cheap, is now made in Chuang Hwa.

So foreign companies making their clothes in Chuang Hwa have a quality control problem too?

So, on a world scale, Nippon doesn't have to worry about being overtaken by Chuang Hwa?

But the U.S. has to worry about all Chuang Hwa products, including the ones made by U.S. companies in Chuang Hwa?

In the broader news context, the basic planetary and human problem of pollution remains a less newsworthy story and a lower priority than pet food, toys, and clothing?

Without clean air, clean water, and fertile land, those things become moot points and academic questions.

...

Governments in so many places, especially the "first" world ones, are having all sorts of meetings, conferences, and studies.

They're expressing their concerns, increasing monitoring, and coming up with new plans, policies, and laws.

It sounds like the insecurity forces are at it again, but that's not the case.

The security services (S.S.) are much more effective in getting what they want almost immediately, unlike these gatherings of hot air.

These gatherings are about protecting the environment and reducing damage to it. There are agreements that something must be done within 43 years, at time of writing.

In contrast, the S.S. doesn't have to wait 43 days to get almost anything that it wants.

Insecurity gets instant gratification. Human species survival is put on hold and has to wait indefinitely. Until it's too late?

...

Environmental news is giving more credibility to my long-standing argument that nation-states are going to have to give up their sovereignty and surrender to the long-range historical, natural behaviours of human beings, such as our natural migratory behaviour.

Global warming is melting the polar ice caps at such an accelerating pace that more and more low-lying lands will soon be flooding.

By soon, some scientists are saying they mean within 32 years, at time of writing.

CBC-TV News shows Environment Canada's chief ice forecaster saying he's now expecting to see an iceless Arctic in his lifetime, instead of leaving that view to his great-grandchildren.

Much of the polar bear population is now expected to disap-pear within 32 years, at time of writing.

The implications for human life and migration are the first news I see on this topic.

Flooding big areas of land, such as the Tokyo Bay area, means more and more people will have to leave their sinking homes and live somewhere else.

Many will have to abandon their nation-states and resume migrating. Nation-states call these people refugees.

NHK-TV news reports that about 200 million people will be left homeless because their homes are sinking under their feet.

In total human terms, that may seem small, less than 3.1 % of the world population of six billion people, at time of writing.

But it's two-thirds of the U.S. population and about 6.2 times more than the Canadian population at time of writing.

It is yet another challenge to the sovereignty claims of Canada's fewer than 40 million people to nearly 10 million square kilometers of the Earth's surface.

Forget about the Canadian government's Arctic sovereignty claims.

Even if the nation-state could bamboozle every adult, adolescent, child, and infant in Canada into getting armed against a huge influx of immigrating humans, the Canadian contingent would be hopelessly outnumbered.

...

NHK News reports current efforts to save Nagano from the scourge of the very destruc-tive tourist industry.

Private vehicles are banned from some areas and visitors are brought in by bus. There's a limit of 100 tourists per day, but that's double the previous number.

Some hotels and other tourism business people complain, but many others realize that if the natural environment is destroyed there will be nothing to attract visitors.

Meanwhile, in Tibet, having failed to conquer the Tibetan locals entirely through military invasion, forced relocation (population dispersion), and repressive rule, Chuang Hwa is finally calling in reinforcements to decisively quash Tibet.

Imitating Bismarck's very successful military technique of making war by building railways, Chuang Hwa's government is using Canadian made Bombardier trains to overwhelm Tibet through an alliance with the tourist industry.

They're sending in a vast, limit-less, invincible, permanent invasion and occupation force composed of suit case wielding, backpack slinging, camera shooting, internet-dwelling troops of tourists.

Of course, they're setting up permanent bases called hotels, with an endless supply of alien provisions, so that the invaders can make themselves at home, whatever the cost to Tibet and all its inhabitants.

Tourist invaders in Tibet are a permanent occupation force that's constantly being replenished and expanded.

Neo-business people applaud the tourist occupation, apparently not understanding the value of preserving the very things that attract people to remote, rural areas, i.e. the remoteness, rural environs, and unique culture therein.

...

A U.K. health department representative on BBC-TV News mentions in passing that alcohol causes cancer.

When I ask my cousin Steve, the cancer researcher, he says he knows nothing about it. He drinks alcohol.

When I bring up the subject in correspondence with a devotee of alcohol, I get the same old line of the alcohol religionism.

The line says that moderate alcohol intake is good for people's health. Except for cancer?

We have a recording of a CBC television programme, originally broadcast twelve years ago, mentioning this kind of pro-alcohol claim.

The programme repeats a report that wine alcohol is a healthy drink.

Updating this report, the programme says drinking grape juice, which contains no alcohol, is equally healthy.

So I'm thinking that the next report probably says that eating grapes is also equally healthy. Sure enough, this fact eventually does make the news.

The beneficial part of the grape is on the underside of the grape peel. There's no added health benefit coming from turning the grapes into either juice or an alcoholic drink.

Conclusion: It's not the wine alcohol or juice that are good for anyone. It's the grapes themselves.

Juice has a higher concentration of sugar, a harmful substance, than grapes and other fruit. Alcohol causes cancer. So just eat grapes for health benefits.

...

According to the U.S. New York Times newspaper, a long established source of news with no history of fiction writing, the Italian government is treating the soccer mob more harshly than the notorious international gangster mob, the mafia.

The Italian government is using its version of U.S. insecurity laws to charge some of the soccer rioters with "terrorist activities".

This makes me wonder why, after a century of terrorizing people around the world, the global crime syndicate, the mafia, is not being charged under the same laws anywhere.

Why aren't organized crime bosses being treated the same way as other "terrorists"?

Why not subject real criminals to the same arbitrary arrest, indefinite detention, torture, confinement, and denial of all legal rights such as a fair trial under the law and due process?

...

In one cold war propaganda commercial that I see on a U.S. TV channel as a child, between cartoons, there's a very short clip of Nikita Khrushchev, the S.U. leader of the day, saying something in Russian and banging his shoe on a desk at the U.N.

His words are translated as, "We will bury you."

This propaganda message is designed to make U.S.ers fear the S.U. and to stir up suspicion and anti-Russian feelings.

Ironically, in Gorbachev's day, U.S. news calls Khrushchev "a reformer".

...

When I'm a child, regular TV channels pre-empt kid's shows whenever adults at television network headquarters think it's necessary to show something important to people, kids or not.

Thus news can and often does interrupt my regular children's show broadcasts.

Then, news is a product of fastidious, nit-picking, zealots of accuracy who uncompromisingly demand independent verification of facts, detail, and objectivity, i.e. hard news editors.

Such editors seem to be getting exiled from specialty TV news channels and excluded from the internet.

In great contrast to my childhood experience, more recent generations of children can watch cartoons and kid's shows all the time, all day, every day, without any interruptions or intrusions from the "outside world", i.e. the non-cartoon and non-kid's show world and news world.

So kids can now grow up knowing nothing about the outside world that adults around them don't mention.

Overly protective adults can almost completely isolate children from everything they need to learn about to become competent, thinking, and influential adults.

Without exposure to legitimate, professional news reporting, children can grow into adults who are more susceptible to Internet "news" from anonymous sources.

It can thus be selective, unsubstantiated, misleading, and/or completely false. And it all too often is just that. It's not news at all. Who's going to know?

...

Children, adolescents, and younger adults are getting some bad news from NHK.

Their artificial diets and irregular eating habits are making them unhealthy and old before their time.

Diet and way of life are turning younger "first" worlders into part of the aging society problem, long before their time.

Medical researchers are finding that people 20 to 30 years old are now getting lower bone density test results and coming down with osteoporosis more than people who are more than 60 years old.

Younger cases of this malady are on the rise. It's just as unusual, unnatural, and bizarre as the unhealthy food and eating habits plaguing younger generations, including mine.

NHK News reports a study of 250,000 women in Nippon in two age groups, 20-30 and 65+.

In the 20-30 group, about 5.6% have osteoporosis. In the 65+ group, about 2.3% have osteoporosis.

The study attributes the higher rate of osteoporosis in younger women to not eating properly, eating the wrong things, and not doing any exercise.

...

Other news reports that memory problems disconnecting humans from their natural needs may be endemic to present day humans.

Kyoto University is publishing the results of memory tests that compare the short-term memories of five and a half year old chimpanzees with K.U. students.

The chimpanzees have better memories. They score 80% while the students' scores decline to 40%. Only older chimps get such lower scores.

Researchers say that humans lost their memories in exchange for something else, maybe language capabilities.

However, our experience is that memory is essential in language learning.

Does this mean chimps evolved from humans?

...

If I'm reading a Spanish-language news story about Brasil correctly, there's finally someone running Brasilia (Lula) who realizes that the favelados are furthering human progress.

Favelados are doing so by creating and developing favelas, which are a natural, creative, inventive form of human settlement.

They need to be encouraged instead of bulldozed and demolished, or pitied and rescued.

As I write while visiting some Rio favelas, the favelados can accomplish so much if they're permitted to invent their own homes and neighbourhoods instead of being rendered homeless and forcibly relocated to housing planned and built by elite professionals and bureaucrats trying to impose their alien ways of life upon the favelados.

(Why use the counterproductive European colonial-national era "white man's burden" approach against favelados?)

Brasil's President Lula, who is considered a radical during my Carioca life, is now saying he wants to extend "infrastructure" to favelas.

That could be all right, so long as the "infrastructure" doesn't hinder favelados' independence, creativity, initiative, and human community-building work.

Humanity can't survive in comfortable, secure captivity. That's fatal to us.

...

NHK News uncritically reports that 1.2 million people in Asia are nouveau riche and control

520 trillion yen. It's a vast monetary fortune.

This report is within the context of a news story about more tourists coming to Nippon from Chuang Hwa and Bharat.

A story buried later in the same television newscast says there are 2.4 billion people living in Chuang Hwa and Bharat.

This story says nothing about the fact that the 1.2 million moneyed people from these same places add up to little more than one per cent of the total population.

However, the second story does mention economic advancement and how it should not be held back because Chuang Hwa and Bharat are "burdened with" masses of unmoneyed people.

So we are told to positively and uncritically evaluate the moneyed tourists while scorning and dismissing the unmoneyed majority as a nuisance holding back the moneyed?

This concept fits in well with the tall tale that people are unmoneyed only because they are stupid, lazy, and unambitious.

It also fits in well with the person back at the Newcastle Science Centre who says he doesn't want to be obliged to wait for others to "catch up with us".

...

A news story about a debate in Toronto schools inspires me to write to the host of CBC television's news programme, "The National".

Of course writing to news organizations is now mostly writing to a vacuum. With rare exceptions, including former news host Barbara Frum, the answer is no reply.

The Toronto debate centres around whether special schools need to be set up emphasizing only the heritage of African-Canadians. Now it's omitted from the school system.

Some people see this as a positive act, while others see it as a neo-segregation. Of course the perspective I express in <u>A Sketch of Terrian History</u> is completely absent from the debate.

From that perspective, all the schools need to be completely changed so that they will no longer concentrate exclusively on the European colonial-national era perspective of the world and history.

Such as change means that there's no need to debate whether or not to create a multitude of special schools devoted entirely to a plethora of non-European era civilizations and world outlooks.

Instead, all schools would centre around the entire human heritage.

Thus the 800 year Moslem era in Europe would receive more attention in all schools than would the 500 years of European era in the world.

I write to the CBC host of "The National" describing the "butterfly news" and "white news only" approach of Canadian news reporting toward the Toronto story and news in general. Here is an excerpt of my letter:

Perhaps mass media news should be called butterfly news, since it flutters from one story to another, stopping only long enough to touch it, before moving on to the next one.

Sure, sometimes butterfly news does go back to the same story again, for another touch or the occasional special report.

This glancing touch news reporting helps explain why CBC News missed an obvious point in the Toronto School District debate about African heritage schools.

The point is - the school system is European-centric.

If it were world-centric, it would start by teaching that every human being is African, according to the anthropologists who found the oldest humanoid remains in Africa, Ardi and Lucy.

A world-centric school system would mention that the British Empire is the only empire that was somewhat larger than the Mongolian Empire, and the Mongolian Empire lasted much longer.

Of course butterfly news isn't the only reason that mass media news missed the obvious in the Toronto schools debate.

The news is also hampered by an apparent "white only news" policy.

Almost every news broadcast in Canada is devoted almost exclusively to the daily reporting of "white news" from the U.S. and Europe.

"World" news reports, if any, are brief and dominated by U.S. and/or European perspectives.

Routine, daily reporting of news directly from Asian, African, and South American sources and perspectives is almost non-existent in Canada.

Some TV5 and BBC World newscasts do provide that news, if only from a European perspective.

A "Foreign Correspondent" show on CBC has little impact.

Foreign correspondents report only extraordinary events or feature items which further distort the alien places they cover.

Finally, when there is a special issue in Canada which could benefit from an outside perspective, such as proportional representation or multiculturalism, CBC News looks only at Europe.

This is an example of a "white news only" special report.

There is no mention of the well-established proportional representation system in Japan.

There is no mention of India's vast experience with multiculturalism and multilingualism, stretching back to antiquity.

How can Canadians be informed if our news reports ignore the world and the perspectives of the world coming directly from lands where more than 80% of humanity live?

...

News provides shallow depth coverage of "security" stories.

No news report that I know about mentions that biometric scanning, computer chip storage, and tracking devices are excellent means of helping terrible villains.

"Security" technology helps dictators to identify, locate, kidnap, torture, and murder dissidents, freedom fighters, pro-democracy leaders, news reporters, intellectuals, elected politicians, and everyone else.

The proliferation of "security" technology thus makes no one safe or secure. Instead, it means that no one can hide out and escape imprisonment, torture, and murder.

That means there can be no future Lech Wałęsa, Nelson Mandela, Steve Biko, Desmond Tutu, Donald Wood, Rigoberta Menchú, Dalai Lama, Daw Aung San Suu Kyi, Mahatma Gandhi, etc.

...

"Security" technology means that people like them can be quietly tracked and eliminated before they can have any impact whatsoever.

They can disappear more rapidly and easily than the children of the "Madres de Mayo" in Buenos Aires.

Of course organized crime can also gain from the spread of biometric scanning and computer chip tracking devices. Witnesses can disappear and jurists can be neutralized.

...

Something called a road improvement tax is levied by Nippon's government. As the name implies, the monies are supposed to go to improving roads.

The tax is added to the price of gasoline fuel for motor vehicles.

However, news reports show large sums of this tax revenue going toward purchasing massage chairs, buying overseas airline tickets, paying for offices with almost no users, along with baseball stadiums and castles.

The news doesn't specify how the money is spent on castles.

When the opposition parties block renewal of this temporary tax measure, the government gets desperate and says henceforth the road improvement tax will not go into road improvement.

It will be spent on other things. So what's new here?

...

In this warming world, northern Nippon has the highest

springtime temperatures since meteorologists start collecting data 130 years ago.

There's no more snow when this news is reported. The next day it snows.

Meanwhile, Miyazaki seems cool, with overnight lows of 8°C to 10°C, and daylight temperatures ranging from 16°C to 20°C.

The yen gets hot too, springing from 124 to 95 per U.S. dollar, the highest rate since our arrival in Miyazaki.

But this time the U.S. currency is also falling to par with the Canadian dollar, for the first time in nearly 30 years, at time of writing.

...

It seems predictable that when the yen peaks the gasoline prices drop as much as 24 yen, but the rising yen gets no credit for it.

Instead, news focuses on the disappearance of the "temporary" road improvement tax.

It disappears in a scandal and dispute between the government and opposition parties.

The tax, as I mention earlier, is being used to buy massage chairs, to pay for overseas travel, and to set up offices with employees who have nothing to do because no one comes to see them.

The government pleads for a return of the tax to discourage gasoline use that's causing air pollution.

At the same time, the government is at an international conference on global warming, talking about buying "carbon credits" from less polluting countries.

That's necessary because Nippon is like all the other "first" world countries.

They're not doing enough to stop the problem and failing to meet the pollution reduction targets they set 11 years earlier.

Raising gasoline prices and taxes until no one can afford to drive gasoline vehicles is a good idea, so long as they also can't drive biofuel vehicles.

I want all the polluting to stop now.

But why contradict a tax on gasoline by using the proceeds as a "road improvement" fund? Improving roads makes it easier to use polluting vehicles more often.

It's easy to prove that the government's story about gasoline taxes cutting pollution is false.

Yes, the news is showing people lining up for cheaper gasoline now.

But every time gas prices increase, the news also shows people lining up at the gas station pumps and saying they're resigned to paying whatever it costs.

Their actions and words are saying they want gasoline at any price, including life itself.

I don't understand their suicidal nihilistic beliefs and behaviours. Whatever happened to humans' natural species survival instincts?

...

But there is some hope in the news too. Seventy per cent of the gasoline stations here claim they're losing money.

During the annual Obon holidays people are taking intercity buses instead of driving themselves. Bus companies report a 61.6% to 150% increase in passengers.

Car owners taking the buses say they didn't realize it is so much easier, more convenient, more comfortable, and much cheaper than driving private vehicles.

Much more remarkable is news from the world capital of consumption, a place notorious for especially polluting motor vehicles spewing out toxic exhaust fumes coming from burning gasoline and bio-fuels.

I mean California, U.S.A. There, people are selling their motor vehicles and going en masse to rapid public transit.

One person interviewed and shown on NHK-TV news says he's saving more than $US800 (800 days of income for a large portion of humanity).

He says he gets to work in moments now, instead of idling

his engine in a traffic jam resembling a long parking lot.

...

Campaigning for an election is already beginning around us, with posters and speeches in the news.

The latest public opinion polls say that 71.4% of the public have an unfavourable view of the current prime minister, while 27.8% are favourable.

The previous prime minister is forced to resign when his popularity hits a minimum of 26.9%. He leaves after only one year in office.

The current prime minister is now in office for only a few months. A month before the northern hemisphere spring equinox here, he's down to only 23% support.

...

Nippon slowly continues to introduce the jury system to its courts. Jurors are already practicing sitting at the front of courtrooms, where judges alone usually sit.

I don't know how popular this system is abroad, but here a public opinion survey says 37% of respondents are unwilling to participate in a jury. Only 15% are willing.

The news report I see doesn't mention how the other 48% feel. Maybe they're undecided or have no opinion. So they would make good jurers?

...

Wherever I go in the world, no matter whether or not I understand little or none of the languages, television news seems to present the same faces in the same voices.

They are polite, calm faces, smiling whenever possible. They're the news hosts' attractively made-up faces, on torsos professionally clothed and heads meticulously coiffed for camera appeal.

They greet viewers in the most pleasant and positive tones of "Good" morning, afternoon, and evening in whatever languages.

News hosts give viewers a welcoming and reassuring feeling to a very rational presentation of the state of the entire world.

The world ranges from the nearest households and neighbourhoods to the farthest and least familiar points of the hori-zons and the universe.

In the end, viewers are thanked and wished well, in either gentle words or positive grimaces, usually showing no negative emotions about the stories told this time.

News hosts and their employers want viewers to watch the news regularly, every day.

Viewers should feel welcome, comfortable, and at home while watching the television news broadcast.

Viewers should also feel as if they have a personal connection with the news hosts, if not the reporters too.

To make this happen, hosts and reporters address each other by their first names. So viewers get to know these total strangers on a first-name basis too.

This personal touch works in my case.

I get a sense of knowing two news hosts when I bump into them and we talk briefly at Van Couverden Public Library and in a department store in Buffalo, New York, (while I'm visiting there from Toronto.)

At the same time, viewers should normally feel that news hosts and the news are clearly separated from each other by more than geographical space or time zones, and by recording and editing time delays.

While news is always out there in the distance, news hosts have to be right here in the viewers' homes.

No matter what's happening in the news, it's kept a safe distance away from the viewers by the buffer of hosts and their neat, polished, shining tables and invisible cameras.

In the news business, hosts have one essential message to convey. They present that message by always remaining cool, calm, and unflappable on camera.

They mustn't lose their composure for a moment, regardless of shocking images or technical failures.

In their general demeanour and their manner of delivering scripted lines, news hosts are always saying this to viewers– "It's okay. Don't worry. Everything is all right."

Finally, whenever and as often as possible, news programmes will try to end in a favourable, relieving way.

The idea behind this approach to news is called, "Leave 'em laughin'."

If the news isn't good, at least it can end by helping viewers to recover from it and to forget its most serious, disturbing, or thought-provoking impacts.

However bad the news in stories may seem, viewers can then feel a sense of relief at the end of the broadcast. Viewers' minds can say to themselves:

"Phew! We're fine. It was all a bad dream.

"Now we can follow the sponsors' advice for a happier life in a better world than the news shows.

"We can take an aspirin, have a drink, munch on some junk food, and buy a new car. Then we'll feel much better.

"We can forget about all the bad news, or at least ignore it until the next news show."

Watching the news becomes much like memorizing a list of items, nonsense syllables or not. Viewers are most likely to remember the first and final items best.

Both items are the faces and voices of the news hosts.

The only other items viewers are expected to remember are the most pleasant and entertaining commercials in between the opening and closing of the news.

So, no matter how outrageous, outlandish, strange, sad, tragic, or violent the news stories may appear to be each day, the television news programme is only repeating, over and over again, the well-known words of Jean-Jacques Rousseau:

"Tout va bien dans le meilleur des mondes."

[These words are written before news becomes part of a website and "yellow journalism" makes a comeback.]

...

Some researchers here in Nippon try to create roads that absorb air pollution.

The objective is not to stop the polluting vehicles, but to compensate for them with very short-term, stop gap measures. It's like "adapting to climate change".

Imagine someone proposing that the best way to stop murder by firearms is to make softer bullets and provide everyone with an impervious head to toe suit of armour.

...

Recent news reports say U.S. movie and television writers are returning to work after a long strike. How is that possible?

If writers are like me, they love writing and can't stop for any reason having nothing to do with writing itself, not even for a strike.

They must be writing secretly during strikes.

...

For me, "OB" is a commercial name of a vaginal hygiene product and "DV" is digital video. But neither OB nor DV mean what I think in the Japanese news speak.

Internet, advertisers, and news people need to use dictionaries, not write new ones.

They all need basic editing, making an effort to keep human languages comprehensible to all users not just the younger generation minority of the moment.

Internet needs people to do the same kind of work as high quality encyclopedia editors and librarians working in collections divisions, i.e. people who can distinguish be-tween works of carefully and well-researched reference ver-sus works of fiction.

Otherwise the internauts and less devoted users can never tell the difference between reality and illusions.

We never know if web site and posting content are information, disinformation, or misinformation.

So everything that internet contains is suspect, unreliable, and should be treated with scepticism, like gossip and rumours.

...

I'm thinking about more causes which only get attention once in a while, during special events and feature issues reports, by the news business.

I mean deaths caused by poverty and disease.

I'm reminded of these causes of death that are killing every day only thanks to NHK-TV news.

It's doing feature stories about Africa during what amounts to an oil for aid conference involving most of Africa's 53 nation-states, currently underway in Yokohama.

I learn that 9.71 million children are dying before they reach five years of age in Africa, according to an interview with someone from the United Nations.

Preventing 9.71 million children from dying means giving all humanity 9.71 million more chances of changing the future.

...

A new U.K. law declares a person a "terrorist sympathizer" if s/he concludes that a terrorist can be the product of the injustice, persecution, and racism such as the incidents that I see in news reports from the U.K. Suffer in silence?

...

Italia takes another big step further along the road to a police state by singling out gypsy children for compulsory fingerprinting.

UNICEF compares this with Italia's Fascist past and says this is a violation of the UN Convention on the Rights of Children.

It's definitely child abuse, on top of the adult abuse engendered by the current insecurity age.

Meanwhile, the U.S. and Nippon continue to fingerprint and take mug shots of certain people including children.

But the worst example is set by the U.K., where children as

young as four years old are getting fingerprinted by the school system, ostensibly as part of pupil registration and as a condition for getting a library card.

However, a U.K. government spokesperson quoted in a U.K. news story says children must be fingerprinted as part of the "war on illegal immigration".

In this "war", human rights are collateral damage?

...

Some news says Chuang Hwa is overtaking the U.S. as the world's worst polluter. Unfortunately, the news fails to mention the details of this event.

The news is neglecting to say that a country with a population of more than a billion is now catching up with a country having only 300 million people, at time of writing.

So the per capita pollution of the U.S. is extreme compared with Chuang Hwa.

...

Two big quakes hit Chuang Hwa's interior and Nippon's northeast, exactly one month apart.

The one in Chuang Hwa kills tens of thousands of people. The one in Nippon kills a thousand times fewer people.

The difference in magnitude is less than a point, but Chuang Hwa's population is larger and the region of northeastern Honshu where the quake hits isn't heavily populated.

The way that homes and highways are ripped apart and buried by the earth is demonstrating how easily entire civilizations can be swallowed up and made to disappear by natural forces.

There are implications for Chuang Hwa's dictatorship.

At time of writing, it's only a couple of months away from staging an olympic games spectacular in Beijing to impress the rest of the world's elite and mesmerize every sports fan into awed, but not odd, inactivity.

This means temporarily shutting down some Chuang Hwa factories to make the pollution less visible. But it doesn't mean rushing to help survivors of the big earthquake.

Chuang Hwa's dictators are treating disaster victims the same way as Burma's military dictators after a recent, very severe typhoon strikes there.

The scenes of so many huge groups of people suffering without adequate supplies, and shelter, sitting pathetically in the mess, waiting for food and water that never comes, reminds me of the way the U.S. elected government of emperor moron leaves the poorest people of New Orleans after the Katrina Hurricane hit a couple of years ago.

The aftermaths of Chuang Hwa's quake and the U.S. hurricane are more evidence that the difference between dictatorship and democracy is being blurred by an elite that only pays lip service to democracy and has no intention of maintaining or improving it for anyone, anywhere.

...

I'm thinking of the Xiang Giang vs. Chuang Hwa situation while local news is reporting events in Brasil to celebrate the 100th anniversary of the arrival of the first settlers, bandeirantes from Kyushu in Brasil.

The news shows interviews with people who look like locals in Nippon but who don't speak the language of Nippon because they are lusophones and Brasileiros/as.

There's a large concentration of these people in São Paulo, Brasil and Gunma, Nippon.

Gunma has signs in both Portuguese and Japanese. Gunma schools provide classes in Portuguese and Japanese language classes for Brasileiro/a children.

It seems unlikely that Brasil's schools provide similar help for Kyushu's bandeirantes 100 years ago.

The challenges and difficulties of the people from Kyushu who leave for Brasil a century ago are depicted in the Brazilian movie "Gaijin".

Brasileiros/as coming here find themselves in a similar language and cultural situation to their ancestors who go to Brasil from Nippon, but more so.

Their ancestors arriving from Kyushu in Brasil have both the advantages and disadvantages of being a visible minority in appearance, language, and culture.

The people already living in Brasil know they're dealing with newcomers who have no knowledge of living in Brasil, its cultures or European language.

However, Brasileiros/as descended from the Kyushu bandeirantes and now residing in Gunma look like the people already here in Nippon.

The more Japanese they appear, the more challenges and difficulties they have here.

The assumptions that these Brasileiros/as are locals here leads to problems and misunderstandings.

Gunma is trying to help.

**Moscow**: In Rio de Janeiro, locals tell me that sítios are free rural plots of land that Brasil's government gives away to encourage people who want to move out of congested cities.

José, the father of my Carioca friend Zita, is a former landless peasant who moves to a big city for employment and income. Now he's living on his own sítio near the city.

There, he grows at least some of his own food.

Sítios are no longer newsworthy when I'm in Brasil, but a similar "daicha" system in Russia remains in the Russian news.

These dwellings on government gift land are such a great idea that, like sítios.

Yet I never hear any mention of "daicha" in all my years of news reading and watching in Canada and everywhere else.

Do I ignore news that I don't find interesting or is all news

U.S. filtered to avoid mention of free land?

Daicha are for weekends, holidays, retirement, or any time that a person wants to return to non-urban, non-toxic sites. The aging, declining population can thus leave cities to rot.

I imagine that it's easy to give away daicha because all land is public-owned during the C.C.C.P. era, ready to give away to private owners when the Russian Federation is born.

Real estate speculators, mortgage dealers, and land holders elsewhere would probably fight against this good idea, even in largely empty Canada. But why?

There's no reasonable, human interest argument against giving everyone a place to live and to grow food for living.

An employeed person with a daicha or sítio no longer needs employment to support her/his basic human needs.

There's no mortgage to pay back for most of the prime years of a lifetime.

Nobody needs employment incomes for food and housing. What they don't grow, they can get by trading crops with their neighbours.

In short, nobody needs full-time, lifelong employment.

This has implications for everyone. It's also a great solution to poverty and homelessness.

...

Years of TV news and political broadcasts during the U.S.A.-C.C.C.P. Cold War, and much later under world-dividing, xenophobic "leaders", show huge tanks, missiles, and massive armies assembling and parading around Red Square, with millions of people and all the Kremlin bosses looking on.

Well, here we are standing in the middle of it.

Red Square is a relatively small square, dwarfed by the one in Beijing.

I don't see how any of the heavy arms or throngs could ever enter or parade through this space of ground, pinned in by buildings and walls. There isn't enough space here.

Who makes the hoax broadcasts, the C.C.C.P., foreign correspondents, propagandists, or all of them combined?

**Vladivostok**: English-language television shows and movies play two languages simultaneously, with Russian drowning out the other.

"Euronews" is all dubbed in Russian. It's a peculiar news programme because it uses only one European language, English.

We can see Canada's prime minister of the moment meeting with the E.U. and French president.

We can also see temperatures in Nippon and Canada, as well as many currency and stock numbers.

We also finally learn the Russian Federation president's name, after months of being unable to figure it out in Nippon's puzzling katakana dialect.

At time of writing, the president is Dimitry Medvedev. Putin is his prime minister.

(We're crossing Russia during a U.S.-investor-bank-led economic collapse. But we don't find out about it until we receive news in a language we understand. Crisis, what crisis? We don't experience it or see news of it in our languages.)

**Tallin-Stockholm Ferry**: Unable to understand the Estonian or Swedish languages, we can comprehend only the visual imagery of our sleeping cabin TV.

We're emerging from a news vacuum to find Nippon's yen much stronger than the highs of our Osaka pass throughs.

The current value is 124 yen, up from 151 yen per Euro before we leave Nippon. The yen is up from 106 to 97 against the U.S. currency.

Oil drops below US$70 per U.S. barrel, after a year of surging toward $200. So food and other prices should drop too!

**L'Île**: This foggy morning, the news reports 20% of the world population consumes 80% of earth's resources.

This story is a repeat broadcast of the news of at least 38 earlier. Apparently no one is tuning in, then or now.

**Richmond (Columbia (Br.)**: We have an encounter with faulty sidewalks, non-responsible government, and self-censoring local newspapers.

On a dry, rainless day, before there's any ice or snow on the ground, Mariko finds herself falling on a hard, concrete sidewalk.

She has two badly bruised knees and scratched hands, which take months to completely heal.

It's surprising, but it's not. We walk all over this city and find uneven sidewalk pavement is the rule, not the exception.

It's not miraculous that thousands of people aren't falling and injuring themselves every day. Most don't walk here.

There are no neighbourhood community centres or commercial facilities, so most of these suburbanites drive everywhere, most of the time.

After reporting Mariko's incident to the city and mayor, we eventually get a letter from the city's insurance agent.

He writes that, according to the provincial supreme court, the city isn't responsible for people falling on the uneven sidewalks. Case closed.

I report the case to the two local weekly publications posing as newspapers. Both completely ignore my report and don't call Mariko to ask her questions.

While I'm searching in their archives for stories about uneven sidewalks, I learn why they aren't interested.

I mean aside from the fact that they probably depend on full page advertizing revenue from the city and may be owned by people close to the current incumbent politicians.

I find a story in one of the "papers" about a woman who has a very serious fall, bloodying herself badly on an uneven sidewalk.

She's very grateful that a passerby helps her get medical attention.

The story is very short and simply an expression of the woman's gratitude to the stranger who rescues here.

There is no background information about the city's reaction and the widespread poor condition of city sidewalks. It's selective and lazy reporting.

...

A feature news item on CBC News from Céline Galipeau of SRC illustrates how the "first" and "third" world exist in one country.

Céline's report is about the "first" and "third" worlds of Bharat, in a place called Dharevi. In Brasil, this community would be called a favela.

In Céline's report, the people with only subsistence lives in Dharevi call it as their home and say they want to remain there.

At the same time, the local "first" world elite's architect-planner sees Dharevi as no more than an abstract urban planning problem needing solving.

Instead of going into the community, sleeping there, and talking at length with the residents, the elite's agent makes on-camera pronouncements and generalizations indicating his ignorance of Dharevi.

He describes Dharevi as a "slum conversion area". He says it needs to be socially and economically rehabilitated.

His objective is to replace a slum with "high scale" housing, i.e. places the current residents cannot afford to own or rent.

Thus he will help "integrate them into society so they can live like ordinary people".

Wow! It's Disraeli's two nations between whom there is no intercourse and no sympathy…

**Montréal**: We're seeing something in the streets before the television news is showing it on screen.

As the last remnants of winter snow decay and turn to water or ice, depending on the ground temperature, the ugliness it all hides comes into view.

As we notice in Gatineau, but on a much vaster scale in the substantially larger urban area of Montréal, all the garbage and all the dog feces that get left, dumped, buried, and camouflaged by snow crystals is now becoming all too apparent.

It's an annual, seasonal problem that can continue so long as there are long, snowy winters here.

We have to watch our step, divert our eyes, and sometimes hold our noses as the ugly gardens of the effluent "first" world society become apparent.

Like many things in this part of the world, it is a problem that goes ignored, unnoticed, and unremedied every year, all the time.

It takes the news reports to embarrass local residents into gradually cleaning up the mess on their doorsteps, after winds heralding the end of winter and the beginning of spring move the lightest debris to the front of someone else's doorstep.

Many years later, we see the same sort of debris in Winnipeg. It's a pan-Canadian winter-spring tradition?

...

During English-language news interviews on television, people who are both answering and asking questions appear to be inventing a new language by ignoring and distorting words already in use.

The vocabulary of this mangled English or manglish, includes words such as mutuality, problematic, systemic, incentivize, strategization, and delegitimize.

I'm not sure whether people with more formal education are trying to reinforce their elite status by making the language mysterious for everyone, or whether people with less formal education are trying to make themselves look more knowledgeable and intelligent by making up new versions of words that work perfectly well in their original form and usage.

Isn't it better for everyone to use the words and expressions that all of us already know and understand, instead of trying to turn them into a code which can only exclude people or make them too embarrassed to say, "What do you mean?"

I only once hear a news interviewer asking anyone that question on the air. The reply is almost snooty.

Oh sure, people who do wonder what the mangled words actually mean can figure them out from context, sometimes.

But isn't communication, and especially the news, supposed to help us all understand what's going on by using straightforward, simple language that we can understand quickly?

If the news is going to permit language mangling, the beginning of each news broadcast should explain vocabulary first, eg. In tonight's news we're reporting on systemic events. The word systemic means.......

Former U.S. president, Bill Clinton's contribution to manglish is well-known and now widely used.

He studies at Oxford University in the U.K. and becomes the first person I ever hear saying, "grow the economy".

My only question is this, "How much watering does the economy require."

Why not conserve water by simply helping the economy (to) grow?

...

For many years I notice news reports becoming obsessed with using the same words over and over again.

When reporters interview people in the news, they repeat the same words as they already hear so much in the news.

Making matters worse, the same words become good for any and all purposes.

The words are overused to the point of making them almost meaningless. At least they lose their impact.

Sometimes I complain to news editors about overusing certain words when there are so many equally appropriate or better words in the dictionaries and thesaurus which punctuate news offices.

One of the current words on my abused list is "devastating".

It's in such common use that it becomes trivialized when describing the European-era created, ongoing, and now accentuated human disaster of Haiti following a very large, destructive, and lethal earthquake.

I can understand using the word devastated to describe the emotions of people who see their loved ones die suddenly and unexpectedly.

I can even stretch that to include people who lose items of sentimental or real value in storms or fires.

But I don't see why children who find themselves unable to take part in team sports, or amateur athletes not winning a trophy, or people who lose a job are also put in the category of "devastated".

They should only be disappointed and depressed, and not forever.

Apart from maybe a job loss for someone who is upset because s/he can never work anywhere again, devastation is a worst case scenario word.

Sporting events are definitely not in the same league or position as the people in Haiti and others who suffer very personal, tragic, and sudden losses.

Diminishing a word by using it too often and as an all-purpose adjective or adverb is also shown in the term "horror story".

Originally, it's probably restricted to horrendously shocking events, such as genocide, the Inquisitions, atomic bombings, and the nasty death camps which are known as the Holocaust.

A "horror story" is also used to mean a terrifying book, audio story, or motion picture.

Now, however, a "horror story" is used for describing solvable problem such as dirty sheets in a hotel during a tourist trip. Complain and change rooms or hotels.

...

Multitasking is supposed to mean a person can accomplish many tasks simultaneously. Sometimes employment advertising lists this as a required job skill.

However, the latest research in the news says multitasking is about short attention spans and lower quality work.

In other words, multitasking is a new way of saying scatterbrain. Scattering a brain prevents it from functioning accurately, efficiently, and at full capacity.

...

During the TV news, the day after Québec's municipal elections, I find out voters in Magog choose mayhem on election day.

Yes, the voters choose mayhem, I mean May Ham, Vicki May Ham. Nobody seems to get the joke because it's in English?

...

Hysterical pseudo-news reports and contriving supporters of the jailkeeper society police state are calling an underwear caper "an attack on America". They mean the U.S.

They've put a failed murder attempt in the same class as the cardboard box cutter killers who used commercial aircraft full of passengers as kamikaze weapons against the U.S. business and military headquarters.

Of course there is no security and the pursuit of it is folly.

It's just like paraphrasing Montaigne's quote, grasp at security and get nothing but air.

In this case it is particularly hot air. But in all the tragic-comedy, pathos, and ridiculous bluster going on, nobody is thinking it all out, as usual.

Or maybe they're just not getting equal access to the microphones in news reports.

...

Television news reporters always try to balance their stories about airport insecurity by interviewing people who both favour and oppose the latest fads in security.

Unfortunately, those in favour always say the same thing and express no doubts or questions about the wisdom, validity, and efficacy of whatever is imposed upon them.

They're merely reflecting their programming and trained responses to everything imposed on their lives.

They accept employment without question, as an unchallengeable good and natural norm. They are passive and accepting, resigned to an unfulfilling existence.

That existence is maximum security.

...

News shows the terrible impact of a 7.1 earthquake in Haiti, very soon after it happens.

The arrival speed of the news teams beats every rescue and aid team, as well as every shipment of food, water, and medical supplies.

How do they do it? Why don't they bring rescue teams and supplies?

Meanwhile, shocked and barely injured foreign residents from "the west" are repatriated by their nation-states just as quickly as the news crews arrive, leaving seriously injured and hungry people behind to starve, suffer, and die in Haiti.

Why do the foreign residents have no qualms about leaving the needy behind instead of offering them their seats in the aircraft and returning to their "first" world isolation wards only after first evacuating all the emergency cases?

The "first" world's greed, incompetence, impotence, stupidity, and indifference to "third" world lives strike again.

Chuang Hwa sends a rescue team to Haiti via Van Couverden.

It arrives in Port-au-Prince before the Europeans, before the U.S., and before other neighbouring countries.

Is that because Chuang Hwa is a dictatorship and thus can move more quickly? Or is Chuang Hwa simply more concerned about helping people in Haiti?

Four days later, a local baby gets evacuated to a hospital in the U.S. for emergency treatment.

This report comes in the same news as a story about a local person with crushed arms. They are amputated because the doctor says there is no other choice.

Without evacuation that's probably true.

In the "first" world, people are told the best thing they can do is donate money. In truth, that's all they know how to do. They spend money without a thought.

It's also the least complicated, low commital, and most distant way of dealing with problems. Throw money at them and they will go away.

Pay and forget the outside world. Hope that "they" will leave "us" alone. The outside world has nothing to do with "us". It doesn't affect "us" at all.

...

One Canadian news report says Chile's 8.8 quake is so severe that it has a miniscule effect on the angle of the earth's axis.

I'm wondering about how much of a cumulative effect the 15 years of big earth-quakes, including and follow-ing Kobe, have on the angle of the axis.

Many miniscule effects can add up to something bigger.

...

The "first" world "baby boomers", including people older, younger, and the same age as me, are actively participating in messing up the environment. That's not news to me.

What I don't realize is that so many of this group are investing in environmental destruction and banking their future on it.

At time of writing, while tonnes of oil spill from an oil well in the waters south of the U.S., destroying life and food supplies, news reports that the oil company drilling is financed by pension fund investments.

In other words, "first" world "baby boomers" have a vested interest in promoting air and water pollution. They're investing in ending human life on earth. It's fatal myopia.

...

Official records show there are about 40,000 people who are more than 100 years old in Nippon.

News reports say some of them are alive only in spirit and in receiving pension money each month, posthumously.

...

News here is full of stories about stranded passengers and airlines losing money, again, from cancelled flights due to a volcanic eruption in Iceland.

I complain to CBC-TV, saying they're not reporting anything about the benefits to the environment of grounding the fleets of petroleum-burning, i.e. air polluting, environment destroying, and global warming planes.

Within a couple of days of my complaint, CBC actually covers this part of the story.

Apparently keeping the planes out of the skies reduces pollution by 90 million tonnes. Hurray for the volcano!

...

A small group of people hiding their identities under black hoods and behind black masks decides to move Volympic demonstrations to "the next level".

They must mean downward.

They pick up heavy metal street boxes for selling newspapers and hurl them through department store windows.

Passersby intervene to try to stop them, verbally, some decrying the wanton destruction of private property.

News focuses on the violence and destruction.

Mercenaries dressed in almost identically black hoods, masks, and combat uniforms, i.e. "private security contractors" "supplementing" the vast police state network of surveillance cameras, police officers, and military personnel, arrive rapidly on the scene, brandishing machine guns, holding them in the ready-to-fire position.

So the objective of the window breakers is to boost the mercenaries, making them look like essential workers and necessary guardians, thus increasing mercenary services sales and raising the stock market value of shares in the mercenary companies?

It's also a successful diversion of the news mass media away from authentic and legitimate protest against real problems.

Cameras and journalists make only very brief, passing reference to the legitimate demonstrations against the lavish and pathetic waste of Volympic spending.

News reports downplay or ignore the actual protest story, adding yet another missed story to the list the the unreported.

Instead the sensational banner headline for the obvious insecurity marketing ploy confrontation is:

"Demonstrations Turned Violent".

Volympic money could go a long way toward financing solutions for the longstanding and solvable poverty, homelessness, drug addiction, and environmental problems facing the Volympic city.

Ignoring this fact means that, for all those supporting the status quo and opposing human progress, the Volympics are a great success.

...

Meanwhile, one of Canada's two major English-language television networks discards the regular news programmes and all other programmes, in this time zone, to broadcast exclusively, I mean only and endlessly, banal interviews with airhead "sports" experts*, while repeatedly replaying and resummarizing Volympic events including both athletic and non-athletic occurrences. (Er, except for the peaceful demonstrators' perspectives on the waste of money.)

(* I mean they aren't talking about the effects of the Volympics on the urban setting, society, or young athletes' minds and bodies.

A truly olympic broadcasting effort should at least interview objective, outside health specialists about the pressure, stress, physiological and psychological effects that young people go through in order to participate in mere games.

We only learn something about such newsworthy problems by talking to a sports competition runner who we meet abroad. Sports reporters should talk to game participants too, and learn.)

Somehow sexual abuse also goes unnnoticed and unreported in sports "news" for generations.

There's a difference between not being interested in sports and being indifferent to the serious human problems facing participants.

...

CBC has a strange habit of talking about multiculturalism and "tolerance". But "tolerance" only seems to mean that

Euroface Canadians need to tolerate the rest.

It may not be an intentional impression, but it comes across that way to me.

I don't understand why the word "tolerance" is appropriate. To me, that word is negative. It means "to put up with" in the sense of something unpleasant, undesirable, annoying.

The CBC usage I'm hearing sounds as if the Eurofaces are somehow inconvenienced in life by the mere presence of non-Eurofaces.

History says otherwise.

The unpleasantness and undesirables disrupting the world for about 500 years are Euroface invaders, not peacefully and slowly migrating humanity from the rest of the world.

If anyone is being tolerant, and running short of tolerance in many places, such as Moslem-centred populations, it is the "third" world.

The "third" world is extremely tolerating the "first". Or should that be - excessively tolerant.

After so many centuries of Euroface violence, violation, and thievery in what is now called the "third" world, it's amazing that the "third" world has any remaining tolerance at all for the intolerable "first".

...

CBC-TV's news-only television network starts more than twenty years before we live in Montréal.

It starts as CBC Newsworld and specializes in non-stop coverage of meetings and hearings while they're happening.

If you're not interested in the particular meeting or hearing, it can be tedious, but it's a good idea.

The cable television companies' CPAC, Canadian Parliamentary Channel takes over, although it tends to lack good programming judgement.

While Pierre Trudeau is speaking to the Senate about Meech Lake, CPAC is broadcasting from the House of Commons, showing a backbencher reading an article from a newspaper out loud.

Or CPAC was supporting the prime minister of the time, by blocking coverage of Pierre.

Most recently, at time of writing, I notice Newsworld becoming repetitive and scatterbrain in its approach to news, playing exactly the same news stories over and over again, with no updates, instead of showing news widely available from around the forgotten, outside world.

I have no idea what's happening in the southern Americas unless I look at summaries in Spanish and Portuguese that I get directly from newspapers from there via the internet.

There is a similar blackout on all of Africa, almost all the time, as well as most of what's happening in Asia and Europe.

Only the most outrageous and provocative headlines come from the outside world, except for the U.S.

The lives of a few hundred people caught in U.S. floodwaters still merit a week of long news stories, while a million people left homeless in Bangladesh get brief, passing mention during the late-night news, if time permits.

When Newsworld changes its name to CBC News Network, the decline of news accelerates.

Ads promoting the new network name call it "faster paced" news.

I write to tell CBC it's ideal for an audience composed entirely of Alzheimer's patients and people with attention span deficiencies.

It's like listening to the same hourly radio news broadcast over and over again, but every ten minutes instead of once per hour.

Major news stories are also interrupted all the time by the most trivial events, such as pancake breakfasts preceding a professional football championship game.

One of Obama's wonderful, intelligent speeches can easily be interrupted to show a "live", "breaking" story about a crowd cheering for victorious hockey players returning from well-played games away.

Anyone, including interviewers, can say anything without thinking or reflection, "live" and around the clock.

One CBC "news" host describes Honduras as a South American country.

What happened to all the news writers and editors? They aren't needed in a world where everything is ad lib and nothing is edited.

Anyone appearing on such a free-for-all mess can take out the time and talk over opponents to mute and muffle them.

It's the anti-60 Minutes, a U.S. CBS News show that starts 20 years before CBC Newsworld.

In that show, all interviews are based on carefully thought out and well written questions delivered by excellent, fast-witted interviewers.

Both questions and answers are recorded well in advance, spliced and pasted together to maximize the information conveyed and to remove the repetition as well as diversionary and delaying tactics of certain interviewees.

Ironically, 60 Minutes features a veteran CBC News reporter' Morley Safer, who is lured away from Canada when 60 Minutes is born.

...

Science and news reports are telling us we can improve and extend our lives by not eating, not breathing, and not sitting. It's easiest not to sit.

...

Television networks shorten their news programmes to summarize sporting events.

I don't understand. Sports fans watch sports events and then sports reports in local news broadcasts, not network news programmes.

People interested in the news want to see news, not summaries of sports they don't watch because they aren't interested in them.

NHK schedules its main sports report for 10 p.m. Saturday nights.

...

Huntsville and Toronto are in the news for hosting one of the very frequent G7/8 meetings and less frequent G20 gatherings.

The Canadian government pays a billion dollars for "secu-rity".

Both places are surrounded and taken over by a multitude of city, provincial, and national police (RCMP). Police are brought in from cities across Canada too.

In Toronto, a huge, long wire and concrete wall is erected, cordoning off not only the meeting place but also the neighbouring apartments and office buildings, including CBC.

Persons coming within five metres of the Toronto wall are required to answer police questions and show identification, or else they can be automatically arrested.

People who sell snacks in the streets are exiled from the meeting zone. Shops in Huntsville and Toronto report huge drops in clientele and income.

Canada's government attempts to justify the insecurity action, its expense, and the much greater cost of the meetings themselves, by saying it all shows Canada's importance in the world and spotlights the country as a place to visit and do business.

Tourists flock to armed camps?

When peaceful demonstrators arrive in front of the Ontario legislative building, far from Toronto's G summit location, the police send in a huge riot squad.

The helmeted, face-guarded, plastic-shielded, armed police police form a blitzkrieg and advance toward the peaceful demonstrators in front of the meeting place of Ontario's democratically-elected government.

As the riot squad pushes forward, its members are making menacing statements and gestures (swinging batons as if about to strike), while ordering the crowd to retreat.

The threatening riot squad charges the people and then stops just short of hitting them. It's a tour de force intimidation against peaceful protesting.

Thousands of demonstrators stand in front of the blitzkrieg, accompanied by reporters and onlookers.

Democratically-elected legislators don't call back the riot squad or ask demonstrators to go home. The Ontario premier's office is silent.

A line of people with cameras stand in front of and beside the police.

I watch a scene like this from late afternoon until mid-evening because even the regular, CBC, CTV, SRC, and TVA television networks start broadcasting a live, uninterrupted report from the scene around Ontario's legislative building

Journalists being told to get out of the way are nervously pulling back, trying to avoid being trampled by the police blitzkrieg charges.

Journalists are saying they don't like violence and understand the need for policing, but the blitzkrieg against peaceful demonstrators also has reporters in shock, saying, "I'm wondering what country I'm in." "This is Canada?"

The police blitzkrieg attack on the peaceful demonstrators deteriorates further the next day. The riot squad begins charging into crowds of peaceful demonstrators.

Police arrest nearly 1,000 people, including bystanders, journalists, and tourists. Some people are merely out for a walk in the park around the legislature.

A few demonstrators sit on the road, with their backs to the police, leaving a safe distance between them and the blitzkrieg.

The demonstrator starts singing Canada's national anthem.

At this precise moment the police riot squad blitzkrieg charges, overrunning the singers, swinging batons.

After the police attack on the passive singers, one of the singers pulls up his shirt to reveal the big red welts on his back from the blitzkrieg's violent attack with clubs.

To my knowledge, there is no public inquiry into the police attack. No public hearings are held with witnesses and victims testifying.

A more than ample supply of news recordings, during hours of broadcasting, is not reviewed by a public investigation into the police riot.

In an attempt to justify the police attacks, Toronto's police chief covers a table with confiscated weapons.

In so doing, he points out that some of the weapons on display are not confiscated during the peaceful demonstration and have no relationship whatsoever to the demonstrations.

So why are they on display? News cameras are expected to edit them out while publishing pictures on television and in newspapers?

This memorable showcase of confiscated weaponry reminds me of Chile's bloodthirsty military dictator, General Pinochet, who invites the foreign news reporters to take pictures of weapons he "discovered".

The general declares the weapons part of an arsenal of opponents of his regime.

He's thus saying that his violent, murderous, oppressive dictatorship of kidnapping and torture is justified, to fight off those heavily-armed opponents.

The general is giving us a preview of Canada's new image showing Canada's importance in the world and spotlighting Canada as an attractive place for tourists and business?

No heads roll at the police department or anywhere else. The story blows over and is forgotten in the news.

The police riot in Toronto becomes a non event. It never happens. It is only a rumour.

The epitaph appears in a major Canadian daily newspaper, which writes an editorial saying that it's nice to be protected, but who will protect us from our protectors?

Then the story disappears... forever? It never happens? It's only rumour, as the Nazi commander says in the film «Schlinder's List»?

...

News shows the U.S. military trying to drum up support for the long U.S. wars in Afghanistan and Iraq.

The U.S. military's advertising department runs a pro-war campaign under the camouflage slogan of "support our troops".

Thus pacifists and other opponents of the wars in Afghanistan and Iraq could be accused of lacking patriotism, which apparently means blind loyalty to the nation-state.

The "unpatriotic" are undermining the morale of people wearing uniforms to defend the nation-state, and foolishly or deliberately aiding and abetting "the enemy".

The U.S. military then, in diplomatic understatement, helps the Canadian military advertising department to adopt exactly the same slogan and war-booster approach.

It slips right past the Canadian mass media news, unnoticed and unreported.

...

During the U.S. wars, for the first time in "peace" time, Canadian news stories feature the head of the Canadian armed forces.

His face and name become familiar, instead of remaining an almost anonymous bureaucratic face and name that few know and which only makes the news for a moment, when appointed and replaced.

At the same time, a former professional hockey player who uses televised hockey games to promote himself and his opinions, and to make controversial statements, such as racist comments about non-anglo hockey players, decides to turn an arena full of hockey fanatics into a pep rally for the military.

He invites the head of Canada's armed forces to make a

grand entrance into the hockey arena, announcing him as a national hero, encouraging loud cheers, as if the military chief were a hockey star.

The ghost of propaganda minister Goebbels would be cheering back stage, gratified that someone is carrying on his tradition of promoting ignorance and its ultimate product, war.

The great diversionary-makers of Rome's coliseums would be delighted too. Don't think. Don't reflect. Just cheer for war.

Eventually the head retires, but his successor is also widely reported and known in the daily news. It is a new era in Canadian government, the military chief era.

In the past, the only famous Canadian military officers are the ones sent as U.N. peacekeepers to the genocide scenes of the former Yugoslavia and Rwanda.

Their work makes them true heroes of peace, not manufactured media stars.

Yet there is never a "support our peacekeepers" campaign in Canada. Canadian Peacekeepers aren't mentioned or boosted at professional hockey games arenas.

...

More recently, news shows a part of the trans-Canada highway that is informally renamed as the route of the returning dead soldiers from Afghanistan.

No such roadway honours the many more peacekeepers.

There is also a new monument that's exclusively for the dead Canadian soldiers killed in Afghanistan, to date 142.

This monument includes the etched-in-stone face of each soldier, plus a write-up.

No such engraved facial monument records the faces of the

multitude of soldiers killed in the big wars of the past century or any other war killing Canadians.

There are always war monuments, not peace monuments, except for the Peace Tower on parliament hill in Ottawa.

...

A recently promoted key agent of the Canadian spy agency, CSIS, reports cases of Canadian military turning over terrorist suspects to the U.S.-created Afghan government for questioning, which includes torture.

When opposition parties in Ottawa ask questions about this report in parliament, the Canadian prime minister replies by accusing the opposition of not supporting our troops and undermining the "mission".

The new armed forces chief says he knows nothing about it. The next battle in this war occurs when the opposition parties insist on seeing all the documents which either support or refute the spy's report.

In response, the government prints out reams of paper composed mostly of photocopies of black felt pen marks, blocking out almost all the content of the documents they represent.

The prime minister then prorogues parliament, i.e. shuts down parliament for three months, saying the government needs time to reorganize its agenda and does not want to meet during the Volympics. Sports replace democracy?

That shuts down the committee hearings about torture reports, the pursuit of documents which either support or refute the reports, etc.

It also cancels all work toward passing legislation the government is pushing.

Three months later, the speaker of the house of commons orders the government to show parliament the uncensored, original documents. He gives a 14 day deadline.

There are meetings among the political parties. When the deadline approaches, opposition parties say progress is being made so the deadline can be extended.

Five months later, parliament closes for a three-month summer break. No document agreement is reached. One opposition party leaves the meetings.

No documents are revealed. Censorship triumphs?

Meanwhile, minister's office staff and public service workers are banned from appearing for questioning at parliamentary hearings.

Only cabinet ministers are permitted to appear.

Canada's spy is left out in the cold.

After all the evasions and all the efforts toward responsible government, for the previous 200 years, all that is left of Canada's government is the slogan, "support our troops".

What torture? What documents? All is forgotten in the news.

...

When people move in Montréal and Miyazaki, they seem to forget to take their cats with them. In Montréal, the SPCA takes care of abandoned cats and sells them.

During a television news interview, an SPCA representative says that a cat fee covers shots and implanting a chip in the cats so they can be located.

Hmm. But according to what the federal and provincial Canadian governments say, while trying to reduce pubic concern over computer chips in passports and drivers licences, people can only know the location of cats if they are 10 cm. away.

So is the SPCA lying, or are the governments lying?

...

CBC News reports that the quality of air is improving in Toronto this summer, apparently due to less air pollution.

So the reduced industrial production and lower automobile sales caused by the economic collapse of the moment is enabling the earth's atmosphere to start repairing itself?

We should use all the company head's bonuses and net worth, plus the stockholders' gains to pay the laid off workers' salaries for improving the air by not being employeed.

...

Is one major "terrorist" in the news merely a murderous business person who is increasing profits for his family business and nation-state dictatorship?

His family owns a construction company. His most notorious crime is destroying buildings full of people. His family profits from new construction contract work.

He is also known for attacks on public transit vehicles full of people.

He's from Saudi Arabia, whose prime income is derived from selling oil to fuel private vehicles with internal combustion engines.

If more people are afraid to use pubic transit, they are more likely to become new customers for oil and internal combustion engines.

If this "terrorist" were truly an opponent of "first" world ways, as all news stories and supporters imply, he wouldn't be targeting public transit at all.

Instead, he would be bombing internal combustion vehicle factories and the highways that their vehicles depend on and use daily.

Since his political and social goals are not reported in the news, despite the many video recordings he sends to the news media, I could easily conclude his real goals are to promote certain businesses and to destroy the world through air pollution.

His name is Ben or Bin something-or-other.

...

At time of writing, CBC News says about 66% of the world population is not on line, i.e. not using the computer internet system.

Only about 21% of the "third" world population is on line.

This is positive, hopeful news for human survival because when people are not mesmerized by screens, their minds are free to think about how to improve the world.

...

**Richmond**: The end of a CBC TV News story gets my attention long enough for me to see a photo of someone being sought by worried parents from another province.

I know the person in the photo. I'm sure it's Ben, the youngest of several guitar and banjo players aboard a train I take to come here from Montréal.

CBC News says anyone knowing the person in the photo should contact the police. I'm of no help because I don't get any information from Ben about where he's staying.

I don't have his e-mail address. But one of the other passengers, Jim, who talks to Ben more than I do, might know how to contact Ben.

So I send an e-mail message to Jim, who writes to me several times after the train ride, and ask him to contact CBC if he knows how to contact Ben.

Just before I leave Richmond en route back to Montreal, Jim tells me I'm right about the photo and he contacts both CBC and the police.

Thus Ben's parents find him. That's all I know before leaving Richmond. This is my first contribution to solving a missing person's case in the news.

**Montréal**: After years of filling Haiti with aid workers and money, the "first" world pours in much more for earthquake relief.

Years later and a year after the big quake, Haiti remains in ruins.

Haiti is thus a monument to the ineffectiveness, ineptitude, impotence, and incompetence of the "first" world.

Then the last of the former Haitian dictators returns to try to stir up the pot further.

He wants to take advantage of the confusion, perhaps regain power, and no doubt steal more money from Haiti. Last time he leaves with $US300 million.

This time he must be planning to take a big chunk of the billions of aid money with him.

He says he wants to run in the current presidential elections, but they are in the middle, between the first round and the second round.

Candidates with fewer votes are already eliminated.

So the former dictator can't possibly run.

The most amazing part of his return is that there are witnesses in Haiti, Montreal, etc. to his crimes against humanity, and he is actually arrested and detained in his hotel room, in a luxurious U.S.-chain-owned hotel in Haiti.

The circumstances of his arrival are bizarre and seem inexplicable, on the surface.

He lives in luxurious exile in France for 25 years before returning to Haiti. He arrives with a diplomatic passport which is about to expire.

The French ambassador says the former dictator has a return airline ticket which he has to use within a few days of arrival in Haiti.

Employees of news-gathering organizations are reporting many theories and rumours, but that's it.

There's very little news about the dictator's arrival in Haiti, or none at all, in English.

The only reason that I'm informed is largely due to the daily, ongoing reporting of the francophone news reporters.

Even when I tune in the NPR U.S. radio network there is only one passing reference to the Haiti dictator story.

There is no news of any government, except the Canadian, warning that the dictator should do nothing to interfere with Haiti's democracy-building process.

...

The news hits us, but not hard, when the current dictator of Tunisia flees while people take to the streets demanding a better form of government.

Although it seems like a distant event, it has more impact on us personally than Haiti.

Sami Fruit, the fruit and vegetable store where we shop, imports many items from northern Africa, including Algeria and Tunisia. For months we buy relatively inexpensive, fresh dates from Tunisia.

After a few days of political demonstrations in that country, the date supply disappears from our store.

...

CBC News says the popular movements currently pushing out the dictators of northern

Africa are a product of dominantly young populations with big food inflation and high unemployment.

The median age in the countries is 18 to 24. The food inflation numbers shown on CBC are much more honest than the ones in Canada and the rest of the "first" world.

CBC says Canada's median age is 44.

The contrast in age is reminding me of my writing when I first arrive in Rio de Janeiro, about the southern Americas and the "third" world being full of younger people, leaving behind the aging, declining "first" worlders.

The anti-dictatorship movement spreads to Libya, Bahrain, Syria, Jordan, and Yemen.

I'm hoping Saudi Arabia and Kuwait will finally be rid of their absolute monarchy dictatorships too.

Even the U.S. and E.U. try to get on the bandwagon against the dictatorships that they enable, empower, and prolong for 30, 40, and more years, at the expense of the local populations and the proliferation of worldwide democracy.

..

In today's news, instability is the new synonym for pro-democracy. Along with it are rebels and sometimes insurgents.

This change of vocabulary comes when Libya gets closer to overthrowing its 40-year dictatorship.

Why? Libya produces only 2% of the world oil supply, and other countries with oil have surpluses, the news says. But somehow petroleum prices start jumping fast due to Libya's pro-democracy, i.e. instability movement.

So people in the "first" world start complaining about Libya.

Scenes of people demanding an end to dictatorship in Libya are suddenly preempted by stories about "instability and unrest in Libya pushing up gasoline prices".

It's yet another example of the "first" world revealing the real reason for its name. People there put themselves first, ahead of democracy and all the rest of humanity in general.

In one news story, international aid organizations warn that increases in oil prices will cause a billion people to starve. That's more than 10% of humanity.

Democracy causes mass starvation? It's like Stalin?

In another news story, the oil companies owning Alberta and the farmers switching from food crops to bio-fuels expect the oil price rises to bring new riches to them.

The billion people who will pay for the riches by starving to death aren't mentioned in this news story.

...

The consequences of falling under the employment system for a lifetime are far worse than my arguments of 30 years before time of writing.

This third year of the current world economic crisis helps prove my basic argument about the bad trade off of getting stuck in employment for the prime years of a lifetime.

According to CBC News, most adults in Canada do not have the means to survive in retirement.

So, in addition to losing all their prime years of life to employers, most employees will now be obliged to continue working for employers well into what are considered the standard retirement age and far beyond.

Nation-states are extending their partnership with employers by officially extending the age of retirement into later years of life too.

This situation brings new meaning to the term lifelong employment, which no longer even theoretically enables people to have retirement at the end, before they get sick and die.

...

Unnoticed news isn't news at all. It's apparent in nature and completely ignored by most societies and nation-states.

SRC Radio's "Semaine Verte" says only 1% of species are monogamous. So lifelong coupling is unnatural.

No wonder there are so many unhappy couples, bad marriages, separations, and divorces, along with abused spouses and abused children.

Societies deny our natural behaviours in even our most basic human relationship, ensuring the continuation of our human form of life.

Meanwhile, a Columbia (Br.) court is deciding the legality of polygamy. It's a decision on whether or not natural behaviour is legal?

The case and news reporting are also flawed because they are suggesting that polygamy means one male with more than one female.

In nature, polygamy is also one female with more than one male. Why distort things more than they are already perverted by unnatural monogamy?

...

One news report says Chuang Hwa is spending more on insecurity than military because it's afraid northern Africa revolts caused by food shortage and inflation could spread.

It reminds me of military dictatorships defending themselves from the general public.

The story goes on to explain that Chuang Hwa is also planning to double food production which means a reversal of rural populations moving to urban centres.

There are stories in the news during my time in Rio de Janeiro about urban people returning to their rural homes after becoming discouraged with city life.

...

SRC's TV programme "La Semaine Verte" says 60% of the world population now lives in Asia; One third of U.S. corn production now goes to bio-fuels; It takes 15 kilos of grain to produce 1 kilo of beef, 6 kilos of grain for a kilo of pork, and $2^{1/2}$ kilos of grain to get a kilo of chicken.

What a waste of corn and other grain.

...

Sendai Nippon has a 9.0 earthquake, it's Sendai's biggest and one of the biggest reported in recorded history. A huge tsunami hits very quickly.

Almost all the news in Canada is about this story.

While news turns most of its attention to Sendai, the nearly toppled dictators of northern Africa and southwestern Asia start to hire mercenaries and send each other troops to slaughter pro-democracy demonstrators.

The G7/8 and "first" world in all its forms responds with its typical impotence and incompetence.

Their failure leaves the road open to their enemies, the "terrorists" who can now say nobody cares except them.

So "terrorists" can send in aid in the form of "freedom fighters" to help the pro-democracy movement and shape it against the "first".

The dictators are already allying themselves like the Nazi and Fascist dictators of Europe do when my parents are young adults; and like those dictators help each other in the civil war of España when my parents are children.

Saudi Arabia's monarchical dictatorship is sending its U.S.-equipped military forces to help Bahrain's monarchical dictatorship kill pro-democracy protesters, giving further credence to the "terrorists" and probably catalyzing and bolstering support for "terrorists".

**Santiago de Cuba**: I see news about an international meeting of an organization I've never heard of and which apparently excludes all "first" world nation-states.

It's called BRICS, named for its five member states, Brasil, Russia, Bharat ("India"), Chuang Hwa, and South Africa.

So BRICS is composed of the two most populous countries in the world; the largest, third largest, and fifth largest countries in the world; the country with the world's largest oil reserves; the two countries with the world's biggest gold reserves; and the currently second and fifth largest economies in the world.

So BRICS is the kingpin in world affairs, regardless of what many people in the "first" world might think of themselves.

Yet I only learn about this group because it's meeting gets a lot of news coverage on the Chuang Hwa television stations we watch in Cuba.

BRICS is founded, without South Africa, two years before we go to Cuba. So why haven't I heard of it before now? I'm so ignorant and/or BRICS is not newsworthy?

...

At time of writing, Chuang Hwa's world conquest by peaceful means is largely unrecognized in the daily news of the "first" world mass media.

It beats armed invasions and arms racing.

CCTV (English) mentions what Mariko and I do observe for years in news stories, i.e. more people seem to be studying Chinese.

We also note stories about Chuang Hwa cornering as much of the world's oil supplies as possible, including those in Africa, via diplomacy, aid, & trade.

...

Every morning I turn on the TV for news, usually tuning in TVE, where there's sometimes an español course.

In Cuba we get news directly from Chuang Hwa, the EU, U.S.C.N.N., Télésur, including TV5 with Canada's SRC Téléjournal.

This particular day is a Sunday, so local and Venezuela television stations are broadcasting the May Day filas (parades).

I'm surprised to see President Raoul Castro walking along the big street passing in front of Plaza de la Revolución, a short walk from here.

I try to see the event from our building's fourth floor windows. I often go there to look at the view beyond the military zone gate on the street just behind us.

Today, I'm not the only one on the fourth.

A nonchalant plain clothes guard, wearing a sports shirt, is sitting on a lounge chair, unlike our regular, friendly, insecurity guards in uniform, who sit out front, smile, wave, and exchange a few words with us.

I quickly realize that I can't see anything of the event I'm trying to see from this vantage.

As I turn to go, the unusual insecurity guard softly tells me not to hang around the windows, for "security" reasons.

Sure, I understand the concern. The U.S. spends decades trying to eliminate Raoul's brother

Fidel. But I can't see anything of the celebrations from here anyway.

What about the fourth floor guests who have the same view?

And, although we see two (unarmed?) green clad soldiers as we walk into the neighbouring university campus, they don't approach us while we're going to the top of a campus building and taking scenic photos from there.

We can't see the plaza where Raoul is walking from there either.

The campus building is at least as high as our building's fourth floor, yet closer to the plaza.

Trees and buildings obstruct our view of today's festivities and give us a great vista of the same Sierra Maestra we can see from our fourth floor.

By the time we walk toward Plaza de la revolución, the street remains filled with people strolling along, wearing red shirts, waving flags and banners in the sun.

The red shirts almost rival Canada Day in Ottawa on parliament hill.

We only approach the fiesta fila as far as the nearby theatre, due to the monotonous, hearing impairing din of over-amplified music and master of ceremonies slogan-chanting.

...

The U.S. world's cable news TV network, in the self-obsessed USA, has only these words drifting past as world footnotes on the TV screen: "Conservatives appear to be winning election in Canada." at time of writing.

Equally self-obsessed European stations have short, summarized stories. Only TV5 shows the SRC election night news cast with all the details.

Some elections get news coverage. Others come out of nowhere on voting day, probably baffling viewers with sudden, surprising news having no background or details.

This is an era when all elections except "ours" are irrelevant and have absolutely no importance. (This is before Aljazeera.)

...

Venezuela's Telesur news insists NATO has gone mad, saying it is suddenly invading Libya for no reason.

Some locals we meet have views reflecting this news.

Meanwhile, all the other channels, including non-NATO CCTV, report the Libyan dictator's attacks on Libyan civilians, causing NATO to bomb the dictator's military installations and the mercenaries he employs.

The discrepancy in reporting is too diverse.

Telesur also reports, in a bottom screen news streamer, that Alquaida is planning to avenge their leader's death at the hands of the U.S. military.

Earlier in the news cycle, this same group is declaring that their leader dies of disease several years before the U.S. kills him. If so, why the vengeance threat?

It's such a crazy contradiction that it puts Telesur's intelligence in question. How can death from illness require revenge? It's sloppy, at best, news-propaganda.

...

As well as being poorly-educated, I'm ill-informed. That's not news to me.

Only today, I'm learning that 12 nation-states found UNASUR three years earlier to integrate themselves. San Martin de los Andes cheers.

Venezuela and other nation-states turn 200 too this year.

Why am I just finding out? (Answer: I'm from the "first" world. The rest of the world isn't newsworthy to us.)

**Montréal**: Attention span deficiency Canadian TV news broadcasting trashes news judgement and objectivity to become particularly airheaded and completely uncritical, starstruck entertainment, non-news whenever a U.K. monarchy representative visits Canada.

Journalism takes a vacation.

I write to CBC News, criticizing it's role in the wide-eyed, bushy-tailed, beaming smile, nearly fainting approach of CBC news staff to the highly staged and artificial U.K. visitors.

At least entertainers work very hard for their fame. They struggle for years to become famous. Monarchs and their families are just born to it. They do nothing to earn fame. They just wave and smile.

Canada's current good-for-nothing monarchy visitors are only here for a stopover, en route to the main event, a gala performance with the authentic U.S. movie star monarchs in Hollywood. Canada is a boring side trip.

Never have so few done so little for so much (U.K., Canadian, Australian, New Zealand, etc.) taxpayers' money.

What world economic collapse, homelessness, poverty, hunger, food riots, revolutions, etc?

That's low priority stuff, minor news on hold until after the "wonderful royals" lovely visit.

Let's be civilized, couth, good-mannered, and polite now. Forget about commoners' problems and riff raff won't you? Enjoy the wondrous pomp and tradition of the layabout elite.

...

"Breaking News" must be reserved for and only about monarchical buttocks and the like.

...

**Portage la prairie**: News value depends on the listener. Some RV dwellers near our tent camp site have a news broadcast playing on their TV.

I overhear news stories such as "Starvation in Somalia", etc. The RV dwellers don't seem to notice. They're talking loudly about something completely unrelated.

Then a story says, "Tourists beheaded" and the RV dwellers go into silent, sudden shock.

Then one exclaims in horror and disbelief, "That's terrible. Those \_\_\_\_ are inhuman!"

So "they" don't value human life, but "we" do? Yes, but "we" only value our own.

...

**Winnipeg**: We're staying in an old hotel (The Marlborough) with some of the 2,000 First Nations refugees in the news who are fleeing the floods in rural areas. We meet some every day.

Aboard an elevator, one of these folks from an isolated community turns her head toward the rear wall and covers her eyes. She doesn't like the elevator and fears it.

To show empathy, I tell her I don't like them either. I get stuck in one in a dumpy old hotel in D.C. (U.S.A.) one time for a few moments.

The Winnipeg elevator fear reminds me of how hesitantly and nervously people in a Malaysian border town next to Singapura step onto escalators. It's another first encounter.

News says the First Nations refugees want to return to their homes; put their children in school because the school year is now underway; and get out of the bad influence of downtown streets in this city.

Winnipeg is a small city, but huge compared with their tiny

communities. News has many stories about poverty, drugs, and gangs in Winnipeg.

**St. Barbe**: We hitch-hike and get a ride all the way from St. Anthony to here. We always try to talk to people picking us up.

I ask our driver if she hears the news story about the big ice berg which has broken off in the north and is heading this way.

She says she never watches, reads, or listens to news.

She says that the only news she knows about is two local fast food chains we've never heard of now opening in St. Anthony. She sounds very excited about this news.

Instead of keeping up with other news, she says that she "only takes care of her family", i.e. children, and works at a hardware store.

She lives in a couple of different areas and places in Newfoundland and Labrador before moving to her current home in St. John's.

She says her husband is francophone from Côte-nord and her kids are in French-language schooling now.

**Hawkes Bay to Deer Lake**: Despite news reports about there being many moose beside the highways, and eye-witness accounts that we're hearing from people like Kevin, our trucker host on this road, and other drivers, we see no moose anywhere along the way.

**Toronto**: We're witnessing, first hand and close up at street level, a major storm in the news. It doesn't seem so bad, but it's cool and rainy.

A highway bus from Montréal dumps us and all the other passengers here in the middle of the night.

The bus station and train station won't open for a few hours, so we're taking shelter along Yonge Street in enclaves in front of a couple of commercial businesses.

Only two panhandlers in the storm approach us and quickly give up.

I'm surprised there are any since the hour and the weather make it very unlikely they'll find anyone to approach.

More surprising is a miserable-looking, wet, hunched up racoon creeping along the sidewalk on the southeast corner of Yonge and Richmond.

We see it from the southwest corner.

There is also a tiny, cockroach-size rat taking shelter under a net metal garbage pail just outside the main western doors of VIA Union Station.

This is the main night life of the storm.

...

According to CBC TV News, there are about 100 "third" world towns in Canada today.

Someone in the news room is discovering that the "first" and "third" are not defined by membership in particular nation-states. Finally!

**Dazaifu**: NHK News says that many people in Nippon stop working in high stress, long hour jobs. Consequently, they're now finding their lives more enjoyable.

They work fewer hours for lower pay and they're getting more time to devote to doing something that they like doing.

They're also gaining closer relationships with their family and friends.

**Fukuoka**: A free trade agreement between Hangoo and the U.S. enables branch plants of Nippon's companies in the U.S. to export products to Hangoo without paying the much higher tariffs imposed on exactly the same products exported directly from Nippon to Hangoo.

NHK-TV News shows the Japanese president of Toyota's U.S. division visiting Hangoo and happily promoting Japanese cars that are made in the U.S.

Nation-state free trade agreements simplify the sales strategies of multinational corporations with plants around the world.

Maybe that's the whole idea.

As someone in Barcelona says to us, about the EU free trade area, during our months in Barcelona, free trade deals are an agreement among companies, not countries.

...

With about 19,000 dead, more than 3,000 still missing, and 450+ unidentified bodies, the eastern Nippon disaster area of one year earlier (Fukushima, Miyagi, and Iwatae) continues to haunt this land.

Commemoratory ceremonies and ongoing news and special TV programmes mark the anniversary for many days, including an appearance by Canadian geneticist and environmentalist Dr. David Suzuki.

There are many lengthy reports about revealing documents describing internal government communication during the disasters; world anti-nuclear power demonstrations; the huge problem of allaying fears about and disposing of débris contaminated with leaked radiation; and, government moves to create tougher regulations defining how much radiation in food stuffs is acceptable.

...

News reports with unblinking, straight-faced reporters regurgitate the incredible claims from unnamed sources, that world "uncertainty" is causing the fuel price increases.

But, at time of writing, this same "uncertainty" is pushing up the yen and making all non-petroleum imports cheaper!

Why not honestly report that someone is artificially increasing petroleum prices to collect more profits, and yen?

...

NHK-TV morning news reports a marvel in company training.

Some companies are sending their young, newly-hired employees to a training session unlike anything I know.

Apparently, many younger people pass so much of their time interacting anonymously and indirectly through computer screens that they develop no interhuman communication skills or social skills.

So the training session tries to help the younger generation of newly-hired employeed by confiscating their cell phones, credit cards, and money, and obliging them to hitch-hike 100 kilometres.

Hitching forces them to talk to people, both to get rides and to carry on conversations during the rides.

Wow! I'm sure hitching helps my communication skills, and in several languages. Bravo trainers!

...

We notice how news is following the same old formula in the U.S.-led G7/8:

There's "this one guy" who is really very, very bad, and if he would just go away, or we could just get rid of him, the world would be transformed, almost overnight, into a wonderful place.

It's not news. It's as dumb as the people weeping and shaking for absolute and obsolete monarchies.

It's a simpleminded distraction from investigating, thinking about, and trying to solve underlying causes of problems facing humanity as a whole entity, not as a species split apart and dislocated by separatist, unnatural nation-states and their barriers to human unity.

I don't hear any reports about all these nasty dictators being part of the European colonial era or Euro Era, U.S.-C.C.C.P. Era legacy, heritage, and traditions.

News reports also revert to the old U.S.A. vs. C.C.C.P. era approaches to covering that "one guy" of the moment's news.

There are endlessly repeated scenes of nasty-looking, almost zombie, goose-stepping soldiers, an apparently invincible military having nothing better to do than parade back and forth across a huge, paved-over, empty parking lot-like area all day and every day, leading and following a massive display of military hardware, especially armoured vehicles and missiles.

These warriors and munitions are ready and able to strike at a second's notice.

The "one guy" has so many soldiers and weapons that he has yet another bunch of them on duty everywhere else in the country simultaneously and aboard all ships at sea that are headed for some other "one guy" land.

All these military menaces are forever ready and poised to strike immediately.

So we must always fear them, remain on constant alert, and stop them by never challenging or questioning huge and limitless military spending.

If it's really that bad, this news leads us to one conclusion:

We should all give up now; surrender and avoid all casualties and futile resistance; and end all military spending because our military is doomed to failure in the face of the ultimate, all-powerful, omnipotent nemesis.

Pre-emptive strikes and sanctions will only make it worse for us in the end. "One guy" will show us no mercy for our foolishness.

This is how the most effective propaganda against us turns out to be our own propaganda.

...

A few days after the commotion in the news caused by U.S. worries that North Korea might eventually be capable of launching a missile with a nuclear warhead, Bharat actually does launch one.

It's a passing story in the news, reported in a neutral, objective manner, mentioning that Bharat is now capable of launching a nuclear strike against Beijing.

There are no outcries from the U.S. or G7/8; no U.N. Security Council meetings expressing outrage or condemnation; and no sanctions proposed against Bharat.

After all, North Korea might create a missile capable of reaching the U.S. capital, not the Chuang Hwa capital.

Someone believes that the radiation from a Bharat nuclear missile striking Beijing, the centre of Chuang Hwa's billion people, would not respect the rules of nature, such as moving air currents, and go around the world?

Whereas a nuclear attack on the U.S. capital, the home of 300-400 million people, must be discouraged and stopped at all cost?

So the U.S.A. again shows it considers itself more valuable and important than the rest of the world.

And most of the rest of the world either remains silent or bows in submission like good courtiers all.

...

On the annual children's day, news features a statistical item illustrating an example of the aging, declining "first" world population.

Sixty-two years before time of writing, $33^{1/3}\%$ of Nippon's population are children. Since then, children's share of the population declines to 13%.

**St. John's**: Many people, including unthinking news reporters and commentators are pointing at "honour killing" as if it were a unique problem in itself, completely detached from all other forms of murder.

"Honour killings" are reported and condemned as if the murderers were killing based entirely on the fact that they belong to only one particular group or type of group of people, or they belong to only one brand of religionism.

In the real world, persons committing murder are no different from one another, whether they are using a religionist excuse or not.

Whether premeditated, spur of the moment, or accidental, murder remains the same crime no matter who commits it. The same applies to all crimes.

So why do only some murders, "honour killings" spark more outrage than other murders solely because they try to use a religionist excuse for killing other people?

The answer is in the question.

If religionism is responsible for the crimes of some people, all religionisms are responsible for the crimes of all people. No type of crime is a product of only one type of person or religionism.

...

David is an interesting, well-informed person who has made his way here due to a series of cut-backs in federal government spending on food inspections.

He's a scientist who works as a food inspector.

Prior to meeting him I hear a news programme stating that municipal water supplies are better than bottled water because municipal water is carefully inspected and controlled, but bottled water is not.

David says bottled water actually is inspected, but it's about the same quality as tap water.

...

Canadians east of Québec are excluded from the late nighttime audience of news broadcasts from Canada's major television networks for more than a hundred years.

Then CTV creates an early edition of its national newscast, with Sandie Renaldo, a long-time late night news host.

Until then, multi-channel cable television systems enables us to watch news from all networks and local channels across Canada, as well as many others from the U.S. and the U.K.'s BBC.

However, before Sandie, there is no regular TV network national newscast conforming to either Atlantic or Newfoundland time zones.

The earliest national newscast available here in St. John's is decided by the Eastern time zone of Ontario and Québec.

So early to late night national newscasts that we can watch at a reasonable hour anywhere else in Canada don't begin until much later here. Some begin after we're asleep.

The same applies to popular entertainment shows. Perhaps the ones originating in the U.S. are delayed because that nation-state isn't as wide as Canada, but there's no excuse for not showing Canadian news and other shows earlier.

My letters complaining about this exclusionist and discriminatory television broadcasting practice are ignored by the Canadian networks, until Sandie's show begins.

Canadians living in the Atlantic and Newfoundland & Labrador time zones are forgotten and ignored by the biggest Canadian TV networks for a long time. They're indifferent.

...

According to a news story seen in passing, the volume of religionist writing called bible in the Hebrew language, meaning simply "book", is being revised for the first time in 500 years.

Apparently there are many grammatical errors.

What does that say about the perfection of the divine origins credited to the human authors and revisers of this book?

...

According to an RDI news report, there are 5,000 delegates, along with 10,000 volunteers, and 16,000 news people at the convention that's to nominate Obama for the U.S. presidency.

So everyone can be interviewed at least once?

...

While the newly elected premier of Québec is making her first speech after the votes are counted, a crazy person at the back of the hall shoots a semi-automatic weapon, some kind of machine gun, killing one person and wounding some others.

It's a very extraordinary event in Canada. The tragedy is not restricted to the death and wounding.

The following day the Canadian television news stations are interviewing mercenaries, asking them if there needs to be more protection for politicians.

It's turning into a business opportunity for them, again.

This same day after, we walk home for lunch from the university and I spot Tom Mulcair in a taxi passing us, pulling up in front of CBC.

He's the NDP leader, leader of the official opposition in Ottawa.

Someone else who looks familiar from television news gets out of the taxi and I point and smile at Mulcair. We wait patiently while Mulcair pays the taxi driver.

When he turns we smile and wave at him. He smiles back. We exchange a thumbs up salute. There is no mercenary or police officer in sight.

We turn our backs and continue to walk away. Mulcair and his companion walk into CBC.

Meanwhile, in Ottawa, the prime minister of the moment continues to go out surrounded by a mercenary/police force around him, as if he were a military dictator.

...

Today's news is that Canada closes its embassy in Iran while the U.S. and E.U. leave theirs open. Strange contrast with the "allies".

To distract attention away from the apparent blunder, Canada's government sends out its immigration minister to repeat news from two years ago.

It's to find and eliminate 3,141 new Canadian citizens who, the government claims, aren't really living in Canada during the waiting period required for citizenship.

When one reporter asks if this doesn't take immigration clerks away from processing applications, the minister says re-sources for immigration work have been increased.

Yet within the same time span, the ministry is claiming it's no longer accepting immigration applications because it wants to clear up the backlog of unprocessed, i.e. unread, applications.

Canadian reporters are so nice to the immigration minister that they enable him to say something preposterous without the least bit of challenge.

He says the citizens and residents being deleted from Canada are "people of means".

They want to work in "havens" abroad while their families live in Canada and benefit from free health insurance and pay local student university tuition instead of foreign student tuition.

The missing questions are these:

1) The government's "investor immigrant" programme is meant to bring in "people of means".

Such people often have business and contractual work abroad as well as homes there. So why invite people to immigrate who you don't really want?

2) If the "wrongdoers" are working in tax havens abroad while their families are here, doesn't that mean a big chunk of the overseas income is going toward paying for their families' living expenses in Canada?

So that tax haven income is being spent in Canada, paying provincial and federal sales taxes at least.

3) Obviously, if the wrongdoers are "people of means" they don't need either free health care or lower tuition fees.

They can afford the best private health care available anywhere in the world. They can afford to send their children to the most expensive and perhaps best universities in the world.

So why would they really need to park their families in Canada?

The "people of means" must be choosing Canada for some other reason.

Maybe they find Canada attractive and simply want to spend most of their tax haven earned money in Canada.

This is why I think the repetition of a two year old news story, with the immigration minister available for about an hour for both a statement and questions from reporters, plus a new, large poster behind him saying, "Canadian citizenship is not for sale", is merely a diversion from the Iran embassy bungle.

...

Seven days of demonstrations for various reasons, (economic, union-management, and religion), look like a world revolution against the "first" world, through the eyes of shocked "first" world reporters telling the stories.

It's more remarkable that stories about a hate film against Moslems gets in the same newscasts as stories about an angry monarchical heir who tries to sue magazines.

Why is the angry monarchical heir mentioned at all? The magazines publish naked photos of the monarchical heir and his spouse.

Thus tragedy mixes with the trivial monarchy news.

...

Canada's prime minister is shown in the news declaring Canada an "energy superpower" that's a more reliable and dependable source of fossil fuels than southwest Asian oil fields.

A few years later, the same government encourages anyone abroad to purchase companies owned by Canadians.

Predictably, the shareholders of a Canadian oil company providing 28% of Canada's oil production are ready to sell.

They accept a $25 per share offer for shares previously selling for $17. The buyer is an oil company owned by Chuang Hwa.

So a major share of the reliable, dependable fossil fuels used by the U.S. is coming from the Canadian "energy superpower" Chuang Hwa state enterprise.

It's a nationalized industry of a government still calling itself "Communist".

So the "conservative" government of Canada is actually a "fellow traveller" of the "international communist conspiracy" now obliging the U.S. to buy "communist controlled" oil supplies from Canada?

Within a day of writing the above, a U.S. cable television news network reports that 29% of the U.S. oil supply comes from Canada.

Canadian oil represents the biggest proportion of the 45% of oil imported by the U.S, the news report says.

...

CBC News reports surveys describing how badly the employeed feel about employment.

The survey finds that 22% of employees are depressed.

Another survey says the employeed who are about to retire, i.e. my generation, want to go into business for themselves so that they can do something they find satisfying/ fulfilling, i.e. be their own bosses, etc.

Obviously, the employed do not find their employment experience personally satisfying, fulfilling, or rewarding.

...

At one point in recent history, new says that about one in eight human beings is going hungry. That's about 800 million people at that time.

Apparently this is an improvement. The previous total was one billion.

Is this good news or did 200 million die of hunger due to world-wide hyper-inflation in food prices thanks to the petroleum countries and companies along with farmers switching from food crops to biofuels to supplement the petroleum burned into toxic gases and the climate change caused by internal combustion engines?

..

According to a U.S. news report about a New York City babysitter stabbing the children in her care to death, children are most often in danger of becoming the victims of people in these categories and in this order: 1) parents; 2) people they know; and 3) babysitters. In comparison, strangers pose the lowest threat to children, about 5%.

So children should be taught that they should only talk to strangers?

...

Late in a daily U.S. CBS News broadcast, the host says "an item catching our attention".

The story, at time of writing, is that the U.S. will be the world's biggest producer of oil in about eight years and will be independent of all imported oil in about 23 years.

That same day and following morning, this item becomes a major news story in Canadian news.

Since 27%-29% of the oil used in the U.S. comes from Canada, and that makes the Alberta oil tar sands economical, it means the current Canadian government's plans to build Canada's economy based mostly on oil sales turns into a pipe dream. Or is that a pipeline dream?

There are boom and bust implications for Newfoundland & Labrador, Nova Scotia, and

Saskatchewan, as well as northern Canada undersea oil exploitation.

In short, it's good news for anyone hoping Canada will no longer be a major contributor to destroying earth's human life-support system. Bravo!

...

According to the news on our battery-powered radio, most of Newfoundland Island is powerless today. We wait and wait again, for 55 hours.

The mayor of this city makes a public statement, trying to keep people calm with some awkward words.

There's no news of the premier of the province.

I joke that she's a probably a "snowbird" off in the southern U.S. for the winter.

She re-emerges after the lights return, but not in person, and only with a story about a provincial government cabinet shuffle.

...

As the blackout stretches out, Mariko and I simultaneously tell each other we're going to CBC, which is on our street, just before MUN, to talk to the newsroom.

Living near a national TV network outlet has its advantages. By chance, come by chance, we find an interested television reporter going in the door when we get to the station.

She's a young, female reporter with "so much makeup!", Mariko says.

"Are you a reporter," I ask. "Yes," she says. "We have an interesting angle on the power outage story," I say.

After listening for a moment, she starts telling us that others agree with our assessment that the blackout seems strange.

The reporter says that a 101 year old who helps set up the original power grid in his youth, tells her there's something wrong with the system. It needs rerouting, he says.

The company knows how to prevent these blackouts but it's not taking action, he says.

I tell the CBC reporter that Miyazaki gets typhoons with the same strong winds as the ones striking here during the storm. Miyazaki gets 300-400 mm rain storms too.

There's even a quake measuring nearly magnitude 5 one time.

Yet we never have a power outage, not even for a moment.

Then the reporter starts noting our names and asking how she can contact us. Good question. We give her our landlord's phone number and address.

The reporter tells me she'll pass the story on to another reporter, who then walks in the front door, by complete coincidence. So I repeat my story, almost word for word.

Reporter two, Robyn Miller, tells us she'll be over to see us that same afternoon and have the story ready for tonight's news. She does exactly what she promises.

She comes alone, lugging a heavy tripod, camera, and bag. Funding cuts by two recent Canadian governments force CBC to make one person do the work of two or three.

It can make reporting less spontaneous and authentic.

Although our words are not distorted, we have to act out lighting candles, putting on mittens, and reading so that the camera can get the action.

A camera operator would be hanging around for a while, recording us doing those things naturally, instead of having us pose.

Robyn is from Ottawa, a graduate of Carleton University School of Journalism. She graduates long after my time there.

We offer to give her a statement in French too, for SRC, but she forgets and doesn't want to turn on the camera again to get something for her francophone reporter colleague here.

I forget to mention my concerns about wasting our winter food supply in the freezer, which could feed a family for a few days.

I talk to Robyn about what I learn at Carleton, i.e. how the most interesting stories can get told when the camera is not turned on.

She gives me her phone number and e-mail address, inviting us to contact her about any other news.

She tells us not to expect more than 10 seconds on the air.

Maybe she's right, after editing out most of what we say. But our air time seems longer, even when interspersed with outdoor shots of electric repair crews, etc.

Our main message gets across – the need for the power company to fix its system so that future power outages will be avoided altogether or minimized.

There is a major error in fact. The story says we work at MUN, not L.E.T.S.

Yet I go to the station with Robyn after she shoots us because she wants me to show a photo of us in Nippon. I provide her with one showing us and the L.E.T.S. logo.

The photo she uses is from the Miyazaki City Hall International Day, when Meg and Miyuki help us run a booth about Canada, featuring the 400th birthday of Québec City.

While I'm using a CBC News computer to get these photos from a USB stick, someone at the floor editor's desk asks me who I am. Robyn vouches for me.

I overhear some chatter among reporters as they arrive and leave from covering news stories.

They're complaining about being underpaid and about stories that do and do not pan out.

Robyn asks us to tell her when the power returns, so I gently note the workplace error in her story in my message.

I tell her not to worry about it, but she replies that the station will correct the error.

I see no evidence of a correction during the next few days,

but I use the error as an excuse for asking Robyn if we can borrow a DVD of the story for our parents.

I would ask anyway, but the error makes it easier.

Robyn says they "don't usually" do so, but I interpret this as meaning there is an exception for people who don't complain angrily about a serious error in fact in a news story about them.

Since there is no electricity this night or the next day until mid-afternoon, we don't see ourselves on TV.

The final day of the power outage I see our story on a MUN library computer and Mariko sees the story on our computer before I get home, just as the power returns.

We have our 10 seconds of fame.

...

News reports about Obama's second inauguration don't jive with what I consider the key lines of his speech. The same is true when I attend Clinton's first inauguration in person.

For me, Obama's key words are these: "Our journey is not complete." "Citizens represent our greatest hope." "Let us answer the call of history."

There is unnoticed symbolism when, after Obama repeats "Our journey is not complete." his microphone picks up the sound of a train horn coming from Union Station on the other side of the U.S. congress building.

Obama is talking about human progress, saying that much is being accomplished but there is still a very long way to go toward improving the world. So we all have to keep working all the time, to try to get there.

He's explicitly and directly talking about advancing all aspects of human equality and peaceful interhuman relations, as well as making sure there is a planetary life-support system to ensure there will be people around to benefit from the advances.

Obama's speech contrasts sharply with Canada's backward path since Pierre Trudeau's retirement.

...

This is the biggest news story since Toronto police arrest someone for pretending to practice witchcraft. Only legitimate witches are acceptable under Canadian law.

The story is coming out of Brasil. One of the world's most tediously boring sports* is creating a boom for language education. (*Only screaming announcers make it sound exciting. The "action" is most players mostly running around doing nothing.)

An international soccer event scheduled for next year is stimulating sex trade workers to learn languages, including English, French, and Italian, so that workers can better serve their clientele.

Apparently vocabulary is the main emphasis.

But, given the very rough-sounding accents of unilingual lusophones in my Rio teaching experience, there should also be a lot of work on pronunciation and tone.

...

One television news broadcaster remarks that the electronic age means people are constantly bombarded with messages and information.

For me, this means the "electronic age" is making the "first" world' situation worse.

The more information and messages it gets the more separated, apart, isolated, incompetent, and impotent the "first" world becomes.

It's so overwhelmed that it doesn't know what to absorb first, so it absorbs little or nothing, while continuing to be completely self-absorbed.

It is paralyzed by its scatter-brained ("multi-tasking") approach to learning nothing about everything and everything about nothing.

...

A U.S. PBS Newshour series, over several days, shows an experiment in one school wherein students are kept out of violent street gangs by special attention to developing personal resistance to getting into gangs.

This helps to keep students out of crime, to stay alive, and to remain out of jail.

Another day, a student from a different school talks about random insecurity checks.

He says that school "security" comes around, picks a student at random, and conducts a complete search of everything in the students desk and hallway locker.

It sounds like what the guards do to prisoners' cells in a penitentiary.

Thus while an experiment in one school encourages students to keep out of prison, insecurity at another school trains students how to be submissive, obedient prison inmates.

...

Hugo Chavez dies in office as Venezuela's democratically-elected president. This news brings condemnation of Chavez.

He has many critics around the world who find nothing good to say about him or anything he does.

When someone you don't like is democratically-elected it means there's something wrong with the democratic process?

It's rigged? Voters disagreeing with the opposition are ignorant and stupid?

At least some news honestly reports that Chavez is born into a materially poor family; goes into the military because that's what you do when you're poor and there is lots of unemployment; tries to overthrow a bad government and consequently goes to jail; is released, runs for president and gets elected several times; takes over the oil industry and uses its revenue to help the materially poor people; and succeeds in making Venezuela the "Latin American" country with the least inequality.

When a USCNN announcer criticizes Chavez for not really being democratic, U.S. civil rights leader Jessie Jackson replies that the first U.S. presidents have slaves and describe the U.S. as democratic.

Years earlier, former U.S. President Jimmy Carter describes the Chavez government as "pure democracy".

Chavez's opponents call him a revolutionary. What's revolutionary about using natural resource money to help the materially poorest people?

And if that is revolutionary, what does it say about oil companies and business people?

The president of the Islamic nation-state of Iran, at time of writing, goes to the funeral of Chavez and is quoted as saying Chavez is in heaven and will return with Jesus Christ to help the world.

What does Muhammad do while this is happening?

...

Every time I hear the word Cardinals in the news I think it's a story about U.S. baseball. But it's about the fact they're electing a new pope in Roma.

The Cardinals, (Or should they be called The Red Caps?), are getting together, flying in from all the cardinal directions, to elect a new pope.

The background story about the newly-elected pope is scarcely getting mentioned during the news media's uncritical frenzy to cover pope election news.

News interviews are dominated by only Vatican experts and insiders.

They don't mention the background story about accusations against the new pope's behaviour during the nasty military dictatorship in his homeland, Argentina.

There is disagreement as to whether the new pope, Frank, is too disinterested, submissive, or implicated in the nasty dictatorship's crimes against humanity.

Whatever the outcome of this debate, the nature of this religionism remains the same unreported story. It's not democratic or a democratic institution, despite "voting".

It's an authoritarian autocracy, headed by an invisible, all-powerful extraterrestrial demanding absolute belief and submission, while ruling through a male only elite responsible only to the alien, not to humanity.

It's a divine right monarchical patriarchal dictatorship selected by demigods.

Why would anyone in such a religionism ruling elite support democracy?

...

A rabbi speaking on a U.S. television news programme tells a story about someone looking around the world and asking "god" why it doesn't send help.

The reply – "I did send help, you."

Unintentionally the religionist is saying the world improves when people see problems and solve them, not when they wait for an extraterrestrial to arrive and fix everything.

...

A trans-Canada oil pipeline, news says, can take advantage of oil refineries in places such as Montréal.

But, according to news we hear while living there, Montréal has shut down most of its refineries in recent years.

...

During the past couple of years, news reports show huge clouds of dust crossing cities in the southern U.S.

There are also stories of months of continuing drought across much of that country.

However, there is no report comparing these events with the ones occurring due to greed, land abuse, and climate change occurring long before, and yet within the lifetimes of my parents.

They live in small town Canada, spending their teens in the "third" world times of a world economic collapse.

In the history of the U.S., that era is the time of the "dust bowl".

I know almost nothing about that until seeing a documentary film called "Dust Bowl" on the U.S. PBS television network.

Overplanting by wheat farmers and "suitcase farmers", who only arrive in the farmland twice a year, to plant and then harvest four million acres of land, destroy the land and leave it to blow away as dust.

Sod-busters?

...

A MUN student comes to us for help and suggestions, after we hear him on CBC Radio news and recognize his name and voice as belonging to someone we meet here.

MUN, acting in the manner I have become accustomed to there, tries to persuade him not to talk to the news reporters after he starts complaining about having to pay an extra $20,000 fee on top of his tuition and mentions getting people to sign a petition in protest.

He gives us all the details of the case he accurately calls "convoluted".

He doesn't have an extra $20,000 and all we can give him is advice on what strategy he might take without risking a kangaroo trial and deportation, or recall by his homeland for activist behaviour.

He calls my words "inspiring". He thanks us. Then his e-mail messages go silent for a long time. (We do hear from him, from undisclosed locations, over the years to come.)

Part of what he says indicates that the Canadian recruiters looking for students abroad are getting lured into corruption.

He confirms what we already know about study-abroad-agents demanding huge fees from students wanting to study overseas, (often just to fill out free application forms and amassing information provided by applicants. We do that at cost, not for money profit, in Miyazaki. This means that we give applicants most of the money we receive from institutions.)

After fleecing the applicants, the agents collect bounty money from overseas too. But there's something we didn't know about.

The recruiters from Canada are invited to go on information junkets abroad, which turn out to be an all-expenses paid luxury trips bankrolled by study-abroad-agents.

No doubt the exorbitant fees charged to student applicants pay the junket bills.

So the junket-takers look the other way when the agents demand huge fees and depict themselves as the only route for applicants who want to ensure they are accepted for study overseas.

Perhaps the junket takers refer applicants and their files to the agents?

I start wondering if consulates and other government offices at home and abroad might not also be getting corrupted.

The former head of Canada's CSIS spy agency did warn about overseas influence on Canadian offices, implying Chuang Hwa. What other nation-states are involved?

...

Calgary and a large area of Alberta receive the latest dividend from putting oil money ahead of the earth's human life-support system.

Heavy rain and overflowing rivers flood vast stretches of land, housing, offices, etc.

News reports three people dead and many thousands so devastated that they'll probably need psychological trauma treatment for the shock.

This is reported as the worst flooding in 100 years in Calgary and its worst disaster in history.

The Alberta premier goes on television using the typically-Canadian, provincialist term "Albertan" to describe victims, constantly substituting it for human identity words such as "people".

CBC and CTV news channels cover this story in excruciating detail, over and over again, every moment of the day and night with en direct, live reports.

It is as if they are reporting the big quake, tsunami, and nuclear accident at Fukushima, Nippon.

Meanwhile, in Bharat, flooding kills 600 to 1,000 people. This story gets passing reference on CBC and CTV news channels.

I write to the news people, complaining that so many news

stories are getting neglected, unreported while the obsession with Calgary and Alberta continues.

It's a sad history of news dating back at least to our first year in Miyazaki, when all news focused on a former U.S. football player accused of murder.

My complaint letter also decries the disproportionate atten-tion being given to Alberta vs. Bharat.

By showing such comparatively little interest in Bharat's 600-1,000 deaths while focusing total attention on Calgary's three deaths, Canadian news appears to be racist coverage.

...

Bolivia's president finds himself on an unexpected visit to Austria while trying to fly home in the presidential jet from meetings with Putin in Moscow.

Other E.U. nation-states deny his plane permission to cross their air space.

When he's forced to land in Austria, he's obliged to leave his government-owned plane while Austrians with police powers search the Bolivian presidential jet.

The president gets the usual police state greeting that Austria affords to tourists?

During our first and last visit, Mariko and I are asked to show passports three or four times while we're simply looking for a train station.

My only questions are these, which I send to the U.S. president's office:

What would the U.S. be doing if a nation-state did the same thing to the U.S. presidential jet?

What implications does this action against the Bolivian presidential jet have for the rule of international law, diplomatic immunity, and safe passage for elected representatives everywhere?

By the end of the day my attention is drawn to Egypt, where tens of millions of people sign a petition asking the president to resign and millions of demonstrators go to the streets to make the same point.

The military take this as a cue to orchestrate a coup d'état, ousting the first democratically-elected president* in the history of Egypt.

He wins by 51.7% of the vote, slightly less than Obama gets for his re-election.

The military dictators claim they are overthrowing the government as the first step in holding new elections. Where have I heard this line before?

As I write since my first days in Rio de Janeiro, how can the hierarchical, follow-orders-without-question military convince anyone that it is somehow competent to intervene in democratic processes and set them on the right course?

All that a coup does in this kind of context is tell the electors in a democracy that there is no need for elections or democratic processes.

If someone elected annoys enough people, they can simply void the elections and cheer the generals when they come in to get rid of the offensive elected.

The deposed president and his party have had all their means of communications and transportation disconnected and blocked by the military, as part of the generals' plans to make sure everyone understands only the military's version of events,. party leaders are arrested.

The military appoints a judge as interim president, as in Dhaka a few years earlier, until new elections can be held. But in Dhaka a dictator was deposed, not an elected government.

There is some indication that the Egyptian general running the coup may be a candidate in the "democratic elections".

He gets his military education in the U.K. and has many connections inside the U.S. military. Did his military friends abroad encourage and support him and his coup?

Officially, the U.S. reacts cautiously, expressing its concern about the coup and calling for elections as soon as possible.

The U.K. says it does not support coups. Deutschland disapproves of a coup against an elected government.

Some commentators interviewed in the news say "It's not really a coup." and, "But in Egypt…".

The U.S. and E.U. nation-states are careful not to use the word "coup" because it would legally require them to impose economic sanctions on Egypt.

So there is much effort to alter semantics and reality to pretend a military coup d'état is not a coup d'état.

Like Brasil's coup d'état when I am 14 years old, this one will probably also be called "the revolution" in the military-based school "history" books.

At least in Brasil, as the biggest protests since Dirétas Já take place, the progressive elected government stays in power, expresses agreement with the crowds, and tries to improve to show it's heeding the voice of the electorate.

…

Meanwhile, in Canada, news reports yoghurt prices increase by 33% while government statistics show the official inflation rate rising to 2% during the past few years.

Sure, like Argentina and Brasil during the military dictatorship years.

A 500% inflation rate was officially only 100% there and then.

The difference is larger in Canada, (16.5 times higher instead of five times higher).

A 2% figure is also being used when we return to Miyazaki via Mokba. But we find flour and rice prices suddenly jump 100% and then more.

…

Corruption in Canadian government becomes more apparent and widely reported in the daily news as Québec's Charboneau Commission obliges two mayors of Montréal and an almost life-long mayor of the city of Laval to resign.

At the same time, Toronto's mayor and his brother are investigated for illegal drug ties, and the unelected senators in Ottawa help themselves to tax monies, as much as they can grasp, to supplement their already hefty salaries.

What are the reactions in Canada to government corruption and bogus official inflation numbers, while multitudes hold protest rallies in the streets of Brasil and Egypt due to the same problems?

Who knows. So many Canadians just want to watch high-priced hockey games and go into the streets to cheer their favourite teams. Pra Frente Canada?

...

U.K. BBC News reports that about 2.5 million people die of air pollution each year.

The previous day, the same news says the U.S. will produce more oil than Saudi Arabia in a few years.

Meanwhile, a business television channel concludes petroleum prices will drop 50% in the U.S. due to expected production there.

Amid the hoorahs of "oil independence", only the faintest voices might be saying, unreported, that cheaper oil means more burning of it and more air pollution, i.e. more death.

Since mega-inflation of food prices is supposedly based on oil prices, even if food prices do not drop when oil prices decline, some might presume food prices will decline by 50% to match oil price drops.

However, climate change already causes widespread drought which lays waste great stretches of agricultural land and reduces food crops during the previous year in the U.S.

So food prices are more likely to increase, due to food scarcity caused by falling oil prices.

Whichever way oil prices go, more people die of air pollution and malnutrition.

The problem is the oil itself, not the price.

...

As in the years that I live under the disappearing military dictators of Brasil and Argentina, elected governments in Canada, the U.S., and E.U. issue inflation rates tremendously lower than the reality we see in the food stores every day for years.

While wheat, corn, and rice prices rise as much as 100%, official government inflation rates of "less than 2%" are reported in the news without a blink from any journalist or business reporter.

Does this mean that news and business reporters i) deliberately ignoring reality; ii) do not shop for food themselves; iii) are simply stupid; iv) or are getting paid off not to ask for honest inflation numbers from elected governments?

Plutocrats own the governments and news rooms?

...

If something "goes viral" on internet, it plagues television "news" channels, and spreads like a cancer, blocking the free flow of information.

...

An announcer on a U.S. cable news network says one of the electronic telephones so much in vogue actually uses, by recharging, more electricity per year than a medium-size refrigerator.

This story goes on to say that new technologies are using 50% more energy than the world aviation industry. So much for environmentally-friendly "progress".

**Buenos Aires**: Local newspapers say "new cold war". So the free world will make a comeback. How? It's deader than the C.C.C.P.

The coup d'état in Egypt is becoming the model of democratic extinction.

**San Rafael**: The worst fire in the history of Valparaíso leaves 11,000 homeless and somehow kills only six people the night we arrive here.

My local friend, Nestor's son, is unaware of this event a full day later since he depends on faulty internet service for his news.

The best source of news is all sources, internet optional and needy extra collaboration from authentic, traceable sources.

**Córdoba**: Cable and internet mean that I no longer depend on Eduardo's short wave radio for odd bits and pieces of news from NHK or CBC International, etc.

I now have too many connections to local and outside information, and lots of U.S. TV shows and movies with either subtitles or dubbed voices.

Yet our friends Ely, Eduardo, and family largely restrict themselves to local news of this city, while Mariko and I watch Telesur and BBC News when the TV is available.

...

Snippets of information from Chilean television stations that we see here say that Santiago has an environmental crisis.

But that's only a caption on screen.

Smiling announcers with traffic scenes behind them have to devote most of their time to the world soccer business championship game results and video highlights.

Sorry, less time for news headlines. What environment?

...

Presidenta Cristina (Kirshner) says Argentina will continue paying the long gone military dictatorship's unpayable debt but not their U.S. hedge funds loan of $US1.5 billion.

Why pay at all? Cristina later recants on BBC News. The hedge funds insist?

Local friend Eduardo says Argentina's debt pre-dates the military nasties.

He says one person loans the nation-state a great deal of money. That person owns a factory in Córdoba and gets a lower tax rate, Eduardo says.

...

A news story says airports are functioning normally in Buenos Aires, but there's a 10-minute traffic delay due to people coming to the centre in cars.

Would this happen in Montréal and Toronto? Not possible! But it does.

...

Telesur celebrates nine years of news broadcasting by starting an English language network. But are anglophones listening to non-"first" world voices?

Venezuelan President Maduro, who succeeds Hugo Chavez when he dies in office, says Telesur will be broadcasting in French, Russian, and Chinese too.

Are the "first" worlders interested in listening?

U.S. cable TV companies already refuse to allow Aljazeera in English to reach U.S.ers, at time of writing.

So much for international accords on the "free flow of information". They mean "down" stream from the "first" world only?

...

Centro de documentación Juan Carlos Garat seems to belong to the Press Union.

The Centro houses a news/ journalism library/archives. There are bound local newspapers (printed on paper) dating back many years. I don't ask how many.
...

News reports that 15% of locals live below the poverty level of 4,000 pesos income in Argentina. That's not many $US at current foreign currency exchange rates, at time of writing.

More than two billion people are living in poverty around the world.

BRICS' bank alternative to the U.S.-centred IMF and World Bank already has deposits from the southern Americas.

...

News reports say that sales are down. Nobody wants to buy anything at currently highly inflated prices, our local friend Eduardo says.

Here, as in the southern Americas during the military dictatorships and as in Canada today, real inflation is far beyond official inflation-based salary and pension rises.

So everyone is worse off.

A big part of the problem here is a tax imposed by "Cristina's" government seven months ago, which more than doubles the prices for everything.

As my Donnacona friend Denis says when the Canadian government imposes a 7% VAT called GST, that tax lowers his standard of living by 7%.

The extra tax revenue in Argentina creates a moneyed-elite nation-state ruling a land of poor people, Eduardo says.

Add the doubling of prices to the government's official bogus 2% inflation to calculate the "official" inflation here, 8%.

This kind of stupid government policy is yet another reason that some locals may start looking for a cleanup reminiscent of Chuang Hwa Mao's permanent war with the military and bureaucrats.

Some locals may now look more favourably on a coup and the revival of a nasty military dictatorship.

Unfortunately, few realize that such a regime would be armed with more than lethal killing weapons this time.

A renewed military dictatorship would be stronger and less likely to leave due to the U.S.-centered insecurity technology that's now so easily available to all potential dictators.

A police state could be permanently installed and imposed indefinitely thanks to U.S. "security" technology. The groundwork is being done around us. (Will there ever be free and open elections in Egypt again, or anywhere else?)

...

At the former military dictatorship's torture centre, La Perla, I talk with our local friend Angel.

I tell him what I learn in Buenos Aires just after the military dictatorship is gone.

Witnesses who I meet then tell me that they hear and see torture victims trying to flee in their neighbourhood.

Angel says that since the military dictatorship then controls and censors all news, reports of victims at that time become rumours passed around and altered in the telling.

It's tragic that torture-murder centres have continued in many nation-states to this very day, right now while we are touring La Perla. Some are run by the U.S. military.

News stories beginning as atrocious accounts could become so unbelievable because – Who would think that anyone would be capable of such terrible acts against anyone?

...

Today' news is that Estela de Carlotto, the head of Abuelas de Mayo in Córdoba is reunited with her 37 year old grandchild who disappears long ago when he's kidnapped by a member of the military dictatorship.

He's the 114th grandchild found alive, to date.

...

At the same time, European parliamentary election results show an increase in votes for separatists in the U.K. and anti-human migration candidates in the U.K. and France.

There are always people in Europe who want to return to the long tragic history of European warfare based on separatism/nationalism/xenophobia.

Many elections occur this year, including ones in Bharat and bogus ones in Egypt, where 45% turnout votes 90% for the general who leads the coup d'état overthrowing the country's first ever democratically-elected government there.

A coup d'état in MuangThai also occurs.

More nation-state military forces who are emboldened by Egypt can thus get their hands on the latest nation-state "security" technology and perpetuate military dictatorships indefinitely, anywhere and everywhere.

...

News is being sidelined by sports in the form of soccer. Mass advertising budgets are sparing no expense to push soccer in every type of TV programming.

The excess of overstated, exaggerated frenzy and popularity are revealed on the right side of page one of a local newspaper.

The soccer propagandists remind me of the military dictatorship pushing the war of Las Malvinas many decades ago.

In fact at least one soccer team photo is used in the war propaganda at that time.

...

Day temperatures defy forecasts by reaching only 16°C instead of 25°C. Evenings cool to 14°C. Mosquito season will soon yield?

Fortunately, news says no more than 21 days of mosquitoes re-main and these ones carry no dengue fever, unlike other times in recent years.

...

Cell phones, computers, and internet servers are almost universally available in the "third" world, in our observations and in news reports showing people in the streets of places we don't yet know.

But potable tap water for all people everywhere remains a futuristic dream.

Electronic devices become more intricate and add more functions, while their prices remain stable or decline in terms of the cost per function.

Yet food remains the same and prices for it jump dramatically in short periods of time.

The survival, nourishment, and fruition of the human species are clearly a low priority in the world economic system.

**St-Roch de l'Achigan**: Puzzling me since our return north, news talks of "Islamic State". I presume they mean Iran, but I'm wrong.

It's the latest group of decapitators who maraud the world, trying to revolt the rest of us.

I soon hear a commentator saying, "The scariest thing about them is that they occupy territory and provide public services."

Oh no! It's another nation-state!?

...

Some of Canada's anglophone "news" people are so poor at their first language that even I notice their mistakes and cringe.

It suddenly occurs to me that Canadian locals having no official language skills, or only poor ones, are like gringos abroad who never bother to learn languages when visiting and living abroad.

But Canadian locals are locals, not tourists! Today television and internet provide ample opportunities to learn and make daily use of both Canadian official languages.

...

In sports "news", a prestigious U.S. college is admitting people to play football even though their reading skills are equivalent to those of an elementary school fourth grader. The college excuses these players from taking college courses.

I have the impression that many sports people behave as if they're still elementary school age and have the related emotional problems, compounded by the frustrations of unnaturally extended adolescence.

My impressions of people in sports also come from seeing and hearing sports enthusiasts and players for years.

I'm concluding that sports players and their entourage might be more susceptible to becoming psychopaths or abusers than other people.

News does report sports players and fanatics arrested for violent crimes against their spouses.

...

News laments the number of children and adolescents committing suicide due to bullying.

In my teens I conclude that living on is far more annoying to the bullies, to my detractors, and to all those who disparage me because they don't know me or because they confuse me with some real problem they're having unrelated to me.

My death would only give them a shallow victory. So I live on a smile broadly.

**Aboard B.C. Ferry**: My sailing is prolonged when the passenger ship I'm aboard is suddenly diverted to help an emergency rescue effort.

Some people are in danger when their small craft capsizes. All ferries and ships in the area are diverted to the scene.

As soon as I hear the public address system announcement that we're being diverted, I phone CBC Radio News to report the mishap and diversion.

The reporter thanks me and says she'll call the coast guard. The story gets about 15 seconds coverage on CBC's nightly TV national news broadcast, "The National".

Fortunately, our vessel is permitted to return to its course because the people in the sea are successfully rescued by another ship.

...

**Richmond**: According to the U.S. P.B.S. Newshour, there are now 600,000 people dying every year from air pollution in Bharat alone. (That's 0.0006% of a billion people.)

That's the same number of people who are homeless in the U.S., at time of writing. (That's 2% of 300 million people.)

Bharat's 600,000 deaths by air pollution far exceed the 3,000+ dying from air pollution in each of Canada's three biggest cities each year.

(But per capita that's almost 0.0003% of 32 million people in Canada at time of writing.)

...

Death is news, but coverage still varies.

In Nigeria, 48 children are killed and 80 are wounded by a terrorist bomber. This story appears half way through a U.S. C.B.S. newscast.

The lead story this same day is about one man shooting one man in Ottawa, Canada. This will mean stricter anti-terror police laws.

Meanwhile, U.S. police shoot dead and strangle to death unarmed African-Americans.

Demonstrators respond by going to shopping centres and freeways.

A U.K. celebrity monarchy tour is also disrupted by the demonstrators. Bravo!

But one shopper in this news story remarks, "What are they doing in our mall?"

During a twelve year period ending the year before last, the U.S. has 45 deaths resulting from "terrorism" and 45,000 deaths from firearms.

Another 33,000 people are killed in motor vehicle accidents.

So "terrorism" should be the top priority of the U.S. government?! People working in that government never notice the news?!

...

Going unnoticed in "first" world news: The military dictators of northern Africa stay in power for 30 years after the Berlin Wall falls.

Accentuating the problem, when a military coup ends Egypt's first short period of democracy, the pre-democracy dictator is acquitted of all charges in court and his militarily-deposed, democratically-elected successor is sentenced to prison for decades.

**Miyazaki:** A 71-year-old local person marks the Shinkansen's 51st anniversary by walking into the first car of a moving one, pouring gasoline over himself, and setting fire to his body in front of passengers sitting and looking in his direction.

He's the only victim besides a woman dying of smoke inhalation between cars.

NHK News starts talking about "security" screening of passengers and bags, but even a "security" expert says only random checks "as a deterrent" are feasible due to passenger load and commuting schedules.

NHK announcers talk of giving up convenience because it could have been a "terrorist" attack.

We hear of no such talk or action after the sarin gas attack in the Tokyo subway about 20 years earlier. People are smarter then?

Unfortunately, nobody in the newsroom is asking why the 71 year old burns himself to death and how any "security" checks could deter anyone's suicide anywhere.

People contemplating suicide need counselling to help, not security screening for them to outwit.

Fear is the worst basis for decision-making and results in only grave errors of judgement and terrible anti-freedom side effects.

Fear-based "security" approaches are merely irrational panic attacks. They are currently destroying all hope of democracy in the world.

...

Richmond (Columbia (Br.) is in the morning news in Nippon, but it's only an old story about Chinese signage (sino-age) there.

A unilingual anglophone is complaining, quite oblivious to the First Nations' feeling the same way about non-First Nations signage, such as crosses, etc.

For "first" worlders, it's always "unjust" when it's not somebody else's problem.

**Van Couverden**: I encounter a neo-Nazi tourist from Germany.

He starts expressing his animosity toward Moslems in the same tones and nuances that his nasty predecessors use to speak of Jews before forcing them into the Warsaw ghetto as a prelude to their train rides to Oscenwisen.

I point out that the Christianist religionist Inquistions in Europe torture and murder Moslems and Jews.

He replies with a dismissive huff, saying that very few people were killed by the Inquistions. I think he says "only a thousand". Yes, Nazis kill tens of millions. He's proud?

So crimes against humanity have an acceptable maximum tally? Sure, that's okay, right?

The neo-Nazi says I must have opinions like mine because I get all my news from the U.S. cable news network. "You should try something out of your comfort zone." he adds.

In fact, I very rarely watch news from that network.

He wants me to read Mein Kampf?

He's assuming a lot for someone just meeting me for the first time.

It's so easy to jump to conclusions and have fixed opinions about Moslems, Jews, and me without knowing anything about any of us.

Only the neo-Nazi makes himself apparent.

...

At time of writing, the relationships between male and female humans become a central topic in the news again.

Much is written and said, but much is missing from the reporting perspective(s).

The male-female relationships affect everything in every life from birth to death.

Yet again, in current news, only the superficial aspects of these relationships are the centre of discussion, not the underlying assumptions and conventions perverting the relationships.

For too long, women and men are treated differently; trained to behave and perceive the world differently; and even nourished differently based entirely and exclusively upon their physiological sexual characteristics.

This is entirely a result of social, cultural, commercial, nation-state, and religionist conventions, i.e. not the long-term natural realities of human life.

**Miramichi**: When a power outage strikes and drags on here, we are literally left in the dark in terms of news.

We conserve our solar energy battery power for light and heat for these winter days.

The blackout is much longer in the Acadien peninsula, which is largely francophone and lower income.  Coincidence?

News reports mention someone going door-to-door to see who needs help.  There is no such knocking here.

Mariko speculates that our neighbours believe we're living comfortably with solar power.

During the final day of the blackout, all of our neighbours leave, going to their forest cabins with wood-burning stoves or staying with family and friends who have electricity.

We don't know enough people to find such refuge.  There are stories of "warming centres", but we know of none are near us.  Surely someone would tell us.

No private or government organizations come around to see who needs help.

Even people we meet while warming up the final day, when the public library opens, don't seem to be aware that the people with electricity could help the people without.

For me this is the typical "first world" mentality.

People freezing in the dark here are of as much concern to people in the "first" world as the hundreds of thousands killed during the past five years of war in Syria.

"First" worlders say, "Isn't that terrible!"

A second later they're back in their routines, isolated from all other reality in the world and universe.

...

A news story reminds me that Québec is advancing more quickly than other provinces in embracing electric vehicles to replace the petroleum companies' highly-polluting internal combustion engine vehicles.

I'm critical of the other provinces for lagging behind and not yet following Québec's lead in pro-environment policies.

Upon hearing my comment, to my surprise, my local friend Guy takes my words as a cue to say that's why Québec doesn't belong in Canada.

I'm surprised because the world's scientists are saying that the world has to unite, not further divide, to solve environmental problems.

A previous U.S. president and a former prime minister of Canada agree with Guy, saying that each nation-state has to come up with different solutions, not work together with other nation-states.

We hang separately instead of together?

...

U.S.ers seem to want guns so that they can shoot each other. The latest incident is at UCLA, a U.S. university. It's a murder-suicide, according to news reports.

The police line up UCLA students surviving the shooting, on their knees with their hands behind their heads and their backs turned to police.

It's a pose used in U.S. movies and television shows as a prelude to an "execution-style" murder.

U.S. ABC News shows the pose twice but without interviews or comments.

...

School children in at least some U.K. schools in the news already have to submit to electronic identification in order to receive their school lunch.

...

News reports about terrorist attacks, such as the frequent mass shootings in the U.S., tell me that s.i.e. Sysiphus routines and habits are literally deadly.

Accidents, mishaps, and terrorist attacks happen mainly when people are robotically doing what they always do where they always are.

They're ideal terrorist targets and prey and so unconscious (somnambulists) that they are the most likely people to become targets, and have accidents and mishaps.

People living outside of such a drone existence are alert, consciously observing and changing their surroundings by curiosity.

They're connected to their urge and need to go into unknown territory to learn and thus progress as humans.

What the drones consider risky, dangerous, and reckless behaviours are thus actually safer, more secure, and a much better, fuller, stimulating, intelligence-using life of thriving as a person.

...

I start writing to news organizations, newspapers, and magazines when I'm 18, 19, or so. I write partisan letters favouring bilingualism and multiculturalism.

Later I write about free trade and other issues.

Much of what I write gets published too, including a pro-immigration letter opposing big, non-refundable fees to merely read applications submitted to Canadian bureaucracy.

More recently, here and now, I write about faulty news and websites.

I realize that's caused by an airhead fixation with "the latest thing" in technology, just like excessive concentration on a single news story while ignoring and reducing coverage of all else in the world.

Stories about the murder trial of a sports star, a U.S. football player in particular, and the death of a rock singer carry on for hours, days, and months in years past.

More obsessive news reporting continues.

A couple of my latest letters go to Aljazeera and NHK.

A younger, female Aljazeera news reporter refers to the pro-democracy leader of Myanmar/Burma as the "lady".

My letter complains that someone who suffers so much for so long under house arrest by military dictators merits using the titles she struggles to earn.

"Lady" demeans her and ignores her life. Men use the word to flatter and limit women. In fact "lady" as a title originates in monarchical dictatorship.

"Lady" refers to someone who is moneyed, idle, and so personally incompetent and inept at doing ordinary things in daily life that she's totally dependent on servants and a male.

Also, like queen, king, prince, princess, and lord, lady is a title gained by birth, marriage, and loyalty, not by making any effort to earn them.

Lady and the rest are not titles awarded for outstanding personal achievement or talent.

Ultimately, such titles originate in battles, murders, treachery, and contributions to such bloodthirsty acts.

There's no positive or earned aspect of such titles, unless violence and deceit are the ruling values.

Offering pomp and tribute to such titles is akin to glorifying other gangster behaviours and mobsters themselves.

My letter to NHK news is also about word usage.

A news reader reports that a U.S. junk food outlet is planning to try to compensate for Nippon's declining population and employeed shortage by recruiting "housewives" for dead end minimum wage jobs.

I write that three or four decades ago, women who work only at home, doing domestic and childcare chores for free are changing their job description title to "homemaker".

I say "housewife" sounds like "house pet", i.e. a loving creature who stays home eating, sleeping, and playing while awaiting the master's return.

It's a glass ceiling vocabulary like "lady" which keeps a woman in her "special" place. She can smile and enjoy her privileged position and status under male rule?

I expect better from the female news reader who is reporting this story.

Shouldn't female news reporters be more aware than male news reporters when it comes to how news vocabulary can depict, reflect, affect, and demean women?

...

Every year, news mentions that millions of people in the "third" world are displaced and their few material possessions are all gone.

They have nothing much beyond some basic clothing.

That's due to disasters, wars, and climate change.

Meanwhile, vast forest fires level luxury homes chock full of possessions in California (U.S.A.). That's all insured and/or covered by government reconstruction assistance.

A victim interviewed by Al Jazeera news laments his great losses – a collection of baseball cards worth $US25,000 and some equally valuable "G.I. Joe" dolls.

"First" world values and generosity are clear from these news stories.

...

Violence is a common way for U.S.ers to resolve disputes, according to their news reports, movies, and television programmes.

U.S.ers can also be very vengeful.

A recent example is how they avenge 3,000 deaths in New York City by taking more than ten times that number of lives in the U.S. wars in Afghanistan and Iraq for 20 years.

In a previous generation, the original Nazis of Deutschland are defeated in six years.

...

A Radio-Canada news story says the coffee companies are now in their tenth year of fighting a court case alleging that their product is carcinogenic.

Why is this story not featured prominently in the news before now? It has implications for so many people.

Mariko reminds me that there's a news story about coffee being carcinogenic 16 years ago, when we're living in the "Ghost House" in Québec City.

The 10 year court case against the coffee companies is like the Tokyo court case against motor vehicle companies' pollution, which suddenly appears in the news after so many years of litigation.

At time of writing, opioid painkiller addiction is dominating the news because it effects about the same number of people in one nation-state as the total number of people dying due to motor vehicle air pollution in a single Canadian city, such as Toronto.

Social drugs like caffeine are downplayed like habitual motor vehicle exhaust pollution.

It's surprising considering what caffeine addicts say all the time.

They say they're hostile or non-functioning until they get their morning caffeine hit. They use caffeine as a wake-up drug to keep alert during the day.

Caffeine addiction seems to be essential for anyone wanting to participate in at least some societies. It's like alcohol used to be in some societies and still is in others.

So inviting other people to socialize, especially when I'm a post-secondary student, means inviting them to "go for coffee".

It's a strange convention for a non-addict like me. If I invite someone to "go for coffee" I know I'm not going to be drinking coffee from the outset.

The other person will always assume I too am a caffeine addict, like "everyone".

When someone replies, "No." to my invitation, that's what I hear. But it's not because the other person isn't a caffeine addict.

If I ask why the other person doesn't want to "go for coffee" I usually hear, "I have a boyfriend." So "a boyfriend" is the antidote to caffeine addiction?

Once I hear "I'm going steady." That means the person is fighting caffeine addiction and steadily succeeding? (It's actually an archaic monogamy pledge from a generation before mine.)

**Fukuoka**: While helping to host some Canadian francophones visiting Fukuoka, we talk about exactly the same news coverage that we all see on SRC-TV here, not in Canada.

We're getting our news from the same source, many thousands of kilometres away, via the U.S. internet system.

That internet extends what I note about the U.S. military radio station (FEN) that Mariko and I hear in Tokyo when we're staying at Kotakemukaihara.

The internet takes FEN-like isolation and enhances it.

Tourists, military, and embassy personnel change their geographic location without leaving their nation-state, and its conditioned mentality.

Nobody, except perhaps language learners knows where s/he is while ostensibly living abroad.

Yet the people I know who never go abroad, and who have cable, satellite, or internet television at home, are strangely the same as the isolated abroad.

The stay-at-homes watch only local TV and only one channel regularly.

Their viewing habits are also uninterrupted by news, local or not.

In Canada they can spend eight months of the year watching hockey games, never knowing what's going on anywhere off the ice.

The least moneyed people have only regular local television stations, until almost mandatory pay TV forces them to stop watching or to pay for stations they rarely or never watch.

It's easy to "dumb down", brainwash, and propagandize people in nation-states, whether they stay home or go abroad. Their viewing habits are very limited. They just watch, they don't do anything.

...

In high inflation times past in Canada and elsewhere, news stories feature employers blaming inflation on the employeed and their unions.

In more recent times, corporate heads talking in the news are blaming fuel prices, "security", "supply chain", and COVID-19 for inflation.

But when wages drop and no longer rise as high as the fast increasing costs of living, news reports the huge incomes being paid to employers and corporate heads.

So what is the true source of inflation not reported in the news? Elite greed.

...

"First" worlders in Canada, the European Union, and the U.S. are in the news decrying the fact that the Russian Federation is meddling with domestic politics abroad and undermining democracy.

Why is this news to people in these parts of the world?

For about 40 years the U.S. and S.U. empires meddle in domestic politics and undermine democracy around the world, especially in the southern Americas and the eastern parts of Europe. It's called the Cold War.

Since that time, the U.S. continues to meddle in other nation-states' internal politics and to undermine democracy, in places such as Ukraine, contributing to triggering the annexation of Crimea and later war in Ukraine.

So to attribute meddling and undermining democracy entirely, exclusively, or largely to the Russian Federation and its democratically-elected president is at least a dishonest argument, at time of writing.

...

The news is full of stories of disruptions in routine daily lives, causing millions of people to flee across nation-state borders.

People born in places such as Syria, Venezuela, Burma, and Somalia are on the move like their human ancestors.

The United Nations and generous people welcome the newcomers, help them, and try to make them feel at home.

But the ultra-nationalist nation-state zealots meet the people migrating with hostility and sometimes violent attacks.

The hostiles call for border closings, barbed wire, huge walls, and military/police action.

The migrating people are blamed for all the nation-state pre-existing ills. "Migrants" are called robbers, parasites, dirty, murderers, and sexual assailants.

This continues the mindless tradition of blaming "foreigners" for unemployment, depleting the ocean's fish supply, COVID-19, and the Bubonic Plague.

It's ironic that the millions of people now attempting to freely cross the entirely arbitrary and artificial boundaries of nation-states are the products of the nation-state itself.

The normal, natural, large-scale human and humanoid migrations of long-term global history, pre-dating the nation-state by hundreds of thousands of years, are now being revived by the nation-state system itself.

"First" world and associate-surrogate nation-states are meddling in the internal affairs of nation-states and undermining the loose fabric holding together nation-states.

The meddling includes invasions, wars, election tampering, climate change, and encouraging repressive regimes such as monarchical and military dictatorships.

...

NHK News shows the latest novelty for school children required to learn English in Japan. It's the "English teacher" robot.

These cute little plastic-bodied, simulated-voice talking computers with permanently fixed, inexpressive faces and emotionless composure fascinate the very young learners of a "living" language.

The bottom-line-induced failure of the L.B.E., (language business establishments devoted to profit not education), and the probable incompetence of their "teaching" staff to make valuable contributions to the advancement of modern language education will not be missed.

Nor will schooled children suffer from not being exposed to the negative energy, behaviours, and mannerisms of malcontent "teachers" who are frustrated because they have no idea how to teach and they live in isolation because they have no interest in language learning when it comes to acquiring the host society's language, eg. Japanese.

However, children schooled by an "English teacher" robot may have a new problem. They will in all likelihood speak English with a robotic accent.

As robotics advance, it might thus become increasingly difficult to distinguish between children and artificial intelligence.

But the current rapid decline in English language spelling, grammar, and usage skills among native speakers will probably make it much easier to recognize the superior language skills of artificial intelligence where English is spoken soon after birth.

...

In Genoa, Italia, a large bridge connecting a major highway between France and Italia collapses, killing and injuring many people and threatening many more living in apartment buildings under what remains of the bridge.

News reports say the bridge is poorly constructed and maintained.

The poor state and maintenance of the bridge is widely known, long before the disaster, news reports say.

This tragic and avoidable event takes me back to the story of my Ottawa dentist.

She says people only work hard if they know they'll get rewarded with money, possessions, and fame.

Without those rewards, people have no motivation to work at all, she says.

Without these essential driving forces, my dentist says, people get lazy, leading to social decay and collapse.

She says that's what capitalism means and that's why it is better than any other system.

Genoa's collapsing bridge and the larger Italia highway system are maintained by at least one private company.

In response to the capitalist-maintained bridge collapse, Italia's government declares a year-long state of emergency, and, according to news reports, plans to put all highways under government control.

So there are no capitalist motivations for building and maintaining a bridge to prevent people from being killed and injured?

Nobody did anything before capitalist incentives, which explains why human beings went extinct eons ago.

**Aside**: There is apparently no capitalist motivation for halting arms production, sales, and use or for preventing wars either.

Ending pollution to maintain the planetary human-life support system is equally lacking in a profit motive? There's no money in keeping humans alive?

...

Canadian news says there's no more highway bus service west of Montréal.

The U.S.-based company providing the service is ending it, saying it can't make enough money on it. This is obviously an attempt to get concessions and money from government.

Unfortunately, other companies' intra-provincial bus services disappear too, making border to border bus service less likely.

This ought to be great news for the train company.

Ticket sales and subsidies previously supporting the bus service could now be put into more trains, more tracks, and more rail service for passengers.

Train fares could be reduced too.

This is also an opportunity to build Shinkansen-like train service along the Québec-Windsor route and between flatland prairie cities.

Instead there is zero reaction from the Canadian government.

Apparently, overland travel in Canada, giving Canadians an opportunity to understand the vastness of the country; to see it in detail; and to meet other Canadians close-up; is of no importance to the nation-state government?

The current "Transport" minister of Canada is a former astronaut who is apparently beyond such earth-bound matters.

He never bothers to even acknowledge letters that I write to him.

**Kazan**: This city has a reputation for being a place where Moslemists and Christianists get along well together, although some news reports say there's a recent diminution in Tartar language schooling.

...

As we leave the land of sake for the land of vodka, the news reports a study saying my lifestyle is the healthiest, like that of my dad and Uncle Lorne.

A comprehensive, worldwide research project by scientists concludes that the best quantity of the alcohol drug to consume is none at all.

Studies link the alcohol drug to some of the most common forms of cancer, i.e. breast and colon.

Prior research, much advertised by alcohol companies, gives the misleading impression that consuming one or two glasses of wine each day is healthy.

Subsequent study reveals that grape juice is just as good and then that the healthy feature is from the grapes themselves. Wine and juice are no better than grapes.

The actual message of the research is that if you drink alcohol you will be healthier if you drink a maximum of one or two glasses per day.

That's later reduced to one or two glass per week.

The same research says that no alcohol is best. So if you don't drink alcohol it's better not to start.

I grow up in a culture where the alcohol drug is a routine and often expected part of socializing.

It's considered a part of reaching legal adulthood by some of my secondary school classmates.

The alcohol drug is so widely accepted, expected, and prevalent that those choosing not to use it are considered odd balls and "rather peculiar", as well as anti-social.

Hard core users mock non-users as puritanical religionist zealots. I do meet some people fitting that description, but I'm not one of them.

One of my cousins who belongs to such a religionist group loses interest in it, quits, and immediately starts drinking alcohol.

One of the alcohol research reports, from CTV National News, adds that two-thirds of the world population do not drink alcohol.

What a surprise! The "first" world, anglo ghetto that I grow up in leads me to believe that my dad, Uncle Lorne, and I belong to a tiny minority.

In the real world we're part of the overwhelming majority.

Only the alcohol companies want to perpetuate this myth through their mass media advertising.

But now that the marijuana drug is legalized in Canada, the same companies have plans for pot drinks. There are also schemes for spiking food with pot additives.

Maybe, like the nicotine companies, the alcohol companies know long before the official research comes out that their products are harmful to human life.

Unfortunately, in the case of the nicotine vendors, it takes 20 to 30 years to start an effective campaign to undermine their market and hold the companies legally accountable.

Meanwhile, governments continue to gain revenue from the addicted by heavily taxing their drugs and not using the proceeds to help addicts.

The same pattern seems to be repeating itself for the marijuana drug product in Canada. How long will it take for this drug to be exposed for detrimental health effects?

One of the most recent news stories about the marijuana drug being used on elderly people should be added to my Virtually Dead volume.

The story recounts how older people with Alzheimer's disease are being given marijuana to calm them down when they suffer angry mood swings.

It's touted as a good thing because it enables health care workers to have more control over the patients.

Great! That's what old, sick people really need, to be drugged into even greater passive submissiveness. Angry vegetables are dangerous.

...

During my first years in the southern Americas, Nippon, elsewhere in Asia, and on the European peninsula I have no idea what's happening beyond my location.

Sometimes I know little about what's going on in some of these locations either, if I lack a bilingual local contact or language skills.

In Lustagoocheehk, Sawaraku, and here my news sources come from Internet broadcasting of radio and television news in languages that I understand.

This broadcasting comes from legitimate news organizations without any particular bias beyond their locations, e.g. "first" world broadcasters.

The main difference in this news receiving experience is due to time zones. So we can watch NHK World during the times we would be sleeping in Nippon.

When it's early morning in Lustagoocheehk and early evening in Sawaraku, it's midday here. We're 800 km. from Moscow, but in the same time zone.

That also means we're an hour later than Paris.

Ten years ago while crossing Russia from Vladivostok to Moscow on the train and thereafter, we're oblivious to the U.S.-led world economic collapse all around us.

This time we're not so calmly isolated from current U.S. worldwide follies. Full internet access provides us with almost all the news sources we get everywhere else.

The only exception is TVA, for some reason, just like SRC's Téléjournal in both Nippon and Canada lately.

For the first time in many months, we can watch the latest SRC Téléjournal here. It's unavailability in Lustagoocheehk and Sawaraku is puzzling.

Lilia, who rents an apartment to us here, provides television that receives channels going into the 700 and 800s.

In our first two days I check them all and finally locate France 24 in French and RT in English.

Unfortunately, only 24 is actual news. R.T. seems satirical, as I expect, then disappointingly amateurish and strangely slant-ed against U.S. Emperor Punchline's detractors, along with all news critical of him.

This slanting makes it seem more likely that Punchline actually is in office due to the Russian Federation's influence on a U.S. presidential election.

R.T. makes me less sceptical about critical concepts being pushed by at least some people in the U.S. about election interference.

We are using Lilia's wifi internet connection and there is no blocking, jamming, or censorship. We can see foreign news that is critical of the Russian Federation government.

Apparently RT is the source of most background consensus news glimpses received by the linguistically-handicapped and isolated anglophone TV news reporters posted here.

Their stories thus fill with superficial impressions and myths approaching propaganda. It's not hard news based on linguistically competent research.

There is too much of this type of reporting from international correspondents. They're talking among themselves.

My personal impressions with disclaimers are more honest and less pretentious.

I make no claim to having definite findings abroad when I have no personal interpreter with language competence.

Mariko says her Russian is very limited and rudimentary. So all I can report from my encounters are voice tones and facial gestures. These are open to gross misinterpretation.

I am limited to conjecture and impressions from visual observations.

But it's still an experience filled with discovery, adventure, and mystery beyond the "guide" books and internet chatter-among-ourselves outsider "certainty".

My concerns about television content here go far beyond RT. A great number of U.S. cable channels are available here in Kazan, as they are in Córdoba four years earlier.

Here the completely U.S. television stations are all dubbed in Russian.

This means spreading the U.S.-only world outlook to generations of Russians, from "Baby TV" to "National Geographic",

"History", and a theme park based channel.

It's far more intrusive and insidious than the old, black and white blatant propaganda content of short wave radio nation-state broadcasting of Cold War times.

Cable TV is indoctrinating elites around the world into discontent and a yearning for the U.S. way-of-life world view.

...

R.T. closely resembles the only blindly pro-Punchline "news" company in the U.S.

It reminds me of the very poorly written English propaganda spewed out during the Cold War when I was a student.

If propaganda is conveyed by poor quality writing and amateurish broadcasting, it will always fail.

RT is currently like the old cable TV channel community shows ridiculed in the old "Saturday Night Live" skits and in two movies called "Wayne's World", but not funny.

...

The fortress in central Kazan, called by the Tatar word "kremlin" in Russia, is a feature of many Russian cities.

For some reason, non-locals equate "kremlin" with the seat of government in Moscow alone. They use "kremlin" to disparage politics not approved by elites abroad.

"The kremlin today decided..." as news reports abroad say.

So "la citadel" decides municipal by-laws in Québec City? Are fortresses elected or unelected?

...

News reports that 87% of the population of Nairobi (Kenya) has some form of "mobile technology" and 50% of the city's populace live in slums. Congratulations technology companies, for improving the world?

...

Murder is an historic part of monarchical dictatorship which still occurs today.

No doubt encouraged by Punchline declaring journalists "enemies of the people", Saudi Arabia's absolute divine right dictatorship murders a U.S. resident Saudi journalist in Turkeye.

This is the final straw for the archaic form of dictatorship?

The Saudi dictators are blockading neighbouring Qatar and demanding that it shut down the excellent Aljazeera news service.

The Saudi dictators are also causing mass starvation and a cholera epidemic in neighbouring Yemen. It's the dictatorship's war against an emerging democracy.

The Saudi dictators make Iran's elected government look like a much better choice as an ally for the G7/8 and associate nation-states which arm and support the Saudi dictatorship instead of challenging it.

Long before the monarchical dictatorship murders the journalist, I write to Krysta Freeland, author of the book Plutocrats and Canada's global affairs minister at time of writing.

I'm complimenting her when the Saudi dictator has a tantrum and decides to sell all his Canadian investments and pull out all of its medical students at Canadian universities.

This tantrum is a result of Freeland criticizing human rights abuses by the dictator.

My message to Freeland is about monarchical dictatorship and how it illustrates the might-makes-right and murderous nature of monarchy itself.

I conclude by saying that no matter how "cute" the "royal" babies and newlyweds may appear, and how "wonderful pomp and ceremony" accompanies them, monarchy cannot escape or deny its legacy of torture, killing, and the mass murder crime against humanity known by the euphemism "war".

I repeat what I say to monarchists in the past, i.e. I prefer democracy to monarchy.

But religionists don't listen to heretics and non-blind-believers.

...

As smog enshrouds Seoul, locals are suddenly appearing in the news saying how worried they are about air pollution damaging their health.

Seven years earlier, 3.7 million people in the world die because of pollution, which includes contaminated air.

...

**Lustagoocheehk**: In A Sketch of Terrian History, I criticize the European calendar year because it starts at the beginning of the northern hemisphere winter instead of spring.

Since life begins in spring, not in winter, I find it strange to start a new year at the time of the winter solstice.

This year, for the first time that I am aware of or remember, three "first" world news reports tell me that at least some non-European calendar makers agree with me.

The northern hemisphere spring equinox is New Year's Day in Kurdish and Persian (Iranian) cultures. Soon thereafter, Buddhists in Burma/ Myanmar start their year.

Bravo intelligent calendar makers!

I hope the news organizations will also report that the Incas, Quechua, and others start their calendars during the southern hemisphere spring equinox.

Leaving ignorance behind always feels so good.

...

According to a U.S. PBS Newshour story from Antarctica, there are several types of penguins.

This bird has been around for 60 million years, which means it sees the dinosaurs come and go.

Unfortunately, due to human poaching of its traditional food supply, a variety of shrimp, and human caused climate change, penguins are in danger.

Among other things, a warming Antarctic climate now includes snow, which makes it more difficult to for penguins to walk. It also suffocates them.

Most types of penguins see their numbers decline 50-75% in only 20 years.

However, one species of penguins could survive because it is adapting. This species is changing its diet to more plentiful fish instead of the increasingly rare shrimp.

...

Mariko and I are looking at a news report about increasing prices on polluting that are being adopted by governments.

In Canada the province of Columbia (Br.) pioneers this pricing about ten years earlier. The province has a thriving economy today.

Six other provinces have their own pricing systems too.

But Ontario drops out when a very "conservative" government opposing conserving the human life-support system is elected.

That's not the issue that elects them. Voters are angry with the incumbents for other reasons and the "conservatives" benefit from the angry votes.

The Canadian government says that the now four provinces not taking decisive action to discourage polluting are automatically subject to a national pricing policy.

Opponents call this pricing a "carbon tax" as if it were merely a fundraising programme to pay down the nation-state's debts.

However, wherever the Canadian pricing policy is imposed, each resident is entitled to a tax rebate which is a sum greater than what they will pay for polluting, if they decrease or stop their polluting behaviour.

Opponents to this concept, both partisans and general public, condemn it as an unfair and unnecessary tax. They vow to vote to end it.

In their vows I see a total lack of interest in making their lives and the world in general a better place, just like the kids who don't study when Mariko and I are studying.

The anti-"tax", conventional path, and not studying people share an anger and/or bitterness.

So they are lashing out at the world instead of trying to become happy by helping their children and grandchildren to enjoy a future of clean oxygen, water, and land to support their lives.

...

Experiments with small children, broadcast by Dr. David Suzuki on the CBC-TV science programme "The Nature of Things" and on the U.S. CBS News programme "60 Minutes" indicate that children are generous and sharing by nature.

That's the most common type of human nature found in the adventures of <u>Terrian Journals</u> too.

...

In U.S. news, the U.S. military reports that its looking into an attack on an oil tanker ship near Iran.

Then the U.S. military shows a video of the Iranian military removing an unexploded weapon from the oil tanker.

Finally, Aljazeera news interviews the ship's owner. He and the oil tanker are Japanese. Nippon trades with Iran and they get along well with it.

Nippon's prime minister is visiting Iran at the time and is well-received. So why would Iran attack a Japanese ship? Removing an unexploded weapon is helpful, not an attack.

So U.S. appointees and allies of Emperor Twit Punchline are attempting mass deception by claiming that Iran is attacking a Japanese ship.

It's another "Gulf of Tonkin", "incubator babies", and "weapons of mass destruction" big lie to drum up support for war against Iran.

These bogus stories are another correct definition of war crimes.

...

An NHK News report indicates the very unwise idea of any jurisdiction trying to impose the same type of anti-Moslem laws now used in Québec.

About 25% of the world's multi-billion population is now Moslem. Native speaker anglophones remain fewer than 10%.

In another news story, NHK reports that a woman in Fukushima is making Moslem gowns and head coverings using old kimonos with beautiful designs.

This could make Moslem clothing a fashion trend for many other women.

...

During our months in Barcelona, Catalunya's capital, there is a separatist movement.

It allies with a then separatist premier of Québec, as I find out in a pamphlet in Barcelona.

In more recent times, Catalan's government tries to separate by holding a referendum. The Spanish government disagrees and declares the referendum illegal.

Consequently, most of Catalunya's voters don't show up at the polls. The results don't reflect a majority vote. But the Catalunya government declares independence.

Faced with intervention by the nation-state government, Catalunya government leaders flee the country and spend some time in exile.

Ironically, they do so in the capital of the anti-separatist European Union.

In a more recent development, there's a trial of the people who flee and some violent rioting in the streets of Barcelona.

A proposed amnesty for the leaders causes heated debate in España's parliament.

A separatist movement begins in Xiang Giang too, apparently because somehow the older people forget the 99 year dictatorship of the U.K. colonial office.

They also never mention it to younger people now in the streets demanding democracy from Chuang Hwa, which replaces the U.K. colonial office? The fact that there is no pro-democracy movement of this type under the U.K. colonial office dictatorship, as far as I know, makes the motivations of the Xiang Giang demonstrators today a departure from 99 years of behaviour.

Perhaps the U.K. colonial office prevents news of rebellion from reaching the news abroad.

I view the Catalunya and Xiang Giang movements as separatists attempting to divide the human community even more than the current revival of nasty regimes.

**Hà Nội**: We don't understand any of the Vietnamese language. But visually, local television news is telling us that there are a lot of meetings going on during our first days here.

One looks like a meeting of the government and/or communist party, based on similar gatherings I see broadcast on Canadian news over the years and in Cuba.

So many of the smaller meetings seem to be within the military. Everyone present is wearing a uniform.

Other meetings are attended mostly by people in white shirts. Bureaucrats?

Few women seem to be taking part in the meetings.

The weather reports are much easier to understand.

We can also see France 24 news and other television stations.

We learn, while staying in Castelo Franco (Italia) a few years earlier, that it's easy to get the wrong impression from news that's not in a language we can understand.

There, we see a story about an apparent illegal drug raid just before some images of older people. We could easily misconclude that seniors are drug smugglers.

**Lustagoocheehk**: In the "war" against COVID-19 the first victim, after truth, is the news. Although Aljazeera does maintain some variety in stories from different parts of the world, others news reporting does not.

Both the Canadian francophone and anglophone all-news television networks sud-denly become a public service instead of pay TV broadcasts.

The lost revenue means that they can only report one story, C-19.

The constant obsession with and repetition of C-19 stories is no doubt traumatizing and causing mental anguish and illness in the minds of people who now find themselves confined most of the day and night to their housing, ranging from tiny apartments to large houses.

Some are more easily manipulated by unscrupulous politicians, such as U.S. Emperor Twit Punchline, who calls for people to rebel and demand the right to shop.

Punchline's supporters gather in close proximity outside and inside government buildings. They're carrying racist symbols and guns made for the battlefields of war.

The emperor wants to become the first dictator of the U.S. since the last U.K. monarchical dictator's rule over that place?

The COVID-19, one-news-story-only reporting goes on for months. It is a rerun of past obsessions and lazy journalism at its worst.

The predecessors include the constant coverage of only: the death of a former U.K. primary school teacher; the murder trial of a former U.S. football player; and, the death by overdose of a U.S. popular singer.

Covering only one story, no matter how important it may seem or actually is, looks unprofessional, irresponsible, and a dereliction of duty on the part of serious journalists.

The job is to cover all the news, not just one story.

If the news is to report only one story it ought to be the impending human species extinction due to climate change.

What story is more news-worthy than that one?

...

A news story on Aljazeera reveals that businesses selling products made by the labours of people in Bangladesh are laying off workers there and not paying them for work already done.

In passing, the news reporter mentions that the regular pay for these Bangladeshi workers is $US100 per month. That's about double the official "salario minimum" paid under the military dictatorship in Brasil about 40 years earlier.

Brasil's actual minimum incomes were closer to $US1 per day at that time.

The Bangladesh incomes in the story are about $US3.33 per day.

These workers are making clothing for sale overseas. The most lucrative market for the people living off the avails of these workers is the "first" world.

The companies buying these garments and their anti-consumerism critics blame the purchasers in the "first" world for wanting "bargain prices" for garments.

Mariko and I pay as little as $C2 for T-shirts in Niagara Falls souvenir ships and in shops close to Toronto's "garment district".

In other places we pay up to $C15 for a T-shirt that's also made in a sweat shop somewhere in the "third" world.

Regardless of how much we pay for a T-shirt, the workers in Bangladesh are still only getting paid $US3.33 per day of work.

According to a brochure* that I pick up when Mariko and I are visiting the Smithsonian National Museum of American History in D.C., 23 years earlier, garment workers in Bangladesh are getting the same income now as then.

(*The Global Production Game! The same brochure says Vietnamese garment workers get the same income. This makes even the cheapest T-shirts in Hà Nội ($2US) seem extraordinarily expensive.)

Today in the "first" world, the price of garments is also the same or higher than then.

Given the fact that transportation fuel costs drop by about 80% in the preceding couple of months, the garment workers in places such as Bangladesh could easily be paid more without interfering with the profit lusting people charging astronomically over-cost prices for garments.

In a good economy, as opposed to the one that cons are trying to bring back, the cost of garments would reflect the incomes of the garment workers.

So if an average garment worker makes only 10 T-shirts per day, the price of the T-shirt would be almost nothing in the "first" world.

Ten T-shirts per day at a pay scale of about $US3.33 per day means a single T-shirt could be sold for about 33.3¢ US.

If garment workers were paid incomes equal to those of U.S. garment workers 23 years earlier, about $80 per day, under a worldwide equal pay for equal work law, a t-shirt made anywhere in the world could be sold for about $US8.

In fact garment workers in Bangladesh can probably make far more than 10 t-shirts a day, which means that the T-shirts they make could be almost given away.

Nobody would be too poor to have a T-shirt.

At the U.S. garment worker pay scale of 23 years earlier, the T-shirts could be sold for much less than $8 each.

So the problem is not with the consumers who want "bargain prices".

The problem is with the garment companies that want to make astronomical profits by cheating both the garment workers and the garment customers.

So it should come as no surprise that the cons and their company supporters now want to bring back "the economy" no matter how many people have to get sick and die from COVID-19.

The well-being of 90-99% of humanity is of no interest to people who value money above human life.

...

Aljazeera remains the only news service I know of that is still covering more than one story in the news. All the others report only about CO-

VID-19 every day and all the time.

It's as if all the journalists go away on holiday and leave only one person to cover the news, so s/he only covers one story.

Journalism is about reporting all the news, not just one story. Otherwise, as one computer company is now showing, most of the news staff can be eliminated.

Yet in all the obsession with virus news only, I note a huge lacking that I'm still waiting to see overcome.

Perhaps I miss the one mention of one fact during the past few months of one-story news, but I have yet to see any news people comparing virus cases with the annual influenza cases.

Surely, having a "pandemic" needs to be explained by comparing it with the number of cases of other diseases and ailments, in recent times and historically.

Without context, news reporting can be meaningless. It enables ignorance, rumour, and misunderstanding to reign instead of helping people decode and understand news.

...

As news reports the renewal of the fight against racism in the world, catalyzed by U.S. police murders and abuse of everyone without pink-white skin pigmentation, I'm not as obtuse as some people born in areas and hues of special status and privilege.

I understand what it feels like to be falsely accused and assaulted by authoritarian figures, as described in pages about my primary schooling in Terrian Journals' Miss Schooling?

Much more recently, in Terrian Journals: Away Team Journals, I learn what it's like to have an abusive mid-age pink-white woman calling a police-like force to come after me by falsely claiming I am "threatening".

I am no more threatening than the African-American encountering a pink-white woman walking her dog, as reported in the news.

She gets fired and the police charge her with making a false report of a crime to an emergency help number. The person calling against me should also be fired.

My experiences may be mild ones and I don't get shot by police, but I nevertheless get a personal taste of what racism victims feel toward their oppressors.

...

News sometimes features interviews with professors who are asked to express their expert opinions on real world events.

My years of daily contact with profs on several campuses lead me to be sceptical and cringe at profs on TV news.

Professors profess knowledge. That doesn't always make them knowledgeable or all-knowing.

Profs are often said to know more and more about less and less and to know less than their students, especially when it comes to life off campus.

Profs who habitually use their students to do their research ad to my concerns about the wisdom of asking profs to make pronouncements, prognostications, evaluations, and predictions.

Expertise and study alone do not necessarily produce reliable outcomes in the natural setting or the unnatural settings of nation-states and societies.

As one space researcher is quoted as saying- We had everything figured out and then actual human behaviour destroyed our model.

Profs may study and learn, but that doesn't make them all-knowing deities of knowledge and understanding.

With these thoughts in mind, I hear Mariko's report of a prof who studies aging and dementia.

He says routine staves off memory loss and strengthens the minds of elderly people. Really?

After 26 years in prison and release at about age 80, Nelson Mandela writes that routine is the enemy of prisoners. It erodes their minds and thinking.

They become zombies of routine. I would say the same about people in standard issue existence. This is probably a contributing factor to dementia.

When the routine of employment is gone, they don't know what to do or think. They forget what it's like to be alive years earlier, due to their dependency on routine.

These are the people the prof is referring to? Their minds are already lost many years before they are elderly.

Mariko's mother and my dad spend most of their lives living routines. Their memory losses are exceptional, according to the prof?

Or do the standard issue people need to maintain the routines enslaving them before they become elderly?

People like me, who seek daily variety even during temporary confinement to routine, require non-routine living to maintain our minds and memories.

Every day is a new experience with new discoveries and new memories to occupy our minds.

Why would someone in a routine standard issue existence need to remember anything. It becomes automatic.

I am far less vulnerable to routine loss than the elderly emerging suddenly from standard issue existence after the prime years of their lives are lost to being held in captivity by employment and societies' conventions and routines.

Note that elderly people we know who are held in "homes" quickly become progressively weaker and feeble-minded in the routines of their institutional "homes".

People in routines don't think because they don't need to think. It's akin to what a trans-Canada railway passenger says to me about not having to think.

Idle passengers in life need only eat and sleep. No survival instincts or thinking are needed. Thus all is lost, including memory.

Besides, their existence isn't very memorable, even to themselves.

People don't remember what it's like to be alive because they are the living dead, often since youth.

Sitting around all day being fed, entertained, etc., in old age, is a continuation of that death, not life.

It's the afterlife of the employeed who never actually live, along with their entourage of dependent partners.

**Tokyo**: News shows the added irony of new compulsory mask laws in both France and Québec, which have bans against Moslems wearing face coverings.

It's poetic justice and irony combined.

Animosity to masks is quite a bad joke in France, a country where partial or complete nudity on beaches is all right but a burkini makes some people "feel uncomfortable".

The European outlook changes considerably since the era when most of them wore old sacks.

Is this why a famous U.S. chain store is called "Sacks"?

**Fukuoka**: News reports that the virus is air borne but I see no stories about second-hand smoke from nicotine delivery devices, leaf burning or vapour type, carrying the virus.

My cancer researcher cousin Steve, in one of the rare bits of communication from his family since our last visit, says the smoke nearest to the nicotine addict can carry viruses.

There is also so much separation, isolation, and disinfectant use now that I wonder if it is lowering our immunity to bacteria and germs.

We build our immunity by exposure to bacteria and germs.

Reducing or eliminating that exposure is surely going to make us all more susceptible to harm during inadvertent exposure.

One news story quotes the president of Peru saying that he's happy to know Peruanos/as are helping to fight COVID-19 by volunteering for tests of potential vaccines.

Another story mentions people in Africa also volunteering for vaccine testing. [Ironically, the greedy "first" worlders are so generous to themselves that they leave almost no vaccine for Africans.]

Wait a minute! "Third" world people are volunteering to develop vaccines for "first" world pharmaceutical companies!

Most residents of the "third" world countries have incomes of $1 to $3 per day.

So the "first" world pharmaceutical companies can offer them more, i.e. very little, to entice volunteers.

Why isn't there an investigative reporter looking into this probable exploitation and life-threatening volunteerism the among "third" worlders, and reporting about it in the news?

"Third" world lives don't matter?

...

What the past calls rebellions, which fail, and revolutions, which succeed at least for a while, now become "mass street demonstrations" or "protests".

Today they seem to be happening everywhere in the news, including MuangThai, Xiang Giang, Belarus', USA (Black Lives Matter), First Nations (Canada), Zimbabwe and other African nation-states, and among the COVID-19 frus-trated.

These street movements might indicate a widespread interest and moves toward direct democracy because political systems and elections fail to serve the human interest.

...

Rather than containing the COVID-19 virus, people are contained as a means to that end by quarantine, isolation, "lock downs", masks, and keeping distant.

Among the beneficiaries are mail order businesses, now called "on line", food delivery companies, and internet entertainment corporations such as Twitter, Facebook, and pharmaceutical drug and supply companies, etc.

One news story reports a surge in "container hotel" demand too.

Instead of being confined to "home", with distracting and annoying "family", people can now retreat to shipping containers converted into hotel accommodation.

...

A news story out of Chuang Hwa more than six months earlier warns that COVID-19 might be able to cross as many as four metres.

Yet in Lustagoocheehk it's two metres. In Sawaraku and Narita, the distance is not that far. Officially it seems to be one metre.

**Lustagoocheehk**: A news story reports that only about 2% of COVID-19 infections can be attributed to people arriving from abroad.

But hypocritical politicians, including an Ontario provincial cabinet minister, sneak away for vacations in warmer climates abroad for a few days and draw the attention of lazy news media's one-story obsession.

So the news rivets attention on almost anyone and everyone who goes beyond Canada's borders.

It's a xenophobic reaction and fear campaign akin to blaming "foreigners" for unemployment everywhere in the world.

Again, since "foreigners" are everywhere, if "foreigners" create unemployment everywhere, how can there be any jobs in the world for anyone, including "foreigners"?

The people who spread diseases are the ones who are sick but who go to work and entertainment centres, such as bars, restaurants, and sports arenas.

The disease spreaders refuse to wear masks and to keep their distance from others.

These culprits are a far larger number of people than the 2% bringing in COVID-19 from some other part of the world.

...

Tens of millions of people in the world now suffer from COVID-19.

The news coverage exceeds the JFK assassination weekend, which is surpassed by the trial of a U.S. football player accused of murdering his spouse and the deaths of a U.S. popular singer and a U.K. princess.

The pandemic will probably be remembered for a long time. But what about the pandemic of a century ago? It too kills millions in many parts of the world.

It must be a front page newspaper story for months during that era.

Yet it gets no mention in any of my schooling text books or my university history courses' required readings.

Why is it that my first knowledge of that pandemic comes from a U.S. Hollywood movie only about 25 years earlier, and I look it up to make sure its not fiction like the film?

That's the "Spanish Flu" and reportedly comes home with

soldiers returning from the 1914 to 1918 war.

My parents are born at the end of that war. As infants they would have no memory of it. But I never hear my very long-lived grandparents talk about it to anyone.

They are in their 20s or 30s during the "Spanish Flu" pandemic. Apparently it's hardest on the youngest people because their immune systems die fighting it.

My elderly grandparents talk about two world wars sometimes, but not about the pandemic of their formative young adult years.

...

According to an SRC RDI news report about the pandemic, 14% of the world's population is getting 50% of the vaccines.

So the "first" world now number well under the 20% of the world population they used to be?

Yet the "first" worlders go on to complain that they are "suffering" from a vaccine shortage and aren't getting their vaccine supplies fast enough.

As an afterthought, when shamed by the WHO, "first" world countries promise to share their surplus, if any, with the "third" world.

There is a world programme to deliver vaccines to the "third" world, but Russia and Chuang Hwa are outpacing it in their generous shipments of their own, non-corporation vaccines to many countries.

The "first" world feels threatened by the potential worldwide influence and good reputation that the generous "second" world Russian and Chinese are gaining.

So, the "first" world becomes a bit generous as "counterpropaganda". The "first" world has "values" of convenience and doesn't like competition.

The "first" sends soon-to-expire vaccines, too many of which are doomed to be thrown away in the "third" world garbage dump of the "first" world.

...

"First" worlders in the news are condemning their elected governments for not securing vaccines for them and delivering them quickly.

My priority for delivering vaccines and inoculating people would be to send the first doses to the "third" world, where more than 80% of humanity lives.

It looks as if Russia and Chuang Hwa agree with me by sending the vaccines they invent in government laboratories to the "third" world.

...

Chuang Hwa's aid now includes supplies of its own COVID-19 vaccine, which is cheaper than the ones made by other capitalist nation-states, which horde their supplies and have a "first worlder first" policy toward COVID-19.

The same applies to Canadian provinces, which now only grudgingly share vaccines with Ontario because its virus cases reach previously unequalled numbers of daily cases.

Ontario goes from fewer than 1,000 cases per day to more than 4,000, and risks having 10-18,000 per day.

But there is something receiving less emphasize in the news which could be the most important reason for the hostility toward Chuang Hwa.

Chuang Hwa is now the world leader in manufacturing, promoting, and increasing the use of green technology, including solar panels, wind turbines, and electric vehicles.

This situation must be intolerable to the U.S. petroleum company oligarchs, who risk losing the ability to increase their fortunes by continuing to destroy the planetary natural system providing life-support for humans.

Does it all boil down to racism against Chuang Hwa? It's not of European origin, so it must be wrong and bad?

...

Meanwhile the "first" world says it will send the leftovers it buys from private pharmaceutical companies to the "third" world

But it sends vaccines with imminent expiry dates, forcing "third" world governments to destroy them.

U.S. President Biden surpasses his promise of 100 million vaccinations for U.S.ers during his first 100 days in office. Instead of 1 million vaccinations per day there are 1.8.

It's not difficult to provide enough vaccine because the U.S. 4% of humanity has 50% of the world supply of vaccines.

At the current rate, the entire U.S. population could be vaccinated at least once within about a month.

Anti-vaccine groups and opponents of measures against COVID-19 slow down the process considerably, leaving tens of millions unvaccinated.

Meanwhile, in Canada, the entire population, i.e. 10% of the U.S. populace is not expected to be vaccinated even once in any less than nine months. Incompetent Canada?

Later, Canada is accused of being one of the world's worst vaccine hoarders.

...

U.S. news says that that country has 4% of the world population and 40% of the vaccine supply.

Nearly 4 million people are vaccinated every day in the U.S. Only a few tens of thousands are vaccinated during the same days in Canada.

Here it's a supply shortage, like in most of the world. Canada's "first" world status isn't giving it an edge. The parties in power in the provinces and Ottawa are blamed.

They represent three of the four national political parties. So no party is best.

Exactly one year after COVID-19 arrives here, P.E.I. still has no one hospitalized and no deaths resulting from the virus. Bravo!

...

The number of doses of vaccine injected in the U.S. grows to nearly four million per day and then surpasses four, long before Biden's 100 day deadline.

Canadian provinces with few COVID-19 cases refuse to share their vaccine supply with provinces hit hard by the pandemic, such as Ontario with 4,000+ new cases per day now.

...

When the U.K., Yisra'el, Canada, and the U.S. report about half their citizens are vaccinated nearly a month before the northern hemisphere summer solstace, during the second year of the pandemic, the U.S. PBS Newshour reports that 75% of the vaccine supply is held by only ten nation-states.

There are nearly 200 nation-states in the United Nations.

During the first year of COVID, very poor nation-state "leaders" dally so much and downplay the virus so much, that COVID-19 has ample time to mutate.

Variants spread everywhere. They are named for where they are first found, but they arise and spread elsewhere without exportation or importation.

When the majority of humanity is not receiving vaccinations, COVID-19 has ample opportunity to grow and mutate.

How long will it be before an increasing variety of mutations become resistant to all existing vaccines?

The ten countries with 75% of the vaccines will find themselves overwhelmed by vaccine-resistant strains of the virus.

...

Yisra'el's extremist yahoo regime boasts that a very large percentage of its national population is already vaccinated using the commercial vaccines. [Third and fourth doses follow.]

But the same extremist regime is blocking delivery of vaccines from Russia to the Palestinians. It's yahoo's final solution for people living in occupied territory.

In world law terms, that's a war crime.

...

Canadian newscasts show long lines of people right here in Lustagoocheehk waiting for something while reporters talk about vaccines.

Three days later I hear radio news reporting a day of free COVID-19 testing in town. When I mention the story to someone working in a supermarket he says it's three days.

We miss all of them. It's not important enough to explain in the news we listen to and watch?

There are no notices on the bulletin boards, such as the one at the supermarket, or anywhere else informing people about the testing.

The boards only have posters about social events and people selling things.

Another day our neighbour Dale says he's just returning from getting his vaccine. He says all we have to do is make an appointment at a pharmacy that's ten minutes walk away.

This is news to us. There are no notices on the bulletin boards about this either.

We only know we can get inoculated because we happen to talk to our neighbour on the right day.

We walk to one of the two pharmacies we pass close to every day and find out.

...

As rumoured in earlier news reports, Canada's government announces that punishing Canadians for exercising their Charter rights will soon end for incoming airline passengers.

Starting early next month, they will no longer be forced to spend thousands of dollars on unmerited and unjustified hotel confinement charges for compulsory stays in hotels normally charging less than $100 per night for $25 rooms.

The new policy only applies to Canadian citizens and permanent residents. Everyone else must still pay.

...

There are many teenaged people running pro-environment and anti-gun movements today. Youth is finally taking over the world?

This has more implications when a news report says that 80% of the people in Iran are less than 30 years old.

...

According to a DPI, Democracy Perception Index survey reported by the U.S. PBS Newshour, people worldwide consider the U.S. the greatest threat to democracy.

About 44% put the U.S. first. About 38% say it's Chuang Hwa. The remaining 28% say Russia. Hm. That adds up to 110%.

...

There are already a number of news reports indicating the range of problems inside Canada's tax department.

The department is increasingly dependant upon the internet for receiving tax returns and exchanging correspondence. Within less than a year, the system is hacked three times.

The department reacts by cancelling access to the tax accounts of nearly a million people.

Another news story says that tax department employees in one major Canadian city are taking bribes. (Montréal)

Yet another news story reports that the tax department provides incorrect information about eligibility for COVID-19 financial assistance.

As a result, 441,000 people who might not qualify are receiving millions of dollars in assistance.

When the government discovers this mistake in tax department information giving, so much money is already distributed that the government decides not to demand its return.

But the tax bureaucracy sends a letter to every one of the 441,000 saying they may have to pay the money back. How much did the letter production and sending cost?

Later the government discovers that hundreds of tax department employees are illegally granting themselves COVID-19 aid money.

The latest news story about the tax department says there's a plan to hire outside contractors to take over the information work of the department.

Will people working for the tax department apply for jobs with the contractor? Will they be the same people who provide wrong information?

Will the tax department bureaucracy use the new contractors as scapegoats for future mistakes while taking the tax information work out of the domain of responsible government?

Private contractors used by the U.S. government, instead of official military personnel, can commit abuses and atrocities for which the U.S. military can honestly deny all responsibility. It's "deniability".

The tax department makes the news again, losing 13 years of court battles with a Saskatchewan company.

The battle costs the taxpayers millions of dollars in lost revenue to pay for the lawyers on both sides all the way to the Canadian Supreme Court.

No price is too high for the taxpayers to pay for the tax department's mistakes?

...

A coup d'état in Burma/ Myanmar is a bigger news story and outrage for all humanity because people whose families originate in that part of the world are in the streets of Canada and other countries denouncing the coup.

The demonstrators inspire me to come up with an idea to help to inform and promote action from humanity everywhere, particularly in small, isolated towns such as Lustagoocheehk.

A store front message window or board could post current, far away human problems to heighten daily awareness for locals everywhere who are routinely passing along the main street every day.

It's different from news which has to be sought out in print or through electronic channels. A message posted in full view of the main street is a constant reminder.

It's not unlike election campaign signs and political messages posted in Canada, Cuba, etc. But it's non-partisan and non-ideological.

...

In the past I consider housing, motor vehicles, and children to be the self-set traps of the employeed and the leverage that employers have for using people.

I now realize that there is a fourth trap and leverage. It's not something new to me. I see it in the news and in my personal experience. It's education money indebtedness.

One of Paul Soloman's "Making Sense" weekly economics reports on the U.S. P.B.S. Newshour broadcast reminds me of the problem and emphasizes it.

I know that post-secondary education student loans put people into debt for years, sometimes for many years, and that they pay them out of their salaries for years.

But the P.B.S. report makes me realize the deeper implications for the first time.

I don't realize these implications because I only see the problem in the abstract. It's beyond my experience. I'm only vaguely aware of our friend Louis Paul's student debt.

Now I understand that although almost anyone can get trapped by mortgage, motor vehicle, and child support payments, only an elite group of students resembling me can get trapped by student loans.

I never need to apply for a student loan and I don't get caught in any of the other traps. So employers never have leverage over me.

...

Aljazeera news reports say that there are "right wing Yisra'el nationalists". They march through the streets shouting, "Death To Arabs!"

It's the nationalists' "final solution" throughout time?

These nationalists can't be the descendants of victims of The Holocaust.

The yahoo running Yisra'el supports invading Palestinian land, turfing out the residents, and building what the United Nations calls "illegal" settlements.

The territory in question is voluntarily ceded to the Palestinians by a late ruler of Jordan, but Yisra'el, particularly un-der yahoo, decides to just take the land for Yisra'el.

Yisra'el needs, as the nasties in Deutschland say, living space. The latest episode in this tragedy involves Yisra'elis evicting Palestinians from their houses, reminding me of the nasties taking over the homes of Polish Jews in the U.S. Hollywood movie "Schindler's List".

This has to be a joke. It can't be serious.

Unfortunately, yahoo later forms a coalition government with like-minded extreme right-wing politicians.

Their supporters want Palestinians to move to neighbouring nation-states.

A few years later, a Palestinian group manages to defy Yisra'el's "iron dome" security system and kill 1,200 Yisra'eli citizens.

Yahoo responds by militarily killing more than 16,000 Palestinians and driving millions of Palestinians out of their homes.

This is yahoo's final solution for Palestinians?

This is the grand finale of the final flareup of more than 75 years of war since the United Nations created Yisra'el?

During these years the word semite, which describes Arabs, Jews, and Phoenicians is redefined to mean only Yisra'elis and others who follow Judaiism.

So anti-semitism is redefined to mean only hatred toward Yisra'elis and others who follow Judaism.

No news reports cover this semantic alteration, automatically eliminating non-Yisra'elis and non-Jews from the semite category.

...

According to Alvin M. Josephy, Jr.'s book about the First Nations in the northern and central Americas - 500 Nations, after learning English, a member of the Cherokee civilization creates a written form for the Cherokee language and founds a Cherokee newspaper.

Faced with this undesirable result, the U.S. elite, in the form of the Georgia militia, shuts down the Cherokee newspaper.

It sounds like the strategy used by military dictatorships everywhere.

So the U.S. constitution's words about freedom of the press, written about 60 years before the militia shuts down the newspaper, only apply to English language newspapers and people of European origin?

**Toronto**: The abundance of people without masks in the Queen Street vicinity and other downtown vias is a big surprise to me.

News stories about crackdowns on public assemblage in Ontario give me the impression that the city police are everywhere, ready to fine people standing too close together or not wearing masks.

In our extensive and detailed walks, essential only for our health, we see no police presence enforcing the "stay at home order". The police are all working from home?

But there are hardly any passengers in the TTC bus and subway cars that we ride after literally landing in the city, from Pearson International Airport to the closest subway station to our lodgings near Osgoode TTC station.

Although it's early evening on a work day night, there are few riders on the Lawrence West to Osgoode Station, Spadina Line route.

I'm using obsolete public transit nomenclature. As I notice during our last visit here, subway lines now go by numbers. But who knows the line numbers and station numbers?

Today's locals know, not former locals like me.

It's like listening to SRC morning radio news in Lustagoocheehk talking about health "zones" one to seven.

Where are the zones? Which zone includes Lustagoocheehk. Nobody ever mentions these essential facts.

**Fukuoka**: Trinity Bellwoods Park has a tent camp of homeless people. I don't take pictures of this hardship.

The surrounding neighbourhood includes supportive identical printed signs asking the city not to evict the campers. I photograph one of the signs.

The tenters have laundry and cooking setups in place around the tents.

Sixteen days later, in Fukuoka, I see a Canadian news report showing a line of police marching on the park camp, forcibly evicting the homeless residents, and erecting wire fences to keep them out.

Apparently twelve campers agree to accept "safer" indoor accommodation. Others say it's "safer" in the park camp.

Police blitzkrieging homeless people looks bad.

Toronto's mayor says the city sends in non-police social assistance workers to offer lodgings to the homeless several times before the police force raid.

Why not offer a tour of alternatives to camp representatives, who could report back to the campers and help them decide where to move?

Police don't solve homelessness. They lack the necessary knowledge and training.

...

Nunavut's member of Canada's parliament says her first term is her last because she's mistreated by parliamentary "security" guards. Racism wins again?

The story is understated by CTV National News. I complain.

The next day there's more coverage, but the "security" department only says it hasn't received a complaint from the MP and they'd be glad to talk to her.

So the victim doesn't complain to the perpetrators and they're be willing to talk to her. Me too, again! Is "security" going to investigate itself?

In so many cases of racial profiling and systemic racism, the head has to apologize and/or resign and the offenders are suspended, fired, and/or tried.

Not on parliament hill?

MP Celina Caesar-Chavannes is a previous victim who is now coming forward.

A couple of days later the story seems to disappear. No special parliamentary hearings are announced to investigate racism against a member of parliament.

...

Experts on the U.S. PBS Newshour say the withdrawal from Afghanistan is based on what the U.S. learned in Viet Nam. It's a rerun of failure?

...

Three recent news stories from different sources are revealing disparities among human beings going well beyond simple basics such as food and shelter.

People living in unmoneyed neighbourhoods in the U.S. are having health problems and dying prematurely because of the extra stress of living in daily fear of survival.

People living in unmoneyed neighbourhoods are also suffering more from climate change's higher temperatures because cities are neglecting them by not planting trees.

Affluent neighbourhoods have big shady trees on every sidewalk and street.

On a larger global scale, the unmoneyed in tropical places who are not the ones causing climate change are losing their food supply and homes to it.

Warming ocean water drives fish to cooler latitudes, leaving the tropical inhabitants without sufficient seafood to sustain themselves.

Floods, fires, and rising sea levels destroy their homes.

...

A U.S. P.B.S. Newshour report shows tiny tots in cap and gown in a procession to celebrate their pre-school "graduation" ceremony.

In my infancy, pre-school goes by the very unpretentious name of "play school". It's organized fun, not an academic programme to determine lifetimes.

Making the most minor events and accomplishments of a lifetime into grand ceremonial occasions tends to cheapen, diminish, and under-rate all that follows.

It rewards the simplest tasks with the first highest awards. It dumbs down awards and awarding.

Is this the intention?

...

"First" world vaccine hoarding is genocide. The "third" world is expendable.

U.S. cases of COVID-19 among the non-vaccinated increase with consumer spending. So they're trying to buy their way to health?

U.S. President Biden says "social" media is "killing people" by allowing misinformation about COVID-19 on "platforms".

One "social" media megacorporation retorts that two million of its users receive accurate information about COVID-19.

But how many users receive the misinformation?

The old game of lying with statistics continues with selective use of statistics. The megacorporation is spreading half truths about itself.

...

Radio-Canada reports that the Canadian health department agrees to agrotoxic company demands that they be permitted to increase the amount of their product used in food production.

The news first reports say that this is only a demand for blueberry farming. Later, news consumers learn that the agrotoxic company wants increases for many other plants.

A commentator in the agricultural/health fields says there is a lack of research about the effects of increasing agrotoxics in many or all food types grown for human consumption.

The elected member of parliament who is the minister responsible for health says that she learns about the agrotoxic decision at the same time as other Canadians, in the news.

She adds that it's not unusual for a minister not to be informed of changes in government policies in her/his ministry.

Admitting that bureaucracy rules a parallel, unelected government is even more troubling than the bureaucracy unilaterally making government decisions.

Later the agriculture minister claims responsibility for the agrotoxic policy change. The agrotoxic company pressure becomes only a coincidence!?

...

Previous generations read the same newspapers and talk about what they read. The same news stories are the common topics of conversation.

The same occurs with radio and television news and entertainment such as sports. In that era there are a limited number of stations, channels, and schedules.

Wherever people share the same language(s), city, nation-state, etc. they have something in common to discuss.

But now people have less and less in common, perhaps almost nothing*.

(*The exception being periods of news obsession with only one story ad nauseum, excluding all else, e.g. celebrity court cases and sudden deaths).

...

As a child, I start watching three or four U.S. national television newscasts and then only watch the CBS Evening News with Walter Cronkite until he retires.

In my childhood, I rarely watch local or national Canadian television news and apparently don't miss anything influencing the world.

Besides, Canada's national newscasts are only aired late at night, while I'm sleeping.

...

I learn more about science (physics) by getting up at 4 a.m. to watch the detailed news coverage of the U.S. Mercury, Gemini, and Apollo space programmes than I learn in all my school science classes, especially physics.

The classes are boring and never mention space science.

...

None of the current affairs that I see on television news are in the social studies and history text books of my time. The classroom ignores the news.

...

The corrupt in Canada need only wait for the hockey playoffs to begin to avoid attracting public attention in the news and to survive scandals in Canada.

News is pre-empted and delayed until late at night in the biggest population centres, unless you switch from the game to the news channels and non-hockey TV networks.

...

There is so much coverage of sports during news broadcasts that it cuts into the time available for covering all other stories of more importance than sports entertainment.

Sports events also preempt both news and other programmes here in Canada.

What a contrast with Nippon, where baseball games are cut short when it's news time on NHK-TV.

That network has a regularly scheduled sports broadcast following the day's regular programmes once a week at the weekend.

But here in Canada, sports takes priority and dominates news, especially hockey games.

Due to the excess coverage, I completely lose interest in sports broadcasting and mute the volume or change the channel almost every time that sports appear.

In this manner I manage to go through the entire hockey season without ever seeing a game or a report about one. I have no idea who makes the playoffs and wins the cup.

It doesn't matter. It doesn't improve the world. It's just big business making money.

...

A very long time after many other parts of the world become mad about soccer, Canadian television news suddenly discovers soccer, starts broadcasting games, and devotes large segments of news programmes to soccer during a world championship.

Before this time, soccer news is an obscure report about U.K. teams only on CBC Radio and buried on, I think, Sunday mornings.

Soccer's very sudden transformation from a hard-core fans-only, obscure, and marginal game into a headline event in Canada is astounding.

It reminds me of how U.S. politicians change Nippon's status in public opinion polls from "greatest ally" to most threatening rival within a few months, when the U.S. wants to sell more goods in Nippon and buy fewer goods from it.

Soccer's remarkable and widespread popularity in Nippon and Canada is a product of very aggressive mass-marketing and propaganda by a world league whose corruption also becomes mainstream news.

In Sumo's Nippon, Canada's hockeyland, and even the baseball and football dominated U.S.A., soccer is becoming another one of the artificial replacements for actual interests (and exercise), brought about through mass manipulation.

Perhaps in the U.S. case it's simply a continuation of existing behaviour. U.S.ers seem ready to buy anything. All the junk food and goods sales prove it.

Selling the soccer world championship games is like staging a bombastic new product advertising campaign, shocking and awing consumers into running out to the nearest vendor to buy the latest thing, i.e. soccer equipment and tickets.

New products and obscure, marginal sports do not become overnight sensations without considerable planning and organizing by a well-financed group of promoters who will do anything, no holds barred, to push their product.

What kind of a parent would induce or encourage its child to become a victim of such a contrived, delusional, and fanatical realm?

Answer: A duped parent rendered mindless and open to hypnotic suggestion by the caretaker society ruling our lives.

...

News reports tells us that some people are now using software to create images which remake people's faces and bodies, to present ideal images of themselves. Whose ideal?

So nobody knows what anyone else really looks like, including themselves.

I already find advertising in St. John's about remaking 60+ year old faces to make them look much younger. Weird! It's only worth doing if the person is truly younger inside.

...

During one Olympic games, in spite of sportscasts devoted only to names, numbers, and nationalities, news leaks out that the competitors, who spend years preparing for the games, are also preparing for a love fest.

Condoms are distributed to all competitors. So they're here for fun and games.

The athletes represent the best and are great role models, sports announcers, fund-raising campaigns, and advertising slogans always declare.

We finally know the activity in which they really excel. When will it be declared an official event, broadcast live?

...

Significant missing news item: When the U.S. asks NATO to help invade Afghanistan under the all-for-one provision of the treaty, all N.A.T.O. members know that Afghanistan never attacks any NATO member.

So the U.S.-led N.A.T.O. invasion does not comply with the provisions of the NATO treaty. It's also fraudulent.

That's now very old unreported news that's obvious from the outset.

There's no justification for invading Afghanistan. There are grounds for co-opting the Taliban government and hunting for the actual perpetrators of the attacks.

The failed U.S. 20 year war against Afghanistan is merely a manifestation of a long-term U.S. foreign policy of monopoly capitalism, world domination, hegemony, vengeance, and reprisals against all comers, whether armed or competitive capitalists.

Most U.S. soldiers die fighting against other capitalists, be they U.K., Confederate, Spanish, Mexican, German, or Japanese. The most recent targets are Iran and China.

When the U.S. can't compete with other capitalists, it attacks them. When the U.S. is defied or attacked, it retaliates with punitive measures.

The U.S. could well declare itself an inheritor of the traditions of the Mongol Khans and the Portuguese gunships off the coast of what they rename Goa.

Instead, the U.S. claims it is following very high ideals and principles.

Yet these loudly espoused motives do not prevent a long tradition of slavery and the racism and discrimination which continues to motivate and drive too many in the U.S., including its elected elites and law enforcement agents.

Yet the U.S. does not enter the wars against Deutschland and the one against Nippon until there are direct attacks against the U.S. or its citizens.

It takes the sinking of a ship called the Lusitania and the U.S. seventh naval fleet to stir up the spirit of vengeance motivating the U.S. to go into battle against Deutschland and Nippon.

The Japanese Imperial Army's atrocities and racism in Chuang Hwa don't stir up U.S. ideals and principles.

Nazi Deutschland's abuse, round-up, and forced relocation of the followers of Judaism and other people to torture and death camps doesn't prompt the U.S. to fight for its ideals and principles in Europe until most of it falls to Naziis.

Nazi Deutschland's complete military conquest of almost every European nation-states with a democratically-elected government doesn't prompt the U.S. to fight for its ideals and principles in Europe.

Nazi Deutschland's non-aggression accords with Fascist dictatorships in España and Italia, along with a similar deal with the C.C.C.P.'s dictator Stalin doesn't prompt the U.S. to fight for its democratic ideals and principles in Europe.

In more recent years, the U.S. ideals and principles do not stop it from encouraging, recognizing, arming, and collaborating with perpetrators of bloody coup d'états and vicious military dictatorships across the southern Americas.

The U.S. does not organize and lead a coalition to bring about regime change in Burma or in northern Africa.

The U.S. invades Afghanistan and Iraq while declaring its high ideals and principles, but tires of the adventures and finally withdraws.

Despite losing every war it enters after 1945, the U.S. has yet to be humbled and chastened by invading and occupational forces from abroad.

The U.S. quietly and almost invisibly pays reparations to Viet Nam after ten years of war, but there is no U.S. experience approaching the renewal of hereditary monarchical dictatorship in France after Napoleon's defeat.

Nor do the U.K. monarchs ever regain their dominion over the U.S.A.

The very severe Versailles Treaty against post-Kaiser Deutschland has no equivalent in U.S. historic experience.

Korean, Chinese, Vietnamese, and Afghan military bases do not control sectors of the U.S.A. or provide support for pacified and allied U.S. troops. Without such humbling and chastening experiences, the U.S. continues to suffer from the 500 year European national-colonial era master race empire delusions of superiority and an almost divine right to world dominion.

Even people dominated by the U.S. are subjected to this contagion.

Downtrodden African-Americans, self-effacing Canadians, and northbound refugees and migrants from various parts of the world are devotees of the concept of the desirability of U.S. world rule.

They perceive the U.S. as a wonderland that embodies high ideals and principles and provides the only ultimate goal of everyone everywhere - material wealth.

Thus one of the most powerful and false myths and scams of modern history is preserved and perpetuated over the world.

It never makes the news. The U.S filters world news and presents it from a U.S.-only perspective for a very long time.

...

Aljazeera news reports a scandal involving the mafia in Tuscony (Italia) making money by illegally dumping toxic waste in land fill, under highways, and in productive agricultural land. Olives and grapes anyone?

...

The U.S. P.B.S. Newshour reports that 60% of U.S.ers do not have university degrees.

When Mariko arrives in Canada to study, C.B.C. News says

only 10% of Canadians have a university education.

Does this at least partially explain why the U.S. elects a madman and why a Crazy Canada Party follows in his footsteps?

...

Every day I see people driving polluting motor vehicles and carrying babies on their backs and fronts as if there were no tomorrow.

Perhaps some of them are aware of news stories about the "unusual" weather, climate change, and how the human life support system is in danger of collapse.

But life goes on. Every day they fill up the gasoline tank at the service station. Every day millions of more babies are born like products on a robotic mass production line.

It must be reassuring to go about daily life routines and to follow conventions unconsciously while automatically believing that tomorrow is on the way and it has a promising future for all who obediently follow the standard issue existence.

This is not optimism. It is role playing.

It manifests an almost* universal religionism. Follow the "good" path in life and you will be rewarded in the afterlife.

(*I write "almost" because I'm not a believer or follower. Nor are others.)

The path of suicidal behaviour goes on and on. It will ensure that there is in fact no tomorrow for human life on earth.

But it doesn't have to be this way.

It just takes a little bit of thoughtful listening and the revival of the human survival instinct that stops self-destructive routines and automatic biological repetition of the way we have "always" done things.

In truth, we have not always done things the way we're now doing them. The polluting motor vehicle is only about a hundred years old. Polluting factories aren't much older.

Human survival and human progress over long term global history is not based on massive self-destructive behaviour.

If we don't stop polluting now, babies will have very short lives.

...

Like the distortions of semantics and "Newspeak" in the book <u>1984</u>, the word "freedom" is now used by groups of people with neo-dictatorial tendencies.

They use "freedom" as a synonym for undermining human rights for most of the world's population so that a minority can continue to rule and enjoy its unwarranted and undeserved special privileges.

...

News from Chile says the Mapuche First Nation is upset by the government's lack of action on their 500 year land claims.

Maps show that my first adventures in the southern Americas are within Mapuche territory. It stretches across a wide area including everything from Bariloche to Bahia Blanca.

Some Mapuche are resorting to violence to regain their territory and the Chilean government is sending in the military to back up military police in response.

Apparently some farmers are losing the land they're working to the Mapuche. Does that include the 100 hectares of land where Ekart was farming, near Pinto?

He's in his eighth year of farming there when we met. That's about 38 years before current time of writing.

He and his European immigrant contemporaries believe that the land they live on is a gift of Chile.

It's like the "free land" or $10 per lot land that Europeans occupied at the invitation of the Canadian government and at the expense of the First Nations of Canada?

So Ekart is learning, like the people he's dusting with his Suzuki vehicle when I visit him, the true identity of the "patrones"? He "doesn't mind" either?

Stolen land doesn't stay stolen forever?

...

News of "vaccination passports" comes out of the newsrooms void that ignores at least the previous 50 years or so of vaccination history.

Nobody in the health departments, politicians' offices, and news businesses seems to remember the yellow cover international vaccination record booklets that people carry when they travel around the world.

That's kind of an important fact to leave out in news coverage of current COVID-19 events.

...

The missing news story about cellular phones and other personal computing devices is the most obvious one that nobody seems to know, including users of these devices.

These technologies are merely PADD, personal advertising delivery devices.

PADD are communications devices used overwhelmingly by advertisers, governments, and video game companies to nab ordinary users.

I include "social media" in the advertisers category.

As one baron of a major "social" media multinational corporation says when he's summoned before a U.S. government panel, his services are paid for by advertisers, not users.

In this respect "social" media is like newspapers, magazines, radio, and television, although most television is pay TV now. "Convenience" and "emergency" are sales pitches that don't reflect reality and account for very little PADD use.

...

A news story about an incident in a Philadelphia (U.S.A.) subway train takes the cyber sublimation to a new low.

First reports say that one passenger sexually assaults another without bringing the other passengers to consciousness.

Instead of trying to help the victim, half conscious celled passengers take videos of the assault and post it on the internet.

A later report says that the people posting the assault were reporting it to the police.

Apparently nobody shouts, "Stop!" or pushes the emergency signal to bring help.

Whatever the details, the assailant is arrested after the assault and the assault does take place without arousing most passengers from cyberia or causing them to help.

Isolation and/or indifference replace humanity in cyberspace?

Thus pollution kills 14 million people per year and COVID kills more than four million people in less than two years?

The U.S. sick society way of life is a world pandemic spread wirelessly.

...

U.S. P.B.S. Newshour reports that people in their 20s and 30s are now perhaps following my lead in rejecting standard issue existence, at least to some extent.

They quit bad jobs with bad employers and won't return to them, ever.

This is creating a "market" in which there is a shortage of employees, forcing employers to offer more than in the recent past.

At least it's a step in the same direction as I go. Many steps remain to be taken. It's like adventure.

...

News reports that the last public pay phone is removed from New York City due to what I call the celled society. This is a shame, a marketing victory, and represents some danger.

The cell phone companies and their allies have succeeded in pulling off the most successful mass sales campaign that I ever see.

The companies persuade massive numbers of people in the U.S. to abandon both home and street phones.

This means that the survivors in at least one popular U.S. environmental disaster film could no longer call rescuers using the public library pay phones. (Day After Tomorrow)

It also means that if anything resembling the Seattle earthquake occurs in New York City, nobody will be able to phone anyone. Cell phones all fail in Seattle during the quake.

If there is a repeat of the financial centre attack, New Yorkers will also be isolated.

...

According to the U.S. P.B.S. Newshour, a "mega-drought" in the southwestern U.S. is reducing the reservoirs providing 75% of the water used in U.S. agriculture.

This is the water supply supporting 60% of the U.S. food supply. (About 50% of the people in the U.S. are obese.)

So the headquarters of the last modern-day empire will soon fall for an unexpected reason, mass starvation?

...

Seven million people in the world die of air pollution every year, according to PBS Newshour. This equals the worldwide three year death toll of COVID-19.

...

News of Betty Windsor's death in the U.K. brings out all the fanatics who adore monarchical dictatorship, including journalists who suddenly forget to report the full story.

Only by chance do I see a story revealing the big tax loss resulting from Betty's death.

Normally, U.K. law requires that the heirs of a deceased person pay a 40% inheritance tax, even under conservative governments. But Betty's heirs pay 0%.

News reports which dare to go beyond this scandal talk of Betty's half billion dollar fortune and say that her estate is worth billions. So her heirs get a tax-free windfall.

At least some news reports, including CBC, do report some of the untidy details, if only in passing.

The "legacy" becomes the biggest non-financial fraud perpetrated against news viewers.

Somehow news writers forget to mention that if someone with a job that actually involves doing almost nothing is credited with accomplishments that s/he never accomplishes or contributes anything to achieving, s/he must also be held responsible for all the ill deeds that s/he does not do or take part in doing.

Meanwhile, there's passing mention of the fact that former U.K.-occupied colonies in Africa don't feel any nostalgia for the ceremonial head of the U.K. occupiers or their enslavement, crimes of genocide, physical abuse, and psychological abuse of Africans.

At the same time, Bharat still wants its jewel back, the one in Betty's crown. U.K. occupiers are jewel thieves.

...

There's no objective or critical information included in the relentless and often subliminal monarchy advertising campaign. The product has no con-tent label. Everyone talks about "The Queen", even U.S. news anchors.

The monarch of Nippon is not called "The Emperor" outside of Nippon. Scandinavian monarchs are also not called "The" king or queen outside their realms.

At the same time, those of us not sharing zealous emotions for monarchy still find ourselves added to the list of loyal subjects of a monarchical head of state in Canada.

Those of us in elected office and public employment are obliged to swear an oath of allegiance to monarchy, even if we are not monarchists.

It seems strange that there is **no** oath of office to Canada, democracy, ethical behaviour, voters, fair-mindedness, conserving Canada's beautiful natural settings, etc.

I respect the right of Canada's non-monarchist elected representatives to choose to swear an oath to all of the above instead of to monarchy or monarchy alone. I am sure that no reasonable monarchist would oppose the reciting of a nobler, challenging, and more demanding oath.

...

The marathon news coverage of the late monarch's funeral not only cost a fortune to taxpayers funding CBC and customers purchasing from CTV advertisers, it smacks of devout monarchist propaganda.

When an entire national news broadcast is devoted to only one story, we are all deprived of information and less well-informed about the important events at home and abroad. In the past, broadcasters simply preempted regular programmes to present a special broadcast on a story of particular significance.

...

According to an NHK World news report, there are now 90,526 centenarians living in Nippon today, including non-local residents. More than 80% of them are women.

In 1970 there were only 130 people more than 100 years old in Nippon.

Nippon is apparently exceptional in terms of its very elderly numbers. I attribute it to the low stress kindness and courtesy that are practised every day here.

Yet women's lives tend to be much more stressful than men due to sexism and relentless ongoing opposition to all steps toward sexual equality. Women are tougher than men?

Unfortunately, as elsewhere, I see that the oldest person alive here, who is 113, appears to be in a vegetative state, according to images depicting her in the news report.

Her mouth is agape. Her eyes are staring at nothing. Her caregivers are speaking very loudly, directly into her ears. Her responses are monosyllabic.

This is not life. This is existence far worse than the standard issue existence Sisyphus.

Such people who are truly no longer alive should not be obliged to exist as virtually zombies by others responsible for their "care".

It is cruel to prolong such existence.

...

Long ago, news reports that people in Europe have compressed or four day work weeks and two-month annual vacations.

At least 44 years ago my parents have flexible hours, meaning they can choose when to start and end each day so long as they are present during "core" work hours.

They also have a non-statutory long weekend every month, which they can use or save (bank) for later or add it to their annual vacation time or regular statutory holidays.

They receive full pay for all their days on and off the job.

So why is CBC-TV News now talking about the four day work week as if it were some experimental novelty now arising, out of COVID-19, for the first time?

Veteran journalists at Carleton University teach me that every news story begins "in the morgue", i.e. the records of previously reported news stories. The morgue is dead?

What has come out of the world pandemic is a system where people work at home instead of at office buildings. It's a long overdue liberation of people from offices.

So now the empty office space can be used to house homeless people and surplus office buildings can be demolished and replaced with public parks.

Under such an urban planning scheme, previously homeless people would be living in former office buildings surrounded by parkland.

Services and entertainment would all be within easy walking distance.

They would be much better off than people housing themselves in dead, motion picture studio back lot suburbs which are dormitories in a community-less desert, where they are totally dependent on polluting vehicles for services.

...

Aljazeera's English-language news network, at least, is

unique among anglophone broadcasters in its frequent mention and detailed coverage of elections everywhere.

The standard "first" world anglophone news broadcasters tend to completely ignore most of the elections in the world if they aren't declared important by a "first" world honcho.

The way that at least the U.S. CBS Evening News covers even Canadian elections is typical.

In the years that I watch that newscast regularly, it does mention that there'll be an election in Canada before it occurs.

When Pierre Trudeau becomes prime minister for the first time, the U.S. news broadcast has two stories.

The first is to compare Pierre's campaign excitement with that of JFK's brother Robert. The second is brief passing mention of the final results.

In recent years, U.S. news has become more aware of the existence of Canada and is now mentioning some events in Canada and the prime minister's name fairly often.

En français and en Español, Canada is also getting coverage in España's 24 hour noticias and TV5 Monde's "journaux".

In contrast to its "first" world news service counterparts, Aljazeera reports elections before they're held, as well as election campaigns and issues as they unfold, and the details of voting and results on election days.

Aljazeera is taking the "first" world news self-isolation out of news reporting.

...

Today's news reports that someone wins a Nobel prize for doing research to find essential differences between humans and the rest of nature.

Is this to justify zoos, hunting, carnivores and vegetarians, sod-busting, pollution, and using non-human animals for research?

In nasty Deutschland, "medical professionals" define some people to be different from "humans" in such a way as to attempt to justify diabolic experiments, torture, other abuse, and mass murder.

Europe's national-colonial era defines all non-Europeans as non-human to justify slavery, genocide, etc. How nasty!

It's far better to look for similarities and commonalities than to seek to divide us all by looking for differences which can justify discrimination, maltreatment, and other negative bad behaviour.

Uniting all that lives should be a norm in the realm of science and the mantra of everyone in the field.

...

Aljazeera news reveals how insincere the N.A.T.O.-centric European Union is about respecting its engagements in the Paris Climate Accord and combating the environmental crisis.

It's clear that destroying the competition of capitalist Russia and capitalist Chuang Hwa is much more important to N.A.T.O.-E.U. than saving the planet's human life-support system.

This is a typical nation-state system attack on humanity, based on deliberately providing and unleashing polluting military weapons and equipment on the environment in Ukraine to win the N.A.T.O. vs. Russian Federation war there.

The war has the positive effect of ending E.U. and other nation-states' access to the world's biggest supply of oil and gas fossil fuels, which is in the R.F.

But the E.U. and others turn this into a new assault on the environment by seeking alternate sources of fossil fuel supplies instead of accelerating development of alternate energy sources.

Both the war and undiminished fossil fuel addiction have vast repercussions, particularly in Senegal, land of the biggest solar power plant in the world.

E.U. nation-states finance the plant, claiming that they do so to compensate Senegal for not exploiting, using, and selling its large reserves of gas.

But the war in Ukraine and the E.U. fossil fuel addiction turn the tide in the other direction, to tsunami heights.

The E.U. now tells Senegal to forget about solar and let E.U. members built gas plants for the sole purpose of fuelling Europe.

Senegal should clearly understand that this is what the lands liberating themselves from the European national-colonial era call neo-colonialism.

The main users and beneficiaries of the gas plants in Senegal are the E.U., not Senegal.

Senegal and other formerly occupied territories will also feel the worst effects of climate change coming from the increased pollution unleashed by the "new sources" of fossil fuels for the "first" world.

...

A news interview with a UN representative indicates how much the elite underestimates the intelligence of the non-elite majority.

According to the U.N. rep, in a single year the Taliban regime in Afghanistan undid all the "progress" of the 20-year war and other interventions of the U.S.-led N.A.T.O. forces.

Clearly any group that can counter so much "progress" in so little time is an insurmountable force. Or the "progress" is very feeble and not rooted where it's planted.

Blaming Taliban for N.A.T.O.'s failure is such a feeble excuse.

It reminds me of European colonial-national era apologists and promoters claiming that they try to "civilize" the "uncivilized" world, but the uncivilized fails to follow.

So lands that are invaded and occupied and people who are subjected to acculturation should be eternally grateful and obedient mimics and parrots of their master's voice?

**Winnipeg**: Local news reports that someone is stabbed to death at the main branch of Winnipeg's public library.

Now the insecurity promoters are reminding locals that they had an airport-like security portal at the library but many people objected so it was removed.

After a month of "discussions", the main branch reopens with the airport-like "security" back, costing about $40,000 a month. Paying any price? City police stand guard too!

News shows the new system in action, with at least one elderly male pushing his walker through the "security" portal.

They're afraid he'll stand upright and take a swing at someone with the walker?!

If one freak stabbing in about 150 years causes this type of extreme reaction, I wonder what two violent events would bring on, strip searches and water-boarding of all library members?

What the world needs now is a Mahatma Gandhi and Martin Luther King, Jr. campaign of peaceful, non-violent civil disobedience to restore human rights and to end the creeping jailkeeper society.

The longer that humanity tolerates and permits "security" laws and measures that are not democratically ratified by referendums requiring 95% approval, the more difficult it becomes to prevent democracy from disappearing altogether.

What end does "security" serve if the final result is a totalitarian dictatorship?

...

News says that at least one of the world's biggest petroleum companies accurately predicts the pending environmental disaster about 50 years ago.

Then, "big oil" pays for research studies which describe exactly what happens ever since.

But the petroleum companies hide their own data and lie about it. They announce that the results of the scientific studies they fund have "inconclusive" results.

Like the nicotine and probably alcohol and caffeine companies, the petroleum oligarchs put money ahead of the survival of the human species.

...

Canada's health departments are poised to oblige alcohol

companies to join the nicotine ones as toxic substances by putting warning labels on alcohol bottles.

The warning labels will tell the world what the alcohol business wants to keep secret. Alcohol causes cancer, heart disease, strokes, etc.

It's not news, its suppressed news, buried by alcohol business advertising campaigns based on alcohol company financed "research" that dishonestly claims their product is good for the health.

Canada's public health authorities finally admit that the best drinking habit is to drink no alcohol. As well as helping to prevent illness and death it has other benefits.

Drinking no alcohol leads to a good night's sleep and better health.

What will happen to the pushy and pushers who religiously insist that a glass of wine or a beer with friends is very healthy?

They'll deny the health warnings, just like pathetic nicotine addicts, ignorant climate change deniers, and reckless anti-vaccine advocates?

...

Merchants are demonstrating why they rank lowest in Nippon's social order, after the samurai, farmer, and artisan.

Several small business people and "experts" talking in news reports say that they expect the current rapid pace of inflation to slow down, but that most prices will not drop to previous levels.

They say it's the "nature of commerce". So the resulting increase in poverty and hunger are collateral damage. If there is a legitimate reason for government regulation, this is it.

Merchants should be forced to reduce prices to pre-hyper-inflation levels when current inflation ends, in order to reduce poverty and hunger.

...

News fails to answer the question: When is a balloon not a weather balloon? When it's a "spy" balloon from Chuang Hwa.

The U.S. suddenly notices that there's some sort of unidentified floating object hovering over its nation-state territory.

The previously invisible object is the size of a dirigible and it's towing two objects "as big as two school buses". Sure, who could miss it? Not the U.S. It's shot down.

Then the U.S. military says three similar objects fly over its territory when Punchline is in office, but nobody notices them until now!? The military admits its myopia?

Of course the military says it doesn't really know what the unidentified floating object is and won't know until the débris from shooting it down is collected.

Yet they're absolutely sure it's a "spy balloon". They're sure they don't know?

Chuang Hwa says its a civilian weather balloon. They are a common tool used by meteorological researchers around the world.

Within a few days, three other mystery objects are shot down by the U.S. military. Two are in the Arctic, one over Alaska (U.S.) and one is over Yukon (Canada). One is over the great lakes marking the Canada-U.S. border in Ontario.

Again, the military knows they are all "spy balloons" from Chuang Hwa, but nobody will know until the military examines the shattered remains and declares it "spy".

It would be easier to examine the débris if the military simply lassoed it, put parachutes on it like a space capsule, and put a small pin in the balloons to bring the objects to Earth gently and intact.

But it's more fun to just shoot them down and watch them crash in the ocean, lakes, or ice? If it moves, shoot first and ask questions later?

Not to be outdone by the renewed Cold War rhetoric, Chuang Hwa says it can see ten U.S. balloons flying over its territory.

Bring on the clowns. Or they are the ones already "leading" the nation-states and losing the balloons from their slapstick acts?

Far beyond all this, suppose that some aliens from another planet are simply having a look around to see if there's any intelligent life on earth.

Shooting down the aliens' "balloons" would surely persuade the trial balloon launchers that there is no life of the sort their seeking on Earth.

Only warlike nation-states would shoot down all the curious objects appearing in the sky.

In the midst of all this manifestation of distrust, animosity, and shooting down the competition in a "capitalist" world, I write to some newsrooms and make a suggestion.

I say that reporters should do some research on the differences between weather balloons and spy balloons and interview some meteorologists for clarification.

Otherwise, news stories will continue to look like rewrites of news releases from the military, always featuring the words "Chinese spy balloon", as if it were absolute fact.

In my note to newsrooms I also predict that the military will put saving face ahead of improving interhuman relations by declaring that the balloons contain technology capable of spying.

Yes, weather balloons are set afloat to spy on the weather and to collect information for climate change research and for improving weather forecasting.

So a half truth can be used to promote more distrust, hostility, and war. This gives the military something to do, i.e. function as the killing machine it is meant to be.

Fortunately, in the end the U.S. admits that the "spy" balloons are, as Chuang Hwa says all along, non-governmental atmospheric research balloons.

But no apology comes from the U.S. Instead, various officials say the balloons are not extraterrestrials. Comedians have more material for jokes.

...

While leaders look skyward for rogue balloons, more people on the ground suffer actual attacks in Toronto, Winnipeg, and elsewhere.

The violence is arbitrary and random, in the streets in the middle of the day and in crowded public transit vehicles. There are stabbings and bear spray attacks on passengers.

Transit drivers are already the targets of violence and now hide behind hard plastic barriers where they can't be so easily attacked.

Passengers remain out in the open and no amount of police presence can protect anyone from an arbitrary, random attack.

"Security" cameras, as usual, are only useful for recording what's happening and providing evidence in court if the assailants remain alive instead of killing themselves or committing suicide by police.

The only protection from violence is prevention, as social workers and others say in news reports.

They say that people confined during the first years of COVID-19 suffer mental health problems that remain undetected and untreated until the sufferers lash out in violent attacks against almost anyone, anywhere.

The increasingly commonplace and murderous mass shootings in the U.S. are another example of the madness, but they predate COVID-19 by a long shot.

The most mysterious ones involve some elderly shooters in the U.S. who have Chinese names and target only other people of Chinese origin.

Nobody is using the words "serial killers" to describe these remarkably alike shootings.

...

We meet someone who reads both Russian and Ukrainian newspapers and who has both ethnicities. When I mention my theory about a Ukrainian civil war, explains more.

He says that Russians and Ukrainians are on both the Russian Federation and the Ukraine Republic sides of the conflict, so there is already a civil war.

The Russia-Ukraine conflict is essentially a civil war, not a war between two distinct nation-states. Thus we learn much from Dima.

With all the very narrow and simplistic reporting coming from linguistically and culturally isolated foreign correspondents and commentators far from the scene, who uncritically parrot and regurgitate the NATO perspective alone, Dima's words are refreshing and help us to expand, broaden, and improve our more objective point of view.

...

Local news reports that a school has to be shut down for a few days because an actual skunk gets into the building and sprays away.

When the school children return to class, the school adopts an animated skunk as its official mascot, prints T-shirts in its honour, and declares a celebration. That clears the air?

All of the above isn't at all strange. Cities have raccoons, weasels, squirrels, rabbits, and rats. So there must be skunks too.

In fact, one of my parents' neighbours tells me that dogs being walked get sprayed by a skunk in that part of town.

So skunks must be everywhere in the urban jungles of at least Canada. No wonder Canadian cities stink.

Cousin Kaeren later tells me that the terrible skunk odour that I notice in cities across the country is coming from a type of marijuana drug. Why would anyone want to inhale the stink of a skunk?! Yuck!

...

**Montréal**: We're at Pierre E. Trudeau Dorval International Airport very early in anticipation of the very long lineups that news reports show at all major airports in Canada.

At some airports, passengers arrive four hours before flight time and miss their flights due to insecurity lineups.

Canadian bureaucracy spokespeople say the "longer than normal" delays in going through the insecurity lines is due to COVID-19, the latest excuse for all incompetence.

The spokespeople also blame passengers, saying that they forget to remove liquids from bags. In fact, during the past several years, no airport insecurity asks us to show liquids.

No spokesperson mentions that London Heathrow Airport (U.K.) announced it no longer had concerns about liquids nearly ten years earlier and told me to bag my liquids.

Blaming others and pandemics is the first refuge of the incompetent and is not an indication of "responsible" government.

The spokespeople try to wiggle out of accepting responsibility by saying that many bureaucrats work at home during the pandemic and have yet to return to working at the airport.

How is the insecurity scanning done from home?

**Winnipeg**: I'm always surprised and disturbed to hear a news report from the vast and dominantly non-anglophone world that features an interview with an ostensibly ordinary local person in the street who just happens to speak English.

My first question is, "Why?

Why ask one of the tiny minority of locals who speak English? It seems to be linguistically lazy reporting and more than potentially inaccurate reporting.

Did this person learn English because s/he's a moneyed local, i.e. a "third" worlder "first" worlder who lives a privileged life in isolation from most locals, their experiences, and views?

Or does s/he work for a U.S. or U.K. diplomatic post? Is she an anglophone spy posing as a local to manipulate news reporters?

Is s/he an anglophone tourist who dresses local and who is simply an uninformed foreign observer like the foreign reporter?

S/he's actually someone from an anglophone country and only shares the same ethnic origin as the locals? She just looks local?

If the answer to any of these questions is "yes", then the news reporters should not be implying that the person being interviewed is a typical local.

News reporters need to know local languages or hire a competent local interpreter to make sure that authentic local opinions are aired, not the views of the elite, the acculturated, or the non-local imposters.

...

LCN, the private national Canadian French-language news network reports two contradictory public opinion surveys on the same subject in Québec.

The first result LCN reports is that about 40% of the people oppose increased immigration. The second result is that 70% think the best worker shortage solution is immigration.

...

Local news and cousin Kaeren tell me that households here have an annual giveaway day.

It's so popular that homeowners put out signs, and lock up things that they want to keep, to prevent passersby from taking away everything they see sitting around outdoors.

**Fukuoka**: Climate change forest fires engulfing most of southern Canada are the new typical summer weather phenomenon.

The wind is blowing smoke from the fires so far that it's filling the air in major Canadian cities and at least Boston and New York city in the U.S.

A CBC News report shows video of the scenes which remind me of New Delhi and Taipei when I'm there.

The smoggy consequences are unpleasant, very unhealthful, and ironic.

City dwellers breathing the polluted air are inhaling the equivalent of half a pack of nicotine smoke per day.

So health departments are warning people to stay home and to wear masks outdoors.

The irony is that, after pretending that COVID-19 is gone and throwing off masks and caution to the wind, the wind is now striking back.

Mariko and I always wear masks, protecting ourselves from all eventualities.

...

When the news shows that a handful of children are found alive in the woods after too many days without bottled water and processed food, the reporters make it sound miraculous.

Yes, it's miraculous that these "third" world children retain their natural human animal ability to sustain themselves in "hostile" nature?

"First world" children would have perished looking for junk food?

...

The most common phrase that I hear in newscasts for downplaying and denying climate change indicates that "mother nature" rules and we "can't do anything about it."

Even news reporters in main stream newscasts indicate that "mother nature" decides everything. So people don't have to decide to change behaviours to promote the survival of the human species?

It's like responding to the question, "How are you?" by saying, "I can't complain and if I did it wouldn't do any good." It's resignation and defeatism.

So give up and die from pollution? Sit idly by and watch the human species go extinct?

That is a solution to climate change. It's the final solution for human animals.

...

Interviews with "experts" are useful as time fillers in the constant news broadcasting cycle.

...

When I'm a child, the United Nations organizes a group that I'm only now finding out about via Aljazeera. I watch news since childhood, so nobody reports it then?

The group is called G77, short for Group of 77, as opposed to the elite minority rulers of the world, the G7.

The G77 starts with 34 nation-state members and grows to 134 today, plus Chuang Hwa. So the group is now called G77+Chuang Hwa.

About 80% of the world population inhabit the 134. Most planetary resources are within the borders of the 134.

The G77 are the original "third" world, i.e. in Cold War semantics, the "non-aligned" with either the U.S. or the now non-existent C.C.C.P.

The C.C.C.P., Chuang Hwa, and associate states are then called the "second" world. It is an abandoned term.

The 134 remain non-aligned by not taking sides in the Russo-Ukraine War, while condemning the Russian Federation for invading Ukraine and while refusing to aid Ukraine.

The 134 are resisting considerable pressure from the U.S. and associate states to support Ukraine.

...

What "first" world governments and news reports call "migrants" are living evidence of a revival of the natural human survival instinct of global movement that does not recognize nation-states' artificial barriers as absolutes.

The difference between past and present human migrations is that in the past they are the natural movement of people during changing seasons and in pursuit of other migrating animals, seasonal edible growing plants, warmer temperatures, etc.

The nation-states distort migration, changing it into a response to artificial stimuli and circumstances caused by the existence of nation-states.

Nation-states cause this distortion in natural human migration by promoting and entrenching inequality among humans, such as: opportunities for achieving fulfilling lives; access to Earth's planetary resources and general wealth; enjoying nutrition and good health; and, a daily peaceful environment for all lives and activities.

The only human equality provided by nation-states is through deliberately not taking effective action to protect and preserve the planetary human life support system.

The resulting equality is human species extinction.

During the calendar year of this writing, more than 400,000 ''migrants'' cross the jungle in Panama en route to Mexico with their real ultimate destination being the U.S.

There are three months left in the year when this statistic is reported by Aljazeera and the USPBS Newshour.

...

Most of the anglophone news, particularly Aljazeera and CBC's daily national newscast become obsessed with the latest Yisra′el-Palestine nation-state war.

I depend of SRC's Téléjournal, along with TVA, 24 Horas, TV5 Monde, NHK World, and PBS Newshour for news everywhere outside of Yisra′el-Palestine.

...

The news I get from the sources which do cover the rest of the news mention an environmental conference in Djakarta. All the other daily news broadcasts don't mention it, while I watch.

...

A farmer in Ontario, appearing on CTV National News, complains about imposing a tax on pollution, with compensation from government.

He says there is "no alternative" to fossil fuels.

So he knows nothing about traditional farming, which uses the energy from water mills and windmills for power. Is he really a farmer?

...

The news I get in Canada and comments I receive from my Cordoba friends Arturo and Diego tell me that Argentina elects a president unfit for office, following past elections in the U.S., Brasil, and some E.U. nation-states.

After struggling so hard to develop democratic forms of government, following years of dictatorships, it's sad to see voters end up with reactionary demagogue regimes, even if its only, I hope, until following elections, as in the U.S. and Brasil.

**Ottawa**: Canada's parliament votes against a bill giving MPs the opportunity to swear an oath to Canada and its populace instead of the U.K.'s monarchy.

This bill is the second of its type in the past two years. This time the 40 member cabinet voted against the bill and 44 non-cabinet members voted against it. So 157 MPs voluntarily voted con and 113 voted in favour.

This is the closest vote in history, so far. News ignores that fact.

Canadian news largely ignores the vote itself. SCR mentions it in French.

In news paying attention to the bill and vote, it is portrayed as an "anti-monarchy" and anti-current U.K. monarch bill.

How frightful! There is no mention of the longstanding indif-ference of most Canadians toward monarchy.

There is also no mention of a public opinion survey, less than one year before the bill and vote, showing that 64% of Canadians say they would vote to abolish monarchy if given the chance to vote in a referendum on monarchy.

But Canadians don't even have the normal, democratic right to choose their head of state, the U.K. monarch, in an election.

In related unreported background to the bill news, for the past 30 years, according to the Canadian citizenship department of the federal government, there have been eight bills proposed to include Canada and democracy in the oath of citizenship and one Charter court challenge to the monarchy oath.

None of the bills become law and when the court case wins in Ontario the author of the case is denied permission to take the case to Canada's supreme court.

So MPs and new citizens must still swear allegiance exclusively to U.K. monarchy, with no mention of democracy, Canada, or the voters.

So, to quote a former Canadian cabinet minster and Canadian ambassador to France, "Canada is not a real country". Canada is also a monarchical colony run by councils responsible only to monarchy, not a real democracy responsible to the voters.

This should be a big story. But it is ignored in Canadian news.

## Where's news

**NASA**: I notice part of a news story about NASA finally building a space platform.

If so, the recent news, at time of writing, about restricting residency rights in the U.K., Nigeria, and India will look incredibly ludicrous and incomprehensible to children learning history 17 years from date of writing, in the 21st century of the European calendar.

The "giant leap" into space could make unemployment rates go to 100 per cent. The term unemployment would be archaic.

Computers would do the idiotic things we call jobs.

Human beings would get to know new worlds and each other better.

Nation-states would be like Canadian provincial governments.

This is already close to the truth in the two major empires' associate states, eg. the European Parliament.

Embassies and consulates then become strictly trade and tourist agencies.

The concept of restricting the free travel of Terrians would be alien.

Cities would be huge theme park entertainment centres.

The necessity of crowding into urban centres for convenience, sustenance, and opportunity would be obsolete.

But meanwhile, with every African deported from Nigeria and every Bengali expelled from India, we can perhaps hear the same cries of disbelief as are heard by i) the U.K.

soldiers who force Canadians in Acadia to leave their homes; and, by ii) the Canadian police who force Canadians of Japanese origin to leave their homes and live in "nice" concentration camps.

We are at one of those fascinating junctures in history, where all is uncertain. Planning is ludicrous.

Being too closely connected to a particular establishment could be like being a dinosaur on cataclysm eve.

We can boldly go in search of the future. We can try new technologies. We can try less rigid forms of social organization, eradicate barriers between Terrians.

Or, we can merely cling to the long-gone past and security illusions of the present.

We can again open the Inquisition courts.

We can again send crusaders to Arabia and find a new Cortez to exterminate the Incans' descendants.

We can again call the non-Europeans "primitive", "savages", "heathens", "pagans", "backward peoples", "underdeveloped", etc.

The result - we thus initiate a new dark age, where innovators are incinerated for "witchcraft".

...

There's a space visitor in Brasil's capital city.

A U.S. space shuttle pilot arrives in Brasilia this week to invite Brasil to send a Brasilero into space. The programme is finally off the ground.

The U.S. executive's "star wars*" scenario is like the conquistadors, or the slaughter of Newfoundland's Beothuk native peoples?

(* movies that remind me of the ancient comic strip "Terry & The Pirates", if it were set in outer space).

Exploration and commerce are accompanied by conquest.

I suppose it's realistic considering that the two empires at time of writing, U.S. and U.S.S.R.

are primarily interested in raw power.

The ideals of Thomas Jefferson and Lenin are window dressing for "manifest destiny" and the revival of the Russian control over Afghanistan, etc. at time of writing.

...The two empires act in ways which reflect the fact that they are the only nation-states without names. U.S.A. and U.S.S.R. are essentially meaningless titles.

Both imply expansionism - any country in the Americas could be a State United with the rest. The Union of Soviet Socialist Republics could encompass the entire planet.

A state and a soviet are mere names for units of government organization.

...Despite Yuri Gargarin and the Soyuz spacecraft, the U.S. makes great strides in space technology, due to the Apollo programme, and gains much economic power with the war-generated decline of Europe.

At time of writing, the U.S.S.R. is number eight in financial debt. It stands beside Poland, which has virtually defaulted on a loan it owes to Brasil, which is number two in debt after Mexico.

...In the raw, the Central American battles thus have nothing to do with political philosophy.

The Soviets are trying to embarrass the U.S. There is no pro-capitalist versus pro-communist battle going on.

The Soviets are taking advantage of the fact that no one likes being a mouse sleeping with an elephant, as Pierre Trudeau put it, decades ago.

The U.S. does the same in Poland and Afghanistan. These small places, like Central America, don't love their imperial neighbours.

...The Soviets use thugs, no doubt, much like the Somosists, i.e. gangster-style mercenaries being used by the U.S.

Somosa is the former Nicaraguan president who tear-gasses children and mothers taking part in a non-violent, sit-down protest some years ago.

Then he gains safe haven in the U.S. state of Florida, sailing through U.S. immigration unmolested.

...The empires are short-term thinkers.

Were it not for nuclear weapons, both Washington and Moscow might already have been sacked.

Perhaps the U.S. is also protected by its benevolence, i.e. permitting democratic elections in Canada, Europe, etc.

...

...Yoga, the "quaint, novel, offbeat, impractical hobby of the counter-culture", is perhaps, in reality a useful tool to counteract space sickness.

The Indians who the Soviet Empire sends into space for propaganda purposes have something valuable to teach us all.

...

News reports that a four million year-old human skeleton is found in Africa this week. We're still discovering life on earth.

...

There's so little money put into the Canadian space programme that one CBC-TV news reader says that the hitch-hiker he picks up near Kennedy Space Centre in Florida (U.S.A.), is a Canadian astronaut.

In a sense, the astronaut is just making space travel more economical and strengthening contact between the general populace and the still elite space travellers.

The USNASA shows that the futures belong to those who can do more with less. People in the "third" world are masterful in this effort.

Eighty per cent of humanity maintains itself for a fraction of the cost-per-person of the "first" world minority.

...

Another N.A.S.A. news story says that, at time of writing, the U.S. space programme is trying to revive itself by supporting a private company using old technology.

That means leftover, 40-year-old Apollo moon rocket parts.

A representative for the company says, during a television newscast, that it's all about using not the newest technology but the "right" technology instead.

He says the "right" technology is very old.

Yes. It's called Soyuz, a spacecraft invented by the C.C.C.P. and which, for a few years, becomes the only way U.S. astronauts and others can get to their space station work place.

...

Nippon's news shows a better way to deal with high energy demands that worsen climate change. The better way is a result of a disaster.

Since the Fukushima quake and tsunami strike, a major nuclear plant there is a shutdown along with all other nuclear power plants in Nippon.

The predictable energy shortage has yet to have any noticeable effects on electricity supplies.

But, at time of writing, a hotter summer is predicted along with power shortages of up to 15% in the biggest cities.

In response the most apparent reaction shown in the news is not a cry for more power plants, it's a successful attempt to reduce the use of electricity.

Office hours start earlier so that employees can begin working during the cooler morning hours, when less air conditioning is required.

Flexible working hours, enabling employees to start earlier and taking stress off the employee transportation system begins about 40 years earlier in Toronto and Vaincouver.

Supermarkets begin opening as early as the ones in Córdoba during the siesta years. Is there hope Nippon will switch to a siesta system?

A shirt manufacturer is producing a new type of dress shirt with fabric which allows air to flow through it and to capture moisture and body odour.

Handheld fan companies are increasing production to compensate for less air conditioning.

More offices are raising the minimum temperature for air conditioning and more employees are wearing the colourful aloha shirts which are now acceptable office wear.

Solar panels on private homes not only cut power needs, the electric companies pay for the electricity put into their grids.

The companies will pay home solar system owners top yen for ten years and a discounted

...

The planned U.S. Orion mission to Mars is in the news. It looks like an Apollo programme rerun from many years earlier, using the knowledge of the C.C.C.P.'s Soyuz.

...

Excited U.S. N.A.S.A. scientists and news reporters show video images of the latest U.S. Mars lander's parachute blowing overhead as the probe approaches the planetary surface.

Then, for some reason there's puzzling over whether the tiny helicopter-drone aboard will be able to take off and fly over the surface.

The question is: Does Mars have sufficient air to enable the flying probe to fly? I find it strange that this question isn't considered before using a parachute.

Parachutes need air too.

While the flying object sent with the Mars probe is readied for possible takeoff, news reports that the wheels on the land-roving part of the probe only move 0.02 km/hr.

I hope the helicopter-drone can move more quickly. Getting this project off and along the ground is so difficult compared with parachuting it to the surface of Mars.

...

There are news stories about using upgraded models of the Apollo programme spacecraft to return to the moon. Other stories say people will be going to Mars in a few years.

This is all old news. It could have happened less than 50 years ago. But the world stopped and started spinning backwards.

Racism and sexism re-emerged.

So did nationalism, cancelling out the planetary consciousness of photos of earth from space, including Earthrise seen from the lunar surface.

Thus, instead of facing a united humanity, COVID-19 can pick off the inhabitants of nation-states who are scrambling to save only the people inside the boundaries instead of all humanity.

Pitting nationalism against a world pandemic is the formula for species extinction.

The only surviving evidence and legacy of the space age are the computers of today, particularly the "Star Trek" "communicators" called "cell phones".

We now have the toys of the space age without the space age they are supposed to serve.

This perspective enables me to see how antique and yet strangely contemporary my writing might appear to readers who graduated from senior secondary school 50 years after me.

Looking back 50 years before my graduation I see the final year of the 1914-18 war, with its world pandemic.

The year that I graduate I have little awareness of that war. I don't know there was a pandemic until nearly 20 years after I graduate.

I don't recall having long conversations with people born in 1850, just my two grandparents who are born in 1880. One of them dies four or five years before my graduation.

But they don't talk about the war or pandemic of a time when they are in their late 30s, early 40s.

I wonder if many people of my generation are talking to 18 to 20 year olds about the space age. Probably not.

They're all playing with their grandchildren and playing the the roles of grandparents, not the teachers of the young.

They leave that education to younger school teachers who also know the space age only as history, not part of their lives.

Today, the space age is confined to, at most, a few pages in the school text books used in history classes.

The space age is a brief period of history which might merit one or two questions in the final exams, just like the 1914-18 war is in my final history tests.

The pandemic marking the end of that war doesn't even merit mention in the text books of my schooling. That gives COVID-19 the opportunity to spread unmolested.

As I watch today's private company rockets blowing up on the launch pads just as government ones do when I'm a child, I realize that I'm not only living through a re-run of a forgotten pandemic, I'm also seeing a re-run of the space age.

Those who don't know history, repeat it and apparently without realizing it.

...

Today's news includes a story about three scientists winning a Nobel Prize for their research into quantum entanglement. Their sharing is an entanglement?

The research includes quantum teleportation, which sounds like the tele-transportation used in the "Star Trek" productions. Apparently it only refers to messages not actual things.

Besides the teleportation, I find something else about the research particularly interesting.

One report says that observation changes what is observed in a broader sense than I already understand in the realm of observing people's behaviours. (source: Big Think)

The research says that measuring a quantum state "can fundamentally alter or determine what you measure". This goes well beyond behaviour.

I interpret this research finding as meaning that observation and action changes what is observed, even if the action is not intrusive or intended to change something.

The research also makes me wonder about a science fiction story combining quantum entanglement, scanning, and 3-D printing.

In "Star Trek" television shows and movies, the "Enterprise" space craft and its crew are sometimes scanned by aliens.

Could the aliens reproduce a duplicate of what they scan, if only to observe and measure the original, and in so doing change everything?

How could this influence and change the original and the duplicate? How could this alter the way they react to each other?

How does the duplication change both the original and duplicate?

### News for the masses: a religiously observed distorted mirror

The mass media foreign correspondent sent abroad seems more like an alien landing on an unexplored planet for a few moments, to collect rock samples before running out of the oxygen and water brought along for the surface walk.

The samples must be collected, packed, and stowed before the liftoff scheduled to make sure that the alien has enough life-support resources to get home safe, healthy, and alive.

Brizola's win in Rio de Janeiro State's gubernatorial election, while the military dictatorship withdraws, attracts a lot of foreign press interest.

I wonder if those reporters are mentioning the request of the military dictatorships' electoral office to hold back election results?

Maybe not.

Maybe the foreign journalists simply write it off as typical "third" world politics, instead of reporting such "banal" details.

After all, there are deadlines and limited space available for the story considerations. Maybe the editor will choose some other story instead, kill this one, or bury it.

Business as usual in the "third" world isn't particularly newsworthy in the north, except as a contrast to the "real" politics of the back home.

Everyone, reporter and audience, knows that and doesn't question such an "obvious given" when giving token coverage to the less important "outside" world, i.e. world outside the "first" world centre of everything.

But Brasil is the third largest country on the American continent, and the U.S. president is planning a visit here.

So maybe the major U.S. mass media, at least, is being polite, looking the other way instead of toward the electoral contest that the locals are supposed to be deciding today, as the military dictatorship withdraws after nearly 20 years in power and democracy is trying to return, six years before the Berlin Wall falls.

### How's news

### Blooper reel

TVA Nouvelles has an annual presentation of funny mistakes and out-takes from its regular daily news shows. It's very honest and amusing.

Other newsrooms need to follow TVA's good example.

Here is some of the content that I find for such a TVA-like self-exposé by the tellers of news:

A murder story becomes magical when the anglophone news reader says that a killer "turned himself into a police box". What a disguise to escape being arrested!

One of the oldest chicken jokes in the world comes to mind when one anglophone script reader says, in a monotonous tone, with no hint of a chuckle, someone was "crossing the street to go to the other side".

Or is this just an exercise in being long-winded?

The anglophone script readers seem to be going far beyond unintended humour.

They're apparently intent on changing not just the English language but also the entire world that it describes.

All the world's problems must have been solved. Not really, but the anglophone news readers say people are "solving issues", instead of problems.

How do you solve an issue?

Apparently something is "generating" concern. Does that mean "causing"? So why not just say so?

At the same time, every problem is now becoming a trouble, such as "computer troubles". This is taking simple engine trouble and trouble-shooting too far.

Try to figure out this phrase: something "caused troubles with the customers".

But if there are no more problems in the world, why is every type of public gathering now called a "rally"?

Even when the event is not a rally at all, but only a calm, restrained, docile meeting of people sitting sedately in the padded chairs of an auditorium, it is called a "rally".

Rallies I see in times past consist of people standing in large, sweaty crowds either cheering and applauding spontaneously and enthusiastically, or following the lead of some kind of cheer leader.

In the mouths of the anglophone script readers, grammar becomes more than incorrect. It becomes a matter of random usage.

In one story, the electors "voted tremendously against" someone or something. How do they do that?

In another story, "a bear seriously inflicted a wound". To my knowledge, a bear is not usually reflecting upon her/himself before, after, or while inflicting wounds.

Measurement becomes totally unclear. An object is described as "two centimeters in size". Objects now have only one dimension? But which one?

Political systems are completely altered with the turn of a word.

Apparently, it has been a month since the latest cabinet in Tokyo is "incorporated". During the next repetition of this news story, the cabinet is "inaugurated".

Why not use the simple description, "sworn in" or "takes office"?

Government offices are being transformed every time the script readers open their mouths.

After decades of deputy-prime ministers in Canada and elsewhere, the script readers unilaterally transform them all into "vice-prime ministers".

It's a corruption story?

The party in power, the group that news broadcasters in Canada simply and routinely call "the government", is being renamed "the ruling party".

It sounds autocratic and dictatorial. It doesn't sound like an elected body.

If the news is about the party in power in Nippon, then why not just say "the Jiminto-Komeito coalition government".

When only referring to the party with the most seats why not call it "the Jiminto government"?

At the same time, everyone working for the government is now called an official. It's a word I associate with football referees and other sports judges or adjudicators.

Instead of saying the police, a government spokesperson, a ministry source, the city clerk's office, etc., all these people are lumped together and given the shorthand title "officials".

Listeners are supposed to guess what kind of "officials"?

Anglophone script readers also seem to be having trouble distinguishing between government offices and corporate executive offices.

Sure, companies do seem to rule over or at least manipulate nation-state governments. But that's unofficial and behind the scenes, rarely overt and open.

Yet one anglophone script reader is calling someone a "company official" instead of a com-pany director, executive, offi-cer manager, spokesperson, etc.

Officials are official, usually government people in certain special jobs. Companies don't have officials.

People in less ostentatious positions are getting changes in their job titles too. The anglophone reader calls one person a "half-time janitor".

Or does this means someone who only works as a janitor during the half-time shows at professional football games?

Physical objects are getting renamed by the script readers. The camera shows a fence and the script reader says it's a "hedge". Glasses needed?

Human progress is getting erased too, by reviving discarded, inaccurate, archaic vocabulary.

Thoughtlessly turning back the clock to the bad old days of rampant, overt sexual discrimination, one anglophone script reader with a U.S. accent, calls police officers "policemen".

There are no more females in the police forces?

Always a marginal area of English usage, sports vocabulary is being sent into a remote exile. Forget about conventions in sportscast word usage.

The sports report is introduced as the sports "section". The

TV folds into a newspaper?

A few years after the most recent olympic games held in Nippon, the pronunciation of Nagano is suddenly changed to Naaa gano.

An anglophone sports report script reader goes through a lengthy, roundabout way of describing professional sports players becoming "free agents" instead of being completely at the mercy of team owners.

But the reader never says "free agent".

There are no more semi-finals, finals, championships, series, or competitions.

Every sporting event, except the U.S. baseball "world" series, now becomes a tournament. I thought that word was for golf.

In other entertainment news...

A music competition is described as "one of the most established", which means exactly what?

Another competition must then be "least established"?

I thought such events could be established or more established, but not most.

Or are we trying to say best known, oldest, most famous, most prestigious, etc.?

The education system is changing altogether. Students in grade eleven are transformed into "second year high school students".

So the readers agree with me that elementary school grades are a forgettable waste of time and can thus be ignored?.

One report says a student is "tripped up", not tripped, by classmates. I get tripped up by words, but never by people. Besides, when I trip, I fall down, not up.

Consumer product labels become incomprehensible.

The very clear words "expiry date" on processed, packaged foodstuff are now described as the "eat-by-date" by an anglophone script reader.

So, to generalize this blanket usage, people are now eating drinks, household chemicals, and medical supplies?

Now for the weather report –

During a story about a tornado, the script reader keeps repeating the word "vortex", but never says "funnel cloud" while supposedly describing in English the first-hand accounts of people who see the tornado funnel cloud.

The anglophone readers go on to say that thunder clouds "generated" the tornado. What's wrong with using the straightforward, quickly understood word "started"?

A "weather official" is then quoted. Does this mean a meteorologist or a forecaster? Is the weather an official entity?

It's hard to imagine a weather report rendered incomprehensible, but the anglophone script readers strike again in the farthest reaches of Nippon.

Apparently, a house in Hokkaido is using "sheets" to prevent rain from leaking through rooves there.

This image of linen is contradicted by a TV camera showing plastic tarp.

"Body warmers" are being delivered to homes without heat. Could this mean a special type of rescue team or large hand warmers?

Reporting from the courtroom –

Somebody is "charged with window-dressing" by the police. I wonder what section of the criminal code describes the crime of window-dressing.

People who decorate display windows in department stores are now criminals?

Employers hiring certain individuals based entirely on their ethnicity, skin pigmentation, or sex, etc., for the sole purpose of avoiding accusations of racism and sexism, are now getting charged with breaking the "window-dressing" law?

Instead of saying that a witness or defendant will be testifying in court and cross-examined by lawyers, s/he is now attending a "questioning session".

Without any court case pending or criminal charges, an anglophone script reader says "allegedly the government".

How about describing a formal allegation and attributing a critical remark before turning to inappropriate, defensive legalese in the news?

Shorthand gibberish is reaching new lows too. What does this mean? –

"Over a week has passed since the advent of the cell phone portability system."

It means a general communications problem to me, regardless of the cell phone.

Weren't cell phones already portable? Isn't advent a bit literary or churchy for a simple newscast?

Broadcast journalists are trained to say "more than", unless describing something that is literally, physically "over" something else.

What's wrong with saying something clear and accurate, such as:

"It's only a week now, since the cell phone companies started making their products more compatible and interchangeable…"

I know this is what the news is supposed to be reporting because Mariko translates a Japanese language version of the story.

In other news…

Something is "expected to start from next year". How about some economy of words? Why use both start and from together when a simple "start" is ample?

Military jargon slips into some news when reports say that a passenger train is "decommissioned". It's secretly an armed train that's transporting troops and weapons?

And finally:

On several occasions one anglophone script reader is ending the regular, daily, 40 minute news programme by calling the entire broadcast a "bulletin". There's no English-English dictionary in the television studio office?

When U.S. news host Walter

Cronkite briefly interrupts regular television broadcasting to announce that JFK is shot, Cronkite says it's a "bulletin".

It's true that news script readers aren't the authors of all the scripts they read, but a newscast, unlike a live and direct report, actually has a written script.

Unless a news story happens suddenly and the script is handed to the newsreader during the broadcast, the reader has time to read, rehearse, and correct a script before broadcast.

So the newsreader is normally the one responsible for making the blatant mistakes listed here.

...

The latest evidence of avoidable non-journalistic reading and failure to look at and edit news scripts beforehand, before actually reading the printed words on the air, makes the readers' English seem like a guessing game.

They seem to be saying, "Guess what word I'm describing in this phrase."

The script readers should be working on quiz shows instead of in news rooms.

One says, "an elevated area of concrete beside the road." The accompanying news camera image shows that the script reader is defining the word "curb".

Why not simply use the widely known word "curb" instead of interrupting the news with a word definition quiz?

News reports are supposed to tell stories using well-written words within an limited time frame.

If time were no object, the news would still be better if it were kept simple and direct, instead of convoluted, long-winded, and puzzling.

Life is too short to waste trying to guess out what words the news script readers are thinking. It's like being force to relive elementary and secondary school.

...

I see the daily, feature network evening news broadcast on one of the original three U.S. television networks.

The announcer says hot weather is causing food in a restaurant to go bad. The closed captioning service shows this as "go bald".

A few moments later there's a report about the dangers of "setting off" fireworks. The caption says the dangers of "setting awful fireworks".

Someone learning English as an additional language will be as puzzled as people who read captions because they have a hearing problem.

News broadcasting live and direct still lags far behind daily news shows in accuracy, clarity, and coherence, compared with well-edited programmes such as U.S. CBS News "60 Minutes".

...

I critique NHK anglophone news readers for their poor script writing, editing, and preparation, but now I find the U.S. PBS Newshour flawed too.

I hear "infuriorating" instead of infuriating; "He got less votes and less seats" instead of fewer; "it's becoming more and more clear" instead of clearer; "in two hours time from now"; and "go through much less doses".

It's not just NHK and PBS. Anglophone news is in trouble.

In other news I hear reporters saying "less people" instead of fewer or a smaller number of people.

A tremendous "amount" of people sounds like an archaeological find involving a mass burial mound full of body parts.

Weirder still are documentaries about people "wilding" the world. They mean, in English, restoring the natural environment and natural species behaviours.

Why not explain what you're talking about instead of trying to reduce it to making up silly shorthand and inventing words that don't exist?

...

Non-answers also plague news broadcasting.

During interviews and analysis panels, apparently reluctant, non-commital, obtuse, and/or uninformed interviewees and commentators are prone to say:

"It's problematique." or "It's systemic." That's the whole answer.

Hearing this answer for many years, I only see one news show host asking what the person means when he says "problematic".

It's a question that needs to be asked every time to glib respondents.

## So and so

A more recent variation in non-answers involves starting every answer to a question with "So."

It sounds as if the respondent is saying, "Hm. I'll say what I'm already planning to say, instead of answering your question."

Or: "I'm not going to answer your question. So here's what I want to talk about instead."

Or worse: "I'm not listening to your question. I'm just going to say the words I memorized before the interview starts."

## What's news

News is everything you didn't know a moment ago, even if everyone else already knows it.

...

When the rain stops the silence is puzzling.

Seeing the garden fill and drain like a bath tub has come to seem normal.

TV news reports showing planned and accidental mud slides, cars bathing, and houses turning into boats are annual routine.

The rainy season, the day and night pounding of waters on our roof, has gone for another year. The silence means I almost think I've gone deaf.

We can look more casually at the little stickers glued beside every tap in Fukuoka – "Don't waste water!" The reservoir is full again.

Reiko, one of my students who lives close to a canal-held river, tells me about having to remove her tatami flooring two years ago, when the stream overflows in the rain.

By coincidence, that's the same year as the southern Brasil flooding which changes my course.

It's surprising not to see the regular sunshine that I come to consider normal during my first months in this city.

Still, it is interesting to see the year's water supply all arriving in one big delivery.

...

While working on a section of my book <u>Mandarinas</u>, about a problem I have with a newspaper subscription in Ottawa, I'm inspired with some thoughts on newspapers themselves.

The newspaper's difference is subscriber participation.

Anyone anywhere can effortlessly switch on a television and turn to channels at will, and either leave the room or fall asleep in front of the screen.

Internet users can browse aimlessly across cyberspace, following "links" to infinity, and "like" anything.

But a newspaper reader, subscriber or not, is someone who deliberately seeks out and reads a specific newspaper printed on newsprint, doing so in a physical geographic place.

Unlike the internet, a newspaper isn't something that's flashed and dangled in front of a reader's eyes until s/he jumps for it like a baby or a cat, and gives it a glance before moving on to a shinier dangling object.

Headlines and/or the newspaper's writing quality or reputation lure in the reader and grab his/her reading attention for at least 12 consecutive minutes a day, according to some research.

That's an eternity for an internet user, a cybernaut, well beyond his/her attention span. If the newspaper reader is a subscriber, s/he expects to find a newspaper at his/her door every day. It's part of his/her daily routine, like a hit of caffeine.

S/he will at least peruse the headlines on the first few pages and read whatever seems most interesting.

S/he will probably turn to the weather and entertainment listings such as movies and sports games.

Everything is well organized in sections and there's a guide on one of the first pages showing what section and page to turn to if a reader wants to read something in particular.

Perhaps s/he'll check out some large and small ads between personal advice columns, comic strips, and horoscopes. The classified pages have a numbered table of contents.

You can find anything very easily. All you need are fingers, thumbs, and eyes. No phone, electricity, batteries, keyboard, or mouse are required.

When a person reads a newspaper, there is no software to purchase that needs frequent updates, upgrades or patches.

Newsprint and paper don't become obsolete or incompatible with fingers and eyes in six months. A newspaper is easily, fully, and safely 100% recyclable.

Poor children recycling newspapers won't be poisoned by toxic chemicals while trying to mine precious metals out of newspapers. There are none.

Newspapers don't need recharging and there is no buffering, "connection lost", or "crash" report. All you need to read a newspaper is daylight or a light bulb.

Newspapers have such "easy access" that they are addictive.

Readers pore over them at breakfast or supper, in train cars, in public parks, and at the workplace during caffeine breaks.

Two complete strangers sitting on different park benches read the same news. If they talk together, they have something in common to discuss.

Newspapers are incredible inventions that are multilingual, multicultural, and worldwide.

Everyone can read a newspaper for free at a public library or out of a garbage pail too. Nobody has to decide between reading a newspaper and having money for food and living.

Newspapers are the ultimate in cheap, full access technology.

The free press is the most democratic and reliable means of getting information about almost anything.

It is run by editors who demand accuracy in both content and presentation.

For the broadcasters of radio, television, and internet, a newspaper is basically a news delivery service. It delivers reporters' stories to readers.

The newspaper's circulation department and the concept of one is unheard of in radio and television news and in cyberspace sites and apps.

Radio, television, and internet are far more "mass" media than a daily newspaper. They lack the circulation department's interest in one mere subscriber.

From the days of free television available by using little more than a simple antenna or a metal coat hanger on top of a TV set to pick up good signals from a number of analog broadcasters, to the time of digital all-pay TV and pay internet servers, broadcasting has no circulation department.

If a viewer can't hear or see the news, it's due to atmospheric conditions, problems with the signal receiver, or the cable/satellite/internet "provider".

Another "condition beyond our control" governing access to broadcasting is poverty.

In the era of digital all-pay TV and pay internet, a person living in poverty cannot be a viewer without going into debt or living in a well funded homeless shelter.

Public libraries with internet may not always be hospitable toward poor homeless people and their sometimes "unpleasant appearance" and "unconventional" behaviours.

News broadcasts aren't discarded on park benches or dropped into garbage cans. Nor are cell phones and computers with access codes visible.

Everyone and no one is responsible for circulation. There is no circulation department.

At the same time, there are circulators, i.e. conveyors of others' messages, e.g. news, who somehow can claim they believe that they are not themselves circulating anything except electronic signals.

This is part of the defence used by "home pages" and "social media platforms" to avoid paying news organizations and journalists for their work.

This is also part of the defence used by "social media platforms" to avoid responsibility for content, within the uncoordinated and disunited demands of public opinion and resulting political pressure.

Taking this argument to its logical conclusion, a newspaper could argue that it provides only paper, ink, and delivery, or a digital facsimile of it on a website.

The words that are transported or transmitted to readers in this manner are not the newspaper's responsibility.

By the same logic, traditionally, radio and television stations are simply transmitting sounds and images in the air as far as the nearest horizons or into outer space, and now only through cables and encrypted satellite signals.

The words and pictures included in the sounds and images are not the radio and television stations' responsibility.

In reality, newspapers, along with radio and television broadcasters, are in fact legally responsible for everything they print and put on the air.

News provider owners, along with their editors, reporters, columnists, and bureaucracy, can be sued in court by readers and people mentioned in stories, for news and editorial comments that smear anyone's character.

The same news people can be held criminally responsible for inciting violence, revealing government bureaucracy secrets, damaging the larger community, etc.

While newspaper, radio, and television share these types of legal liability, the owners of internet "websites", "platforms", and providers seem to believe that they are simply "paperboys" and radio/TV set sales and delivery people.

Thus, to date, "platform" and provider mega-corporations are claiming that they are exempt from legal liability and regulation for the content available by means of their corporations.

They seem determined to equate themselves with paperboys and radio/TV set sales, rental, and delivery truck people.

So "platform" and provider mega-corporations claim they are not liable for the script, sounds, and images that they deliver.

All of these internet media delivery people are private companies with corporate bureaucracies performing non-governmental public services.

The only participation by government bureaucracy in their affairs is confined to government programme advertising, government sites using the companies, and some government regulation, e.g. business licences, & attempting to collect internet company corporate income taxes.

"Platform" and provider mega-corporations are thus, by and large, subject only to the government requirements that are applied to companies in general.

They don't have to apply for, get approval for, or renew public broadcasting licenses, or face routine license challenges by the general public who complain to a government regulator of licences, as do radio and television companies.

There appears to be little or no international or universal government regulation for "platform" and provider mega-corporations.

At best, members of the general public can be denied access to services by these giants, for not agreeing to the "conditions of service" dictated by the giants alone.

If you don't accept "cookies", i.e. surrender your right to privacy, you are denied access to the news.

Imagine a "paperboy" not handing you a newspaper because you refuse to give him/her a report about everything you do while you are not reading the paper.

This "paperboy" is the advertiser paying fees to the internet "platforms".

Although newspapers, radio, television, and internet all depend on advertising, only newspapers need a circulation department to attract advertisers.

Special private bureaucracies conduct ratings surveys to provide radio and television with "certified" audience totals to attract advertisers.

"Platform" and provider corporations simply track and collect data on "users" and provide it to the advertisers.

There is no need for circulation or ratings agencies or departments.

Instead of looking at total circulation numbers, "platforms" and advertisers look at "user" circulation, collecting information about everywhere that a "user" goes in cyberspace.

The "user" her/himself is the circulation.

Imagine a world in which advertisers pay newspapers, portable radio makers, and mini-TV sets manufacturers to tell advertisers where you shop, what you buy, and everything else about you.

Silly idea, but it's now effectively true about advertisers. They pay for reports on your shopping habits and a personal dossier about you.

The closest the old media get to merely tracking receivers' shopping is to pay newspapers to print coupons and to pay broadcasters to invite listeners and viewers to call stations to get free coupon via the post office.

It's so primitive and labour intensive compared with targetted tracking technologies.

Nowadays, attention span deficiency and the scatterbrain behaviour that the "platform", provider and technology products create, encourage, and enhance, under the innocuous and yet complementary-sounding label "multi-tasking", is a free-for-all advertiser's feast.

It doesn't matter what the cybernaut is paying attention to for a nano-second.

So long as the advertiser is always there to keep tabs on the cybernaut and to bombard her/him with ads in a variety of forms beyond what can be created using newspapers, radio, and TV, there is no need for circulation numbers or ratings data.

The habitual and loyal reading of particular newspapers and listening to particular radio stations and broadcasts, and watching particular television channels & programmes is no longer relevant.

Content no longer matters. It's completely irrelevant to advertisers. Watch or read anything you like. All you have to do is give us your full attention. Stare at the screen. Ads are everywhere.

You will read, listen, view, and buy. Resistance is futile!

OF course, in this context, news and information are redundant. News is only one "click" among billions, no different from any other. So news can be down-played and left to decline.

Internet "news" can include unlimited and unrestricted poor writing, inaccuracies, and overtly biased reporting that's would be difficult to find in print at a reputable newspaper devoted to good journalism and high editorial standards.

It doesn't matter. It's only news. Nobody who is electronically distracted for a lifetime will ever notice the news or its glaring defects.

There is no need for a "next edition" with a correction or retraction of a flawed story.

Play all the same news, all the time. Who will notice? The same "breaking news" repeats over and over again, going into reruns.

It repeats like a cucumber or a uncontrollable breaking wind.

Poor news reading and unedited news stories that are "streamed live" and recorded forever, can be replayed on an eternal loop, on demand.

It's irrelevant to the internet, its advertising trackers, and the somnambulant cybernaut.

It's only news. All that matters is a few seconds of attention to expose the cybernaut to the corporate ad.

Contributing to this situation and going around the traditional news corporations, manufacturers and governments promote the use of "platforms" to receive "information".

In this way, corporate/ government bureaucracy also promotes the sale of both "platform" and provider services as well as the manufacture and sale of electronic devices needed for getting access to "platform" and provider services.

Government bureaucracy support and boost "platform" and provider services, and their technology, free of charge to the mega-corporations providing them.

In so doing, government bureaucracy contributes to making communication appear more democratic while it is actually becoming more bureaucratic and less accessible.

There is also an ever increasing risk of government corruption through favours, kick-backs, and pay-offs to bureaucrats and politicians who are effectively acting as sales agents for platforms.

Need a government service or public information? Buy a device and load the app.

Every time that a bureaucrat, politician, or public corporation subscribes to and encourages members of the general public to purchase a device to get an app or to visit a website, the provider makes money.

At what point will a provider demonstrate its gratitude to the under-budgetted and over-worked "public service" entities, and in what form?

At the same time, "feedback" forms, named for the interference and sound distortion caused by placing the broadcaster's microphone in too close proximity to the broadcaster's loud speaker, all too often include only fixed question and answer formats, e.g. FAQ.

"Contact us" loops link back to themselves, giving little or no opportunity for full expression or comments and questions.

As bureaucracy is prone to say: Fill out our form by answering only our questions using only our answers. "Open" questions and answers are only appropriate if they are of benefit to the government/corporate bureaucracy.

Do not write outside the lines or in this space.

...

All too often, politicians spin their tales and "news" organizations uncritically repeat them, as if journalism were a propaganda or public relations office of government/corporate bureaucracy.

This is particularly evident in U.S. stories depicting Chuang Hwa corporations as always bad and, by implication, the U.S. corporations as always good.

In fact most news organizations in the U.S. are corporate U.S.A.

...

**War monuments**

The time of writing is 40 years after the U.S. bombs the city of Fukuoka.

Television news shows an interview with an older person living here at the time. He points out a repaired hole in one of Ohori Koen's beautiful bridges.

I go to the park to see it for myself. It's hard to believe that any nation-states could use such a lovely place for dropping bombs.

This news reminds me of a discovery I make in Seoul, capital of Hangoo.

I find a statue near city hall depicting a warrior who leads the fight against a Nippon army's invasion of Hangoo a few hundred years ago.

The non-locals are always the unprovoked aggressors.

Fukuoka remembers only the Mongols who try to invade Nippon on the coast here.

"Our" side is always defending itself from others.

### Advertising holding up news

**Toronto:** For many years, CTV National News is notorious for commercials promoting powerful fossil fuel burning motor vehicles, counteracting all the news stories about air pollution.

**Bogotá, Rio de Janeiro, Singapura**: Old nicotine television commercials are still running on television in the cool Colombian capital, years after they're banished from the tube in Canada and the U.S.

Advertisements in news/sports papers show Eiffel's Statue of Liberty holding a pack of the product over the skyline of New York City.

Movie theatres in Rio's Cinélandia run nicotine commercials before every newsreel and movie.

Everyone entering Téatro Municipal, Rio's miniature of l'Opéra de Paris, is handed a fancy pack of nicotine at the doors.

Fortunately, actually using the product is banned in the theatre auditoriums. It's a fire hazard.

More than a decade later, Singapura is screening and running a commercial featuring an apparent mock-up of N.A.S.A.'s Mission Control in Houston (U.S.A.).

All the N.A.S.A. personal cheer when a spacecraft is successfully launched. Then they all start lighting up and inhaling a nicotine product.

Nicotine is out of this world, or it just takes you away from life as we know it?

**Rio de Janeiro**: In pre-internet times, I make one of my rare trips to the Canadian consulate to look at news in the papers and telex reports.

I notice that trade among all nation-states is comparatively low at the moment.

Also, global migration is being severely restricted by governments. This suggests an increase in nationalism, parochialism, racism, and ideologism.

At the same time, there are suggestions for more exchanges of university personnel across national borders, and a training deal with some north-African country.

I suggest a better course would be to encourage free migration for all, around the world for both people and goods.

National identity inhibits the natural migration of people and substances. We become prisoners of our mere artifact, the nation-state.

...

Every TV show that I see in Rio, except the news, is preceded by a picture of a government censor form, describing censorship, if any (usually none), and recommending a minimum age for viewing.

Most shows produced here are soap operas of the Masterpiece Theatre type.

Like Canadian TV, most other series are from the U.S.A., but dubbed with Portuguese voices here.

There are so many different Brasileiro network newscasts.

Newspapers are linked with TV and radio networks, like in Canada and the U.S., but here they carry the same names, such as Jornal do Brasil and Radio Jornal do Brasil.

Network television generally comes from the big city, São Paulo, the most populous city in South America. The networks usually have names or letters.

They are Bandeirantes, TVS, O Globo, and TVE, the educational station.

TVE has a "how to speak Portuguese correctly" feature, which I need.

A new network, run by the magazine empire Manchette, is due to begin soon.

Saturday and Sunday TV are devoted to Chacrinha and Silvio Santos.

Chacrinha wears clown-like clothing and hosts a teenage music programme, complete with adolescent screamers and their idols.

Silvio Santos hosts what seems to be an endless afternoon of duplicates of U.S. quiz shows.

There are even excerpts from the inane Gong Show, from "Hollywoogee", as they say here.

(Many years later when some try to recruit Santos as a presidential candidate, he declines, saying that he's just an entertainer. This leaves the field clear for another clown, Bolsonaro.)

We can almost be sure that anyone we visit on the weekend will have their TVs on and tuned to Chacrinha or Santos shows, O Globo's "best TV".

These are not my Carioca friend Zita's favourite programmes.

In fact, she watches very little television before I arrive and adjust her antenna so that her TV set can pick up all the local channels.

## World News

A global news service would make the moment's state of humanity the lead item.

This item would state the birth and death estimates up to the moment.

For death estimates, the mortalities would be listed under causes, e.g. diseases: yellow fever xxx; cancer xxx; ebola xxx; e-coli xxx; malaria xxx; AIDS xxx, influenza xxx, COVID, etc.; wars: names of belligerents xxx; hunger: names of nation-states xxx; pollution: air xxx; water xxx; land xxx; accidents: land motor vehicle xxx; water vehicle xxx; aircraft xxx; murder: xxx; etc.

These daily listings could become a major influence on all readers and viewers, including government and corporate, if not cause of attempted censorship or statistics manipulation.

How many nation-state chiefs make speeches against all war deaths?

The northern hemisphere's Remembrance Day, and the like, unknown in parts of the southern hemisphere that I frequent on that day in the past, praises mass murder victims and trained killers who live as peaceful human beings until the nation-states force them to wear uniforms and use deadly weapons.

## Local & National News

Local news would be a universal category, not attached to any particular local geographic location. There would be no need for an international news category.

All nation-states' news would be national news. It's both semantically and planetarily more accurate as opposed to present categories, which are separatist illusions.

## My Pre-Newsworld News Lineup

Thirteen years before CBC creates CBC Newsworld, a constant and continuous news broadcasting television network, I write to Harry Boyle at the Canadian Radio-Television Commission and <u>Saturday Night Magazine</u> with an idea.

"When I was back in high school I used to write essays about many things, including television's future. That was before I thought of cablevision as any more than a better TV aerial.

"One essay talked about the world-uniting possibilities of TV, about such things as constant, live satellite TV coverage of the Mona Lisa and other wonders of the world.

Television watchers could tune in their favourite parts of the world 24 hours a day." I write.

"...It's nice to know that such tuning in is nearly economically feasible today.

"The advent of national cable regulatory bodies can be a factor contributing to the world-tuning possibilities of television.

"As a cable regulator within a multinational, multi-regional country, Canada, the CRTC has even more potential for world-tuning than other national bodies.

"Within Canada our many cultures and regions can have constant exposure to each other through channel allocation regulations for cable.

"Canadian television watchers can be permitted to tune in to at least one TV station from every province.

"This would mean that a Vancouver resident could tune in local news and locally-centred broadcasts from nine other Canadian centres.

"Watching a locally-produced TV programme or news story about Alberta's Pacific Western Airlines purchase is very different if you can tune in to local stations in Vancouver, Edmonton, and Ottawa the same day.

"It's like reading the Vancouver Sun, Edmonton Journal, and Ottawa Citizen the same day.

"Dependence on centralized network productions and news reduces local events and people to mush.

"The many times I've crossed Canada I've found local TV programmes as much a novelty as being a visitor in the cities and towns themselves.

"You'd save me a lot of travel by letting me watch other Canadian local stations in Vancouver.

"People in Ottawa might spend 3:00 to 3:30 p.m., their time, watching BCTV noon news and Ida Clarkson instead of Gilligan's Island, Hogan's Heroes, Leave It To Beaver, or the like.

"During the two years I lived in Ontario, I enjoyed being able to see regional news on Ontario's Global TV.

"It would help national unity if B.C. people could tune into Global News 10 p.m. Edition at 7 p.m. Pacific Time each night, and see rural Ontarians complaining about Toronto.

"Okanagan fruit growers could see what their counterparts in the Niagara area were doing today.

"And there are countless other examples.

"Late night local news from Toronto and Montreal would come to B.C. at about 8:30 p.m. Pacific Time each night.

"Football and hockey are live and direct, why not other local events too?

"Any event broadcast nationally becomes a national event.

"National unity should come from putting locals in touch with other locals, not from imposing network interpretations down our throats.

"We need realities, not generalizations and stereotypes.

"The novelty of being able to tune in any province, any time might lower our interest in the mush entertainment of mass programming.

"Who needs Kojak when you can watch a show about today's events on East Hastings?

"Why watch Cher when you can watch the Yonge Street Strip?

"Why watch Little House on the Prairie when you can see community building and family farms in Saskatchewan?

"Mass mush from the networks could lose its audience.

"Cable and Anik, or other satellites, can unite real-life Canadians in real-life localities instead of the mythical faceless Canadian that networks aim at in mass programming.

"The next logical step would be to make television from countries all over the world available in Canada, via satellite and cable converters.

"There is a market for every language in the various communities of Canada. Note the success of Vancouver Radio CJVB.

"We can tune in to TV produced by local stations in Seattle, Spokane, Buffalo, etc. and begin to feel an affinity toward people who live there.

"We get TV shows live from small parts of the Moon and Mars, which networks can't reduce to mush.

"We see a picture of a Martian rock which a camera just happens to see, not a picture of a Martian rock which a network decides is typical and likely to appeal to some anonymous audience.

"Perhaps we would feel a greater affinity toward our fellow citizens in Edmonton, Regina, Winnipeg, Toronto, Montreal, Saint John, Charlottetown, Halifax, St. John's, and Whitehorse if we could see these people for ourselves, as they present themselves in local TV.

"We can remove ABC, NBC, and CBS from cablevision altogether. But we'll still have mush, albeit Canadian mush, from CBC and CTV.

"And we won't know our fellow citizens of Canada, or the world, any better than we do now.

"Let's have the world's first non-network, a network of unconnected local TV programmes - live and direct.

We now return you to your regular network programming.

...

There is no reply from <u>Saturday Night Magazine.</u> However, the CRTC's Diane Rhéaume does reply, two months later.

She writes that my "approach to broadcasting" is "naive" but "extremely fascinating".

She says my suggestion is tech-nically feasible but asks who would pay for such a system which might only attract "a small portion of the popula-tion".

Within four years of her letter, the U.S. CNN goes on the air.

The internet and daily cable TV access to local stations across Canada arrives much later.

## Communiqués & non-communiqués from "home" and "abroad"

The reporting of news depends on the news reporters, the editors, and the receivers.

Both reporters and editors remain close to news receivers, no matter how far away the story setting may be.

Certain conventions and concepts of what news is palatable to the news readers and audience prevail.

In news media dependent upon advertising revenue to survive, the relationships between news collectors and recipients is accentuated.

A reporter or editor who strays too far from what is palatable to the news receivers risks costing the advertisers customers.

When advertisers withdraw their support for news media, the media loses the revenue it needs to survive.

The farther away the story happens, the more visible the relationship among news reporters, editors, and receivers becomes.

Certain conventions and palata-ble news considerations come into more obvious play.

These factors are more evident when the "home" news receivers are contrasted with the "away" receivers.

A U.K. news team proves this point in Vancouver, a place I refer to as i) Vaincouver, due to the aggressively and uncritical chauvinistic locals I encounter there over a ten year period; and, ii) Van Couverden, for the original family name of the Dutch-U.K. sailor that the city is named after.

The U.K. news team does an honest and objective report on the downtown poverty and drug addiction area of downtown, an area that is well-known, at least by reputation, to all who live in the city.

An uproar among residents of the city ensues. Instead of acknowledging a long-standing problem; admitting it is being neglected; thanking the news crew for putting a spotlight on a problem long in need of solving; and, urging the municipal government to try harder to solve it, city residents condemn the news people reporting the story.

The U.K. news team is vilified in ferocious terms for "unobjective" reporting that doesn't show the local attractions, and so harms the tourist industry.

Lesson for news reporters and editors: Don't be honest, show reality, or hope to encourage news receivers to take action to help improve things?

Of course, since the news team is from the U.K., the news receivers there have nothing personal invested in some place too far away for them to easily visit anyway.

Vancouver is just some foreign place that's not as good as here. There's no place like home.

This is also the typical reception likely to come from stories about problems reported in news from home and abroad

For the most part, they aren't the reader's problems unless they impinge upon daily life routines.

This doesn't mean the reporters and editors covering news can safely disconnect from their own perceptions or those of the news receivers.

News reporters, editors, and receivers reflect each other and their local origins.

They cannot objectively separate themselves from themselves.

"Everyone knows" comes into play all the time. There are certain non-professional consenses framing all news reporting, editing, and receiving.

If there is a consensus that we live in the "greatest", "best", "most beautiful", or "super natural" place on Earth, everything goes well in the best of all worlds.

This means that everywhere else in the world will inevitably have problems and they are destined to be far less well off than here at "home".

So an "accurate" and "objective" news report can never imply, suggest, or blatantly say that "we" have any roll in creating and neglecting problems abroad or in making the people living there less well off.

People and places abroad are not as well off as here because of their poor locations and because people there are not like "us".

This is why "they" all want to immigrate here or arrive as refugees and enter illegally.

They know that if they live here and behave properly, like us, their lives will be wonderful.

Any news reporter or editor unable to understand these central "values" of "home" will lose most of the local news receivers, or become the objective of scorn and pity.

Thus following locally-held beliefs, conventions, and consenses are the key factors in journalistic career self-preservation and the news organization's business model.

### Secret "Monitor"?

I reply to an ad on the NHK World website. NHKW wants people abroad to view six of its programmes every month, including one newscast, and to provide NHKW with comments on each one.

The title of this type of viewer is "monitor", as in the screen of an old desktop computer or a prestigious, well-written, and highly-respected newspaper that is somehow put out by a religionist group called "Christian Science".

If there really are oxymorons, as opposed to the regular variety, this group name is among them.

Being a captive of bureaucracy, like all media of communication, NHKW wants me to fill out forms with details.

Initially, NHKW also wants everything delivered by encrypted e-mail.

I fill out a form and become one of the chosen few, or many. I don't know how many NHKW monitors are out there.

But to sign my name and write the date on the form accepting the monitor position, I have to use a secret code. The same applies to reading the instructions sheet and to receiving the monitor's forms.

I find this awkward, challenging, and silly.

I explain that I'm not involved in espionage and my opinions are no secret. NHKW relents.

Fortunately, NHKW is headquartered in Nippon. Thus my perspective on "secret code" is received, understood, acknowledged, and recognized as valid.

My sincere flattering words in the letter I write to NHKW, plus the coincidence of "Respect For The Aged Day" when I write, convince NHKW that I don't need to use codes.

When a coded message is sent to me in error, NHKW writes an apology to me the next day and includes forms not encrypted to require any secret code to read and use them.

Such is common sense and respect for others in Nippon.

I imagine that at least slightly older and senior NHKW staff instruct the younger technical staff to grant my wish to communicate without secret codes.

As <u>Terrian Journals</u> attests, I make no secret of my perspectives, so why would I send "monitor" forms in code?

The "monitor" forms ask me to provide overall and specific category impressions, along with a one to five rating number ranging from "5-excellent" down in each category.

There's a small space for optional comments alongside.

The biggest demand of the form is the 130 to 180 word overall comment about each of the six programmes viewed.

At first, only one of the six shows appears to be compulsory, the news. That suits me perfectly. Then it's dropped to "optional". I'm too critical?

I often write to NHKW and other news broadcasts when I want to make a comment about lacking coverage, alternate perspectives, unasked questions, language usage, or missing content.

I don't know how many words I write in each case. So far, mostly newspapers print me.

Only a couple of CBC Radio broadcasts, in Vancouver and Saskatoon, read and play me.

The non-news NHKW broadcasts I "monitor" are recommended and my choice.

So it's not challenging. I'm an amateur viewer of TV and internet TV shows for a long time before getting a "monitor" role.

...

The U.S. P.B.S. Newshour reports a nature revival project in Argentina to restore endangered species to their natural behaviours and habitats.

The species include jaguar, seals, and others. At least one species is released from a zoo and retrained to help it bring back its natural behaviour and survival instincts.

While watching this news report, I quickly realize that humans can also benefit from this type of release and training.

Humans, through too many generations of existing in isolated immobile housing, nation-state captivity, and what I dub the "caretaker society" which is now the "jailkeeper society", have lost their natural survival skills and instincts.

Despite, in some cases espousing otherwise, human beings, particularly "first" worlders, are now as indifferent to healthy living and to the planetary human life support system as the breeded cattle lowing in meadows under trees.

Their "lives" are only about being milked and butchered, much like human lives.

Human captivity in "security", "comfort", and routines is rendering us docile, submissive, and compliant, leading us along the road to species extinction.

Our lives are milked along the way until our lifetimes are effectively slaughtered.

So many of us pass lifetimes merely waiting to die.

...

Aljazeera news reports that the fossil fuel polluters have more lobbyists in Glasgow than the number of nation-state delegates attending.

It's the 26th annual United Nations sponsored conference on the environment. They all fail. Ditto all that follow.

...

My 90+ year old mother hears CBC-TV news announcers saying that if she wants complete news on various topics she must "go to" CBC.ca.

CTV news and others say, "for the complete interview go to our website".

News only goes to those who pay for internet and its evil cousin, digital pay TV.

So if you don't buy a computer, pay for internet or cable, and/or buy a cellular phone, you will not be informed.

And if you have those gadgets you are at high-risk of being misinformed or disinformed by an assortment of charlatans?

What happened to the nation-state speeches about "the free flow of information"?

The "information highway" is a toll road.

Before the era of techno-ruled news media, you could at least get a newspaper left on a park bench or a bus seat or rustle one out of a garbage can for free.

...

Unlike the heydays of free news on the radio and television, and in discarded printed newspapers, we now pay for advertising at least twice for news and everything else.

We pay once by purchasing the product advertised and we pay once more for receiving the advertising through the electronic devices that we buy and via the internet services we pay for every month.

At least with radio and analog television the listeners and viewers only paid for their signal receiving devices once and those devices functioned well for many years, if not decades.

...

The effective communications "service" fee amounts to paying for the advertising being broadcast on top of the products' purchase prices.

But now we pay for the advertising of products that we never buy, don't want, and don't use.

Even the most environmentally-friendly people who are only taking public transit or who are driving electric cars are assaulted by and paying for fossil fuel and polluting vehicle advertising.

And attention to the advertising is obligatory.

Whereas a newspaper or magazine reader can flip beyond full page advertisements and cover smaller ads by folding pages and placing fingers and palms strategically over ads while holding up a printed periodical, a "smart" phone holder finds advertising is constantly in his/her face.

Ads are everywhere s/he looks or even glances, even between the paragraphs of text that s/he is actually trying to read. Ads are constantly blocking and distracting her/his attention.

**Québec**: SRC news shows a group of apparently pro-pandemic activists blocking the streets of Ottawa and preparing to do the same elsewhere.

Why do the opponents of anti-COVID-19 health measures be-lieve that they have a special right to demonstrate anywhere they wish, any time they wish, and indefinitely, and that nobody else is entitled to do the same thing?

Who else can demonstrate when the "special group" blocks the roads and whistles, shouts, and knocks down anyone with a different opinion and anyone who is trying to report the news?

When the "special group" shouts "freedom" and "liberté" they mean exclusively for themselves, not for anyone else and definitely not for all.

...

The group is receiving millions of dollars and carrying U.S. and U.S. civil war era separatist "confederate" flags.

Nazi flags and at least one flag of former U.S. emperor twit punchline are brandished and waved with enthusiasm by the mob.

SCR's Téléjournal nightly newscast exposes one of the mob organizers as a former advisor to the former U.S. emperor.

The U.S.-like extremists are blocking the 911 emergency services phone line in Canada. They support fire and death too?

Are the Fenians on the way? It's "54' 40" or fight" all over again?

...

I see thugs shouting at television news reporters while they are trying to report events. I see others blowing horns and whistles to silence the news reporters.

I see a TVA reporter knocked down by one extreme right-winger. Another TVA reporter is surrounded by thug-like people.

In Surrey (Columbia (Br) thugs are caught on camera knocking a news crew's camera to the ground and spitting on the journalists.

This is classic Nazi black shirt and Fascist brown shirt thuggery and bullying that I read about in history books about the prelude to the 1930s/40s wars.

We already have to fight against the return of racism and the suppression of women's rights. In the U.S. voter rights are being diminished. Now we have to push back Nazis again?

Nasties wait until the positive achievements of human progress go out of memory and try to reverse them all.

...

"Smart" TV is blocking access to news in Canada. It's a device that looks like a television but is not a television.

The ones we see in Toronto, Québec City, and Winnipeg accommodation do not include all of Canada's TV networks.

Here in Québec City there is only one national French language television station available through the "smart" TV in our apartment.

But that's only repeated rebroadcasting of old news programmes such as SRC's evening news.

There is no TVA. When I try to add TVA I can only get "TV America", a U.S. channel I know nothing about.

This "TV" goes far beyond the usual U.S. acculturation efforts of Hollywood movies and the U.S. cable network news channel.

Even France 24 is only available in English, not its original French language broadcast.

All of the non-U.S. broadcasting that we watch on the internet, except Aljazeera, is only available on the tiny computers we're carrying, not on "Smart" TV.

Where are the "Canadian content" rules and "language police" when you need them?

(Two years later I finally get to see TVA and TV5 Monde on "smart" TV, in Saint-Boniface, Manitoba. It's because I complain to the Canadian government?)

...

Although there is no wifi internet access at our current location, cell phones function and there is television reception, bringing us the news. I note one particular developing news story.

Unable to compete with the capitalist Russian Federation and capitalist Chuang Hwa, the N.A.T.O.-G7 clique tries to freeze out the competition and kill it off by "sanctions".

Escalating a dangerous and increasingly deadly monopoly game, N.A.T.O. invites Nippon and Hangoo to a "North Atlantic" meeting.

This pushes capitalist Russia and capitalist Chuang Hwa closer together.

N.A.T.O.-G7's attempt to reignite the Cold War creates a situation either breaking into a final "first" world war or/and the founding of a Russian Federation-Chuang Hwa ruled world order.

N.A.T.O.-G7 moves backfire. All "for Ukraine"!? Daft!

...

News becomes the first victim of wars in Ukraine and Palestine.

When Russia complains about attacks against ethnic Russians in Ukraine, it's wrong for Russia to assemble troops and invade Ukraine.

But when Yisra'el complains about an attack against Yisra'elis living near the western Palestine-Yisra'el border, it's okay for Yisra'el to assemble troops and invade Palestine.

After the first two years of fighting in Ukraine, Russia is held responsible for killing 10,000 Ukrainians.

In only two months of fighting in Palestine, Yisra'el is responsible for killing 16,000 Palestinians.

The Russian president is tried in absentia and convicted of war crimes. A worldwide warrant is issued for his arrest. If he sets foot outside the Russian Federation (R.F.), he risks arrest and incarceration.

The Yisra'eli prime minister has no trial or conviction for war crimes. He's free to go almost anywhere in the world unmolested.

When he leaves office he will face charges in Yisra'eli courts for other crimes. Thus he uses his invasion as a means to stay in office.

The Russo-Ukraine war begins when, instead of reflecting upon itself and showing a reasonable understanding of the concerns of the R.F., N.A.T.O. accuses the R. F. of threatening Ukraine.

The R.F. stations 100,000 troops on the Ukraine border as a show of strength, reflecting distrust of the way former victims of the C.C.C.P. are transforming the E.U. and N.A.T.O. into an anti-Russian-Federation alliance.

The R.F. agrees to withdraw its forces if N.A.T.O. agrees not to expand into Ukraine and thus become a more imminent threat on the R.F.'s borders.

It's a reasonable offer.

N.A.T.O. refuses the request outright. Instead, N.A.T.O.'s main members threaten to reduce the Federation's ability to function as an increasingly capitalist country.

Is this crisis really about the capitalist R.F. becoming too much of a formidable competitor challenging the status quo monopoly long held by other leading capitalist nation-states?

Before the Russo-Ukraine war, the R.F. is becoming the main supplier of fossil fuels to the E.U.

It's an echo of the way the other leading capitalist nation-states are reacting toward capitalist Chuang Hwa's increasing strength and challenge to the status quo monopoly.

Capitalist Chuang Hwa is becoming the leader in computer and solar power technology when the U.S. and its associate states ban and slap tariffs on leading Chinese high-tech products and services, and block their sales and services abroad. (Huawei & TicToc)

While the U.S. internet and "social" media mega-corporations spread everywhere and collect data about people around the world for marketing and political influence, capitalist Chuang Hwa is condemned for doing exactly the same thing.

...

A former resident of what is previously called "East Germany" tells me that during the Cold War she could listen to radio news from both the C.C.C.P. and the U.S.

She knows both sides are propaganda. She says that she only believes the parts of news stories that are the same when broadcast from both sides.

Unfortunately, early in the Russo-Ukraine war, it becomes more difficult for many people to hear both sides and to decide what is true vs war propaganda from both sides.

The E.U. bans R.T. from Russia, a mediocre and amateurish news station which I first see in Kazan.

Two of Canada's major cable TV companies copy the U.S.-lead removal of RT. They call R.T. "Russian propaganda".

Whatever happened to "freedom of the press". U.S. right-wing news and misinformation is still available around much of the world.

There is a certain amount of truth coming from both anti-R.F. and anti-R.T. sources.

Blocking R.T. makes it much more difficult to distinguish between information and propaganda coming from the anti-R.F. news reports.

Fortunately, I can still watch R.T. on the internet and through the TV screens at our apartment. But for how long?

Whenever I do so, broadcasts from other sources, even entertainment, become stop and go.

That means I have to push the

play button every few seconds because the broadcast stops in mid-sentence. Is this a result of anti-Russian or pro-Russian hacking?

If the removal of RT by cable services is justified due to Russia's invasion of Ukraine, then so too is the removal of the U.S. Fox News, which encourages and promotes the mob invasion of Ottawa and armed mob invasions of Canadian border posts.

...

Honest reporting in the face of armed forces and propaganda has to try harder.

I see Canadian news reporters who should know better who are now uncritically and unreflectively parroting anti-R.F. propaganda.

What about striving for "objectivity" or at least reporting more than one side of a story?

Journalistic principles are abandoned altogether during war?

...

U.S. multinational "social" media mega-corporations threaten to ban all Canadian news from their internet services. They refuse to comply with Canadian and international copyright law.

All of the internet corporations republishing and rebroadcasting news authored by others must be subject to the same legal requirements and responsibilities as all publishers and broadcasters, such as but not limited to obeying copyright law, obtaining written permission from authors for reproduction of their works in part or in full, paying royalties to authors, and complying fully with Canadian content rules.

Otherwise, multinational internet mega-corporations supplant and replace the Canadian news and government. A corporate dictatorship totally replaces a democratic leaning system.

...

Today's news says the IMF loans to nation-states don't work and people end up worse off than before the loans.

Why is this news now? Ignorance.

When I'm in the southern Americas for the first time. it is already particularly and visibly evident that IMF loans don't help and actually make things worse for most people.

I see it in the supermarkets of Rio de Janeiro, Córdoba, and elsewhere. In Córdoba, store clerks are changing the prices of goods two or three times a day.

...

The IMF's failure and my observations of it bring up an important point about my role in the "first" versus "third" worlds.

I can be seen and depicted as some "first" world dilettante who goes to the "third" world to exploit economic hardships, particularly currency devaluations.

That would be true if I was aware of the economic situation in the "third" world in the sense of daily shopping economic impact before I get there.

But I know nothing about it until I get there, just as I know nothing about Canada's narrow immigration policies until I go to Canada with non-Canadians.

As a typically unaware "first" worlder I only know what the news reports in passing reference about the "third" world and popular perceptions of the "third" world.

From those sources I have a vague notion that there are a lot of poor people, they have difficult lives, and the "first" world is trying to help out.

It's simplistic at best and a half-truth or false portrayal of reality. It conjures up images of starving masses who are incapable of helping themselves or generally inept.

This is a typical "first" world image of the "outside" world.

This clears me of charges of going to the "third" world with a premeditated plan to exploit other people's difficulties. Such malfeasance is beyond my knowledge.

I have no such evil plans or motivations for going to the "third" world.

In a less defensive and positive sense, my presence in the "third" world is an amazing eye-opener and self-education project that evolves from my life up to then.

Going to the "third" world for extended periods of time, instead of superficial lark tourist trips in cloistered tours and accommodation, is an unexpectedly enriching journey.

I mean enriching in the most profound sense, not merely financial gain or amassing the meaningless, attention-diverting, and stress filled trinkets called "possessions".

In the "third" world I learn so much more than I could ever hope to learn in the "first" world cocoon and in the tourist industry bubbles.

I learn a lot and tell the stories that unfold as I do, as they happen. I tell the stories of the ignored and invisible majority of the world's people living in most of the world.

At worst and at best, the economic benefits and opportunities that I gain in the "third" world are a de facto "third" world subsidized education.

The subsidized education is for a "first" worlder who, despite an exceptional formal university education in both depth and breadth, is an almost typically ignorant "first" worlder in regard to the "third" world.

I say "almost" because I am truly exceptional in the sense that I actually do try to learn about the "third" world by effectively and literally leaving the "first" world behind by deliberately choosing to live in the "third" world and getting to know the non-elite instead of my "first" world elite counterparts who are living abroad or who are local born elite "third" worlders, i.e. actually "first" worlders..

...

Without perceived credibility, there would no longer be any university professors invited to appear in news broadcasts to express "learned" opinions on current affairs.

Their broad and comprehensive theoretical knowledge, based on years of research involving talking to other academics and inattentively perusing their writings, which are based entirely upon research models and sitting in offices and libraries thinking profoundly, would be lost.

The significance of these isolated academic "experts" appearing in news broadcasts is already lost on me. Frankly it makes me cringe.

They are literally fish out of water. "Outside" air disagrees with them.

The exceptional contacts that academics do have with the "outside" world are mainly with people who are mostly in the 18 to 24 year old age group.

Even when this age group is proportionately a larger part of the general populace, they cannot help an academic to understand the broader outside world where most news occurs.

...

New York City news reports passengers are stranded in airports with no food, drink, or accommodation. Climate change storms cause disruptions, losses, and anger. Airlines go silent and hide from public view.

The same is happening in major city Canadian airports.

The news also dramatically emphasizes the fraudulent fallacy that baggage "security" exists in air transportation.

News cameras reveal very large floor spaces crammed with luggage which airlines have lost track of and are unable to easily return to passengers.

So if anything dangerous is already inside the bags, or added in the chaos, nobody knows about it. Nobody knows who handles whose bags.

While airline passengers and increasingly smaller carry-on bags are put through a gauntlet of tagging, document presentation, "security" gates, etc. it's obvious that nobody is keeping track of the exact location, ownership, and "security" of all baggage at all times.

...

One news source says, with a straight face, that Ukraine is desperate for fossil fuels to heat its homes and other buildings because winter is so cold there.

The announcer, who lives in Nippon but not Hokkaido, reports, without apparent thought, that the average temperature in the first month of winter is -3° C in Ukraine.

In most of Canada and the Russian Federation, as well as some northern U.S. states, and the iced-over Abashiri coast of Hokkaido, -3°C is a warmer day of winter, in fact balmy.

Ukraine winter news needs to be put into the truly cold context of the harsh objective reality experienced by millions of people every winter.

## Tomorrow's News Yesterday

A U.S. oil company holds an essay contest to honour that nation-state's 200th birthday. The contest asks writers to depict the world of one hundred years in the future.

I'm 25 to 26 the year of the contest.

I write, in part: 100 years from now, language, libraries, and news may no longer exist.

A technological advancement in the encyclopedia will likely replace these things as well as radio, television, and telephone...

And all human beings will be encyclopedists.

All that has been publicly thought and known will be stored in enormous information banks.

The who, what, when, where, and how of past and present will be available instantly to all.

Contradictory whys and their discrepancies will also be available.

Anyone will be able to record a thought or event. Contradictory reports will be supplemented, automatically, with information from other reports they contradict.

An infinite cross-reference computer index will provide

access to everything from semantic definitions to complex formulae.

The chief problem for users will be learning how to make extremely selective requests for information.

Everyone will be his/her own news editor, deciding all the news that's fit to know.

# VOLUMES FROM MYTHBREAKER

## Pre-Terrian Journals:

Explorations Of Inner & Outer Space
Out of Context
Terrian Journals Origins

## Terrian Journals series:

### Core volumes

A Sketch of Terrian History
Terrian Journals' How To Make The Nation
Terrian Journals' 500 Years In Louis Bourbon's Few Hectares
Full Employment: Not Fulfilling Terrian
Caretaker Society
Terrian Journals: Living as a Newcomer
Middle Earth Journals
Re discovery Journals
Fukurokuju No Kasumi Journals
Sabbatical Journals
Departure Journals
Adventuredate Unknown Journals
Away Team Journals
Searching For South Journals
Inonakanokawazu Journals
КАЗАНЬ Journals
Exile Journals
Tenjin Journals
Next Journals

## Theme Volumes

Terrian Journals for the Misguided
Terrian Journals' News To Me
Terrian Journals' N.S.R.: Not Spying, ...Really!
TJ JNG: Terrian Journals' Jokes Nobody Gets
Terrian Journals' Half Serious
Terrian Journals' Disbelief
Terrian Journals' House Trap
Terrian Journals' Virtually Camping
Terrian Journals' Crystal Virtually Dead
Terrian Journals' Maximum Insecurity
Terrian Journals' Mandarinas
Terrian Journals First Anthology
Terrian Journals Second Anthology

## Archway series:

Archway: Six Year Book of Dreams
Archway: Lifetime Rhyme
Archway: Life Before Dreams
Archway's Valentine Love
Archway's Garden Rhymes
Archway's Christmas New Years Rhymes

## Education Titles:

Language Learning Secrets
Trying To Teach Languages In The L.B.E. World
An Adult Book About Education
Terrian Journals' Miss Schooling?

## Fiction:

Terrian Journals'
Political Science Fiction

www.ingramcontent.com/pod-product-compliance
Lightning Source LLC
Chambersburg PA
CBHW070746230426
43665CB00017B/2266